BUSINESS ESSENTIALS
(SUPPORTING HNC/HND AND FOUNDATION DEGREES)

Business Law

Course Book

In this December 2007 first edition

- activities, examples and quizzes

- practical illustrations and case studies

- index

- fully up-to-date as at December 2007

- coverage mapped to the Edexcel Guidelines for HND/HNC Unit 5 and Specialist Units 25, 27 and 28

BPP
LEARNING MEDIA

BUSINESS ESSENTIALS

First edition September 2007

ISBN 9780 7517 4477 4

British Library Cataloguing-in Publication Data

A catalogue record for this book is available from the British Library

Printed in Great Britain by WM Print
45-47 Frederick Street
Walsall, West Midlands
WS2 9NE

Published by
BPP Learning Media Ltd
BPP House, Aldine Place
London W12 8AA

www.bpp.com/learningmedia.com

We are grateful to Edexcel for permission to reproduce the Guidelines for
the BTEC Higher Nationals in Business.

BPP Learning Media acknowledges the contribution of Ian Kilbey, LLB
LLM, senior lecturer in law at de Montfort University, who acted as a
consultant for the chapters of this book on EU law.

NOTES

CONTENTS

LEARNING MEDIA

INTRODUCTION

This is the first edition of BPP Learning Media's dynamic new **Business Essentials** range. It is the ideal learning solution for all students studying for business-related qualifications and degrees, and the range provides concise and comprehensive coverage of the key areas that are essential to the business student.

Qualifications in Business are traditionally very demanding. Students therefore need learning resources which get straight to the core of the topics involved, and which build upon students' pre-existing knowledge and experience. The BPP Learning Media Business Essentials range has been designed to meet exactly that need.

Features include:

- In-depth coverage of essential topics within business-related subjects
- Plenty of activities, quizzes and topics for class discussion to help retain the interest of students and ensure progress
- Up-to-date practical illustrations and case studies that really bring the material to life
- A glossary of terms and full index

In addition, the contents of the chapters are comprehensively mapped to the **Edexcel Guidelines**, providing full coverage of all topics specified in the HND/HNC qualifications in Business.

Each chapter contains:

- An introduction and a list of specific study objectives
- A summary diagram and signposts to guide you through the chapter
- A chapter roundup, quick quiz with answers and answers to activities

Further resources

Lecturers whose colleges adopt the Business Essentials range (minimum of ten copies for each relevant unit) are entitled to receive **free practice assignments and answers** for the units concerned. While remaining under the copyright of BPP Learning Media, these can be copied and distributed to students as desired.

BPP Learning Media CD Roms will also be available early in 2008 to complement some titles within the series. These provide interactive learning modules for the key topics in the subject.

BPP Learning Media
2007

Other titles in this series:

Generic titles

Economics *

Accounts *

Business Maths *

Core units for the Edexcel HND/HNC Business qualification

Unit 1	Marketing
Unit 2	Managing Financial Resources and Decisions
Unit 3	Organisations and Behaviour
Unit 4	Business Environment
Unit 5	Business Law *
Unit 6	Business Decision Making
Unit 7	Business Strategy
Unit 8	Research Project

Specialist units (endorsed title routes) for the Edexcel HND/HNC Business qualification

Units 9-12	Finance
Units 13-16	Management
Units 17-20	Marketing
Units 21-24	Human Resource Management
Units 25-26	Company and Commercial Law *

* CD Roms available spring 2008.

For more information, or to place an order, please call 0845 0751 100 (for orders within the UK) or +44(0)20 8740 2211 (from overseas), e-mail learningmedia@bpp.com, or visit our website at www.bpp.com/learningmedia.

If you would like to send in your comments on this Course Book, please turn to the review form at the back of this book.

STUDY GUIDE

This Course Book includes features designed specifically to make learning effective and efficient.

(a) Each chapter begins with a summary diagram which maps out the areas covered by the chapter. You can use the diagrams during revision as a basis for your notes.

(b) After the main summary diagram there is an introduction, which sets the chapter in context. This is followed by learning objectives, which show you what you will learn as you work through the chapter.

(c) Throughout the Course Book, there are special aids to learning. These are indicated by symbols.

Signposts guide you through the text, showing how each section connects with the next.

Definitions give the meanings of key terms. The **glossary** at the end of the Course Book summarises these.

Activities help you to test how much you have learnt. An indication of the time you should take on each is given. Answers are given at the end of each chapter.

Topics for discussion are for use in seminars. They give you a chance to share your views with your fellow students. They allow you to highlight holes in your knowledge and to see how others understand concepts. If you have time, try 'teaching' someone the concepts you have learnt in a session. This helps you to remember key points and answering their questions will consolidate your knowledge.

Examples relate what you have learnt to the outside world. Try to think up your own examples as you work through the Course Book.

Chapter roundups present the key information from the chapter in a concise format. Useful for revision.

NOTES

(d) The wide **margin** on each page is for your notes. You will get the best out of this book if you interact with it. Write down your thoughts and ideas. Record examples, question theories, add references to other pages in the book and rephrase key points in your own words.

(e) At the end of each chapter, there is a **chapter roundup**, and a **quick quiz** with answers. Use these to revise and consolidate your knowledge. The chapter roundup summarises the chapter. The quick quiz tests what you have learnt (the answers often refer you back to the chapter so you can look over subjects again).

(f) At the end of the text, there is a **glossary of key terms** and an **index**.

PART A

THE LEGAL SYSTEM

BPP
LEARNING MEDIA

Chapter 1:
ENGLISH LEGAL SYSTEM AND SOURCES OF LAW

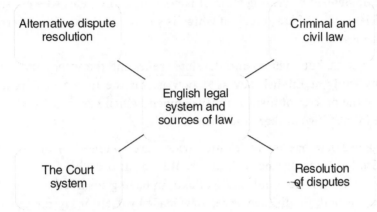

Introduction

In order to understand fully the topics of contract, employment and tort law it is vital that you first have an appreciation of the English legal system and are familiar with the terminology used.

Your objectives

In this chapter you will learn about the following.

(a)   The role of law within society

(b)   The difference between civil and criminal law

(c)   How disputes may be resolved by the courts, by tribunals and by arbitration

1 CRIMINAL AND CIVIL LAW

Law can be summarised as a body of rules for the guidance of human conduct, imposed upon and enforced among the members of a particular state in order to enable the state to function. If there is no legal system it is likely that chaos will ensue, as can sometimes be seen in countries where civil war causes the system of law and order to be abused and ultimately to break down.

We are all subject to the law. Its consequences affect us all on a daily basis, whether we are buying a house, buying goods in a shop (ie entering a consumer contract), entering a contract of employment or driving a car. It is not only individuals who are subject to the law: the different types of law, much of which is specific to them, also govern companies and other business units.

The law is not static but changes and develops, reflecting the values and institutions of each era. Any study of English law as it now is (for the time being) requires a brief explanation of the process of historical development which has made it what it is, which we shall give in these two background chapters.

Although English law has many features which are common to other national legal systems, it also has some distinctive features of its own. It differs from the law of many Western European countries (and also Scotland) in having absorbed only a small amount of Roman law. Second, English law is case law made by decisions of the courts to a much greater extent than the law of many other countries. We shall look at the rules applied to case law in Chapter 3.

1.1 Public and private law

One basic division of law is between public and private.

Public law governs relations between an individual citizen and the state. Examples include:

(a)   The **criminal law**, which will be discussed in greater detail shortly

(b)   **Constitutional law**, which is the law governing matters such as the operation of Parliament and the frequency with which general elections must be held

(c)   **Administrative law**

Private law, which is also known as **civil law**, is the law governing relations between citizens themselves. Examples include:

(a)   The **law of contract**, which you will cover in some depth later in this text

(b)   The **law of tort**, which is the law covering the legal duty of people towards each other, such as the law of negligence. This is also covered later in this book.

(c)   The **law of trusts**, dealing with the disposal of a person's property according to their wishes

(d)   **Property law**, that is the rules on the buying, selling and holding of property and

(e)   **Family law**, concerned with issues such as divorce, custody of children and wards of court.

1.2 Civil and criminal law

The distinction between criminal and civil liability is central to the legal system and to the way in which the court system is structured. The objectives of each category of the law, although closely connected, are different.

A **crime** is conduct prohibited by the law. The **State** (in the form of the Crown Prosecution Service) is the usual prosecutor in a criminal case because it is the community as a whole which suffers as a result of the law being broken. However, private individuals may also prosecute (although this is rare). Persons guilty of crimes are **punished by fines or imprisonment**.

In a criminal trial, the **burden of proof** to convict the accused rests with the prosecution, which must prove its case **beyond reasonable doubt**. A criminal case might be referred to as *R v Shipman 2000*. The prosecution is brought in the name of the Crown (R signifying Regina, or the Queen). Shipman is the name of the accused or defendant.

Civil law exists to **regulate disputes** over the rights and obligations of persons dealing with each other. The State has no role in a dispute over, for instance, a breach of contract. It is up to the persons involved to settle the matter in the courts if they so wish. The general purpose of such a course of action is to impose a settlement, sometimes using financial **compensation** in the form of the legal remedy of damages, sometimes using **equitable remedies** such as injunctions or other orders. There is no concept of punishment; it is more a case of righting a wrong.

For example, the civil law can deal with matters as major as the ownership of a fleet of tankers, in a multi-million pound case lasting for months, or as seemingly minor as the height of a hedge between neighbours.

In civil proceedings, the case must be proved on the **balance of probability**. The party bearing the burden of proof is not required to produce absolute proof, nor prove the issue beyond reasonable doubt. He must convince the court that it is more probable than not that his assertions are true.

Terminology is different from that in criminal cases; the claimant sues the defendant, and the burden of proof may shift between the two.

The main areas of civil liability for this syllabus is **contract** between persons.

Definition

> **Standard of proof**: the extent to which the court must be satisfied by the evidence presented.

> **Activity 1**   **(5 minutes)**
>
> Why do you think that the standard of proof in criminal trials does not have to be beyond *all* doubt?

Activity 2   **(5 minutes)**

While driving, Martin exceeded the speed limit and crashed into the wall of Andrew's house, causing damage worth £5,000. What legal actions, either criminal or civil, may arise as a result of his actions?

---

2   RESOLUTION OF DISPUTES

Most people think that legal disputes are resolved purely by going to court. It is true that there is a well-established hierarchy of courts, the precise structure of which depends on whether the matter is dealt with under civil or criminal procedures, but alternative means of resolving disputes are becoming increasingly popular. The use of mediation, conciliation, tribunals and arbitration is often seen as quicker, cheaper and more focused than the traditional routes through the Courts, although recent reforms to the conduct of civil proceedings have helped to streamline the procedure.

3   THE COURT SYSTEM

The diagrams opposite set out the basic structure of the courts. The structure is different for criminal and civil cases, although as you can see from the diagram, some of the courts have both criminal and civil jurisdiction. The courts are discussed in more detail below.

3.1   Civil structure

The diagram below sets out the English **civil court structure**. This applies to cases arising in contract and tort, the two areas of law covered in this Unit. It is worth your having a basic understanding of how such cases are handled.

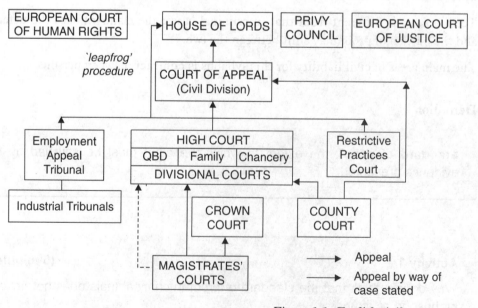

Figure 1.1: English civil court structure

3.2 The County Court

Jurisdiction

County Courts have **civil jurisdiction** only but deal with almost every kind of civil case. The practical importance of the County Courts is that they deal with **the majority of the country's civil litigation**.

The County Court is involved in:

(a) **Contract and tort claims,** so the areas of law covered in this book (defamation of character is not included)

(b) **Equitable matters** concerning trusts, mortgages and partnership dissolution

(c) **Disputes concerning land**

(d) **Undefended matrimonial cases**

(e) **Probate matters** (disputes over the terms of a will)

(f) **Miscellaneous matters** conferred by various statutes, for example the Consumer Credit Act 1974

(g) Some **bankruptcy,** company winding-up and admiralty cases

(h) All **small claims** and **fast-track cases** under the civil procedure rules, and some multi-track cases.

3.3 Civil procedure rules

Civil procedures encourage parties to consider **alternative methods** of dispute resolution and to avoid **expensive litigation**, resolving cases **quickly and without unnecessary confrontation.** Early settlement of disputes is encouraged during proceedings.

The Court has the power to control every aspect of the litigation process, shifting responsibility away from the litigants and their advisers. The Court is intended to be a place of **last resort** and not a place of first resort.

There are two principal areas in which the civil procedure rules are relevant:

- Tracking
- Case management

Tracking

After a defence has been filed, the case will be allocated to one of three tracks.

(a) In the **small claims track,** claims of no more than £5,000 will be heard. These are cases that are to be dealt with quickly and informally, often without the need for legal representation or for a full hearing.

(b) The **fast-track** is for claims of between £5,000 and £15,000 where the trial is to last no longer than one day. These are subject to a simplified court procedure and a fixed timetable designed to enable the claim to be determined within 30 weeks.

(c) Under the **multi-track,** claims of over £15,000 which are to be managed by the courts will be heard.

Case management

After allocation, the court will give directions setting out the procedures to be followed in bringing multi-track cases to trial. These will be an initial 'case management conference' to encourage parties to settle the dispute or to consider alternative dispute resolutions (such as mediation or arbitration). Features of the procedures include the following.

(a) A **pre-action protocol**, which entails setting out the claim in full to the defendant in an attempt to negotiate a settlement. The emphasis is placed on co-operation to identify the main issues. Failure to co-operate may lead to cost penalties, regardless of the eventual outcome of the case.

(b) A strict **timetable** for exchange of evidence is set by the court, including witness statements and relevant documents. Those holding themselves out as potential expert witnesses should be prepared to arrange their affairs to meet the court's commitments (*Matthews v Tarmac Bricks and Tiles Ltd 1999; Linda Rollinson v Kimberly Clark Ltd 1999*).

(c) A three-week **trial window** is allocated once the defence has been received. This does not change and the trial can fall anytime within the three-week period.

(d) There are cost **penalties** for failing to meet any deadline or date set by the court.

These civil procedure rules are subject to **continuous review** and update. A lot of legal terms previously in common usage have been replaced, for example a 'counterclaim' is now referred to as a 'Part 20 claim' and a 'payment into court' is referred to as a 'Part 36 claim'.

There is a senior judge with overall responsibility for civil justice, known as the **Head of Civil Justice**. His appointment is designed to raise the status of civil justice, which had long been in the shadow of the criminal justice system.

FOR DISCUSSION

In 1996 a survey by the National Audit Office found that although 94% of claimants in the Small Claims Court obtained judgement in their favour, only 54% recovered all or part of their claim and 36% recovered nothing.

Appeals

From the county court there is a right of appeal direct to the Civil Division of the Court of Appeal for multi-track cases. In most other cases an appeal goes to the relevant Division of the High Court.

Staffing

A **circuit judge** presides, being a barrister of at least ten years' standing. A **district judge**, who must be a solicitor or barrister of at least seven years' standing, assists the circuit judge.

Activity 3   **(10 minutes)**

Penny sues Desmond for breach of contract, asking for and obtaining damages of £10,000. In which court would this case be heard? Suppose the sum involved was £3,000. Would that make any difference to your answer?

3.4 The High Court

The **High Court** is organised into three divisions.

- Queen's Bench Division
- Chancery Division
- Family Division

Queen's Bench Division (QBD)

(a) *Civil jurisdiction*

The Queen's Bench Division deals mainly with common law matters such as actions based on contract or tort. It is the largest of the three divisions, having 73 judges. It includes a separate **Admiralty Court** to deal with shipping matters, and a **Commercial Court** which specialises in commercial cases.

(b) *Supervisory role*

The QBD can issue orders to other lower courts to take or desist from particular actions.

(c) *Criminal (appellate) jurisdiction*

The division hears some appeals from the county court, from the magistrates' courts (by way of case stated) and from the Crown Court.

Chancery Division

This division deals with traditional equity matters.

- Trusts and mortgages
- Revenue matters
- Bankruptcy (though outside London this is a county court subject)
- Disputed wills and administration of estates of deceased persons
- Partnership and company matters

There is a separate **Companies Court** within the division which deals with liquidations and other company proceedings and a patents court established under the Patents Act 1977.

Family Division

This division deals with matrimonial cases, family property cases, and proceedings relating to children (wardship, guardianship, adoption, legitimacy etc). The division hears appeals from magistrates' courts and the county court on family matters.

Appeals

Appeals are made from the High Court as follows.

(a) *Civil cases*

Appeals may be made to the **Court of Appeal (Civil Division)** or to the **House of Lords**, under what is known as the (rarely used) **'leapfrog'** procedure. For the leapfrog procedure to be followed, all parties must give their consent to it, and the case must involve a point of law of general public importance.

(b) *Criminal cases*

Appeals are made direct to the House of Lords where the case has reached the High Court on appeal from a magistrates' court or from the Crown Court.

Staffing

The High Court is staffed by *puisne* (pronounced 'puny') High Court judges. QBD is presided over by the Lord Chief Justice. Chancery is nominally presided over by the Lord Chancellor, in practice it is the Vice Chancellor. Family Division is presided over by its President.

3.5 Criminal structure

The diagram below sets out the **English criminal court structure.**

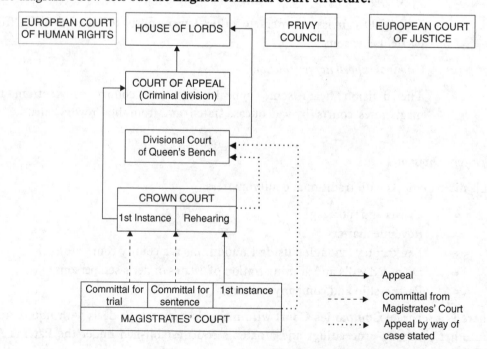

Figure 1.2: English criminal court structure

3.6 Magistrates' courts

Magistrates' courts are the inferior criminal courts. In addition they exercise certain family law, administrative law and minor civil functions such as licensing and local authority rates.

Criminal jurisdiction

Magistrates' courts deal with **criminal cases** as follows.

(a) They try summarily (without a jury) all minor offences.

(b) They conduct **committal proceedings,** which are preliminary investigations of the prosecution case, when the offence is triable only on **indictment** (by a Crown Court). For example, all cases of murder, although it is a serious offence, will start in the magistrates' court and then be committed to the Crown Court.

Definitions

> **Summary offences** are minor crimes, only triable summarily in magistrates' courts, for example speeding, pickpocketing.
>
> **Indictable offences** are more serious offences that can only be heard in a Crown Court. Examples include murder and arson. Some offences are '**triable either way**'. This means that the defendant can choose whether to be tried summarily by the magistrates, or by a jury in the Crown Court. Some types of burglary or robbery are triable either way.

The maximum penalties which **magistrates** may impose on a defendant convicted summarily of a criminal offence are **six months' imprisonment** or a **fine (or compensation to victim) of up to £5,000.** However, they can commit a person convicted of a summary offence to Crown Court for sentencing, so that a larger penalty may be imposed.

Civil jurisdiction

Magistrates' civil jurisdiction includes family proceedings (financial provision for parties to a marriage and children, the custody or supervision of children and guardianship, and adoption orders), various types of licensing, and enforcement of local authority charges and rates, for example the early opening of pubs in the UK during the Rugby World Cup in 2003.

Appeals

A defendant convicted on a **criminal charge** in a magistrates' court has a general right to a rehearing by a Crown Court.

On **family matters,** appeals are to a divisional court of the Family Division of the High Court.

Staffing

Lay magistrates are not legally qualified and they sit part-time. They are appointed by the Lord Chancellor and are assisted by a legally qualified clerk, who must be a solicitor or barrister of at least five years' standing. **Stipendiary magistrates** must be solicitors or barristers of at least seven years' standing. They are full time magistrates and sit in cities. Lay magistrates sit two or three to a court, while stipendiary magistrates sit alone.

Activity 4   **(10 minutes)**

Agatha is being prosecuted for an offence that is triable either way. She elects to be tried summarily in the magistrates' court, as she thinks that this will ensure that she cannot be sentenced to more than six months' imprisonment or fined more than £5,000. Is she right?

Give reasons for your answer.

3.7 The Crown Court

The Crown Court is theoretically a single court forming part of the **Supreme Court**, but in fact it comprises **local courts** in 90 large towns and also the **Central Criminal Court** (the Old Bailey, scene of many high profile trials) in London.

Criminal jurisdiction

It tries all indictable offences with a jury and hears appeals and deals with committals for sentencing from magistrates' courts.

There are four classes of offence triable in the Crown Court.

(a) **Class 1 offences** are the **most serious offences** such as murder and treason. A High Court judge must preside.

(b) **Class 2 offences** include **serious** offences such as rape and manslaughter. Cases are usually presided over by a High Court judge.

(c) **Class 3 offences** are **less serious** offences which must be tried on indictment. Examples are robbery and grievous bodily harm. A High Court judge, circuit judge or recorder may preside.

(d) **Class 4 offences** are those offences which may be tried on **indictment or summarily** (triable either way) such as burglary and reckless driving. Usually a circuit judge or recorder presides, though a High Court judge may do so.

Civil jurisdiction

The Crown Court deals with a few types of civil cases, being appeals from the magistrates' court on matters of affiliation, betting, gaming and licensing.

Appeals

From the Crown Court there is a right of appeal on criminal matters to the Criminal Division of the Court of Appeal. An appeal by way of 'case stated' on a point of law may also be made to a Divisional Court of the Queen's Bench Division.

Staffing

A High Court Judge, a circuit judge or a recorder may sit in the Crown Court, depending on the nature of the offence being tried. All indictable offences will be heard by a judge with a jury of between ten and twelve persons.

3.8 The Court of Appeal

The two branches of the law, civil and criminal, come together in the Court of Appeal and the High Court.

A **court of first instance** is the court where the case is originally heard in full. The **appeal court** is the court to which an appeal is made against the ruling or the sentence.

If the appeal court finds in favour of the appellant the original decision is **reversed** ie the result is changed, but the law is not. This is different from **overruling** which happens when a higher court finds a lower court's decision to be wrong in law and in future the law is changed.

Civil Division of the Court of Appeal

The Civil Division of the Court of Appeal can hear appeals from the High Court, county courts, and from certain other courts and special tribunals. It reviews the record of the evidence in the lower court and the legal arguments put before it. It may uphold or reverse the earlier decision or order a new trial.

Criminal Division

The Criminal Division of the Court of Appeal hears appeals from the Crown Court. It may also be invited to review a criminal case by the Home Secretary or to consider a point of law at the request of the Attorney General. Such appeals can have a widespread effect: in early 2004 a decision of the Court of Appeal meant that the government undertook to review over 250 cases of suspected child murder, which could in fact have been cot death.

Appeals

Appeals lie to the House of Lords, with the leave of the House of Lords or the Court of Appeal, on a point of law.

Staffing

The **Lord Justices of Appeal** are promoted from the High Court. In the Criminal Division, the **Lord Chief Justice** presides. In the Civil Division the **Master of the Rolls** presides.

3.9 The House of Lords

The House of Lords has two separate roles, and it is important that these are not confused.

(a) It has a **legislative role,** as one of the two Houses of Parliament. It approves, delays or argues against, all proposed Acts of Parliament.

(b) It has a **judicial role,** as the highest appeal court of the legal system, hearing appeals from both the civil and criminal divisions of the Court of Appeal.

Judges are usually promoted from the Court of Appeal to be members of the House of Lords. They are known as **Lords of Appeal in Ordinary,** or **Law Lords.** Five judges normally sit together, though there may only be three.

The Constitutional Reform Act 2005

The **Constitutional Reform Act 2005** which received Royal Assent on 24 March 2005 and that is expected to come into effect in 2008, will sever the link between the **legislative** and **judicial** functions of the House of Lords.

A **Supreme Court** of the United Kingdom will be established consisting of **twelve judges** known as *'Justices of the Supreme Court'* and its members will include a **President** and a **Deputy President.** The initial members will be the Lords of Appeal in Ordinary who are in tenure at the time.

Its **role** will be the same as the existing House of Lords judicial function, however it will extend into other matters outside the scope of this Course Book.

The House of Lords will continue with its current **legislative role** once the Supreme Court has been established.

3.10 European Courts

As we shall see later in this chapter, European Union law has a significant impact on English law.

The European Court of Human Rights

The European Court of Human Rights is the **supreme court** of those European states who have signed up to the **European Convention of Human Rights.** Any individual who alleges that their human rights have been violated can bring an action against those responsible.

Since the **Human Rights Act 1998** (see Chapter 3), the UK has incorporated the European Convention of Human Rights into UK law, enabling enforcement to be exercised by UK courts.

The European Court of Justice

The **European Court of Justice** has the role of **interpreting** European Treaty law and ensuring it is **observed.** European laws are enacted in the UK and are therefore directly applicable to **individuals** and **businesses** within the UK. Cases are usually between nation states or European institutions, however, individuals **can appeal** to the ECJ if they are affected personally.

The European Court of Justice is a court of first instance from which there is no appeal. The jurisdiction of the European Court falls under four main heads.

- Legal matters arising from the acts or omissions of member states, such as failure of a member state to fulfil its treaty obligations.

- Rulings on legal issues affecting persons which arise from EU law.

- Actions brought against EU institutions by member states, individuals or companies.

- Disputes between the communities and their employees.

When a legal issue affecting persons which arises from EU law comes before the Judicial Committee of the House of Lords, which is the final court of appeal in the UK, the Judicial Committee is obliged to refer it to the European Court for a ruling.

Thereafter the English court (duly instructed as to the meaning) must apply the rule to the case before it.

The Court consists of judges appointed for six-year periods on recommendation of member states. They are assisted by **Advocates-General** who submit reasoned argument on the issues before the Court. The Court gives a single judgment.

EU law in the UK

The directives to which Parliament must ultimately conform are issued as a result of negotiation and often agreement between the UK government and the other governments of the EU.

The UK government in turn is dependent on the support of a majority of Members of Parliament to retain office. To that extent, Parliament has indirect influence on the EU law-making process.

The House of Lords acknowledged the supremacy of EU law in the Factortame litigation.

> *Factortame Ltd v Secretary of State for Transport (No 2) 1991*
> *The facts:* Article 52 of the Treaty of Rome prohibits discrimination against the nationals of another EU member state. The Merchant Shipping Act 1988 requires 75% of directors and shareholders in companies operating British-registered fishing vessels to be British. Certain UK companies controlled by Spanish nationals and fishing in British waters were unable to meet these conditions. They brought a claim against the UK government on the grounds that the Act was incompatible with EU law.

> *Decision:* the ECJ laid down that EU law must be fully and uniformly applied in all member states.

3.11 The Privy Council

The **Judicial Committee of the Privy Council** is the final Court of Appeal for certain Commonwealth countries. Their decisions are also important to cases heard in the UK as they have **persuasive influence** over hearings concerning points of law applicable under the UK's jurisdiction.

Activity 5   **(10 minutes)**

List the court (or courts) to which an appeal may be made from each of the following:

(a) The County Court
(b) The High Court (civil cases)

(Refer to the court structure diagram in Section 3.1.)

---

4   ALTERNATIVE DISPUTE RESOLUTION

The court system is not always the most effective means to resolve disputes, although improvement to civil procedures makes it more attractive now. The key means of alternative dispute resolution (ADR) are various tribunals, and arbitration.

4.1   Tribunals

Employment tribunals

Employment tribunals (formerly industrial tribunals) are governed by the Employment Tribunals Act 1998 and have a wide jurisdiction over most disputes between **employee and employer**. Each tribunal is staffed by a legally qualified **chairman** and two other persons, one representing the employer and one representing the employee. Here are some examples of typical cases.

- Disputes about redundancy pay
- Complaints of unfair dismissal
- Questions as to terms of contracts of employment
- Equal pay claims and disputes over issues such as maternity pay
- Appeals against health and safety notices
- Complaints about sex, race and disability discrimination
- Disputes over trade union membership

There is a right of appeal to the **Employment Appeal Tribunal**.

Employment Appeal Tribunal

This is a court of equal status with the High Court. It hears appeals from tribunals mainly on employment matters.

A **High Court judge** and two **lay assessors** from a panel appointed on the Lord Chancellor's recommendation sit. From the EAT there is a right of appeal to the Court of Appeal.

Social security appeal tribunals

The Social Security appeal tribunals is the first level of external review of decisions made by Centrelink, the administrative body, and the Child Support Agency, regarding social security, family assistance, education and training payment, and child support.

16

Lands tribunal

This tribunal deals with disputes over the value of property, for example for compulsory purchase. It is usually composed of three members, being experienced lawyers and qualified valuation experts.

Supervision of tribunals

The working of the system of tribunals is supervised by a **Council on Tribunals**. In many instances there is a statutory right to appeal from a tribunal to a higher court on points of law. The High Court may also make prerogative orders to prevent or remedy errors and injustices.

4.2 Arbitration

This is increasingly becoming a popular alternative to litigation in the courts, and it is now quite common for contracts, especially large commercial contracts, to contain provision for voluntary arbitration in the event of a dispute arising between the parties to the contract. This can be very helpful as referring the dispute to arbitration means that it will be handled by an independent expert (or panel of experts) who fully understand the legal ramifications. It also provides advantages such as privacy for the parties involved.

Proceedings in arbitration are less adversarial and confrontational in nature than court hearings (where one party is 'opposed' to the other) so it is more likely that a compromise will be found, meaning that the concept of 'winners and losers' is less pronounced.

Unless otherwise agreed, a hearing before an arbitrator follows the same essential procedure as in a court of law. However, following the Arbitration Act 1996, the arbitrators and parties can settle on the **form** of the arbitration.

The Arbitration Act 1996

The Arbitration Act 1996 aimed to introduce **greater speed and flexibility** into the arbitration process, in particular by conferring upon the parties the right to make their own agreement on virtually all aspects of the arbitration (s 1). It contains provisions for the **appointment and removal** of arbitrators, and the power to appoint **experts** (s 37), advisers and assessors. It turned the courts' role into a **supervisory** rather than an interventionist one. Under this Act, the parties may choose to dispense with formal hearings and strict rules of evidence and procedure (s 46).

Under the 1996 Act, an arbitration agreement is a **separate agreement** which can outlive the original contract that gave rise to the arbitration proceedings.

The main advantage of the arbitration procedure is **privacy**, since the public and the press have no right to attend a hearing before an arbitrator.

Compulsory arbitration

In addition to voluntary arbitration as described above, compulsory arbitration may be enforced in the following circumstances.

(a) Certain statutes (Acts of Parliament) provide for arbitration on disputes arising out of the provision of the statute.

(b) The High Court may order that a case of a technical nature shall be tried (or investigated with report back to the court) by an Official Referee or other arbitrator.

Chapter roundup

- Law is a fundamental part of a civilised society and governs the relationships between individuals among themselves and between individuals and the state.

- People are prosecuted under the criminal law for offences committed against the state, and a penalty is imposed.

- Individuals (or companies) sue each other under the civil law to receive compensation for some kind of loss or damage suffered. The purpose is not punishment but the righting of a wrong.

- There is a hierarchy of civil and criminal courts. In broad terms those lower down in the hierarchy have a right to appeal to those above. The operation of the civil courts depends largely on the financial value of the case under consideration.

- Going to court is not the only means of resolving a dispute. Tribunals deal with specific cases involving employment and other specialised areas, and arbitration provides a highly effective alternative to litigation.

Quick quiz

1 Give two examples each of public and private law.

2 What degree of proof is required in a civil case?

3 What matters are dealt with in the small claims track?

4 Which Court hears appeals arising from decisions of the Court of Appeal?

5 In which court will a criminal case start to go through the legal process?

6 What are the advantages of arbitration over court action?

Answers to quick quiz

1   Public law: Criminal law
                       Constitutional law
    Private law: Contract law
                       Law of tort
                                   (see para 1.1)

2   Proof on the balance of probability. (para 1.2)

3   Claims worth less than £5,000. (para 3.3)

4   The House of Lords. (paras 3.4 and 3.9)

5   Magistrate's court. (para 3.6)

6   Reference to detail
    Use of experts
    Privacy
    Compromise
    Confidentiality
    Speed and economy
    Decisions are binding   (para 4.2)

Answers to activities

1   Nothing can be proved beyond *all* doubt.

2   Martin could be prosecuted under the criminal law for speeding, and also sued by Andrew under the civil law for damages for the damage caused to Andrew's house.

3   The case for £10,000 would probably be heard in a fast-track case in the County Court. If the amount involved was £3,000 it would probably be dealt with as a small claims track case.

4   This will not ensure a lower sentence, as Agatha could be convicted in the Magistrates' Court but then committed to the Crown Court for sentencing.

5   (a)   The Civil Division of the Court of Appeal (for multi-track cases) or the High Court.

    (b)   The Civil Division of the Court of Appeal or the House of Lords.

Chapter 2:
LEGAL ADVICE, FUNDING AND LEGAL PERSONNEL

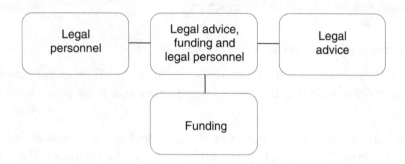

Introduction

In this chapter, we turn our focus from the English legal system, with its national spread, to the interaction between you and the system. You may wish to obtain legal advice as an individual or on behalf of a business entity that you are connected with, for example a company or a partnership. You will need to establish how to obtain legal advice, and how the cost of this advice might be funded.

Your objectives

In this chapter you will learn about the following.

(a)   Where to go to obtain legal advice

(b)   How legal services are funded

(c)   The different types of legal personnel that you may encounter

1   LEGAL ADVICE

The Legal Services Commission was created under the Access to Justice Act 1999 and replaced the Legal Aid Board. It is responsible for the administration of two schemes in England and Wales, Community Legal Service Direct (CLS Direct) and the Criminal Defence Service (CDS). For many individuals, these services provide a useful first reference point for access to legal advice. Meanwhile, other individuals will contact a solicitor for advice and business people too are likely to use a firm of solicitors for advice. Those who are less familiar with the legal system, or whose circumstances are quite specific, may well encounter other sources.

1.1   Community Legal Service Direct (CLS Direct)

Community Legal Service Direct has replaced the old civil legal aid scheme and is designed to provide wide public access to information and advice, together with details of funding.

CLS Direct has developed local networks of people and organisations giving legal help and advice, for example lawyers, Citizens Advice Bureaux, law centres and local councils. There are also national organisations which are legal helplines. The CLS legal Advisor Directory of legal information and advice providers is available on the official website at clsdirect.org.uk. Most have the CLS Specialist Quality mark.

1.2   Criminal Defence Service (CDS)

The Criminal Defence Service replaced the old system of criminal legal aid. It guarantees people under police investigation or facing criminal charges access to legal advice. It is run by the CDS in partnership with criminal defence lawyers and representatives. Support may be provided by solicitors in private firms, or by solicitors, accredited representatives and administrators employed by the Public Defender Service (PDS). Staff at the PDS are available round the clock to:

- Give advice to people in custody
- Represent clients in court

There are three levels of support.

(a)   **Advice and assistance**, which covers advice and assistance from a solicitor on criminal matters.

(b)   **Advocacy**, which covers some case preparation and initial representation at court.

(c)   **Representation** for criminal offences.

A **duty solicitor** is available at a police station to help during questioning and at a Magistrates' Court and is provided to offer free legal advice. This scheme is designed for those individuals who do not have their own solicitor.

Advice and assistance

Advice and assistance covers help from a solicitor including giving general advice, writing letters, negotiating, getting a barrister's opinion and preparing a written case. It enables people of limited financial means to get help from a solicitor.

Advocacy

This covers the cost of a solicitor preparing the accused's case and initial representation in certain proceedings in both the Magistrates' Court and the Crown Court.

Representation

Representation covers the cost of a solicitor to prepare the accused's defence before he goes to court and to represent him there, including dealing with issues such as bail.

Representation is *not* available to bring a private prosecution – that is, bringing a criminal case against another person.

1.3 Other sources

There are many ways of finding a solicitor in order to obtain legal advice. The following is not an exhaustive list.

(a) Through the www.clsdirect.org.uk website, which gives access to the online CLS Legal Advisor Directory

(b) The Law Society's Directory of Solicitors and Barristers

(c) By going to a local solicitor's office

(d) By asking at a local Citizens' Advice Bureau or law centre

(e) By asking a trade union official

(f) By asking a friend or relative

Activity 1 **(1 hour maximum)**

Visit the www.clsdirect.org.uk website and see how long it takes you to identify how you might obtain advice on one of the following in your area.

(a) Making a will
(b) A family dispute
(c) Obtaining some money you are owed

---

2 FUNDING

Funding is available, as a general rule, to those of limited financial means, through the CLS Fund or the CDS respectively. The person must apply for CLS Fund help from legal advisers who have the CLS Specialist Quality mark award and who display the CLS logo. An individual cannot apply directly to the fund.

Other methods of funding might include the following.

(a) Advice from a Citizens Advice Bureau or Law Centre is often free of charge.

(b) A solicitor might offer a half-hour of free legal advice to a new client.

(c) Some solicitors offer a first consultation at a fixed price.

(d)   Some solicitors will provide advice free of charge in certain situations. This is referred to as '*pro bono*' work.

(e)   Membership of a trade union may give an entitlement to free legal advice.

(f)   Some insurance policies especially those offered by motoring organisations, cover free legal advice and services.

(g)   Some lawyers operate on a 'no win, no fee' basis. This is also referred to as a conditional fee.

CLS Fund

Whether the CLS Fund will support a particular case depends on whether it meets criteria that are applied according to the Lord Chancellor's priorities. These are set in the Funding code.

The CLS Fund may provide funding in the following areas.

- Divorce
- Housing matters such as rent or mortgage arrears, repairs, eviction
- Welfare benefits
- Credit, debt, buying goods
- Immigration, nationality or asylum
- Jobs/discrimination at work
- Family and children
- Challenging decisions of public bodies such as the Benefits Agency or the Home Office
- Mental health
- Actions against the police
- Criminal negligence
- Care in the community provided by a Social Services or Health Care Authority

No win, no fee

If a case goes to court, some lawyers will agree either to reduce or waive their charges if their client loses the case. This is called a 'no win, no fee' (or conditional fee) agreement. If the client wins the case, he will have to pay the lawyer what is know as a 'success' fee along with the usual costs like the lawyer's expenses and the court's fees. However, he should be able to claim these costs and the success fee back from the other side. If he loses the case, he will not usually have to pay his own lawyer's fees, but he may have to pay the expenses and the other side's legal costs. He may be able to take out insurance to cover these costs.

CDS funding

A law practice must be registered with the CDS in order to provide advice under it. Funding of the various levels of advice is as follows.

A client applying for help with a magistrates court case must satisfy both a **means test** and an interests of justice test.

The **means test** is such that those in receipt of income-based jobseekers' allowance, income support or a guaranteed State Pension Credit automatically qualify as does anyone under 16 and anyone aged 16 to 18 in full-time education. Otherwise, the client needs to have a weekly income below a certain amount. Also, they must not have capital worth over a certain figure.

The factors to be taken into account in the **interests of justice** test are detailed in the Access to Justice Act 1999.

3   LEGAL PERSONNEL

In this chapter, we review the role of solicitors and barristers. The role of the judiciary was described in Chapter 1.

3.1   Solicitors

A solicitor provides a range of legal services to companies, organisations and individuals on a wide range of legal issues, in diverse areas of practice. The majority of solicitors work in private practice but there are other opportunities in industry and in the public sector.

Private practice

Within private practice there are a number of areas where a solicitor might work.

(a)   **High street firms** – concentrate on work with the local community and individuals. Typically this would include matrimonial, conveyancing and wills.

(b)   **Niche firms** – law firms that specialise in a variety of areas of law from Admiralty to Trust.

(c)   **Medium-sized firms** – these firms work with individuals and commercial businesses.

(d)   **Large commercial firms** – mainly based in major cities, these concentrate on work with large commercial businesses.

Qualifying as a solicitor

The Law Society is the body that makes the rules on education and training of solicitors. To qualify as a solicitor the individual must:

- Either complete a three-year law degree, or a one-year full-time Common Professional exam (CPE), or a post-graduate Diploma in Law

- Undertake the Legal Practice Course (one or two years)

BPP
LEARNING MEDIA

- Complete a two-year training contract with an approved solicitor or other approved organisation, such as a local authority

The training contract is the final stage of qualification for a career as a practising solicitor. A training contract takes two years and many training contract providers divide this training amongst different departments or 'seats' (usually four) to give the trainee a breadth of experience that better enables him to make a decision on specialisation after qualifying.

Outside private practice

The majority of solicitors and barristers are employed in private practice but this is changing. Other areas where a solicitor's qualification is often useful or essential are described below.

(a) **Commerce and industry** in the UK. They offer in-house specialist legal knowledge to large organisations such as utilities, finance and industrial companies. Some companies offer training contracts (and pupillages for barristers) but it is more usual to move into industry work on qualification.

(b) The **Crown Prosecution Service** (CPS) also offers pupillages and training contracts for students who have completed their law school training.

(c) The **Government Legal Service** (GLS) consists of qualified lawyers and legal trainees employed in over 40 government organisations. The GLS take a small number of trainee solicitors and barristers each year and can offer sponsorship. Trainees may be trained in more than one government department and pupil barristers are able to spend some of their pupillage in chambers.

(d) There are many **local government opportunities**. All councils have legal departments staffed by solicitors – and some barristers – to advise on a wide range of topics from employment to land purchase, through to prosecution of rogue traders and suppliers. There is no national recruitment scheme, as each local authority is a separate employer and will advertise and recruit according to their own policy.

3.2 Barristers

Barristers are specialist lawyers, who are expected to have expertise in advocacy, the provision of written advice and the drafting of documents. Barristers research specific points of law and precedents, prosecute or defend cases in court and draft opinions and pleadings.

The majority of work is in private practice although opportunities also exist in the Employed Bar: in industry and in the public sector. There are many specialist areas that a barrister can practise in from Admiralty, Landlord and Tenant to Revenue.

Qualifying as a barrister

The Bar Council is the body that makes the rules on the education and training of barristers. To qualify as a barrister the individual must:

- Either complete a three-year law degree, or take the one-year CPE

- Join one of the four Inns of Court then complete the one-year Bar Vocational Course (two years part-time) before being 'called to the Bar'

- Undertake a one-year pupillage

Pupillage

Pupillage involves a twelve-month period of practical supervision under an experienced barrister and can be in chambers or in industry or with organisations such as the Government Legal Service. The first six months is non-practising with pupils shadowing their pupil master. The next six months is spent practising with pupils undertaking their own cases. This second six months can be spent at the same chambers but this is often spent at another 'set'. There are also opportunities to use other external training such as marshalling (shadowing a judge) to satisfy, with the prior approval of the Bar Council, all or part of the practising six months of pupillage.

Activity 2   **(30 minutes)**

Look on the Internet or in your local area business telephone directory or Yellow Pages for details of solicitors' firms. See how far you can distinguish between the specialisations of the different firms.

Chapter roundup

- The Legal Services Commission is responsible for the administration of the Community Legal Service Direct and the Criminal Defence Service. These have replaced the old system of legal aid.

- Funding is usually available only to those of limited financial means. Some lawyers take cases on a conditional fee basis.

- Lawyers practice as solicitors or barristers. There are separate routes to qualification for each.

Quick quiz

1   The Public Defender Service (PCS) is part of the community Legal Service Direct. True or false?

2   What is the duty solicitor scheme?

3   What does *pro bono* mean?

Answers to quick quiz

1   False. It is part of the Criminal Defence Service (see para 1.2)

2   A scheme under which a solicitor is available at a police station or a magistrates' court to give advice to an individual who has been detailed or arrested on suspicion of a criminal offence. (para 1.2)

3   A solicitor may agree to do work free of charge, or *pro bono*. (para 2)

Answers to activities

1   There is no specific solution to this activity.

2   There is no specific solution to this activity.

Chapter 3:
SOURCES OF LAW AND RULES OF INTERPRETATION

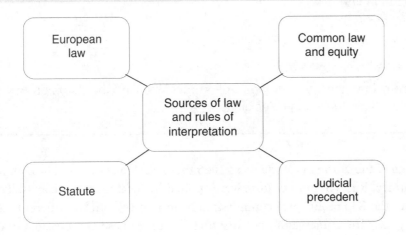

Introduction

There are three main sources of law with which you need to be familiar if you are fully to understand the detailed areas of the law which are covered in the forthcoming chapters. The first is judicial precedent, or case law, which is the law that is created as a result of the decisions of the courts. The second is statute, which is the law created by Acts of Parliament. The third is European law. It is important for you to understand the role of European law in the UK.

Throughout this Course Book, you will find references to cases to illustrate the legal principles and rules which you will learn, and also to statute (shown for example as *Companies Act s 368*). You will find reference to European Regulations, which have the force of law in the UK, and Directives which must be implemented by national legislation.

Judicial precedent and statute are often referred to as the **legal** sources of law. There are also two important **historical** sources of law, common law and equity, from which much of case law springs, and we introduce the chapter with a brief review of the role of equity today.

Your objectives

In this chapter you will learn about the following.

(a) The doctrine of judicial precedent and when it is and is not applied

(b) The importance of statute and the means by which legislation is made

(c) The importance of delegated legislation

(d) Rules of statutory interpretation

(e) An introduction to the role of EU law

(f) The difference between common law and equity and the role of equity today

1 COMMON LAW AND EQUITY

English law has developed in an unbroken progression over a period of some 900 years. English law's historical sources are those procedures, rules and ways of thinking which have given rise to today's current sources of law. The most important historical sources of law are common law and equity. It is important to have some understanding of these sources before studying judicial precedent.

1.1 Common law

Definition

> **Common law**: the body of legal rules developed by the common law courts and now embodied in legal decisions.

At the time of the Norman Conquest in 1066 there was no system of law common to the whole country. Rules of local custom were applied by local manorial courts. To improve the system, the King sent royal commissioners on tour (circuit) to different parts of the realm to deal with crimes and civil disputes. In time these commissioners developed rules of law, selected from the differing local customs which they had encountered, as a common law (ius commune) which they applied uniformly in all trials (before the King's courts) throughout the kingdom.

The procedure of common law could be unsatisfactory. A claimant might lose his case owing to a minor technicality of wording, be frustrated by specious defences, deliberate delay or corruption, or find himself unable to enforce a judgement given in his favour because there was no suitable common law remedy. As a result, the doctrine of equity was developed.

Definitions

> **Claimant**: the person who complains or brings an action asking the court for relief (used to be called the plaintiff).
>
> **Defendant**: the person against whom a civil action is brought or who is prosecuted for a criminal offence.

1.2 Equity

Citizens who could not obtain redress for grievances in the common law courts petitioned the King to obtain relief by direct royal intervention. The principles on which the Chancellor (on behalf of the King) decided points were based on fair dealing between two individuals as equals. These principles became known as equity. The system of equity, developed and administered by the Court of Chancery, was not an alternative to the common law, but a method of adding to and improving on the common law.

Definition

Equity: a source of English law consisting of those rules which emerged from the Court of Chancery to supplement (but not replace) the common law.

This interaction of common law and equity produced three major changes.

(a) **New rights**. Equity recognised and protected rights for which the common law gave no safeguards. If, for example, Sam transferred property to the legal ownership of Tom to pay the income of the property to Ben (in modern law Tom is a trustee for Ben), the common law simply recognised that Tom was the owner of the property and ignored Tom's obligations to Ben. Equity recognised that Tom was the owner of the property at common law but insisted, as a matter of justice and good conscience, that Tom must comply with the terms of the trust imposed by Sam (the settlor) and pay the income to Ben (the beneficiary).

(b) **Better procedure**. Equity could be more effective than common law in bringing a disputed matter to a decision.

(c) **Better remedies**. The standard common law remedy for the successful claimant was the award of monetary compensation, damages, for his loss. Equity was able to order the defendant to do what he had agreed to do (specific performance), to abstain from wrongdoing (injunction), to alter a document so that it reflected the parties' true intentions (rectification) or to restore the pre-contract status quo (rescission).

Definitions

Specific performance: an equitable remedy in which the court orders the defendant to perform his side of a contract.

Injunction: an equitable remedy in which the court orders the other party to a contract to observe negative restrictions.

Rectification: an equitable remedy in which the court can order a document to be altered so that it reflects the parties' true intentions.

Rescission: an equitable remedy through which a contract is cancelled or rejected and the parties are restored to their pre-contract condition, as if it had never been entered into.

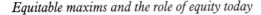

Equitable maxims and the role of equity today

The development of equity was based on a number of equitable maxims (or principles). These are still applied today if an equitable remedy is sought. The following are examples.

(a) **He who comes to equity must come with clean hands**. To be fairly treated, the claimant must have acted fairly himself. For example, in the case *D and C Builders v Rees 1966* the defendant could not plead a defence of equitable estoppel because she had tried to take advantage of the claimant's financial difficulties.

(b) **Equality is equity**. The law attempts to play fair and redress the balance; hence what is available to one person must be available to another. As an example, equity does not allow the remedy of specific performance to be granted against a minor (ie a person under the age of eighteen), and it does not allow a minor to benefit from the remedy either.

(c) **Equity looks at the intent, not the form**. However a person may try to pretend that he is doing something in the correct form, equity will look at what he is actually trying to achieve. For example, if an agreed damages clause in a contract is not a genuine estimate of likely loss, equity will treat the clause as a penalty clause, and it is less likely to be awarded to the injured party.

The relationship between common law and equity

Until the 1870s, common law and equity were administered in separate courts. However, the Judicature Acts of the 1870s enabled them to be administered in the same court, and a judge is able to apply to a case whichever principles he thinks fit.

In the case of a conflict between the two, however, **equity will prevail**. It is sometimes described as 'a gloss on the common law' in that where a common law decision would produce an unfair, or inequitable, result, equity can be applied to avoid that outcome.

2 JUDICIAL PRECEDENT

The development of common law and equity has led to one of the main legal sources of law, case law, and has an influence on much of the other main source, legislation.

2.1 *Stare decisis*

Both common law and equity are the product of decisions in the courts. They are judge-made law but based on a principle of consistency. Once a matter of principle has been decided (by one of the higher courts) it becomes a precedent. In any later case to which that principle is relevant the same principle should (subject to certain exceptions) be applied. This doctrine of consistency, following precedent, is expressed in the maxim stare decisis, 'to stand by a decision'.

Judges inevitably create law. Sometimes an Act of Parliament will deliberately vest a wide discretion in the judiciary. In other cases there may be no statutory provision and no existing precedent relevant to the particular dispute. Even so, the doctrine of judicial precedent is based on the view that it is not the function of a judge to make law, but to decide cases in accordance with existing rules.

It is generally accepted that consistency is an important feature of a good decision-making process. Similar cases should be treated in the same way. However, the passage of time, or changing circumstances, may cause a case to offer a solution which no longer appears just. One of the main functions of the higher courts is to give an authoritative decision on disputed questions of law. A court's decision is expected to be consistent (or at least not unjustifiably inconsistent) with previous decisions and to provide an opinion which the parties, and others, can use to direct their future relationships. This is the basis of the system of **judicial precedent**.

Judicial precedent depends on the following.

(a)   There must be adequate and reliable reports of earlier decisions.

(b)   There must be rules for extracting from an earlier decision on one set of facts the legal principle to be applied in reaching a decision on a different set of facts.

(i)   The principle must be a proposition of law.
(ii)   It must form part of the *ratio decidendi* of the case.
(iii)   The material facts of each case must be the same.

(c)   Precedents must be classified into those which are binding and those which are merely persuasive. This depends primarily on the respective status of the preceding court and the later one.

2.2   *Ratio decidendi*

A judgement will start with a description of the facts of the case and probably a review of earlier precedents and possible alternative theories. The judge will then make statements of law applicable to the legal problems raised by the material facts. Provided these statements are the basis for the decision, they are known as the *ratio decidendi* of the case. The *ratio decidendi* (reason for deciding) is the vital element which binds future judges.

Definition

> ***Ratio decidendi***: the reason for a decision.

If a judge's statements of legal principle do not form the basis of the decision, or if his statements are not based on the existing material facts but on hypothetical facts, they are known as *obiter dicta* (said by the way). A later court may respect such statements, but it is not bound to follow them. They are only of persuasive authority.

Definition

> ***Obiter dicta***: statements made by a judge 'by the way'.

It is not always easy to identify the *ratio decidendi*. The same judgement may appear to contain contradictory views of the law in different passages. In decisions of appeal courts, where there are three or even five separate judgements, the members of the court may reach the same conclusion but give different reasons. The ratio may also be mingled with *obiter* statements. Many judges help by indicating in their speeches which comments are *ratio* and which are *obiter*.

NOTES

Activity 1 (10 minutes)

A case hinges upon whether clementines are oranges. The judgement contains the remark 'clementines are oranges, just as peanuts are nuts'. How does this remark illustrate the distinction between *ratio decidendi* and *obiter dicta*?

Distinguishing the facts

Although there may arguably be a finite number of legal principles to consider when deciding a case, there are necessarily an infinite variety of facts which may be presented. Apart from identifying the *ratio decidendi* of an earlier case, it is also necessary to consider how far the facts of the previous and the latest case are similar. Facts are never identical. If the differences appear significant the court may 'distinguish' the earlier case on the facts and thereby avoid following it as a precedent.

Not every decision made in every court is binding as a judicial precedent. The **court's status** has a significant effect on whether its decisions are binding, persuasive or disregarded. You may want to refer back to the court structure diagrams in Chapter 1, Sections 3.1 and 3.4 while you read the table below.

Court	Bound by	Decisions binding
Magistrates' Court	• High Court • The Court of Appeal • House of Lords • European Court of Justice	• No one • Not even itself
County Court	• High Court • The Court of Appeal • House of Lords • European Court of Justice	• No one • Not even itself
Crown Court	• High Court (QBD) • The Court of Appeal • House of Lords • European Court of Justice	• No one • However, its decisions are reported more widely and are more authoritative

The High Court
consists of divisions:
• **Queen's bench**
• **Chancery**
• **Family**
	• Judge sitting alone
	  – The Divisional Court
	  – The Court of Appeal
	  – House of Lords
	  – European Court of Justice
	• Judges sitting together
	  – Any Divisional Court
	  – The Court of Appeal
	  – House of Lords
	  – European Court of Justice
		• Judge sitting alone
		  – Magistrates' court
		  – County court
		  – Crown Court
		
		• Judges sitting together
		  – Magistrates' Court
		  – County Court
		  – Crown Court
		  – Divisional Courts

BPP
LEARNING MEDIA

Court	Bound by	Decisions binding
The Court of Appeal	• Own decisions • House of Lords (subject to an exception below) • European Court of Justice	• All inferior English courts • Itself (subject to the exception)
The House of Lords	• Itself (except in exceptional cases) • European Court of Justice	• All English Courts • Itself (except in exceptional cases)
The European Court of Justice	• No one • Not even itself	• All English Courts

EU law

Apart from binding precedents as described above, reported decisions of any court (even if lower in status) may be treated as persuasive precedents: they may be (but need not be) followed in a later case. If, in a case before the House of Lords there is a dispute about a point of European Union (EU) law, it must be referred to the European Court of Justice for a ruling. English courts are also required to take account of principles laid down by the Court of Justice in so far as these are relevant. The Court of Justice does not, however, create or follow precedents as such.

Overruling a precedent

A court of higher status is not only free to disregard the decision of a court of lower status in an earlier case. It may also deprive it of authority and expressly overrule it. This does not affect the outcome as regards the defendant and claimant in the earlier decision; it only affects the precedents to be applied in later cases.

Avoiding precedent

Even if a precedent appears to be binding, a court may decline to follow it:

(a)   By distinguishing the facts (as described above)

(b)   By declaring the *ratio decidendi* obscure, particularly when a decision by three or five judges gives as many different ratios

(c)   By declaring that the previous decision was made *per incuriam*, that is without taking account of some essential point of law, such as an important precedent

(d)   By declaring the precedent to be in conflict with a fundamental principle of law

(e)   By declaring the precedent to be too wide

Activity 2 (10 minutes)

A brings an action against B and the case is finally settled in favour of B in the Court of Appeal.

Fifteen years later C brings an action against D on similar but slightly different facts and the case of A v B is the only relevant precedent.

If C v D reaches the House of Lords, consider whether the case of A v B is binding.

2.3 The advantages and disadvantages of precedent

Many of the strengths of judicial precedent also indicate some of its weaknesses. Generally the arguments revolve around the principles of consistency, clarity, flexibility and detail.

Certainty. The whole point of following binding precedent is that the law is decided fairly and predictably. In theory therefore it should be possible to avoid litigation because the result is a foregone conclusion. However, judges are often forced to make illogical distinctions to avoid an unfair result which, combined with the wealth of reported cases, serves to complicate the law.

Clarity. Following only the reasoning in ratio statements should lead to statements of principle for general application. In practice, however, the same judgement may be found to contain propositions which appear inconsistent with each other or with the precedent which the court purports to follow.

Flexibility. The real strength of the system lies in its ability to change with changing circumstances since it arises directly out of the actions of society. The counter argument is that the doctrine limits judges' discretion and they may be unable to avoid deciding in line with a precedent which produces an unfair result. Often the deficiency may only be remedied by passing a statute to correct the law's failings.

Detail. Precedents state how the law applies to facts, and it should be flexible enough to allow for details to be different, so that the law is all-encompassing. However, judges often distinguish cases on facts to avoid following a precedent. The wealth of detail is also a drawback in that it produces a vast body of reports which must be taken into account; again, though, statute can help by codifying rules developed in case law.

Practicality. Case law is based on experience of actual cases brought before the courts. This is an advantage over legislation which is often found wanting when tested. However, unfair precedent may be created that may be difficult to avoid or overrule.

3 STATUTE

Legislation is made by **Parliament** (or in exercise of law-making powers delegated by Parliament). Until the United Kingdom entered the European Community in 1973 the UK Parliament was completely **sovereign**.

In recent years however, UK membership of the European Community has restricted the previously unfettered power of Parliament. There is an **obligation**, imposed by the Treaty of Rome, **to bring UK law into line with the Treaty itself and with Directives.**

Regulations, having the force of law in every member state, may be made under provisions of the Treaty of Rome.

Parliamentary sovereignty gives rise to a number of consequences. Parliament may

- **Repeal** earlier statutes
- **Overrule** or modify case law developed in the courts, or
- **Make new law** on subjects which have not been regulated by law before.

In practice, Parliament usually follows certain **conventions** which limit its freedom.

No Parliament can legislate so as to **prevent** a future Parliament changing the law.

The judges have to **interpret** statute law and they may find a meaning in a statutory rule which those Members of Parliament who promoted the statute did not intend.

The **validity** of an Act of Parliament cannot be questioned.

> *Cheney v Conn 1968*
>
> *The facts:* The claimant objected to his tax assessment under the Finance Act 1964 because some of the tax collected was used to fund the manufacture of nuclear weapons. He alleged that this was contrary to the Geneva Conventions Act 1957 and in conflict with international law.
>
> *Decision:* The 1964 Act gave clear authority to collect the taxes.

However, the judge may declare an Act to be 'incompatible' with the European Convention on Human Rights.

3.1 Types of legislation

In addition to making new law and altering existing law, Parliament may make the law clearer by passing a **codifying** statute (such as the Sale of Goods Act 1979) to put case law on a statutory basis, or a **consolidating** statute to incorporate an original statute and its successive amendments into a single statute (such as the Employment Rights Act 1996 or the Companies Act 2006).

Legislation can also be **categorised** in the following ways.

- **Public Acts**; legislation that affects the **general public**

- **Private Acts**; legislation that affects **specific individuals and groups**

- **Enabling legislation; empowers a specific individual or body** to produce the detail required by a parent Act. For example, a parent Act may outline a particular report that it requires companies to produce. Enabling legislation would leave the detail of how the report should be put together and it contents to an individual or body that is suitably qualified. See **delegated legislation** in paragraph 2.5.

3.2 Parliamentary procedure

A proposal for legislation is originally aired in public in a Government green paper. After comments are received a white paper is produced, which sets out the aim of the legislation. It is then put forward in draft form as a bill, and may be introduced into either the House of Commons or the House of Lords, the two Houses of Parliament.

When the bill has passed through one House it must then go through the same stages in the other House.

In each House the successive stages of dealing with the bill are as follows.

(a) **First reading:** publication and introduction into the agenda: no debate.

(b) **Second reading:** debate on the general merits of the bill but no amendments at this stage.

(c) **Committee stage:** the bill is examined by a standing committee of about twenty members, representing the main parties and including some members at least who specialise in the relevant subject. The bill is examined section by section and may be amended. If the bill is very important all or part of the committee stage may be taken by the House as a whole sitting as a committee.

(d) **Report stage:** the bill as amended in committee is reported to the full House for approval. If the Government has undertaken in committee to reconsider various points it often puts forward its final amendments at this stage.

(e) **Third reading:** this is the final approval stage at which only verbal amendments may be made.

When it has passed through both Houses it is submitted for the **Royal Assent** which in practice is given on the Queen's behalf by a committee of the Lord Chancellor and two other peers. It then becomes an Act of Parliament (or statute). It comes into effect at the start of the day on which Royal Assent is given, or (if the Act itself so provides) at some other time or on a commencement date set by statutory instrument.

Most bills are public bills of general application, whether introduced by the Government or by a private member. They are referred to as **Government bills** or **private members' bills** respectively. An example of the latter is the Abortion Act 1967, sponsored by David Steel MP. Private members' bills are often brought on matters of conscience such as fox hunting.

If the House of Commons and the House of Lords disagree over the same bill, the House of Lords may delay the passing of the bill for a maximum of one year (except for financial measures, such as the annual Finance Act). It may veto any bill which tries to extend the life of Parliament beyond five years, and it may veto any private bill.

Activity 3   **(10 minutes)**

Many countries have a Bill of Rights, which cannot be changed by normal legislative procedures. What aspect of Parliamentary sovereignty would make it difficult to give a Bill of Rights for the UK such a secure position?

3.3 Delegated legislation

To save time in Parliament it is usual to set out the main principles in the body of an Act as numbered sections and to relegate the details to schedules (at the end of the Act) which need not be debated, though they are visible and take effect as part of the act. But even with this device there is a great deal which cannot conveniently be included in acts. It may, for example, be necessary, after an Act has been passed, for the Government to consult interested parties and then produce regulations, having the force of the law, to implement the Act, to fix commencement dates to bring the Act into operation or to prescribe printed forms for use in connection with it. To provide for these and other matters a modern act usually contains a section by which power is given to a minister, or a public body such as a local authority, to make subordinate or delegated legislation for specified purposes only.

Definition

Delegated legislation: rules of law made by subordinate bodies to whom the power to do so has been given by statute.

Delegated legislation appears in various forms. Ministerial powers are exercised by **statutory instrument** (including emergency powers of the Crown exercised by **Orders in Council**). Local authorities are given statutory powers to make **bye-laws**, which apply within a specific locality.

Delegated legislation is important for a number of reasons.

(a)   Without delegated legislation, Parliament would be overwhelmed by the volume of work. Even now, the government of the day is frequently unable to fulfil all its proposals for new legislation within the allotted period. This enables Parliament to concentrate on the broader principles of the legislative framework, rather than getting bogged down in details.

(b)   The use of delegated legislation enables new laws to be passed much more quickly, especially advantageous in times of emergency.

(c)   The subject of new legislation is often highly detailed, technical and complex. It makes sense, therefore, for the exact content and wording to be arrived at by consultation with professional, commercial or industrial groups outside parliament.

(d)   It also means that the primary legislation is less voluminous because the details are left to other delegated legislation documentation.

(e)   Delegation leads to greater flexibility, because regulations can be altered later without the need to revert to Parliament.

There is also some disadvantage inherent in passing legislative powers into the hands of persons outside Parliament itself. The volume of delegated legislation means that it can become difficult for Parliament to keep track of the effect of the legislation that it has enabled. Also, although Parliament is ultimately responsible for the legislation that is in force, it is likely that much of the detail has actually been drafted and finalised by individual ministers or by civil servants. Since civil servants are unelected, the degree to which lawmaking powers should be delegated to them is a matter for some debate.

It is therefore important that delegated legislation is properly controlled and that control is exercised by the courts and by Parliament.

Control over delegated legislation

Parliament does exercise some control over delegated legislation by restricting and defining the power to make rules and by keeping the making of new delegated legislation under review. Some statutory instruments do not take effect until approved by affirmative resolution of Parliament. Most other statutory instruments must be laid before Parliament for 40 days before they take effect. During that period members may propose a negative resolution to veto a statutory instrument to which they object.

There are standing Scrutiny Committees of both Houses whose duty it is to examine statutory instruments with a view to raising objections if necessary, usually on the grounds that the instrument is obscure, expensive or retrospective. They cannot object to its nature or content.

As explained above, the power to make delegated legislation is defined by the Act which confers the power. A statutory instrument may be challenged in the courts on the ground that it is *ultra vires*, that is that it exceeds the prescribed limits, or on the ground that it has been made without due compliance with the correct procedure. If the objection is valid the court declares the statutory instrument to be void.

Definition

> **Ultra vires**: beyond their powers.

The **Human Rights Act (HRA)** does not give courts power to strike out primary legislation which is contrary to the HRA. However, as **secondary legislation**, delegated legislation is not affected and courts **are permitted** to **strike out** any delegated legislation that runs contrary to the HRA.

> **Activity 4**   **(10 minutes)**
>
> An Act of Parliament gives the Chancellor of the Exchequer power to fix the rate of tax on land values by statutory instrument. The Chancellor issues a statutory instrument extending the tax to the values of shareholdings. Consider whether the statutory instrument could be challenged.

3.4 Statutory interpretation

We have already stated that judges have a role to play in interpreting whether a case law precedent should apply to cases before them. They also have to interpret statute law.

There are a number of situations which might lead to a need for statutory interpretation.

(a) **Ambiguity** might be caused by an error in drafting.

(b) **Uncertainty** may arise where the words of a statute are intended to apply to a range of factual situations and the courts must decide whether the case before them falls into any of these situations.

(c) There may be **unforeseeable developments**.

(d)   The draft may use a **broad term**. Thus, the word vehicle may need to be considered in relation to the use of skateboards or bicycles.

There is a series of rules concerning how a judge should interpret statute. In general, he is required to consider the purpose of the statute so that it achieves its purpose. Following the incorporation of the European Convention on Human Rights and Fundamentals Freedom into UK law in the form of the Human Rights Act 1998, the UK is required to interpret statute in a way that is compatible with the Convention, as far as is possible.

There are a number of different sources of assistance for a judge in his task of statutory interpretation. These are the **principles of statutory interpretation** and consist of:

- Rules
- Presumptions
- Other aids (intrinsic or extrinsic)

Rules of statutory interpretation

In interpreting the words of a statute the courts have developed a number of well-established general principles.

(a)   The **literal rule** means that words should be given their plain, ordinary or literal meaning. Normally a word should be construed in the same literal sense wherever it appears throughout the statute.

(b)   The **golden rule** means that a statute should be construed to avoid a manifest absurdity or contradiction within itself. By way of example, there is a principle that a murderer cannot benefit under his victim's will. In the case of *Re Sigsworth 1935* the golden rule was applied to prevent a murderer from inheriting on the intestacy of his mother (his victim) although he was her only heir on a literal interpretation of the Administration of Estates Act 1925.

(c)   The **mischief rule** states that if the words used are ambiguous and the statute discloses, in its preamble, the purpose of the statute, the court will adopt the meaning which is likely to give effect to the purpose or reform which the statute is intended to achieve. This is called a 'purposive approach'.

(d)   The **contextual rule** means that a word should be construed in its context: it is permissible to look at the statute as a whole to discover the meaning of a word in it. The courts have been paying more attention to what Parliament intended in recent times. This is in order that the courts apply the law for the purpose for which it is enacted by Parliament. A more purposive approach is also being taken because so many international and EC regulations come to be interpreted by the courts.

(e)   The **purportive approach:** the Statute's words are interpreted with reference to the context and purpose of the legislation, ie what is the legislation trying to achieve?

(f)   The *eiusdem generis* **rule**: Statutes often list a number of specific things and end the list with more general words. In that case the general words are to be limited in their meaning to other things of the same kind as the specific items which precede them.

Presumptions of statutory interpretation

Unless the statute contains express words to the contrary it is assumed that the following presumptions of statutory interpretation apply, each of which may be rebutted by contrary evidence.

(a) **A statute does not alter the existing common law**. If a statute is capable of two interpretations, one involving alteration of the common law and the other one not, the latter interpretation is to be preferred.

(b) **If a statute deprives a person of his property**, say by nationalisation, he is to be compensated for its value.

(c) **A statute is not intended to deprive a person of his liberty**. If it does so, clear words must be used. This is relevant in legislation covering, for example, mental health and immigration.

(d) **A statute does not have retrospective effect** to a date earlier than its becoming law.

(e) **A statute does not bind the Crown**. In certain areas, the Crown's potential liability is great and this is therefore an extremely important presumption.

(f) **A statute has effect only in the UK**. However a statute does not run counter to international law and should be interpreted so as to give effect to international obligations.

(g) **A statute cannot impose criminal liability** without proof of guilty intention. Many modern statutes rebut this presumption by imposing strict liability, say for dangerous driving under the Road Traffic Act.

(h) **A statute does not repeal other statutes**.

(i) Any point on which the statute leaves a **gap or omission** is outside the scope of the statute.

Other assistance in interpretation

The Interpretation Act 1987 defines certain terms frequently found in legislation. The Act also states that, unless a specific intention to the contrary exists, the use in a statute of masculine gender terminology also includes the feminine, and vice versa. Similarly, words in the singular include plurals, and vice versa.

Intrinsic aids to statutory interpretation consist of the following.

(a) The **long title** of an Act, which may give guidance as to the Act's general objective.

(b) The **preamble** of an Act often directs the judge as to its intentions and objects.

(c) **Interpretation sections** to Acts. Particularly long, complicated and wide-ranging Acts often contain self-explanations; for instance, s 207 of the Financial Services Act 1986 defines 'authorised persons' and 'recognised investment exchanges' for its purposes.

(d) **Sidenotes**. Statutes often have summary notes in the margin.

Intrinsic aids are those words contained in the Queen's Printer's copy of the statute. **Extrinsic** aids are those found elsewhere.

Extrinsic aids include the following.

(a) Reports of the Law Commission, royal commissions, the Law Reform Committee and other official committees.

(b) *Hansard*, the official journal of UK Parliamentary debates. This follows a decision of the House of Lords in *Pepper v Hart 1992* where the House of Lords decided that it is acceptable to look at the original speech which first introduced a bill to ascertain its meaning, but only if the Statute is ambiguous or obscure, or its literal meaning would lead to absurdity.

4 EUROPEAN LAW

You will find further detailed coverage of European law in Part E of this Course Book.

The sources of Community Law may be described as primary or secondary. The **primary sources of law** are the foundation treaties themselves.

- The **Treaty of Paris 1951,** which established the **ECSC**
- The **First Treaty of Rome 1957**, which established the **EEC**
- The **Second Treaty of Rome 1957**, which established **EURATOM**

Secondary legislation takes three forms, with the Council and Commission being empowered to do the following:

- Make regulations
- Issue directives
- Take decisions

They may also make recommendations and deliver opinions although these are only persuasive in authority.

Direct applicability and direct effect

To understand the importance of regulations, directives and decisions, it is necessary to appreciate the distinction between **direct applicability** and **direct effect**.

Community law which is directly applicable in member states comes into force without any act of implementation by member states. Law has direct effect if it confers rights and imposes obligations directly on individuals.

4.1 Regulations

Regulations have the force of law in every EU state without need of national legislation. In this sense regulations are described as **directly applicable**. Their objective is to obtain uniformity of law throughout the EU.

Definition

> **Regulations** apply throughout the Union and they become part of the law of each member nation as soon as they come into force without the need for each country to make its own legislation.

Direct law-making of this type is generally restricted to matters within the basic aims of Treaty of Rome, such as the establishment of a single unrestricted market in the EU territory in manufactured goods.

Acts of implementation are actually prohibited, in case a member state alters the scope of the regulation in question.

4.2 Directives

Definition

> **Directives** are issued to the governments of the EU member states requiring them within a specified period (usually two years) to alter the national laws of the state so that they conform to the Directive.

Thus the Financial Services Act 1986 embodied certain Directives on company securities and the Companies Act 1989 (now consolidated in the Companies Act 2006) gives force to the Eighth Directive.

Until a Directive is given effect by a UK statute it does not usually affect legal rights and obligations of individuals. The wording of a Directive may be cited in legal proceedings, but generally **statutory interpretation has been a matter for the UK courts**. However, as noted above, under the Human Rights Act 1998, the courts are now required to interpret UK legislation in a way which is compatible with the European Convention on Human Rights.

Directives are the most significant and important means of importing continental law into the UK legal system.

4.3 Decisions

Decisions of an administrative nature are made by the European Commission in Brussels.

Definition

> A **decision** may be addressed to a state, person or a company and is immediately binding, but only on the recipient.

4.4 Legislative procedure

Proposals for EU legislation are drafted by the Commission. These drafts are referred to member states for comments. The directives are also debated in the preparatory stage by the European Parliament. The final stage is the consideration of a Directive by the Council of Ministers. The Council authorises the issue of the Directive and the member states must then alter their law accordingly.

Chapter roundup

- Case law is the application of reported cases to later cases.

- Decided cases can fix the law for the purposes of future cases heard before certain courts, through the doctrine of precedent.

- The binding element in an earlier decision is the *ratio decidendi*, not the *obiter dicta*.

- The House of Lords binds all courts except itself. The Court of Appeal and a Divisional Court of the High Court bind themselves and all lower courts.

- A court can avoid following a precedent on several grounds.

- Statute law is made by Parliament, which, subject to the UK's membership of the European Union, has unfettered legislative powers.

- Much detailed legislation is delegated to Government departments exercising powers conferred by Acts of Parliament.

- Judges have to interpret statutes in order to apply the law.

- There are a number of rules and presumptions of statutory interpretation.

- The European Commission is a significant source of UK law.

- EU law is primary (the foundation treaties) and secondary (regulations and Directives).

Quick quiz

1 How was the Common Law first developed?

2 Give some examples of equitable maxims.

3 Can *obiter dicta* in a case have any influence on the outcome of subsequent cases?

4 What does it mean to say that a court's decision was taken *per incuriam*?

5 What is meant by Parliamentary sovereignty?

6 Why is delegated legislation essential?

Answers to quick quiz

1   Through justices sent by the King to administer the same law to everyone. (see para 1.1)

2   He who comes to equity must come with clean hands'.

Equality is equity'.

Equity looks to the intent rather than the form'. (para 1.2)

3   It can be persuasive, but it is not binding. (para 2.2)

4   Without taking some essential point into account. (para 2.3)

5   Parliament can make any law, but cannot prevent a future parliament from changing the law. Judges are bound by parliament. (para 3)

6   To enable governments to introduce all legislation needed, otherwise there would not be enough time. (para 3.2)

Answers to activities

1   'Clementines are oranges' is the *ratio decidendi* (ie the decision in the case). 'Peanuts are nuts' is an *obiter dictum*, an additional comment which is not central.

2   The House of Lords in C v D could disregard the Court of Appeal decision in A v B or even over rule it. Alternatively the case A v B might be distinguished on its facts.

3   No Parliament can bind its successors.

4   It would be *ultra vires* (ie beyond the powers of the Chancellor).

PART B

THE LAW OF CONTRACT

Chapter 4:
INTRODUCTION TO
THE LAW OF CONTRACT

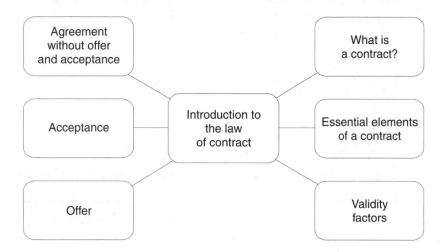

Introduction

A contract is an agreement which legally binds the parties to it. Consider the contracts that you may have entered into as an individual, when buying a house for example, or starting work. Similarly, a business will enter into contracts when it deals with property or takes on new staff.

Restrictions on the individual's freedom to make contracts have been developed to protect the disadvantaged, particularly in their dealings with large or monopolistic organisations. An example is the Sale of Goods Act 1979, which implies certain terms into contracts for the sale of goods, which cannot be excluded in consumer sales. A seller is bound by these terms even though he has never agreed to them, or may never have even thought of them.

The first essential element of a binding contract is **agreement**. To determine whether or not an agreement has been reached, the courts will consider whether one party has made a firm offer which the other party has accepted.

In most contracts, **offer and acceptance** may be made orally or in writing, or they may be implied by the conduct of the parties. The person making an offer is the **offeror** and the person to whom an offer is made is the **offeree**.

The **particular significance of offer and acceptance is that a binding contract is thereby formed,** so that new terms cannot thereafter be introduced into the contract unless both parties agree. From this moment on, the terms of the contract appear from the offer and acceptance, rather than from the unexpressed intentions of the parties.

NOTES

Your objectives

In this chapter you will learn about the following.

 (a) The nature of a contract
 (b) The classification of contracts
 (c) The essentials of a valid contract
 (d) What 'an offer' is in law
 (e) How it is distinguished from other things
 (f) What 'acceptance' is in law
 (g) How it is distinguished from other things
 (h) How acceptance must be communicated to create agreement

1 WHAT IS A CONTRACT?

Definition

A **contract** may be defined as an **agreement which legally binds the parties**.

A party to a contract is bound because he has **agreed** to be bound. The underlying theory, then, is that a contract is the outcome of 'consenting minds'. Parties are not judged by what is in their minds, but by what they have said, written or done.

Many principles of modern contract law are strongly influenced by the events and important cases of the nineteenth century. However, a number of **developments in the twentieth century** should be brought into consideration.

1.1 Inequality of bargaining power

It is almost invariably the case that the two parties to a contract bring with them differing levels of bargaining power. The law will intervene only where the stronger party takes unfair advantage of his position.

It is almost invariably the case that the two parties to a contract bring with them differing levels of **bargaining power**. Many contracts are made between experts and ordinary consumers. The law will intervene **only** where the former takes **unfair** advantage of his position and not simply because one party was in an inferior bargaining position. **Freedom of contract** is a term sometimes used and can be defined as follows.

> *'The principle that parties are completely unrestricted in deciding whether or not to enter into an agreement and, if they do so, upon the terms governing that relationship. In practice, this is not always the case because one may be in a much stronger economic position, and legislation has been introduced in order to redress the balance.'*

1.2 The standard form contract

Mass production and nationalisation have led to the standard form contract.

Definition

The **standard form** contract is a standard document prepared by many large organisations and setting out the terms on which they contract with their customers. The individual must usually take it or leave it: he does not really 'agree' to it. For example, a customer has to accept his supply of electricity on the electricity board's terms; individuals cannot negotiate discounts.

One of the main problems with standard form contracts occurs when the dominant party tries to exclude liability for the terms in the contract. The legislation protecting consumers in such situations, the Unfair Contract Terms Act, is covered later in this Course Book.

1.3 Consumer protection

In the second half of the twentieth century, there was a surge of interest in **consumer matters** mainly because of mass production and aggressive marketing. There is a greater need for **consumer protection**. Consumer interests are now served by consumer protection agencies, which include government departments (the **Office of Fair Trading**) and independent bodies (the **Consumers' Association**) and legislation.

Public policy sometimes requires that the freedom of contract should be modified. For example, the Consumer Credit Act 1974 and the Unfair Contract Terms Act 1977 both regulate the extent to which contracts can contain certain terms.

Consumer protection is covered in detail in the BPP Learning Media Business Essentials Course Book Company and Commercial Law.

2 ESSENTIAL ELEMENTS OF A CONTRACT

In order to be valid and enforceable by the law, a contract must contain certain key elements. These are as follows.

2.1 Agreement

The first essential feature of a contract is that the parties have made an agreement. This is determined by the rules of **offer** and **acceptance** which will be outlined in Chapter 4.

2.2 Consideration

The second essential element is that the agreement, or the obligations assumed by each party, must be supported by consideration from the other party. We will cover the rules of consideration in Chapter 5.

2.3 Intention to create legal relations

The last essential element is that the parties to the agreement intend that their promises be legally binding. In Chapter 6, we discuss intention to create legal relations and the capacity of certain groups of people to enter contracts.

3 VALIDITY FACTORS

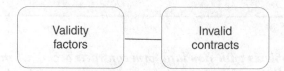

If one of the three essential elements of contract is not present, there is no contract. However, even if all three essential elements are present, the validity of a contract may be affected. The validity of a contract may be affected by the following factors.

(a) **Form.** The general rule is that a contract may be in any form (written or oral, for example). However, a minority of contracts have to be made in a particular form.

(b) **Genuine consent.** The validity of a contract may be affected if a person has been misled into a contract, or if the parties have come to agreement, but are actually at cross-purposes, ie one of them is mistaken as to the precise nature of the contract. This is covered further in Chapter 8.

(c) **Capacity.** some persons, for example children, only have limited capacity to enter into contracts. This is covered further in Chapter 6.

(d) **Content.** A contract must be complete and precise in its terms. We will discuss this in Chapter 7.

(e) **Legality.** The courts will not enforce a contract which is deemed to be illegal or contrary to public policy. This is covered further in Chapter 8.

3.1 Invalid contracts

A contract which is affected by such 'vitiating factors' exists, but may be **void, voidable** or **unenforceable**. It is important that you understand the difference between these terms.

Definitions

(a) A **void contract** is **not a contract** at all. The parties are not bound by it and if they transfer property under it they can sometimes (unless it is also an illegal contract) recover their goods even from a third party.

For example, A sells goods to B, who sells them on to C. B then fails to pay A for the goods and disappears without trace. If A can demonstrate that he was genuinely mistaken as to the identity of B and would not have dealt with him had he known who B really was, then A can recover the goods which were subject to the original contract from C. This is because the law takes the view in such a situation that the original contract between A and B was no contract at all and of no effect.

Therefore C, who was an innocent third party acting in good faith, has to return the goods to A and either bear the loss or find and sue B.

(b) A **voidable contract** is a **contract which one party may avoid**, that is terminate at his option. The contract is treated as valid unless and until it is avoided. Property transferred before avoidance is usually irrecoverable from a third party.

For example A sells goods to B on 1 June. On 8 June B sells them onto C. On 10 June, it is discovered that B had made a misrepresentation in the original contract between A and B and A seeks to recover the goods. Given these dates, A cannot do so, as the goods have been sold on to C *before* A tries to avoid the original contract, and at the time that B sells them he (B) still has good title.

If on the other hand, B did not sell the goods on to C until 12 June, which is after A seeks to avoid the original contract with B, that original contract has already been avoided, and B would not be able to pass good title on to C.

(c) An **unenforceable contract** is a **valid contract** and property transferred under it cannot be recovered even from the other party to the contract. If either party refuses to perform the contract, the other party cannot compel him to do so. A contract is usually unenforceable when the required evidence of its terms, for example, written evidence of a contract relating to land, is not available. Unenforceable contracts are only problematic if a dispute over the contract arises.

The life of a contract

Once a valid contract has been formed, it remains in existence until **discharged**, usually in one of four ways. The most common means of discharge is **performance**, where both parties fulfil their contractual obligations. The most common problem arises where there is a **breach of contract**, whereby one party fails to carry out their side of the contract properly.

NOTES

3.2   Form of a contract

As a general rule, **a contract may be made in any form**. It may be **written**, or **oral**, or **inferred** from the conduct of the parties. For example, a customer in a self-service shop may take his selected goods to the cash desk, pay for them and walk out without saying a word.

Writing is not usually necessary except in the following circumstances.

- Some contracts must be by deed.
- Some contracts must be in writing.
- Some contracts must be evidenced in writing.

Contracts by deed

A contract by deed must be in **writing** and it must be **signed**. Delivery must take place. Delivery is conduct indicating that the person executing the deed intends to be bound by it.

These contracts must be by deed.

- Leases for three years or more

- A conveyance or transfer of a legal estate in land (including a mortgage)

- A promise not supported by consideration (such as a covenant, for example a promise to pay a regular sum to a charity)

Definitions

> A **contract by deed** is sometimes referred to as a specialty contract. Any other type of contract may be referred to as a **simple contract**.

Contracts which must be in writing

Some types of contract are required to be in the form of a written document, usually signed by at least one of the parties.

These contracts must be in writing.

- A **transfer of shares** in a limited company
- The sale or disposition of an **interest in land**
- **Bills of Exchange** and **cheques**
- **Consumer credit** contracts

A contract for the sale or disposition of land promises to transfer title at a future date and must be in writing. The conveyance or transfer must be by deed and will therefore also be in writing.

In the case of consumer credit transactions, the effect of failure to make the agreement in the prescribed form is to make the agreement unenforceable against the debtor unless the creditor obtains a court order.

Contracts which must be evidenced in writing

Certain contracts may be made orally, but are not enforceable in a court of law unless there is written evidence of their terms. The most important contract of this type is the contract of **guarantee**.

Note. This is the first chapter in which you have seen detailed references to cases. They are usually presented with the claimant's name first, and then the name of the defendant. The names may sometimes be reversed where the case has gone to appeal and the original defendant is now bringing the appeal.

4 OFFER

4.1 Definition

> An **offer** is a definite promise to be bound on specific terms.

Certainty of the offer

An apparently vague offer can be made certain by reference to the parties' previous dealing.

> *Gunthing v Lynn 1831*
> *The facts*: the offeror offered to pay a further sum for a horse if it was 'lucky'.
>
> *Decision*: the offer was too vague and no contract could be formed by any purported acceptance.

> *Hillas & Co Ltd v Arcos Ltd 1932*
> *The facts*: the claimants agreed to purchase from the defendants '22,000 standards of softwood goods of fair specification over the season 1930'. The agreement contained an option to buy a further 100,000 standards in 1931. The 1930 transaction took place but the sellers refused to supply any wood in 1931, saying that the agreement was too vague to bind the parties.
>
> *Decision:* the wording used, and the previous transactions, showed a sufficient intention to be bound. There was therefore a valid contract.

A definite offer may be made to a **class** of persons or to **the world at large**.

> *Carlill v Carbolic Smoke Ball Co 1893*
> *The facts*: the manufacturers of a patent medicine published an advertisement by which they undertook to pay '£100 reward ... to any person who contracts ... influenza ... after having used the smoke ball three times daily for two weeks'. The advertisement added that £1,000 had been deposited at a bank 'showing our sincerity in this matter'. The claimant read the advertisement, purchased the smoke ball and used it as directed. She contracted influenza and claimed her £100 reward. The manufacturers argued a number of defences, including the following.

(a) The offer was so vague that it could not form the basis of a contract as no time limit was specified.

(b) It was not an offer which could be accepted since it was offered to the whole world.

Decision: the court considered these two defences as follows.

(a) The smoke ball must protect the user during the period of use. The offer was not vague.

(b) An offer to the public can be accepted so as to form a contract.

Carlill is an extremely important case that you must learn.

4.2 Supply of information

Only an offer in the proper sense may be accepted so as to form a binding contract. The supply of information will not be considered to be an offer.

> *Harvey v Facey 1893*
> *The facts*: the claimant telegraphed to the defendant 'Will you sell us Bumper Hall Pen? Telegraph lowest cash price'. The defendant telegraphed in reply 'Lowest price for Bumper Hall Pen, £900'. The claimant telegraphed to accept what he regarded as an offer; the defendant made no further reply.
>
> *Decision*: the defendant's telegram was merely a statement of his minimum price if a sale were to be agreed. It was not an offer and no contract had been made.

If, in the course of negotiations for a sale, the vendor states the price at which he will sell, that statement may be an offer which can become accepted eventually.

> *Bigg v Boyd Gibbons 1971*
> *The facts*: in the course of correspondence the defendant rejected an offer of £20,000 by the claimant and added 'for a quick sale I would accept £26,000 .... if you are not interested in this price would you please let me know immediately'. The claimant accepted this price of £26,000 and the defendant acknowledged his acceptance, stating that he had given instructions for the sale to his solicitor.
>
> *Decision*: in this context the defendant must be treated as making an offer (at £26,000) which the claimant had accepted.

Reference to a more detailed document will not necessarily prevent a statement from being an offer.

> *Bowerman and Another v Association of British Travel Agents Ltd 1996*
> *The facts*: The case arose out of the insolvency in 1991 of a tour operator through whom a school party had booked a holiday. The party claimed a full refund under the ABTA scheme of protection. The ABTA scheme did not extend to one item, namely the holiday insurance premium and this was explained in ABTA's detailed handbook. The claimant argued that the 'ABTA promise' (to refund holiday expenses, widely advertised in the press) constituted an offer to the public at large,

and that offer was accepted when the holiday was booked with the relevant tour operator.

Decision: The public had been encouraged by ABTA to read the written 'ABTA promise' as creating a legally binding obligation to reimburse all the expenses of the holiday.

A statement of intention

Advertising that an event such as an auction will take place is not an offer to sell. Potential buyers may not sue the auctioneer if the auction does not take place: *Harris v Nickerson 1873*. This is an example of a statement of intention which is not actionable.

4.3   An invitation to treat

Where a party is initiating negotiations, he is said to have made an invitation to treat.

Definition

> An **invitation to treat** is an indication that someone is prepared to receive offers with the view to forming a binding contract. It is not an offer in itself.

There are four types of invitation to treat.

- Auction sales
- Advertisements
- Exhibition of goods for sale
- An invitation for tenders

Auction sales

An auctioneer's request for bids is not a definite offer to sell to the highest bidder. The bid itself is the offer, which the auctioneer is then free to accept or reject: *Payne v Cave 1789*. Acceptance is indicated by the fall of the auctioneer's hammer. Where an auction is said to be 'without reserve' (minimum price) the auctioneer is offering the goods for sale, and the bid is the acceptance: *Barry v Davies 2000*.

Advertisements

An advertisement of goods is an attempt to induce offers and is therefore classified as an invitation to treat.

> *Partridge v Crittenden 1968*
> *The facts*: Mr Partridge placed an advertisement in *Cage and Aviary Birds* magazine containing the words 'Bramblefinch cocks, bramblefinch hens, 25s each'. The RSPCA brought a prosecution for offering for sale a protected species in contravention of the Protection of Birds Act 1953. The justices convicted Partridge. He appealed to the Court of Appeal.
>
> *Decision*: the conviction was quashed. The prosecution could not rely on the offence of 'offering for sale', as the advertisement constituted an invitation to treat. He was therefore not making an offer.

The circulation of a price list is also an invitation to treat: *Grainger v Gough 1896*. It cannot be an offer because 'if it were so, the merchant might find himself involved in any number of contractual obligations to supply wine of a particular description which he would be quite unable to carry out, his stock of wine of that description being necessarily limited.'

Activity 1   **(2 minutes)**

In *Carlill v Carbolic Smokeball Co 1893*, the company published an advertisement for its patent medicine in which it undertook to pay £100 to anyone who, having used the medicine, became ill with influenza within a limited period thereafter.

At what time was the contract between Mrs Carlill and the company made?

A   When she read the advertisement
B   When she bought the patent medicine
C   When she used the medicine and caught influenza
D   When she notified the manufacturer of her claim

Exhibition of goods for sale

Displaying goods in a shop constitutes inviting customers to make offers to purchase, or an invitation to treat.

> *Fisher v Bell 1961*
> *The facts*: a shopkeeper was prosecuted for offering for sale an offensive weapon by exhibiting a flick knife in his shop window.
>
> *Decision*: according to the ordinary law of contract, the display of an article with a price on it in a shop window is merely an invitation to treat. Therefore he was not offering the knife for sale, but rather inviting offers from potential purchasers. The shop keeper would then be able to either accept or reject the offer.

> *Pharmaceutical Society of Great Britain v Boots Cash Chemists (Southern) 1952*
> *The facts*: certain drugs containing poisons could only be sold 'under the supervision of a registered pharmacist'. The claimant claimed this rule had been broken by Boots who put supplies of these drugs on open shelves in a self-service shop. Boots contended that there was no sale until the customer brought the goods to the cash desk and offered to buy them. A registered pharmacist was stationed at this point.
>
> *Decision*: The court found for the defendant (Boots) and commented that if it were true that a customer accepted an offer to sell by removing goods from the shelf he could not then change his mind and put them back because to do so would constitute breach of contract.

Invitation for tenders

A tender is an estimate submitted in response to a prior request. When a person tenders for a contract he is making an offer to the person who has advertised a contract as being available. If you want an extension built on your house, you might obtain tenders from three different builders. You therefore receive three offers and you decide which one to accept.

> **Activity 2**   **(10 minutes)**
>
> Bianca goes into a shop and sees a price label on a CD for £15. She takes the CD to the checkout, but the till operator tells her that the label is misprinted and should read £20. Bianca maintains that she only has to pay £15. How would you describe the price on the price label in terms of contract law?

FOR DISCUSSION

As seen in the *Partridge v Crittenden* case, the general rule is that an advertisement will not be interpreted as an offer. However, in *Carlill's case* the advertisement by the Carbolic Smoke Ball Co was construed as an offer that could be accepted by Mrs Carlill's act. What factors do you think a judge would consider relevant in determining whether an offer has been made?

4.4 Termination of offer

The key way that an offer is terminated is by being **accepted**, thereby creating agreement. An offer is **terminated** so that it may no longer be accepted in any of the following circumstances.

- Rejection
- Lapse of time
- Revocation by the offeror
- Failure of a condition to which the offer was subject
- Death of one of the parties

Rejection

Outright rejection terminates an offer. A counter-offer also terminates the original offer.

> *Hyde v Wrench 1840*
> *The facts:* W offered to sell his farm for £1,000. H offered £950 (a counter-offer) which W rejected. A few days later H said he would buy for £1,000. W refused to sell and H maintained that they had a contract.
>
> *Decision:* the counter-offer of £950 had rejected the original offer to sell of £1,000.

Counter-offer

Acceptance must be **unqualified agreement to the terms of the offer**. A purported acceptance which introduces any new terms is a counter-offer, which has the effect of terminating the original offer.

NOTES

Definition

> A **counter-offer** is a final rejection of the original offer. If a counter-offer is made, the original offeror may accept it, but if he rejects it his original offer is no longer available for acceptance.

A counter-offer may of course be accepted by the original offeror.

> *Butler Machine Tool Co v Ex-cell-O Corp (England) 1979*
> *The facts*: The claimant offered to sell tools to the defendant. Their quotation included details of their standard terms. The defendant 'accepted' the offer, enclosing their own standard terms. The claimant acknowledged acceptance by returning a tear-off slip from the order form.
>
> *Decision*: The defendant's order was really a counter-offer. The claimant had accepted this by returning the tear-off slip.

Request for information

It is possible to respond to an offer by making a **request for information**. Such a request may be a request as to whether or not other terms would be acceptable – it is not a counter-offer.

> *Stevenson v McLean 1880*
> *The facts*: The defendant offered to sell iron at '40s net cash per ton, open till Monday'. The claimant enquired whether he would agree to delivery spread over two months. The defendant did not reply and (within the stated time limit), the claimant accepted the original offer. Meanwhile the defendant had sold the iron to a third party.
>
> *Decision*: There was a contract since the claimant had merely enquired as to a variation of terms.

Lapse of time

An offer may be expressed to last for a **specified time**. If there is no express time limit set, it expires after a **reasonable time.** What is reasonable depends on the circumstances of the case.

> *Ramsgate Victoria Hotel Co v Montefiore 1866*
> *The facts*: the defendant applied to the company in June for shares and paid a deposit to the company's bank. At the end of November the company sent him an acceptance by issue of a letter of allotment and requested payment of the balance due. The defendant contended that his offer had expired and could no longer be accepted.
>
> *Decision*: the offer was for a reasonable time only, so the offer had lapsed.

Revocation by the offeror

The offeror may revoke his offer at any time before acceptance: *Payne v Cave 1789*.

If he undertakes that his offer shall remain open for acceptance for a specified time he may nonetheless revoke it within that time, unless by a separate contract he has bound himself to keep it open for the whole of the specified time.

> *Routledge v Grant 1828*
> *The facts*: the defendant offered to buy the claimant's house for a fixed sum, requiring acceptance within six weeks. Within the six weeks specified, he withdrew his offer.
>
> *Decision*: the defendant could revoke his offer at any time before acceptance, even though the time limit had not expired.

Revocation may be an express statement to that effect or may be an act of the offeror indicating that he no longer regards the offer as in force. His revocation does not take effect **until the revocation is communicated to the offeree**. This raises two important points.

While posting a letter is a sufficient act of acceptance (as we shall see shortly), it is not a sufficient act of revocation of offer.

> *Byrne v Van Tienhoven 1880*
> *The facts*: the defendants were in Cardiff; the claimants in New York. The sequence of events was as follows:
>
> 1 October   Letter posted in Cardiff, offering to sell 1,000 boxes of tinplates.
> 8 October   Letter of revocation of offer posted in Cardiff.
> 11 October Letter of offer received in New York and telegram of acceptance sent.
> 15 October Letter confirming acceptance posted in New York.
> 20 October Letter of revocation received in New York. The offeree had meanwhile resold the contract goods.
>
> *Decision*: the letter of revocation could not take effect until received (20 October). Simply posting a letter does not revoke the offer until it is received. Therefore there was a binding contract.

While acceptance must be communicated by the offeree, revocation of offer may be communicated by any third party who is a sufficiently reliable informant.

> *Dickinson v Dodds 1876*
> *The facts*: the defendant, on 10 June, wrote to the claimant to offer property for sale at £800, adding 'this offer to be left open until Friday 12 June, 9.00 am'. On 11 June the defendant sold the property to another buyer. The intermediary between Dickinson and Dodds informed Dickinson that the defendant had sold to someone else. On Friday 12 June, before 9.00 am, the claimant handed to the defendant a formal letter of acceptance.
>
> *Decision*: the defendant was free to revoke his offer and had done so by sale to a third party; the claimant could not accept the offer after he had learnt from a reliable informant of the revocation of the offer to him.

Where an offer is meant to be accepted by conduct (a **unilateral** contract), it has been held that it cannot be revoked once the offeree has begun to try and perform whatever act is necessary.

> *Errington v Errington 1953*
>
> *The facts*: a father bought a house for his son and daughter-in-law to live in. He paid the deposit, and the son and daughter-in-law were to make the mortgage repayments. The father told them that the house would be theirs when the mortgage was paid off. The son subsequently left his wife, who continued to live in the house.
>
> *Decision*: The Court of Appeal ruled that the father could not eject the daughter-in-law from the property. Lord Denning said 'The father's promise was a unilateral contract – a promise of the house in return for their act of paying the instalments. It could not be revoked by him once the couple entered on the performance of the act ...'.

Failure of a condition

An offer may be conditional in that it is dependent on some event occurring or there being a change of circumstances. If the condition is not satisfied, the offer is not capable of acceptance.

> *Financings Ltd v Stimson 1962*
>
> *The facts*: the defendant wished to purchase a car, and on 16 March signed a hire-purchase form. The form, issued by the claimants, stated that the agreement would be binding only upon signature by them. On 20 March the defendant, not satisfied with the car, returned it to the motor dealer. On 24 March the car was stolen from the premises of the dealer, and was recovered badly damaged. On 25 March the claimants signed the form. They sued the defendant for breach of contract.
>
> *Decision*: the defendant was not bound to take the car. His signing of the agreement was actually an offer to contract with the claimant. There was an implied condition in this offer that the car would be in substantially the same condition when the offer was accepted as when it was made.

Termination by death

The death of the **offeree** terminates the offer.

The **offeror's** death terminates the offer unless the offeree accepts it in ignorance of the offeror's death, and the offer is not of a personal nature: *Bradbury v Morgan 1862*.

5 ACCEPTANCE

5.1 Definition

> **Acceptance** is the unqualified agreement to the terms of the offer.

Acceptance may be by express words or by action (as in *Carlill's* case). It may also be inferred from conduct.

> *Brogden v Metropolitan Railway Co 1877*
> *The facts*: having supplied coal for many years to the defendant, the claimant suggested there should be a written agreement. The claimant continued to supply coal under the terms of the draft agreement but no version was ever signed. The claimant later denied that there was any agreement between him and the defendant.
>
> *Decision*: the conduct of the parties indicated that they both agreed to the terms of the draft. The draft agreement became a binding contract as soon as the defendant ordered and the claimant supplied coal.

Silence as acceptance

There must be some act on the part of the offeree to indicate his acceptance.

> *Felthouse v Bindley 1862*
> *The facts*: the claimant wrote to his nephew offering to buy the nephew's horse for £30.15s, adding 'If I hear no more about him, I consider the horse mine at that price'. The nephew intended to accept his uncle's offer but did not reply. He instructed the defendant, an auctioneer, not to sell the horse. Owing to a misunderstanding the horse was sold at auction to someone else. The uncle sued the auctioneer in conversion (a tort alleging wrongful disposal of another's property).
>
> *Decision*: the action failed. There could be no acceptance by silence in these circumstances. The claimant had no title to the horse and could not sue in conversion.

Unsolicited goods

Goods which are sent or services which are rendered to a person who did not request them are not 'accepted' merely because he does not return them to the sender. His silence is not acceptance of them, even if the sender includes a statement that he is deemed to have agreed to buy and/or pay unless he rejects them: Unsolicited Goods and Services Act 1971. The recipient may treat them as an unsolicited gift.

5.2 Acceptance 'subject to contract'

Acceptance '**subject to contract**' means that the offeree is agreeable to the terms of the offer but proposes that the parties should negotiate a formal contract. Neither party is bound until the formal contract is signed. Agreements for the sale of land in England are usually made 'subject to contract'.

Acceptance 'subject to contract' must be distinguished from outright acceptance made on the understanding that the parties wish to replace the preliminary contract with another at a later stage. Even if the immediate contract is described as 'provisional', it takes effect at once.

> *Branca v Cobarro 1947*
> *The facts*: a vendor agreed to sell a mushroom farm under a contract which was declared to be 'a provisional agreement until a fully legalised agreement is signed'.
>
> *Decision*: by the use of the word 'provisional', the parties had intended their agreement to be binding until, by mutual agreement, they made another to replace it.

5.3 Letters of intent

Definition

A **letter of intent** is a means by which one party gives a strong indication to another that he is likely to place a contract with him.

Thus a building contractor tendering for a large construction contract may need to sub-contract certain (specialist) aspects of the work. The sub-contractor will be asked to provide an estimate so that the main contractor can finalise his own tender.

Usually, a letter of intent is worded so as not to create any legal obligation. However, in some cases it may be phrased so that it includes an invitation to commence preliminary work. In such circumstances, it creates an obligation to pay for that work.

> *British Steel Corpn v Cleveland Bridge and Engineering Co Ltd 1984*
> *The facts*: the defendants asked the claimants to supply nodes for a complex steel lattice-work frame, and sent the claimants a letter of intent, stating their intention to place an order on their standard terms. The claimants stated that they were unwilling to contract on such terms, but started work, and eventually completed and delivered all the nodes. They sued for the value of the nodes and the defendants counter-claimed for damages for late delivery.
>
> *Decision*: since the parties had not reached agreement over such matters as late delivery, there was no contract, and so there could be no question of damages for late delivery. However, since the claimants had undertaken work at the request of the defendants and the defendants had accepted this work, the claimants were entitled to a reasonable remuneration for services rendered.

5.4 Acceptance of a tender

As we saw earlier, an invitation for tenders is an invitation to treat. There are two distinct types of tender.

(a) A tender to **perform one task**, such as building a new hospital, is an offer which can be accepted.

(b) A tender to **supply or perform a series of goods or services**, such as the supply of vegetables daily to a restaurant, is not accepted until an order is placed. It is a standing offer. Each order placed by the offeree is an individual act of acceptance creating a separate contract. Until orders are placed there is no contract and the tenderer can terminate his standing offer.

> *Great Northern Railways v Witham 1873*
> *The facts*: the defendant tendered successfully for the supply of stores to the claimant over a period of one year. In his tender he undertook 'to supply ... such quantities as the company may order from time to time'. After making some deliveries he refused to fulfil an order which the claimant had given.
>
> *Decision*: he was in breach of contract in refusing to fulfil the order given but might revoke his tender and need not then fulfil any future orders within the remainder of the twelve-month period.

5.5 Counter-offers and requests for information

As we saw earlier, a counter-offer does not constitute acceptance; it is the making of a new offer which may in turn be accepted or rejected. Nor is a request for further information an acceptance.

Activity 3 **(1 hour)**

In January Elle offered to buy Jane's boat for £3,000. Jane immediately wrote a letter to Elle saying 'For a quick sale I would accept £3,500. If not interested please let me know as soon as possible.' Elle did not see the letter until March when she returned from a business trip but then replied. 'I accept your offer. I trust that if I pay £3,000 now, you can wait until June for the remaining £500.' On receiving the letter, Jane attached a 'sold' sign on the boat but forgot to reply to Elle. Is there a contract between Elle and Jane? If so, what are its terms?

Activity 4 **(5 minutes)**

Mike offered to sell Barry his car for £5,000. Barry agreed but said he would pay by five instalments of £1,000 per month. Mike then sold the car to Catherine. Barry plans to sue Mike for breach of contract. Will he succeed?

NOTES

5.6 Communication of acceptance

The general rule is that acceptance must be **communicated** to the offeror and is **not effective until this has been done**.

Waiver of communication

The offeror may, by his offer, dispense with the need for communication of acceptance. In *Carlill v Carbolic Smoke Ball Co 1893*, it was held that it was sufficient for the claimant to act on the offer without previously notifying her acceptance of it. This was an example of a **unilateral contract**, where the offer takes the form of a promise to pay money in return for an act.

Prescribed mode of communication

The offeror may call for acceptance by specified means. Unless he stipulates that this is the only method of acceptance which suffices, then acceptance by some other means equally expeditious would constitute a valid acceptance: *Tinn v Hoffmann 1873*. A telegram or even a verbal message could be sufficient acceptance of an offer inviting acceptance 'by return of post'. This would probably apply now also to acceptance by fax machine or e-mail.

> *Yates Building Co v R J Pulleyn & Sons (York) 1975*
> *The facts*: the offer called for acceptance by registered or recorded delivery letter. The offeree sent an ordinary letter which arrived without delay, at the same time as a registered or recorded delivery letter would have arrived.
>
> *Decision*: the offeror had suffered no disadvantage and had not stipulated that acceptance must be made in this way only. The acceptance was valid.

No mode of communication prescribed

The offeree can use any method but must ensure that his **acceptance is understood** if he chooses an **instantaneous method of communication**.

> *Entores v Miles Far Eastern Corporation 1955*
> *The facts*: the claimants sent an offer by telex to the defendants' agent in Amsterdam and the latter sent an acceptance by telex. The claimants alleged breach of contract and wished to serve a writ.
>
> *Decision*: the acceptance took effect (and the contract was made) when the telex message was printed out on the claimants' terminal in London. A writ could therefore be issued.

5.7 The postal rule

The offeror may expressly or by implication indicate that he expects acceptance by means of a letter sent through the post. The **postal rule** states that, where the use of the post is within the contemplation of **both** the parties, the acceptance is complete and effective as soon as a letter is **posted**, even though it may be delayed or even lost altogether in the post.

Adams v Lindsell 1818

The facts: the defendants made an offer by letter to the claimant on 2 September 1817 requiring an answer 'in course of post'. The letter of offer was delayed and reached the claimants on 5 September; they immediately posted a letter of acceptance, which reached the defendants on 9 September. The defendants could have expected a reply by 7 September, and they assumed that the absence of a reply within the expected period indicated non-acceptance and sold the goods to another buyer on 8 September.

Decision: the acceptance was made 'in course of post' and was effective when posted. The contract was made on 5 September, when the acceptance was posted.

The intention to use the post for communication of acceptance may be deduced from the circumstances without express statement to that effect.

Household Fire and Carriage Accident Insurance Co v Grant 1879

The facts: the defendant handed a letter of application for shares to the claimant company's agent in Swansea with the intention that it should be posted to the company in London. The company posted an acceptance (letter of allotment) which was lost in the post, and never arrived. The defendant was called upon to pay the amount outstanding on his shares.

Decision: the defendant had to pay. The contract between the company and him had been formed when the letter of allotment was posted, regardless of the fact that it was lost in the post.

Under the postal rule, the offeror may be unaware that a contract has been made by acceptance of his offer. If that possibility is clearly inconsistent with the nature of the transaction, the postal rule is excluded and the letter of acceptance takes effect only when received. In particular, if the offer stipulates a particular mode of communication, the postal rule may not apply.

Holwell Securities v Hughes 1974

The facts: Hughes granted to the claimant an option to purchase land to be exercised 'by notice in writing'. A letter giving notice of the exercise of the option was lost in the post.

Decision: the words 'notice in writing' must mean notice actually received by the vendor; hence notice had not been given to accept the offer.

Acceptance of an offer may only be made by a person authorised to do so. This will usually be the offeree or his authorised agents.

Powell v Lee 1908

The facts: the claimant successfully applied for a post as a headmaster. Without authorisation, the claimant was informed of the appointment by one of the managers. Later, it was decided to give the post to someone else. The claimant sued for breach of contract.

Decision: he failed in his action for breach of contract. Since communication of acceptance was unauthorised, there was no valid agreement and hence no contract.

NOTES

Activity 5 (10 minutes)

Jarvis wrote to Cocker on 1 April offering to sell him his mountain bike for £2,000, and asking Cocker to reply by post. Cocker received the letter on 2 April and the same day posted a letter of acceptance. On 3 April, Jarvis telephoned Cocker to say he was increasing the price to £2,500, but Cocker is insisting on buying at £2,000. What is the legal position?

Acceptance by email

The law is unclear as to when an acceptance sent by email becomes effective Communication of acceptance is not instantaneous using this method. Instead it should be linked to when the offeror actually saw the email, or should have read it, or might have been expected to read it.

Reward cases

The question arises as to whether contractual obligations arise if a party, in ignorance of an offer, performs an act which fulfils the terms of the offer. If A offers a reward to anyone who finds and returns his lost property and B, in ignorance of the offer, does in fact return it to him, is B entitled to the promised reward? In fact there is no contract by which A is obliged to pay the reward to B.

> *R v Clarke 1927*
> *The facts*: a reward of £1,000 was offered for information leading to the arrest and conviction of a murderer. C, an accomplice, gave the necessary information. He claimed the reward, admitting that he had acted only to save his own skin.
>
> *Decision*: his claim failed. Although he had seen the offer, it was not present in his mind when he acted.

However, acceptance may still be valid even if the offer was not the sole reason for the action.

Cross-offers

If two offers, identical in terms, cross in the post, there is no contract: *Tinn v Hoffmann 1873*.

Unilateral contracts

The question arises as to whether contractual obligations arise if a party, in ignorance of an offer, performs an act which fulfils the terms of the offer. If A offers a **reward** to anyone who finds and returns his lost property and B, in ignorance of the offer, does in fact return it to him, is B entitled to the promised reward? There is agreement by conduct, but B is not accepting A's offer since he is unaware of it.

BPP
LEARNING MEDIA

R v Clarke 1927
The facts: a reward was offered for information leading to the arrest and conviction of a murderer. If the information was provided by an accomplice, he would receive a free pardon. C claimed the reward, admitting that he had acted to save his own skin and that all thought of the reward had passed out his mind.

Decision: there could not be acceptance without knowledge of the offer.

However, acceptance may still be **valid** even if the offer was not the sole reason for the action.

Williams v Carwardine 1833
The facts: a reward was offered to bring criminals to book. The claimant, an accomplice in the crime, supplied the information, with knowledge of the reward.

Decision: as the information was given with knowledge, the acceptance was related to the offer.

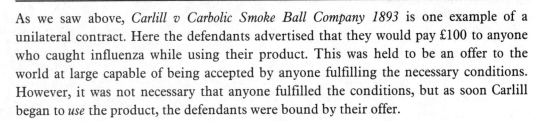

Activity 6   **(20 minutes)**

John offers to sell his car to Ahmed for £2,000 on 1 July saying that the offer will stay open for a week. Ahmed tells his brother that he would like to accept the offer. Unknown to Ahmed, his brother informs John of this on 4 July. On 5 July John, with his girlfriend present, sells the car to Gina. John's girlfriend tells Ahmed about this later that day. The next day, Ahmed delivers a letter of acceptance to John. Is John in breach of contract?

As we saw above, *Carlill v Carbolic Smoke Ball Company 1893* is one example of a unilateral contract. Here the defendants advertised that they would pay £100 to anyone who caught influenza while using their product. This was held to be an offer to the world at large capable of being accepted by anyone fulfilling the necessary conditions. However, it was not necessary that anyone fulfilled the conditions, but as soon Carlill began to *use* the product, the defendants were bound by their offer.

An ordinary offer can be revoked at any time before complete acceptance and, once revoked, can no longer be accepted (*Routledge v Grant 1828*). However, in the case of a unilateral contract, the courts have held that an offer cannot be revoked once the offeree has begun to perform whatever act is necessary (*Errington v Errington 1953*).

6   AGREEMENT WITHOUT OFFER AND ACCEPTANCE

Because the courts cannot ascertain the intentions of the parties, they must rely on what the parties **say or do**. In certain cases they may go beyond what can be inferred from the words and actions of the parties and **construct** a contract.

Clarke v Dunraven 1897
The facts: the owners of two yachts entered them for a regatta. Each undertook in a letter to the Club Secretary to obey the Club's rules, which included an obligation to pay all damages caused by fouling. The defendant's yacht fouled the claimant's yacht, which sank. The claimant sued for damages. The defendant argued that his only liability was under the Merchant Shipping Act 1862 and was therefore set at £8 per ton.

Decision: a contract had been created between the parties when they entered their yachts for the regatta, at which point they had accepted the club's rules. The claimant was entitled to recover full damages.

6.1 Collateral contracts

Definition

> A **collateral contract** is a contract the consideration for which is the making of some other contract. If there are two separate contracts between on the one hand A and B and on the other hand A and C, on terms which involve some concerted action between B and C, there may be a contract between B and C.

There is a contract between B and C despite the absence of direct communication between them.

Shanklin Pier Ltd v Detel Products 1951
The facts: the defendants gave assurances to the claimants that their paint would be satisfactory and durable if used to repaint the claimant's pier. The claimants in their contract with X for the repainting of the pier specified that X should use this paint. The paint proved very unsatisfactory. The claimants sued the defendants for breach of undertaking. The defendants argued that there was no contract between the claimants and themselves.

Decision: the contract between the claimants and X requiring the use of the defendant's paint was the consideration for a contract between the claimants and the defendant.

NOTES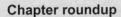

Chapter roundup

- The three essential components of a contract are offer and acceptance, consideration and the intention of the parties to create legal relations

- A void contract is one which has no legal effect at any time: neither party can obtain rights or obligations under it

- A voidable contract is one which is valid unless and until it is avoided

- An unenforceable contract is one which is valid but which cannot be enforced by either of the parties should something go wrong

- The first essential element of a binding contract is agreement. This is usually evidenced by offer and acceptance.

- An offer is a definite promise to be bound on specific terms, and must be distinguished from the mere supply of information and from an invitation to treat.

- An offer is terminated, and no longer open for acceptance, in the following circumstances.

    - Rejection by the offeree
    - Lapse of time
    - Revocation by the offeror
    - Failure of a condition to which the offer was subject
    - Death of one of the parties

- Acceptance must be unqualified agreement to all the terms of the offer. It may be by express words or inferred from conduct. Inaction does not imply acceptance.

- A counter-offer is a rejection of the original offer.

- Acceptance is not effective until communicated to the offeror, with two exceptions.

    - The offeror may waive the need for communication of acceptance by making an offer to the entire world.

    - He may indicate that he expects acceptance through the post.

- In the latter case, the 'postal rule' applies: acceptance is complete and effective as soon as notice of it is posted.

Quick quiz

1   What is a standard form contract?

2   What are the three essentials of a valid contract?

3   Define void, voidable and unenforceable contracts.

4   What case illustrates the principle that an offer may be made to the world at large?

5   What is an invitation to treat?

6   Can a third party communicate revocation of an offer?

7   What happens when an offeree accepts an offer but applies different terms to it?

8   What does the postal rule say?

Answers to quick quiz

1   Contract produced by large companies setting its own compulsory terms. (see para 1.2)

2   • Intention to create legal relations
     • Offer and acceptance
     • Consideration   (Section 2)

3   (a)   A **void** contract is **not a contract** at all. The parties are not bound by it and if they transfer property under it they can sometimes (unless it is also an illegal contract) recover their goods even from a third party.

     (b)   A **voidable** contract is a **contract which one party may avoid**, that is terminate at his option. The contract is treated as valid unless and until it is avoided. Property transferred before avoidance is usually irrecoverable from a third party.

     (c)   An **unenforceable** contract is a **valid contract** and property transferred under it cannot be recovered even from the other party to the contract. If either party refuses to perform the contract, the other party cannot compel him to do so. A contract is usually unenforceable when the required evidence of its terms, for example, written evidence of a contract relating to land, is not available. Unenforceable contracts are only problematic if a dispute over the contract arises.

                                                            (para 3.1)

4   *Carlill v Carbolic Smokeball Co. 1893.* (para 4.1)

5   An indication that someone is prepared to receive offers. (para 4.3)

6   Yes, as long as he is reliable. (para 4.4)

7   A new offer is created which can be either accepted or rejected. (para 5.5)

8   The acceptance is effective as seen as it is posted, as long as the post is the expected means of communication. (para 5.7)

Answers to activities

1   When she used the medicine and caught influenza. This was acceptance of the offer which, because it was to the entire world, had dispensed with the need for communication of acceptance. The answer is C.

2   A price label is an invitation to treat (*Fisher v Bell 1961*) ie an invitation to the customer to make an offer which the shop can either accept or reject.

3   Elle's offer of £3,000 is an **offer**. Many offers are in fact made by prospective purchasers rather than by vendors. Jane's letter forms a **counter-offer**, which has the effect of terminating Elle's offer: *Hyde v Wrench 1840*. Elle may now accept or reject this counter-offer.

    There is nothing to indicate that Jane's (counter) offer is not still open in March. An offer may be expressed to last for a **specified time**. It then expires at the end of that time. If, however, there is no express time limit set, it expires after a **reasonable time**.

    Elle's reply, using the words 'I accept your offer' **appear conclusive. However they are not**. The enquiry as to variation of terms does not constitute acceptance or rejection: *Stevenson v McLean 1880*. The effect of Elle's reply is probably best analysed as being a **new counter-offer** including terms as to deferred payment, which **Jane purports to accept by affixing a 'sold' sign**. The court would need to decide whether, in all the circumstances, acceptance can be deemed to have been communicated.

    Following *Butler Machine Tool Co v Ex-Cell-O Corp (England) 1979*, the **counter-offer introduces new terms**, that is, price. The price is therefore £3,500. As to **date of payment**, it would appear that the attachment of a 'sold' sign to the boat is confirmation that the revised terms proposed by Jane are acceptable.

4   No. By introducing the payment terms, Barry has rejected Mike's original offer and made a counter-offer to buy the car for £5,000 but pay over five months. Mike is free to accept or reject this, and by selling to Catherine, rejects Barry's offer.

5   Cocker can enforce the contract. The post is seen as the means of acceptance and, following the postal rule, Cocker has accepted. There is a contract.

6   Communication of acceptance may only be made by a person authorised to do so (*Powell v Lee 1908*), therefore Ahmed's brother's purported acceptance is not valid. Revocation of an offer may be communicated by a reliable informant (*Dickinson v Dodds 1876*), so Ahmed is made aware of the revocation on 5 July. His attempted acceptance on 6 July is therefore not valid.

    As there was no consideration to support any separate agreement to keep the offer open for a week, John is free to sell the car to Gina.

Chapter 5:
CONSIDERATION

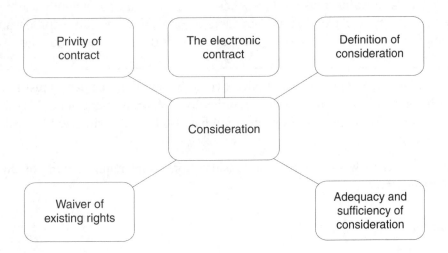

Introduction

Consideration is also one of the three essential elements of a binding contract. The principle is that the parties to a contract must each provide something, whether money, the provision of a service or some other form of contribution to the contract. A contractual promise is one which is not purely gratuitous. If a window cleaner telephones you and promises as a special promotion to clean your windows tomorrow for free, but then fails to turn up, you cannot sue him for breach of contract. This is because there is no contract, because you have provided no consideration.

Your objectives

In this chapter you will learn about the following.

    (a)   The nature of consideration

    (b)   The rules governing past consideration

    (c)   The rules governing adequacy of consideration

    (d)   The rules governing sufficiency of consideration

    (e)   The rules governing the doctrine of promissory estoppel

    (f)   The rule of privity of contract

1 DEFINITION OF CONSIDERATION

There have been a number of case law definitions of consideration, for example from *Currie v Misa 1875*.

Definition

'A valuable **consideration** in the sense of the law may consist either in some right, interest, profit or benefit accruing to one party, or some forbearance, detriment, loss or responsibility given, suffered or undertaken by the other.'

Using the language of purchase and sale, it could be said that one party must know that he has bought the other party's promises either by performing some **act** of his own or by offering a **promise** of his own. Consideration has also been described as 'the price of the other person's promise'.

There are a very few situation when consideration is not required. One of these is a **specialty contract**.

Definitions

A **specialty contract** is one where consideration is not a compulsory element. An example is the granting of a deed, such as a deed of covenant in favour of a charity. The charity does not have to provide any consideration in return.

This is in contrast to a **simple contract** (most types of contract) which is one where consideration is provided by both sides.

It is sometimes said that valid consideration may be **executed** or **executory**, but it **cannot be past**. These terms are explained below.

1.1 Executed consideration

Definition

Executed consideration is a performed, or executed, act in return for a promise.

If, for example, A offers a reward for the return of lost property, his promise becomes binding when B performs the act of returning A's property to him. The claimant's act in Carlill's case in response to the smoke ball company's promise of reward was thus executed consideration.

1.2 Executory consideration

Definition

> **Executory consideration** is a promise given for a promise, not a performed act.

If, for example, a customer orders goods which a shopkeeper undertakes to obtain from the manufacturer, the shopkeeper promises to supply the goods and the customer promises to accept and pay for them. It would be breach of contract if either withdrew without the consent of the other.

1.3 Additional rules for valid consideration

As well as being either executed or executory, there are **additional** rules that must be met for consideration to be valid:

- **Performance must be legal,** the courts will not enforce payment for illegal acts

- **Performance must be possible,** agreeing to perform the impossible is not a basis for a binding contract

- **Consideration must pass from the promisee,** (see privity of contract later in this chapter)

- **Consideration must be sufficient but necessarily adequate,** (see Section 2 in this chapter)

1.4 Past consideration

Both executed and executory consideration are provided at the time when the promise is given.

Definition

> Anything which has already been done before a promise in return is given is **past consideration** which, as a general rule, is not sufficient to make the promise binding.

Re McArdle 1951
The facts: under the terms of a will, children were entitled to a house after their mother's death. In the mother's lifetime one of the sons and his wife lived in the house with the mother. The wife made improvements to the house. The children later agreed in writing to repay to the wife the sum of £488 'in consideration of your carrying out certain alterations and improvements' to the property. At the mother's death they refused to do so.

Decision: the work on the house had been completed before the documents were signed. At the time of the promise the improvements were past consideration.

If there is an existing contract and one party makes a further promise, no contract will arise. Even if such a promise related to the previous bargain, it will be held to have been made upon past consideration.

Roscorla v Thomas 1842

The facts: the claimant agreed to buy a horse from the defendant at a given price. When negotiations were over and the contract was formed, the defendant told the claimant that the horse was 'sound and free from vice'. The horse turned out to be vicious and the claimant brought an action on the warranty.

Decision: the express promise was made after the sale was over and was unsupported by fresh consideration.

Exceptions to the doctrine of past consideration

In three cases past consideration for a promise can make the promise binding.

(a) Past consideration is sufficient to create liability on a **Bill of Exchange** (such as a cheque) under s 27 Bills of Exchange Act 1882.

(b) After six (or in some cases twelve) years the right to sue for recovery of a debt becomes statute barred by the **Limitation Act 1980**. If, after that period, the debtor makes written acknowledgement of the creditor's claim, the claim is again enforceable at law. The debt, although past consideration, suffices.

(c) When a request is made for a service this **request may imply a promise** to pay for it. If, after the service has been rendered, the person who made the request promises a specific reward, this is treated as fixing the amount to be paid under the previous implied promise.

Lampleigh v Braithwait 1615

The facts: the defendant had killed a man and had asked the claimant to obtain for him a royal pardon. The claimant did so, 'riding and journeying to and from London and Newmarket' at his own expense. The defendant then promised to pay him £100. He failed to pay it and was sued.

Decision: the defendant's request was regarded as containing an implied promise to pay, and the subsequent promise merely fixed the amount.

The third exception above has been somewhat revised by the courts, so that both parties must have assumed throughout their negotiations that the services were ultimately to be paid for.

Re Casey's Patents 1892

The facts: A and B, joint owners of patent rights, asked their employee, C, as an extra task to find licensees to work the patents. After C had done so, A and B agreed to reward him for his past services with one-third of the patent rights. A died and his executors denied that the promise made was binding.

Decision: the promise to C was binding since it fixed the 'reasonable remuneration' which A and B by implication promised to pay before the service was given.

Activity 1   **(10 minutes)**

Which of the following is valid consideration? Try to state the law to justify your answer.

(a) An action six months ago for which the person who carried it out is now demanding payment.

(b) A promise to pay for goods in six months' time.

(c) A request to someone to clean your windows.

---

2   ADEQUACY AND SUFFICIENCY OF CONSIDERATION

The law says that consideration need not be adequate but it must be sufficient. This means that the consideration need not be of equal value to the parties to the contract, but it must be of some value to the parties involved. This does not have to be financial or monetary value, although obviously in many contracts it often is.

In a basic contract for the sale of goods, one party will provide money as his consideration, and the other party will provide the goods.

2.1   Adequacy

The courts have always made it clear that parties to a contract are expected to look after themselves, and the courts will not protect them if all they have done is made a 'bad bargain' and accepted inadequate consideration. Therefore, if someone sells their car, worth £10,000, for £2,000, they cannot expect the courts to step in, unless there has been some element of fraud or misrepresentation in the run up to the contract.

The courts will not seek to weigh up the comparative values of the promises.

> *Thomas v Thomas 1842*
> *The facts*: by his will the claimant's husband expressed the wish that his widow should have the use of his house during her life. The defendants allowed the widow to occupy the house (a) in accordance with her husband's wishes and (b) in return for her undertaking to pay a rent of £1 per annum. They later said that their promise to let her occupy the house was not supported by consideration.
>
> *Decision*: compliance with the husband's wishes was not valuable consideration (because there was no economic value attached to it), but the nominal rent was sufficient consideration, even though inadequate as a rent.

The value of forbearance

Forbearance, or the promise to give something up or to stop doing something, can be adequate consideration, if it has some value or amounts to giving up something of value. For example, a contract in which one party promises to give up smoking would probably have adequate consideration.

However, although consideration need not be adequate it must be **sufficient**.

2.2 Sufficiency

The term **sufficiency of consideration** means that the consideration must be something more than the party involved was already intended to do. It must be deemed actually to be consideration. For example, the performance of an existing legal duty cannot be regarded as consideration, as the person involved would be going to do it anyway.

> *Chappell & Co v Nestle Co 1960*
> *The facts*: as a sales promotion scheme, the defendant offered to supply a record to anyone who sent in a postal order for 1s.6d and three wrappers from 6d bars of chocolate made by them. The claimants owned the copyright of the tune. They sued for infringement of copyright. In the ensuing dispute over royalties the issue was whether the wrappers, which were thrown away when received, were part of the consideration for the promise to supply the record. The defendants offered to pay a royalty based on the price of 1s.6d per record, but the claimants rejected this, claiming that the wrappers also represented part of the consideration.
>
> *Decision*: the wrappers were part of the consideration as they had commercial value to the defendants.

As stated earlier, forbearance or the promise of it may be **sufficient** consideration if it has some value, or amounts to giving up something of value.

> *Horton v Horton 1961*
> *The facts*: under a separation agreement, the defendant agreed to pay his wife (the claimant) £30 per month. Under the deed this amount was a net payment after deduction of income tax; for nine months the husband paid it without any deduction so that the wife had to make the deductions herself. He then signed a document agreeing to pay such amount as 'after the deduction of income tax should amount to the clear sum of £30'. He paid this for three years, then stopped, pleading that the later agreement was not supported by consideration.
>
> *Decision*: the later agreement was supported by consideration: the wife could have sued to have the original agreement rectified, but did not.

Performance of existing contractual duties

Performance of an **existing obligation** imposed by statute is **no consideration** for a promise of reward.

> *Collins v Godefroy 1831*
> *The facts*: the claimant had been subpoenaed (ie summoned to court) to give evidence on behalf of the defendant in another case. He alleged that the defendant had promised to pay him six guineas (£6.30) for appearing.
>
> *Decision*: there was no consideration for this promise, as the claimant was obliged to appear by law. He failed in his claim for the six guineas.

But if some extra service is given, that is sufficient consideration.

> *Glasbrook Bros v Glamorgan CC 1925*
> *The facts*: at a time of industrial unrest, colliery owners, rejecting the view of the police that a mobile force was enough, asked and agreed to pay for a special guard on the mine. Later they repudiated liability saying that the police had done no more than perform their public duty of maintaining order.
>
> *Decision*: the extra services given, beyond what the police in their discretion deemed necessary, were consideration for the promise to pay. If the judgement of the police authorities had been that a special guard was necessary, they would not have been entitled to charge for it.

Where one party's actions lead to the need for heightened police presence, and the police deem this presence necessary, they may also be entitled to payment.

> *Harris v Sheffield United F.C. Ltd 1988*
> *The facts*: the defendants argued that they did not have to pay for a large police presence at their home matches.
>
> *Decision*: they had voluntarily decided to hold matches on Saturday afternoons when large attendances were likely, increasing the risk of disorder. (An important factor here was that the police were required to be inside the football club's premises.)

Performance of more than existing contractual duties

If there is already a contract between A and B, and B promises additional reward to A if he (A) will perform his **existing duties**, there is **no consideration** from A to make that promise binding. A assumes no extra obligation and B obtains no extra rights or benefits.

> *Stilk v Myrick 1809*
> *The facts*: two members of the crew of a ship deserted in a foreign port. The master was unable to recruit substitutes and promised the rest of the crew that they should share the wages of the deserters if they would complete the voyage home short-handed. The shipowners however repudiated the promise.
>
> *Decision*: in performing their existing contractual duties the crew gave no consideration for the promise of extra pay and the promise was not binding. The lack of two crew members did not mean that the remaining crew were doing more than their existing duty.

If a claimant does **more** than perform an existing contractual duty, this **may amount to consideration.**

> *Hartley v Ponsonby 1857*
> *The facts*: 17 men out of a crew of 36 deserted. The remainder were promised an extra £40 each to work the ship to Bombay. The claimant, one of the remaining crew-members, sued to recover this amount.
>
> *Decision*: the large number of desertions made the voyage more hazardous, and this had the effect of discharging the original contract. The claimant had a new contract, under which his promise to complete the voyage formed consideration for the promise to pay an additional £40.

Recent developments

The courts appear to be taking a slightly different line in recent years on the payment of additional consideration. It may be that where the party providing the additional reward has received a 'practical' benefit that will be treated as consideration even if, in law, he has received no more than he was already entitled to under the contract.

> *Williams v Roffey Bros & Nicholls (Contractors) Ltd 1990*
> *The facts*: the claimants agreed to do carpentry work for the defendants, who were engaged as contractors to refurbish a block of flats, at a fixed price of £20,000. The work ran late and so the defendants, concerned that the job might not be finished on time and that they would have to pay under a penalty clause in the main contract, agreed to pay the claimants an extra £10,300 to ensure the work was completed on time. They later refused to pay the extra amount.
>
> *Decision*: the fact that there was no apparent consideration for the promise to pay the extra was not held to be important, and in the court's view both parties derived benefit from the promise. The telling point was that the defendants' promise to pay the extra mount had not been extracted by duress or fraud: it was therefore binding.

> *Re Selectmove 1994*
> *The facts*: a company which was the subject of a winding-up order offered to settle its outstanding debts by instalment. An Inland Revenue inspector agreed to this proposal. The company tried to enforce it.
>
> *Decision*: despite the verdict in *Williams v Roffey Bros & Nicholls*, the court followed *Foakes v Beer* (see below) in holding that an agreement to pay in instalments is unenforceable.

Performance of existing contractual duty to a third party

If A promises B a reward if B will perform his existing contract with C, there is consideration for A's promise since he has obtained a benefit to which he previously had no right, and B assumes new obligations.

> *Shadwell v Shadwell 1860*
> *The facts*: the claimant, a barrister, was engaged to marry E (an engagement to marry was at this time a binding contract). His uncle promised the claimant that if he married E (as he did), the uncle would during their joint lives pay £150 pa until such time as the nephew was earning 600 guineas (£630) working as a barrister (which never transpired). The uncle died after eighteen years, owing six annual payments. The claimant claimed the arrears from his uncle's executors, who denied that there was consideration for the promise.
>
> *Decision*: the nephew had provided consideration as he was initially under a duty only to his fiancée, but by entering into the agreement he had put himself under obligation to the uncle too.

Activity 2   **(5 minutes)**

Which of the following is true of consideration?

(a) It must be of adequate and sufficient value.
(b) It must move from the promisee.
(c) It must never be past.
(d) It must be given in every binding agreement.
(e) It may be performance of an existing obligation.

3 WAIVER OF EXISTING RIGHTS

Particular complications arise over sufficiency of consideration for promises to **waive existing rights,** especially regarding rights to common law debts.

3.1 The rule

If X owes Y £100 but Y agrees to accept a lesser sum, say £80, in full settlement of Y's claim, that is a promise by Y to waive his entitlement to the balance of £20. The promise, like any other, should be supported by consideration. If it is not, it is not binding.

> *Foakes v Beer 1884*
> *The facts*: the defendant had obtained a court judgement against the claimant for the sum of £2,091. Judgement debts bear interest from the date of the judgement. By a written agreement the defendant agreed to accept payment by instalments of the sum of £2,091, no mention being made of the interest. Once the claimant had paid the amount of the debt in full, the defendant claimed interest, claiming that the agreement was not supported by consideration.
>
> *Decision*: she was entitled to the debt with interest. No consideration had been given by the claimant for waiver of any part of her rights against him.

3.2 Exceptions to the rule

There are, however, exceptions to the rule that the debtor (denoted by 'X' in the following paragraphs) must give consideration if the waiver is to be binding. These exceptions concern variation of the original contract terms.

(a) If X offers and Y accepts anything to which Y is not already entitled, the extra thing will be sufficient consideration for the waiver. This may be for example:

    (i) Goods instead of cash: *Anon 1495* or
    (ii) Payment before the date payment is due: *Pinnel's case 1602*.

(b) If X arranges with a number of creditors that they will each accept part payment in full settlement, that is a bargain between the creditors. X has given no consideration but he can hold the creditors individually to the agreed terms: *Wood v Robarts 1818*.

(c) If a third party (Z) offers part payment and Y agrees to release X from Y's claim to the balance, Y has received consideration from Z against whom he had no previous claim.

Welby v Drake 1825
The facts: D owed W £18. D's father paid W £9 in settlement of the debt, and W had agreed to accept that amount. W then sued D for the remaining £9.

Decision: W could not recover the additional money, because the father, as a third party, had paid the original sum on the faith of the discharge of the sum from a further liability.

(d) The principle of **promissory estoppel** (see below) may prevent Y from retracting his promise with retrospective effect.

Activity 3   **(5 minutes)**

Hugo agreed to drive his friend Laurence (a nervous passenger) to Cardiff. He said that if Laurence paid him £25, he would not exceed the speed limit on the motorway. Is this promise enforceable?

3.3 Promissory estoppel

The equitable concept of **promissory estoppel** operates to prevent a person rescinding (ie going back on) his promise to accept a lesser amount. He cannot retract his waiver with retrospective effect, though it may permit him to insist on full rights in the future.

Central London Property Trust v High Trees House 1947
The facts: in September 1939, the claimants let a block of flats to the defendants at an annual rent of £2,500 pa. It was difficult to let the individual flats in wartime, so in January 1940, the claimants agreed in writing to accept a reduced rent of £1,250 pa No time limit was set on the arrangement but it was clearly related to wartime conditions. The reduced rent was paid from 1940 to 1945 and the defendants sublet flats during the period on the basis of their expected liability to pay rent under the head lease at £1,250 only. In 1945 the flats were fully let. The claimants demanded a full rent of £2,500 pa, both retrospectively and for the future. They tested this claim by suing for rent at the full rate for the last two quarters of 1945.

Decision: the agreement of January 1940 was a temporary expedient only and had ceased to operate early in 1945. The claim was upheld. However, had the claimants sued for arrears for the period 1940 to 1945, the 1940 agreement would have served to defeat the claim.

Definition

> **Estoppel** operates when a person, by his words or conduct, leads another to believe that a certain state of affairs exists. If the other person, relying on that belief, alters his position to his detriment, the first person is **estopped** (prevented) from claiming later that a different state of affairs existed.

In the *High Trees* case, if the defendants had sued on the promise, they would have failed for want of consideration. The principle is '**a shield not a sword**', ie it is a defence, which does not create new rights.

> *Combe v Combe 1951*
> *The facts*: a wife obtained a divorce. Her ex-husband promised that he would make maintenance payments of £100 per annum. The wife did not apply to the court for an order for maintenance, but this forbearance was not at the husband's request. No maintenance was paid and the wife sued on the promise. In the High Court the wife obtained judgement on the basis of the principle of promissory estoppel. The ex-husband appealed.
>
> *Decision*: The Court of Appeal said that promissory estoppel 'does not create new causes of action where none existed before. It only prevents a party from insisting on his strict legal rights when it would be unjust to allow him to enforce them'. The wife's claim failed.

From this it can be seen that promissory estoppel applies only to a voluntary waiver of existing rights.

> *D and C Builders v Rees 1966*
> *The facts*: the defendants owed £482 to the claimants. The claimants, who were in acute financial difficulties, reluctantly agreed to accept £300 in full settlement. They later claimed the balance.
>
> *Decision*: the debt must be paid in full. Promissory estoppel only applies to a promise voluntarily given. The defendants had been aware of and had exploited the claimants' difficulties. In this important case it was also held that payment by cheque (instead of in cash) is normal and gives no extra advantage which could be treated as consideration for the waiver under the rule in *Pinnel's case*.

Summary

Promissory estoppel is one of the most complex legal doctrines you will encounter in this book. In summary, three elements are required if promissory estoppel is to apply:

- A waiver of rights by one of the parties to the contract
- The other party must rely on that waiver to some extent
- Some special or unusual circumstances must apply

These three components can be clearly illustrated by the *High Trees* case, as follows.

- Central London Property trust waived their right to the full rent while subletting was difficult

- High Trees relied on that waiver by in turn reducing the rents charged to their tenants

- The situation arose because of the war: an unusual set of circumstances

4 PRIVITY OF CONTRACT

If you don't provide consideration, you cannot sue on the contract. This is a critical rule in contract law, and reflects the fact that consideration is essential.

This maxim means that **only the person who has paid the price of a contract can sue on it.** If, for example, A promises B that (for a consideration provided by B) A will confer a benefit on C, then C cannot as a general rule enforce A's promise.

> *Tweddle v Atkinson 1861*
> *The facts*: the claimant married the daughter of G. On the occasion of the marriage, the claimant's father and G exchanged promises that they would each pay a sum of money to the claimant. The agreement between the two fathers expressly provided that the claimant should have enforceable rights against them. G died without making the promised payment and the claimant sued G's executor for the specified amount.
>
> *Decision*: the claimant had provided no consideration for G's promise. In spite of the express terms of the agreement he had no enforceable rights under it and was not therefore 'privy to the contract'.

In *Tweddle's* case each father as promisee gave consideration by his promise to the other, but the claimant was to be the beneficiary of each promise. Each father could have sued the other but the claimant could not sue.

The rule that consideration must move from the promisee overlaps with the rule that only a party to a contract can enforce it. Together these rules are known as the principles of **privity of contract**.

No-one may be entitled to or bound by the terms of a contract to which he is not an original party. A person is regarded as a party to the contract if he provides consideration.

4.1 The rule

As a general rule, only a person who is a party to a contract has enforceable rights or obligations under it. The following is the leading case in this area:

> *Dunlop v Selfridge 1915*
> *The facts*: the claimant, a tyre manufacturer, supplied tyres to X, a distributor, on terms that X would not re-sell the tyres at less than the prescribed retail price. If X sold the tyres wholesale to trade customers, X must impose a similar condition on those buyers to observe minimum retail prices (such clauses were legal at the time though prohibited since 1964 by the Resale Prices Act). X resold tyres on these conditions to the defendant. Under the terms of the contract between X and Selfridge, Selfridge was to pay to the

claimant a sum of £5 per tyre if it sold tyres to customers below the minimum retail price. They sold tyres to two customers at less than the minimum price. The claimant sued to recover £5 per tyre as liquidated damages.

Decision: the claimant could not recover damages under a contract (between X and Selfridge) to which it was not a party.

Definition

> **Privity of contract** is the relation between the two parties to a contract. Third parties who are not privy to the contract generally have no right of action. This is true even if they receive benefits under it.

Effect on third parties

In these circumstances the party to the contract who imposes the condition or obtains a promise of a benefit for a third party can usually enforce it, but damages cannot be recovered on the third party's behalf unless the contracting party is suing an agent or trustee. Only nominal damages can be given if the contract was only for a third party's benefit. Other remedies may be sought however.

> *Beswick v Beswick 1968*
> *The facts*: X transferred his business to the defendant, his nephew, in consideration for a pension of £6.50 per week and, after his death, a weekly annuity to X's widow. Only one such annuity payment was made. The widow brought an action against the nephew, asking for an order of specific performance. She sued both as administratrix of her husband's estate and in her personal capacity as recipient.
>
> *Decision*: as her husband's representative, the widow was successful in enforcing the contract for a third party's (her own) benefit. In her personal capacity she could derive no right of action.

Exception to the third party rule

Where the contract is one which provides something for the enjoyment of both the contracting party and third parties, such as a family holiday, the contracting party may be entitled to recover damages for his loss of the benefit.

> *Jackson v Horizon Holidays Ltd 1975*
> *The facts*: Mr Jackson booked a holiday with Horizon for himself and his family. Various things went wrong and the holiday did not meet the claims of the brochure, and Mr Jackson sued for damages for his own loss and disappointment and that of his family.
>
> *Decision*: he was successful in claiming all of the damages as the contract was made not only for Mr Jackson himself but also for the benefit and enjoyment of his family. This judgement has been fairly widely criticised.

FOR DISCUSSION

Do you think that the judgement in *Jackson, v Horizon Holidays* was fair, or do you think it breached legal principles? What source of law (from Chapter 2) do you think is demonstrated here?

If the contract is broken and the claimant seeks damages on the other parties' behalf he can also recover for the loss suffered by those other people: *Woodar Investment Development Ltd v Wimpey Construction (UK) Ltd 1980.*

4.2 Exceptions

There are a number of real or apparent exceptions to the general rule of privity of contract.

(a) *Implied trusts*

Equity may hold that an implied trust has been created.

Gregory and Parker v Williams 1817
The facts: P owed money to G and W. He agreed with W to transfer his property to W if W would pay his (P's) debt to G. The property was transferred, but W refused to pay G. G could not sue on the contract between P and W.

Decision: P could be regarded as a trustee for G, and G would therefore bring an action jointly with P.

(b) *Statutory exceptions*

(i) There are statutory exceptions which permit a person injured in a road accident to claim against the **motorist's insurers** (Road Traffic Act 1972) and which permit husband or wife to **insure his or her own life** for the benefit of the other under a trust which the beneficiary can enforce (Married Woman's Property Act 1882).

(ii) The provisions of the Contract (Rights of Third Parties) Act 1999 has had a significant impact on the rights of third parties, see below.

(c) *Agency*

(i) In normal circumstances the **agent** discloses to a third party with whom he contracts that he is acting for a principal whose identity is also disclosed. The agent has no liability under the contract and no right to enforce it.

(ii) If a person enters into a contract apparently on his own account but in fact as agent on behalf of a principal, the doctrine of the **undisclosed principal** determines the position of the parties. An undisclosed principal may adopt a contract made for him by an agent. Until such time as the principal takes this action, the agent himself may sue the third party.

(d)   *Covenants*

A restrictive covenant, which a third party may enforce, may run with land. For example, if the owner of a house is bound by a covenant not to cut down trees on the land, any subsequent buyer of that house will also be bound by the same covenant.

(e)   *Assignment*

(i)   A party to a contract can **assign** or transfer to another person **the rights** contained in the contract. He cannot assign the burden of his contractual **obligations**.

(ii)   A legal assignment must be absolute, it must be in writing, and notice must be given to the other party: s 136 Law of Property Act 1925. It is **not possible** to assign:

(1)   A **right of action**, which is a claim for unliquidated damages for breach of contract

(2)   **Rights which are personal** to the original parties to the contract.

(f)   *Foreseeable loss to the third party*

Linden Gardens Trust Ltd v Lenesta Sludge Disposals Ltd (1994)
The facts: Linden Gardens contracted with the defendants for work to be done on their property. The defendants knew there was the likelihood that the property would be transferred to a third party soon after. After the transfer it became apparent that the workmanship amounted to breach of contract. As the third party had no action against the defendants due to the rules on privity, Linden Gardens took action in their place.

Decision: as the transfer was in the contemplation of both parties the original beneficiary could claim full damages on behalf of the third party.

Activity 4   **(10 minutes)**

Julia arranges a party for her daughter Tamsin's 21st birthday, and books the band 'Mardi Gras'. On the day, the band fail to turn up and Tamsin is distraught. Who can sue them for breach of contract?

4.3   Contracts (Rights of Third Parties) Act 1999

The Contracts (Rights of Third Parties) Act 1999 gives third parties statutory rights under contracts in certain circumstances.

There is a two-limbed test for the circumstances in which a third party may enforce a contract term:

- Whether the contract itself expressly so provides

- Where the term confers a benefit on the third party, unless it appears that the contracting parties did not intend him to have the right to enforce it.

The third party must be expressly identified in the contract by name, class or description, but need not be in existence when the contract is made (for example, an unborn child or future spouse). The Act enables a third party to take advantage of exclusion clauses as well as to enforce 'positive' rights.

5 THE ELECTRONIC CONTRACT

It could be said that the case of *Byrne v van Tienhoven*, dating from 1880, is an early example of an **electronic contract**. In that case, the sending of an acceptance by telegram was an important action in a chain of events leading to the formation of a contract. Since then, technology has permitted such actions to become **almost instantaneous**. Fax messages, e-mails and use of the internet may all play a part in the communication of offers and purported acceptances.

This is a potentially wide ranging topic and the law is still in its infancy. Below is a summary of the issues which will need to be considered.

(a) **In writing**? There are two main reasons why contracts need to be in writing.

(i) A written contract provides evidence of the terms of the contract.

(ii) The requirement of formality allows a weaker party to 'think twice' before entering into a transaction.

An electronic contract meets the reasoning behind the requirement for writing, and can thus be said to be in writing.

(b) **Signed?** In 2000 the UK government passed legislation to give legal effect to 'digital signatures', thereby giving an electronic contract the same status as contracts in more traditional formats.

(c) **Timing of acceptance.** A contract comes into existence when an offer is accepted; in the case of acceptance by letter, this is when the letter is posted not when it is received. Internet e-mail shares many of the qualities of conventional mail – it is not usually instantaneous and may be subject to delay. Therefore the postal rule, with any problems arising from it, probably applies, although the point has not been tested.

(d) **Consideration.** Difficulties with credit card payments have slowed the growth of electronic commerce. The Internet is largely insecure, and this may cause problems when it comes to payment.

Activities on the internet are largely **unregulated** at the moment, but this is likely to change, as governments recognise the business opportunities available and the EU seeks to **protect consumers. Basic legal principles** must therefore be applied.

Of course, the internet is much more than simply a means of sending and receiving messages. As the commercial applications of the **world wide web** have been exploited, a new 'shop front' has been developed. Some sites are highly automated and software handles ordering, stock checking, payment processing and despatch confirmation without human involvement.

There are risks associated with leaving commercial transactions to automated IT programs. Eliminating human intervention and fully automating the sales process, for example, can increase the likelihood of errors. A notable recent example is the Argos website in the UK which offered television sets for £2.99, rather than £299.

The following are some of the **practical legal issues** that must be faced by a **seller** when contracting online.

- Websites should be constructed as shop windows, that is, **invitations to treat** rather than offers.

- **Terms and conditions** governing electronic transactions should be made explicit and clear.

- **An indication of interest** by a purchaser visiting the website should be understood by both parties to be **an offer,** not an acceptance, which the seller is then free to accept or reject.

- Sellers can continue to use **disclaimers of liability**, clearly displayed on the website, subject to the usual **consumer protection laws** on unfair terms.

- The **law and jurisdiction** governing the transaction should be made clear, for example, 'All transactions are governed by English law'.

- The seller should make sure that any **web pages do not contravene local laws** (for example, those relating to advertising standards) in the countries targeted.

- A **time limit** should be set for all offers made on the website, which should take account of potential delays in receiving emails.

Chapter roundup

- 'A valuable consideration in the sense of the law may consist either in some right, interest, profit or benefit accruing to one party, or some forbearance, detriment, loss or responsibility given, suffered or undertaken by the other.' *Currie v Misa 1875*.

- Consideration may be executed (an act in return for a promise) or executory (a promise in return for a promise). It may not be past, unless one of three recognised exceptions applies.

- Consideration need not be adequate, but it must be sufficient. This means that what is tendered as consideration must be capable in law of being regarded as consideration, but need not necessarily be equal in value to the consideration received in return (for example a peppercorn rent).

- The principle of promissory estoppel was developed in *Central London Property Trust v High Trees House 1947*.

- As a general rule, only a person who is a party to a contract has enforceable rights or obligations under it. This is the doctrine of privity of contract, as demonstrated in *Dunlop v Selfridge 1915*.

Quick quiz

1   What is executed consideration?

2   What is past consideration?

3   Give three situations where past consideration may make a promise binding.

4   What point of law is illustrated by *Chappell & Co v Nestle Co 1960?*

5   Summarise the facts of *Stilk v Myrick 1809* and *Hartley v Ponsonby 1857*, showing the distinction between them.

6   List two situations in which a debtor need not give consideration for a creditor who promises to accept a lesser sum in full settlement of a debt to be bound by his promise.

7   What is the doctrine of promissory estoppel?

8   What is privity of contract?

9   Give the name of a case which illustrates the rule that consideration must move from the promisee.

Answers to quick quiz

1   An act which has been performed (executed) in return for a promise. (see para 1.2)

2   Anything which has been done before a promise is made to do something in return. (para 1.4)

3   Bills of exchange
     Elapse of time
     Request for services (para 1.4)

4   Consideration need not be adequate. (para 2.2)

5   In *Stilk v Myrick*, two of the crew deserted, and the fact that the rest of the crew sailed the ship home was not sufficient consideration. In *Hartley v Ponsonby*, half of the crew deserted. The sailing home of the ship by the remainder *was* sufficient consideration for the wages promised. (para 2.2)

6   Part payment by a third party.
     The offer of something different, eg goods instead of cash. (Section 3)

7   It prevents someone going back on a promise to accept less consideration in certain circumstances. (para 3.3)

8   The rule that only the parties to a contract (ie those who provide consideration) may sue on it. (Section 4)

9   *Tweddle v Atkinson, 1861* (Section 4)

Answers to activities

1   (b) and (c). (a) is not as consideration is past. (b) is executory consideration and (c) gives rise to an implied promise to pay, as in *Lampleigh v Braithwait 1615.*

2   (b) only. Consideration need only be sufficient, it need not be adequate (a). It can be past in limited circumstances (c). It need not be given in a contract by deed (d). Performance of an existing obligation cannot support a new contract (e) because there is no extra obligation.

3   No, as by keeping within the speed limit, Hugo is doing no more than his existing legal duty. He is not doing anything 'extra'.

4   Only Julia, as she was privy to the contract, while Tamsin is not.

Chapter 6:
INTENTION AND CAPACITY

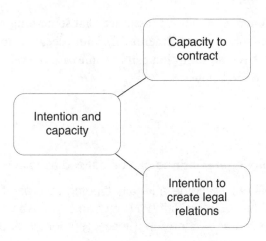

Introduction

An agreement is not a binding contract unless the parties intend to create legal relations and have the capacity or ability to do so. 'Legal relations' can be defined as the willingness to be bound by the terms of the contract. Where there is no express statement as to whether or not legal relations are intended (as may be said to be true of the majority of contracts), the courts apply one of two presumptions:

(a) Social, domestic and family arrangements are *not* usually intended by the parties involved to be binding;

(b) Commercial agreements *are* usually intended to be legally binding.

Anyone entering a contract has to have the capacity to do so, otherwise it can be argued that they are not acting in full understanding of what they are doing. The law seeks to protect such groups of people, most notably those aged under 18, known as minors.

Your objectives

In this chapter you will learn about the following.

(a) The rules governing when spouses enter a contract with each other
(b) The rules governing commercial agreements
(c) The rules governing capacity to contract

1 INTENTION TO CREATE LEGAL RELATIONS

Where there is no express statement as to whether or not legal relations are intended, the courts apply one of two **rebuttable presumptions** to a case.

- Social, domestic and family arrangements are not usually intended to be binding.

- Commercial agreements are usually intended by the parties involved to be legally binding.

The word 'presumption' means that it is assumed that something is the case, for example it is presumed that social arrangements are not deemed to be legally binding. 'Rebuttable' means that the presumption can in some cases be refuted, as, for example, in some of the cases described below.

Definition

> **Intention to create legal relations** can be defined as follows.
>
> 'An agreement will only become a legally binding contract if the parties intend this to be so. This will be strongly presumed in the case of business agreements but presumed otherwise if the agreement is of a friendly, social or domestic nature.'

1.1 Domestic arrangements

Husband and wife

The fact that the parties are husband and wife does not mean that they cannot enter into a **binding contract** with one another. Contrast the following two cases.

> *Balfour v Balfour 1919*
> *The facts*: the defendant was employed in Ceylon. He and his wife returned to the UK on leave but it was agreed that for health reasons she would not return to Ceylon with him. He promised to pay her £30 a month as maintenance. Later the marriage ended in divorce and the wife sued for the monthly allowance which the husband no longer paid.
>
> *Decision*: an informal agreement of indefinite duration made between husband and wife whose marriage had not at the time broken up was not intended to be legally binding.

> *Merritt v Merritt 1970*
> *The facts*: the husband had left the matrimonial home, which was owned in the joint names of husband and wife, to live with another woman. The spouses met and held a discussion, in the course of which he agreed to pay her £40 a month out of which she agreed to keep up the mortgage payments. The wife made the husband sign a note of these terms and an undertaking to transfer the house into her name when the mortgage had been paid off. The wife paid off the mortgage but the husband refused to transfer the house to her.

Decision: in the circumstances, an intention to create legal relations was to be inferred and the wife could sue for breach of contract.

Where agreements between husband and wife or other relatives relate to **property matters** the courts are very ready to impute an intention to create legal relations.

Relatives

Agreements between other family members may also be examined by the courts.

> *Jones v Padavatton 1969*
> *The facts*: the claimant wanted her daughter to move to England to train as a barrister, and offered to pay her a monthly allowance. The daughter did so in 1962. In 1964 the claimant bought a house in London; part of the house was occupied by the daughter and the other part let to tenants whose rent was collected by the daughter for herself. In 1967 the claimant and her daughter quarrelled and the claimant issued a summons claiming possession of the house. The daughter sued for her allowance.
>
> *Decision*: there were two agreements to consider: the daughter's agreement to read for the bar in exchange for a monthly allowance, and the agreement by which the daughter lived in her mother's house and collected the rent from tenants. Neither agreement was intended to create legal relations.

Other domestic arrangements

Domestic arrangements extend to those between people who are not related but who have a **close relationship** of some form. The nature of the agreement itself may lead to the conclusion that legal relations were intended.

> *Simpkins v Pays 1955*
> *The facts*: the defendant, her granddaughter and the claimant, a paying boarder, took part together each week in a competition organised by a Sunday newspaper. The arrangements over postage and other expenses were informal and the entries were made in the grandmother's name. One week they won £750; the paying boarder claimed a third share, but the defendant refused to pay on the grounds that there was no intention to create legal relations.
>
> *Decision*: there was a 'mutuality in the arrangements between the parties', amounting to a contract.

1.2 Commercial agreements

When business people enter into commercial agreements it is presumed that there is an intention to enter into legal relations unless this is **expressly disclaimed** or the **circumstances indicates otherwise.**

> *Rose and Frank v Crompton 1923*
> *The facts*: a commercial agreement by which the defendants appointed the claimant to be its distributor in the USA contained a clause described as 'the Honourable Pledge Clause' which expressly stated that the arrangement was 'not subject to legal jurisdiction' in either country. The defendants terminated the agreement without giving notice as required, and refused to deliver goods

ordered by the claimants although they had accepted these orders when placed.

Decision: the general agreement was not legally binding as there was no obligation to stand by any clause in it. However the orders for goods were separate and binding contracts. The claim for damages for breach of the agreement failed, but the claim for damages for non-delivery of goods ordered succeeded.

The words relied on by a party to a commercial agreement to show that legal relations are not intended are not always clear. In such cases, the **burden of proof** is **on the party seeking to escape liability**.

Edwards v Skyways Ltd 1964
The facts: in negotiations over the terms for making the claimant redundant, the defendants gave him the choice either of withdrawing his total contributions from their contributory pension fund or of receiving a paid-up pension. It was agreed that if he chose the first option, the defendants would make an ex gratia payment to him. He chose the first option; his contributions were refunded but the ex gratia payment was not made. He sued for breach of contract.

Decision: although the defendants argued that the use of the phrase ex gratia showed no intention to create legal relations, this was a commercial arrangement and the burden of rebutting the presumption of legal relations had not been discharged by the defendants.

1.3 Statutory provisions

Procedural agreements between **employers and trade** unions for the settlement of disputes are not intended to give rise to legal relations in spite of their elaborate content: s 179 **Trade Union and Labour Relations (Consolidation) Act 1992**.

1.4 Letters of comfort

For many years, holding companies have given '**letters of comfort**' to creditors of subsidiaries which purport to give some comfort as to the ability of the subsidiary to pay its debts. Such letters have always been presumed in the past not to be legally binding.

Kleinwort Benson Ltd v Malaysia Mining Corpn Bhd 1989
The facts: the claimants lent money to the defendant's subsidiary, having received a letter from the defendant stating 'it is our policy to ensure that the business is at all times in a position to meet its liabilities to you.' The subsidiary went into liquidation, and the bank claimed against the holding company for the outstanding indebtedness.

Decision: the letter of comfort was a statement of existing policy and not a promise that the policy would continue in the future. Because both parties were well aware that in business parlance a 'letter of comfort' imposed moral and not legal responsibilities, it was held not to have been given with the intention of creating legal relations.

1.5 Transactions binding in honour only

If the parties state that an agreement is '**binding in honour only**', this amounts to an express denial of intention to create legal relations.

> *Jones v Vernons Pools 1938*
> *The facts*: the claimant argued that he had sent to the defendant a football pools coupon on which his predictions entitled him to a dividend. The defendants denied having received the coupon. A clause on the coupon stated that the transaction should not 'give rise to any legal relationship … but … be binding in honour only'.
>
> *Decision*: this clause was a bar to an action in court.

Activity 1 (5 minutes)

A widow tells her adult son that he can stay at her house temporarily so long as he does his share of domestic chores. Consider whether there is likely to be a contract under which accommodation is supplied in return for housework. Give reasons for your answer.

Activity 2 (10 minutes)

Which of the following scenarios do you think gives rise to the intention to create legal relations?

(a) Jenny, a student, offers to pay her brother Jim if he will help her with an assignment. Jim has helped but Jenny will not pay up.

(b) Mary and her friend Bridget regularly play bingo together. When they started doing so, they both signed a piece of paper to the effect that if either of them ever won more than £100, the money would be shared equally. Mary has now won £70,000 and is refusing to pay any proportion of it to Bridget.

(c) Dave, a taxi driver, agrees to take Brian to the airport. Brian will pay the full fare. Dave now says that he would rather go to watch a football match and will not therefore be taking Brian.

2 CAPACITY TO CONTRACT

Capacity refers to the fact that the law regards some groups as being unable to enter into binding contractual arrangements, because they might not be in a position to fully understand the agreement they have entered into.

2.1 Minors

The legal capacity of minors (persons under the age of eighteen) is determined by the Minors' Contracts Act 1987. A contract between a minor and another party may be one of three types.

- A **valid** contract is binding in the usual way.

- A **voidable** contract is binding unless and until the minor rescinds the contract.

- An **unenforceable** contract is unenforceable against the minor unless he ratifies (adopts) it – but the other party is bound.

Two sorts of contract are valid and binding on a minor: a contract for the supply of goods or services which are **necessaries**, and a **service contract** for the minor's benefit.

If goods or services which are necessaries are delivered to a minor under a contract made by him, he is bound to pay a reasonable price for them: s 3 Sale of Goods Act 1979. Necessaries are defined in s 3 Sale of Goods Act 1979 as goods or services **suitable** to the condition in life of the minor and to his **needs** at the time of sale and delivery.

(a) **Suitability** is measured by the living standards of the minor. Things may be necessaries even though they are luxurious in quality, if that is what the minor ordinarily uses. Food, clothing, professional advice and even a gold watch have been held to be necessaries.

(b) The second test is whether the minor requires the goods for the personal **needs** of himself (or his wife or child). Goods required for use in a trade are not necessaries, nor are goods of any kind if the minor is already well supplied with them.

Nash v Inman 1908
The facts: N was a London tailor who sued I on bills totalling £145 for clothes, including eleven fancy waistcoats. It was conceded that the clothes were suitable, but it was shown that he already had plenty of them.
Decision: the clothes were not necessaries.

A **service contract** for the minor's benefit which contains an element of education or training is the other type of contract which is binding on a minor.

Doyle v White City Stadium 1935
The facts: D, who was a minor, obtained a licence to compete as a professional boxer. Under his licence (which was treated as a contract of apprenticeship) he agreed to be bound by rules which could withhold his prize money if he was disqualified for a foul blow (as in fact happened). He asserted that the licence was a void contract since it was not for his benefit..

Decision: the licence enabled him to pursue a lucrative occupation. Despite the penal clause, it was beneficial as a whole.

Voidable contracts of a minor

A minor may enter into a contract by which he acquires an interest of a continuing nature. Such contracts are **voidable** by the minor during his minority and within a reasonable time after attaining his majority. If no such steps are taken, the contract is binding. Examples of voidable contracts are:

- Contracts concerning **land** – for example, leases
- Purchases of **shares** in a company
- **Partnership** agreements

A contract of this type does not require any kind of ratification by the minor on his majority. It remains binding unless he **repudiates** it within a reasonable time.

> *Edwards v Carter 1893*
>
> *The facts*: a marriage settlement was made under which the father of the husband to be agreed to pay £1,500 per annum to the trustees. The husband to be, who was a minor at the time of the settlement, executed a deed under which all property which he might receive under his father's will would also be vested in the trustees. He attained his majority one month later, and three-and-a-half years later his father died. A year after this, he repudiated the agreement.
>
> *Decision*: the repudiation was too late and was ineffective.

The effect of repudiation is to relieve the minor of any contractual obligations arising after the repudiation. The key to liability or recovery of sums paid may well depend upon whether the minor received **consideration**.

> *Steinberg v Scala (Leeds) 1923*
>
> *The facts*: the claimant bought shares in the defendant company but repudiated the contract after paying some of the money. The company agreed to remove her name from the register of members but refused to refund her money.
>
> *Decision*: the claimant had benefited from membership rights as consideration, and was not entitled to a refund.

Unenforceable contracts of a minor

All other contracts entered into by a minor are described as **unenforceable** – the minor is not bound (though he may ratify it) but the other party is bound.

Where a contract is voidable and is repudiated by the minor, or where it is unenforceable and is not ratified by the minor, any **guarantee** of the contract given by a capable (ie adult) person is still valid. In addition, a minor may be required to return property which he acquired under a repudiated or unenforceable contract.

A minor is generally liable for his **torts** (ie wrongful acts causing loss or damage to others). He will not, however, be liable if he commits a tort in procuring a contract which is not binding on him. If he were liable, the other party would effectively be able to enforce such a contract.

> *R Leslie Ltd v Sheill 1914*
>
> *The facts*: an infant obtained a loan of £400 by means of a fraudulent misstatement of his age.
>
> *Decision*: he could not be compelled to repay it, as this would constitute enforcement of the contract.

FOR DISCUSSION

The law relating to minors' contracts has remained unchanged for decades. Do you think that it should be changed? Would you retain the same amount of protection for minors?

NOTES

2.2 Companies

The capacity of a company to contract may be restricted by one of its 'constitution documents', the memorandum of association. An act by the company which exceeds its capacity is said to be *ultra vires*.

The purpose of this is to protect the shareholders of a company and its creditors, to prevent the directors from causing the company to enter contracts that might be to the detriment of the interests of the shareholders and creditors.

Company law, including the capacity of companies to contract, is covered in the BPP Learning Media Business Essentials Course Book Company and Commercial Law.

Chapter roundup

- An agreement is not binding unless the parties intend to be bound by it.

- Legal relations are not normally intended in domestic situations (although there are exceptions to this).

- Legal relations are presumed to be intended in commercial agreements, unless clearly indicated otherwise.

- Some legal persons may have restricted capacity to contract, for example minors and companies.

Quick quiz

1   Contrast *Balfour v Balfour* with *Merritt v Merritt* and explain why they had different outcomes

2   What general rule applies in commercial agreements?

3   What contracts made by minors are valid?

Answers to quick quiz

1   In *Balfour v Balfour*, the couple were still married at the time of the agreement, so it was not legally binding. In *Merritt v Merritt*, the couple were legally separating, so the agreement was legally binding. (see para 1.1)

2   They are presumed to be legally binding. (para 1.2)

3   Contracts for the supply of goods and services which are necessaries.
    Service contracts for the minor's benefit. (para 2.1)

Answers to activities

1   No there is unlikely to be a contract, as in this domestic situation legal relations are unlikely to be intended.

2   (a)   The parties to a social or domestic arrangement are presumed not to have intended to create legal relations. A brother and sister would be regarded as being within a 'domestic' situation. Therefore Jim will not be able to enforce the agreement.

    (b)   On the face of it, this would appear to be a domestic arrangement, as it involves two friends socialising together. Therefore there would not be an intention to create legal relations. However, given that Mary and Bridget both signed a piece of paper stating what should happen, it can be argued that legal relations were intended. Bridget should be able to claim half of Mary's winnings.

    (c)   This would appear to be a commercial agreement and the intention to create legal relations is therefore presumed. Brian should be able to act against Dave for breach of contract.

Chapter 7:
TERMS AND EXCLUSION CLAUSES

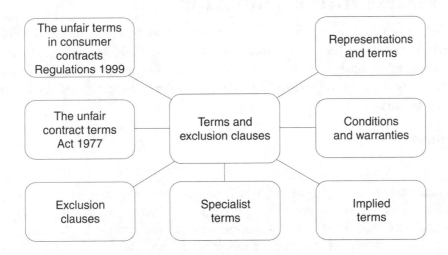

Introduction

As a general principle the parties may by their offer and acceptance include in their contract whatever terms they like, but certain legal rules apply and the law may modify these express terms in various ways.

(a)   The terms must be sufficiently complete and precise to produce an agreement which can be binding. If they are vague there may be no contract.

(b)   Statements made in the pre-contract negotiations may become *terms* of the contract or remain as **representations** to which different rules attach.

(c)   The terms of the contract are usually classified as **conditions** or as **warranties** according to their importance.

(d)   In addition to the express terms of the agreement, additional terms may be implied by law.

(e)   Terms which exclude or restrict liability for breach of contract (exemption or exclusion clauses) are restricted in their effect or overridden by common law and statutory rules.

Your objectives

In this chapter you will learn about the following.

(a)   The effects of incompleteness in the terms of a contract

(b)   The distinction between representations and contract terms

(c)   The concepts of condition, warranty and innominate term

(d)   How terms may be implied into a contract

(e)   Some examples of specialist terms in a contracts

(f)   The limitations on the effectiveness of exclusion clauses

(g)   How exclusion clauses may fail to be effectively incorporated into a contract

(h)   How exclusion clauses are interpreted

(i)   The main provisions of the Unfair Contract Terms Act 1977

1   REPRESENTATIONS AND TERMS

In addition to the final contract, many statements may be made during the process of negotiation that often leads to the formation of a contract. It is important to be able to establish whether what has been written or said actually amounts to a contract term or whether it is simply a representation. **Statements may be classified as terms or as representations**.

Definition

> A **representation** is something which induces the formation of a contract but which does not become a **term** of the contract. The importance of the distinction is that different remedies are available depending on whether a term is broken or a representation turns out to be untrue.

If something said in negotiations proves to be untrue, the party misled can claim for **breach of contract** if the statement became a **term** of the contract. (If the pre-contract statement was merely a **representation** then the party misled can claim misrepresentation; this usually results in a lesser remedy than in cases of breach of contract.) There are a number of factors that a court may consider in determining if a statement is or is not a term.

The court will consider **when** the representation was made to assess whether it was designed as a contract term or merely as an incidental statement. The court will also look at the **importance** the recipient of the information attached to it.

> *Bannerman v White 1861*
> *The facts*: in negotiations for the sale of hops the buyer emphasised that it was **essential** to him that the hops should not have been treated with sulphur adding that, if they had, he would not even bother to ask the price. The seller replied explicitly that no sulphur had been used. It was later discovered that a small proportion of the hops (five acres out of 300) had been treated with sulphur. The buyer refused to pay the price.
>
> *Decision*: the representation as to the absence of sulphur was intended to be a **term** of the contract.
>
> *Routledge v McKay 1954*
> *The facts*: the defendant, in discussing the possible sale of his motorcycle to the claimant, said on 23 October that the cycle was a 1942 model; he took this information from the registration document. On 30 October the parties made a written contract which did not refer to the year of the model and the purchaser had not indicated that the age of the cycle was of critical importance to him. The actual date was 1930.

Decision: the buyer's claim for damages failed. The reference to a 1942 model was a **representation made prior** to the contract

If the statement is made by a person with **special knowledge** it is more likely to be treated as a contract term.

Dick Bentley Productions v Arnold Smith Motors 1965
The facts: the defendants sold the claimants a car which they stated to have done only 20,000 miles since a replacement engine and gear-box had been fitted. In fact the car had covered 100,000 miles since then and was unsatisfactory.

Decision: the defendants' statement was a term of the contract and the claimants were entitled to damages.

Oscar Chess v Williams 1957
The facts: the defendant, when selling his car to the claimant car dealers, stated (as the registration book showed) that his car was a 1948 model and the dealers valued it at £280 in the transaction. In fact it was a 1939 model, worth only £175, and the registration book had been altered by a previous owner.

Decision: the statement was a mere representation. The seller was not an expert and the buyer had better means of discovering the truth.

1.1 Express terms

Definition

> An **express term** is a term expressly agreed by the parties to a contract to be a term of that contract. In examining a contract, the courts will look first at the terms expressly agreed by the parties.

An apparently binding legal agreement must be **complete in its terms** to be a valid contract.

Scammell v Ouston 1941
The facts: the defendants wished to buy a motor-van from the claimants on hire-purchase. They placed an order 'on the understanding that the balance of purchase price can be had on hire-purchase terms over a period of two years'. The hire-purchase terms were never specified.

Decision: the court was unable to identify a contract which it could uphold because the language used was so vague.

It is always possible for the parties to leave an essential term to be **settled by other means,** for example by an independent third party.

It may be agreed, for instance, to sell at the open market price on the day of delivery, or to invite an arbitrator to determine a fair price. The price may be determined by the course of dealing between the parties.

Where an agreement appears vague or incomplete, the courts will seek to uphold it by looking at the **intention of the parties**: *Hillas & Co Ltd v Arcos Ltd 1932*. If the parties use standard printed conditions, some of which are inappropriate, such phrases may be disregarded.

Nicolene v Simmonds 1953
The facts: the claimant offered to buy steel bars from the defendant. A contract was made by correspondence, in which the defendant provided that 'the usual conditions of acceptance apply'. The defendant failed to deliver the goods and argued that there had been no explicit agreement.

Decision: the words should be disregarded. The contract was complete without these words; there were no usual conditions of acceptance.

1.2 Oral evidence of contract terms (parol evidence rule)

Where a contract is in **writing**, and all the necessary terms are present, the courts will interpret the terms of the contract by reference to the **written document only**. They will not admit oral evidence to add to, vary or contradict written terms. This is known as the **parol evidence rule**.

Hawrish v Bank of Montreal 1969
The facts: a solicitor gave to a company's bank a personal guarantee 'of all present and future debts' of the company. He later sought to give evidence to show that the guarantee applied only to a particular overdraft existing when the guarantee was given.

Decision: such evidence was inadmissible.

There are the following exceptions to the rule.

(a) Oral evidence may be given of trade practice or custom: *Hutton v Warren 1836*.

(b) The parties may agree orally that their written consent should not take effect until a **condition precedent** has been satisfied, for example, a written contract to buy a house subject to a verbal agreement that it would take effect only if the purchaser's surveyor gave a satisfactory report: *Pym v Campbell 1856*.

(c) Oral evidence may be given as an addition to a written contract if it can be shown that the document was not intended to comprise all the agreed terms.

SS Ardennes (Cargo Owners) v SS Ardennes (Owners) 1951
The facts: the claimants were orange-growers in Spain and the defendants were shipowners. A printed bill of lading provided that the ship might go 'by any route...directly or indirectly' to London. The shipowners' agent had given a verbal undertaking that the vessel would sail direct from Spain to London. The ship sailed via Antwerp, so that the oranges arrived late and a favourable market was missed.

Decision: evidence might be given of the verbal undertaking as a term overriding the bill of lading.

Activity 1 **(5 minutes)**

A contract contains a term which states that the price shall be £50,000 unless the parties agree otherwise within seven days of the contract's being signed.

Does this invalidate the contract? Give reasons for your answer.

---

2 CONDITIONS AND WARRANTIES

2.1 Definitions

The terms of the contract are usually classified by their relative importance as conditions or warranties.

Definitions

Condition: a term which is vital to the contract, going to the root of the contract.

Warranty: a less important term. It does not go to the root of the contract, but is subsidiary to the main purpose of the agreement.

2.2 Effects

Non-observance of a condition will affect the main purpose of the agreement. Breach of a condition entitles the party not in breach to treat the contract as discharged. Breach of a warranty only entitles the injured party to claim damages.

The following two cases are very useful in highlighting the difference.

> *Poussard v Spiers 1876*
> *The facts*: Madame Poussard agreed to sing in an opera throughout a series of performances. Owing to illness she was unable to appear on the opening night or on the next few days. The producer engaged a substitute who insisted that she should be engaged for the whole run. When Mme Poussard had recovered, the producer declined to accept her services for the remaining performances.
>
> *Held*: failure to sing on the opening night was a breach of condition which entitled the producer to treat the contract for the remaining performances as discharged. Singing on the opening night could be regarded as fundamental to the contract.

Contrast that with:

> *Bettini v Gye 1876*
> *The facts*: an opera singer was engaged for a series of performances under a contract by which he had to be in London for rehearsals six days before the opening performance. Owing to illness he did not arrive until the third day

BPP
LEARNING MEDIA

before the opening. The defendant refused to accept his services, treating the contract as discharged.

Held: the rehearsal clause was subsidiary to the main purpose of the contract. The contract did not fail because the singer missed some of the rehearsals. Breach of the clause must be treated as breach of warranty, so the producer was bound to accept the singer's services. He had no right to treat the contract as discharged and must compensate the claimant, though he could claim damages (if he could prove any loss) for failure to arrive in time for six days' rehearsals.

Consider also:

Schuler v Wickham Machine Tool Sales 1973
The facts: the claimants entered into a four-year contract with the defendants giving them the sole right to sell panel presses in England. A clause of the contract provided that it should be a condition of the agreement that the defendants' representative should visit six named firms each week to solicit orders. The defendants' representative failed on a few occasions to do so and the claimants claimed to be entitled to repudiate the agreement on the basis that a single failure was a breach of condition giving them an absolute right to treat the contract as at an end.

Held: such minor breaches by the defendants did not entitle the claimants to repudiate. The House of Lords construed the clause on the basis that it was so unreasonable that the parties could not have intended it as a condition (giving the claimants a right of repudiation) but rather as a warranty. Thus the claimants were themselves in breach of contract leaving the defendants with a claim for damages against them.

Determining whether a contractual term is a condition or a warranty is clearly very important. Classification depends on the following issues.

(a)   Statute often identifies implied terms specifically as conditions or warranties. Such identification must be followed by the courts. An example is the Sale of Goods Act 1979 which states, for example, that in a contract for the sale of goods there is an implied condition that the seller has the legal authority to sell.

(b)   Case law may also define particular clauses as conditions, for example a clause as to the date of 'expected readiness' of a ship let to a charterer: *The Mihalis Angelos 1971*.

(c)   Where statute or case law does not shed any light, the court will consider the intention of the parties **at the time the contract was made** as to whether a broken term was to be a condition or a warranty.

2.3   Innominate terms

Where the term broken was not clearly intended to be a condition, and neither statute nor case law define it as such, it cannot necessarily be assumed that the term is a warranty. Instead, **the contract must be interpreted in the light of the specific situation**; only if it is clear that in no circumstances did the parties intend the contract to be terminated by breach of that particular term can it be classed as a warranty. Such intention may be **express** or be **implied** from surrounding circumstances. Where it is not clear what the effect of breach of the term was intended to be, it will be classified by the court as innominate, intermediate or indeterminate (the three are synonymous).

The consequence of a term being classified as innominate is that the court must decide what is the actual effect of its breach. So it does not fall neatly into the classification of either condition or warranty and therefore cannot follow the rules for those. If the nature and effect of the breach is such as to deprive the injured party of substantially the whole benefit which it was intended he should obtain under the contract, then it will be treated as a breached condition, so that the injured party may terminate the contract and claim damages.

> *Hong Kong Fir Shipping Co Ltd v Kawasaki Kisa Kaisha Ltd 1962*
> *The facts*: the defendants chartered a ship from the claimants for a period of 24 months. A term in the contract stated that the claimants would provide a ship which was 'in every way fitted for ordinary cargo service'. They were in breach of this term since the ship required a competent engine room crew which they did not provide. Because of the engine's age and the crew's lack of competence the ship's first voyage was delayed for five weeks and further repairs were required at the end of it, resulting in the loss of a further fifteen weeks. The defendants purported to terminate the contract so the claimants sued for beach of contract on the grounds that the defendant had no right to terminate; the defendants claimed that the claimants were in breach of a contractual condition.
>
> *Decision*: the term was innominate and could not automatically be construed as either a condition or a warranty. The obligation of 'seaworthiness' embodied in many charter party agreements was too complex to be fitted into one of the two categories. The term would be construed in the light of the actual consequences of the actual breach. The ship was still available for 17 out of 24 months. The consequences of the breach were not so serious that the defendants could be justified in terminating the contract as a result. The defendants were in breach of contract for terminating it when they did.

Activity 2   (10 minutes)

A company contracts for the purchase of 200 mobile telephones 'immediately suitable for use in the UK'. Assume that this term is innominate. How would the court classify it if:

(a) The telephones supplied required tuning to particular frequencies, a task taking two minutes for each one?

(b) Use of the telephones supplied was illegal in the UK, and they could not be modified to make their use legal?

How did you arrive at that conclusion?

3 IMPLIED TERMS

There are occasions where certain terms are not **expressly** adopted by the parties. Additional terms of a contract may be **implied** by law: by custom, statute or the courts to bring efficacy to the contract. Implied terms may override express terms in certain circumstances such as where they are implied by statute.

Definition

An **implied term** is a term deemed to form part of a contract even though not expressly mentioned. Some such terms may be implied by the courts as necessary to give effect to the presumed intentions of the parties. Other terms may be implied by statute, for example, the Sale of Goods Act.

3.1 Terms implied by custom

The parties may enter into a contract subject to **customs** of their trade. Any express term overrides a term which might be implied by custom.

> *Hutton v Warren 1836*
> *The facts*: the defendant landlord gave the claimant, a tenant farmer, notice to quit the farm. He insisted that the tenant should continue to farm the land during the period of notice. The tenant asked for 'a fair allowance' for seeds and labour from which he received no benefit because he was to leave the farm.
>
> *Decision*: by custom he was bound to farm the land until the end of the tenancy; but he was also entitled to a fair allowance for seeds and labour incurred.
>
> *Les Affreteurs v Walford 1919*
> *The facts*: a charter of a ship provided expressly for a 3% commission payment to be made 'on signing the charter'. There was a trade custom that it should only be paid at a later stage. The ship was requisitioned by the French government and so no hire was earned.
>
> *Decision*: an express term prevails over a term otherwise implied by custom. The commission was payable on hire.

3.2 Terms implied by statute

Terms may be implied by statute. In some cases the statute permits the parties to contract out of the **statutory terms**. In other cases the statutory terms are obligatory: the protection given by the Sale of Goods Act 1979 to a consumer who buys goods from a trader cannot be taken away from him.

3.3 Terms implied by the courts

Terms may be implied if the court concludes that the parties intended those terms to apply to the contract.

> *The Moorcock 1889*
> *The facts*: the owners of a wharf agreed that a ship should be moored alongside to unload its cargo. It was well known that at low water the ship would ground on the

mud at the bottom. At ebb tide the ship settled on a ridge concealed beneath the mud and suffered damage.

Decision: it was an implied term, though not expressed, that the ground alongside the wharf was safe at low tide since both parties knew that the ship must rest on it.

A term of a contract which is left to be implied and is not expressed is often something that goes without saying; so that, if while the parties were making their bargain an officious bystander were to suggest some express provision for it, they would say 'why should we put that in? That's obvious' : This was put forward in *Shirlaw v Southern Foundries 1940*. The terms is required to give **efficacy** to the contract, that is, to make it work in practice.

The court may also imply terms because the court believes such a term to be a 'necessary incident' of this type of contract.

> *Liverpool City Council v Irwin 1977*
> *The facts:* The defendants were tenants in a tower block owned by the claimants. There was no formal tenancy agreement. The defendants withheld rent, alleging that the claimants had breached implied terms because *inter alia* the lifts did not work and the stairs were unlit.
>
> *Decision:* Tenants could only occupy the building with access to stairs and/or lifts, so terms needed to be implied on these matters.

Where a term is implied as a 'necessary incident' it has precedent value and such terms will be implied into future contracts of the same type.

4 SPECIALIST TERMS

There are many specialist terms which are used in contract law, often relating to specific business situations.

4.1 *Force majeure*

Force majeure clauses are also sometimes referred to as hardship clauses.

Definition

> **Force majeure clauses** are inserted into contracts, sometimes as a matter of routine, when the parties can foresee that difficulties are likely to arise but the parties cannot foresee their precise nature or extent.

This is especially common in the engineering or building trades.

The subject matter of force majeure clauses can range from the effect of an engineering component being unavailable, so that a contract cannot be completed in its current form, to such 'acts of God' as a ship sinking with all of the contract's necessary supplies on it.

4.2 Price variation clauses

As you have already seen, once a contract has been established, any change to the contract can only be achieved if both of the parties provide some form of fresh consideration, effectively therefore making an additional contract on top of the one which already exists.

Therefore it is difficult for one party to amend the price of the goods subject to the contract once it is in existence.

However, some contracts may include in them a clause stating that the price may be varied. If this were in itself a contractual term in a contract between businesses, it would be valid. This type of clause is especially likely where the subject of the contract is some commodity whose price fluctuates, such as sugar, or where the contract is not likely to be fulfilled for some time.

A practical example is seen in the cases where people make hotel and other bookings to celebrate major events such as the Olympic Games a long time in advance (in many cases years in advance) but the price is not finally fixed until much closer to the event. The purchasers involved would have an opt-out clause to enable them not to buy, but if they did proceed with the contract they would be bound by the contractual price.

Price variation clauses in contracts between businesses and consumers (consumer contracts) may be regarded as an unfair contract term, an issue we shall return to later.

4.3 Retention of title clauses

The terms of a retention of title clause provide that where goods are sold, the seller can retain title to the goods (in other words still be the legal owner of them) until he is paid for them by the purchaser. The seller retains legal title even where possession of the goods passes to the seller. The advantage of this is that if the purchaser becomes insolvent, or for some other reason does not pay, the seller can recover the goods.

The goods, once recovered, may not be in as good condition as they were at the time of sale, and hence not worth as much, but it does give the seller some protection against losing all the value of his goods.

The Romalpa case

Retention of title clauses are often called *Romalpa* clauses after the first big case on the issue.

> *Aluminium Industrie Vaassen BV v Romalpa Ltd 1976*
> *The facts*: Romalpa purchased aluminium foil on terms that the stock of foil (and any proceeds of sale) should be the property of the Dutch supplier until the company had paid to the supplier all that it owed. Romalpa got into financial difficulties and a receiver was appointed. The receiver found that the company still held aluminium foil and proceeds of selling other stocks of foil, and had not paid its debt to the supplier. The receiver applied to the court to determine whether or not the foil and the cash were assets of the company under his control as receiver.
>
> *Decision*: the conditions of sale were valid. The relevant assets, although in the possession of the company, did not belong to it. The receiver could not deal with these assets since his authority under the floating charge was restricted to assets of the company.

Further issues

The extent to which a *Romalpa* clause protects an unpaid seller depends to a great extent on the wording of the actual clause. A retention of title clause may be effective even though goods are resold or incorporated into the buyer's products so as to lose their identity if it expressly states that they can be used in these ways before title has passed: *Clough Mill Ltd v Martin 1985*.

Unless the clause expressly retains title even after resale or incorporation, the supplier is not entitled to a proportionate part of the sale proceeds of the manufactured product: *Borden (UK) Ltd v Scottish Timber Products Ltd 1979*. Where there is no express provision, resale or incorporation is conversion of the supplier's property but a third party will still get good title.

If the buyer resells the goods when there is an express provision allowing resale before title passes, the proceeds of sale are held by the buyer as trustee for the supplier, but this can only be acted on if the right is registered as a charge on the buyer's assets.

One critical point about retention of title clauses is their communication. As with other contractual terms, they must be adequately communicated to the other party to the contract *before* the contract is entered into. A party who is expected to be bound by a retention of title clause must be aware of it prior to entering the contract, otherwise he cannot be expected to be bound by it.

Many companies include their retention of title clauses on their invoices. This is too late, as an invoice is not a pre-contractual document, and the contract has already been made by the time the invoice is sent to the purchaser. In order to be legally valid, a retention of title clause should be on a document such as an order form, or in a statement of terms sent out before the contract is agreed.

4.4 Liquidated damages clauses

To avoid calculations or disputes later over any amount payable, the parties to a commercial contract may include in their contract a formula – **liquidated damages** – for determining the damages payable for breach.

A genuine pre-estimate of loss

In construction contracts it is usual to provide that if the building contractor is in breach of contract by late completion a deduction is to be made from the contract price The formula will be enforced by the courts if it is '**a genuine pre-estimate of loss**'.

> *Dunlop Pneumatic Tyre Co Ltd v New Garage & Motor Co Ltd 1915*
> *The facts*: the contract imposed a minimum retail price. The contract provided that £5 per tyre should be paid if they were resold at less than the prescribed retail price. The defendant did sell at a lower price and argued that £5 per tyre was a 'penalty' and not a genuine pre-estimate of loss.
>
> *Decision*: in this case the formula was an honest attempt to agree on liquidated damages and would be upheld.

Compare this with:

> *Ford Motor Co (England) Ltd v Armstrong 1915*
> *The facts*: the defendant had undertaken not to sell the claimant's cars below list price, not to sell Ford cars to other dealers and not to exhibit any Ford cars without permission. A £250 penalty was payable for each breach.
>
> *Decision*: since the same sum was payable for different kinds of loss it was not a genuine pre-estimate of loss and was in the nature of a penalty.

Penalty clauses

Penalty clauses may look similar to liquidated damages clauses, but are designed to intimidate, rather than just to make good a loss.

A contractual term designed as a **penalty clause** to discourage breach is **void** and not enforceable. Relief from penalty clauses is an example of the influence of equity in the law of contract.

> *Bridge v Campbell Discount Co 1962*
> *The facts*: a clause in a hire purchase contract required the debtor to pay on termination, a sum which amounted to two thirds of the HP price and additionally to return the goods.
>
> *Decision*: this was a penalty clause and void since the creditor would receive on termination more than 100% of the value of the goods.

Penalty clauses in consumer contracts may fall under the Unfair Control Terms regulations, which we shall return to later.

A court deciding whether a clause in a commercial contract is for liquidated damages or is a penalty clause will consider:

- How the contract refers to the clause
- Whether it is a genuine pre-estimate of loss
- That a stipulated amount of damages is not necessarily disproportionate simply because it greatly exceeds the actual loss sustained
- Whether the parties' bargaining power was so imbalanced that one party effectively dictated the terms

Generally, because of the principle of freedom of contracts, courts are reluctant to interfere with such clauses in commercial contracts.

Activity 3 **(10 minutes)**

A qualified accountant undertakes to prepare a client's tax return. The accountant then finds that the tax return form has been redesigned, and that his computer system cannot cope with the new design. Consider whether he could claim that there was no term in the contract stating that he should be able to prepare a return in the new form, and that he is therefore not obliged to do so.

5 EXCLUSION CLAUSES

To be enforceable, a term must be validly incorporated into a contract. Because most disputes about whether a term has been incorporated arise in the context of exclusion clauses, much of the relevant case law surrounds exclusion clauses. In this section, we will examine the ways in which the courts may determine:

(a) Whether an exclusion clause (as a contract term) has been **validly incorporated** into the contract; and

(b) If so, how the exclusion clause should be **interpreted**.

Definition

> **Exclusion clause**: a clause in a contract which purports to exclude liability altogether or to restrict it by limiting damages or by imposing other onerous conditions. They are sometimes referred to as **exemption clauses**.

There has been strong criticism of the use of exclusion clauses in contracts made between manufacturers or sellers of goods or services and private citizens as consumers. The seller puts forward standard conditions of sale which the buyer may not understand, but which he must accept if he wishes to buy. With these so-called **standard form contracts,** the presence of exclusion clauses becomes an important consideration.

For many years the courts demonstrated the hostility of the common law to exclusion clauses by developing various rules of case law designed to restrain their effect. These are described in this section of the chapter. To these must also be added the considerable statutory safeguards provided by the **Unfair Contract Terms Act 1977** (UCTA). These are considered in the next section of this chapter.

The statutory rules do permit exclusion clauses to continue in some circumstances. Hence it is necessary to consider both the **older case law** and the **newer statutory rules**.

The **courts** have generally sought to protect consumers from the harsher effects of exclusion clauses in two ways.

(a) Exclusion clauses must be **incorporated** into a contract before they have legal effect.

(b) Exclusion clauses are **interpreted** strictly. This may prevent the application of the clause.

5.1 Incorporation of exclusion clauses

The law seeks to protect customers (usually the weaker party to the contract) from the full force of exclusion clauses. They do this by applying the 'letter of the law' to see if such clauses have been incorporated correctly. Where there is uncertainty the clauses may be excluded from the contract.

Such uncertainty can arise in several circumstances.

- The document containing notice of the clause must be an **integral part** of the contract.

- If the document is an integral part of the contract, a term may not usually be disputed if it is included in a document which a party has **signed**.

- The term must be put forward **before** the contract is made.

- If the contact is not signed, an exclusion clause is not a binding term unless the person whose rights it restricts was made **sufficiently aware** of it at the time of agreeing to it.

- **Onerous terms** must be sufficiently highlighted (it is doubtful whether this applies to signed contracts).

Contractual documents

Where the exclusion clause is contained in an unsigned document it must be shown that this document is an integral part of the contract and is one which could be expected to contain terms.

Chapelton v Barry UDC 1940
The facts: there was a pile of deck chairs and a notice stating 'Hire of chairs 2d per session of three hours'. The claimant took two chairs, paid for them and received two tickets which were headed 'receipt' which he put in his pocket. One of the chairs collapsed and he was injured. The defendant council relied on a notice on the back of the tickets by which it disclaimed liability for injury.

Decision: the notice advertising chairs for hire gave no warning of limiting conditions and it was not reasonable to communicate them on a receipt. The disclaimer of liability was not binding on the claimant.

Thompson v LMS Railway 1930
The facts: an elderly lady who could not read asked her niece to buy her a railway excursion ticket on which was printed 'Excursion: for conditions see back'. On the back it was stated that the ticket was issued subject to conditions contained in the company's timetables. These conditions excluded liability for injury.

Decision: the conditions had been adequately communicated and therefore had been accepted.

Signed contracts

If a person **signs** a document containing a term he is held to have agreed to the term even if he had not read the document. But this is not so if the party who puts forward the document for signature gives a misleading explanation of the term's legal effect.

L'Estrange v Graucob 1934
The facts: the defendant sold to the claimant, a shopkeeper, a slot machine under conditions which excluded the claimant's normal rights under the Sale of Goods Act 1893. The claimant signed the document described as a 'Sales Agreement' and including clauses in 'legible, but regrettably small print'.

Decision: the conditions were binding on the claimant since she had signed them. It was not material that the defendant had given her no information of their terms nor called her attention to them.

Curtis v Chemical Cleaning Co 1951
The facts: the claimant took her wedding dress to be cleaned. She was asked to sign a receipt on which there were conditions which she was told restricted the cleaner's liability and in particular placed on the claimant the risk of damage to beads and sequins on the dress. The document in facts contained a clause 'that the company is not liable for any damage however caused'. The dress was badly stained in the course of cleaning.

Decision: the cleaners could not rely on their disclaimer since they had misled the claimant. She was entitled to assume that she was running the risk of damage to beads and sequins only.

Activity 4   **(5 minutes)**

A contract between P and Q includes a clause excluding P's liability in certain circumstances. When Q enquires as to the meaning of this clause, P replies that he does not wish to provide an oral interpretation, but that Q must read the clause for herself. Q reads the clause and signs the contract. P later seeks to rely on the exclusion clause, and Q claims that P should have interpreted the clause for her. The clause itself is not misleadingly phrased. Consider whether Q is likely to be able to prevent P from relying on the clause.

Unsigned contracts and notices

Each party must be aware of the contract's terms before or **at the time of entering into the agreement** if they are to be binding.

Olley v Marlborough Court 1949
The facts: a husband and wife arrived at a hotel and paid for a room in advance. On reaching their bedroom they saw a notice on the wall by which the hotel disclaimed liability for loss of valuables unless handed to the management for safe keeping. The wife locked the room and handed the key in at the reception desk. A thief obtained the key and stole the wife's furs from the bedroom.

Decision: the hotel could not rely on the notice disclaiming liability since the contract had been made previously and the disclaimer was too late.

Complications can arise when it is difficult to determine at exactly **what point in time** the contract is formed so as to determine whether or not a term is validly included.

Thornton v Shoe Lane Parking Ltd 1971
The facts: the claimant wished to park his car in the defendant's automatic car park. He had seen a sign saying 'All cars parked at owner's risk' outside the car park and when he received his ticket he saw that it contained words which he did not read. In fact, these made the contract subject to conditions displayed obscurely on the premises. These not only disclaimed liability for damage but also excluded liability for injury. When he returned to collect his car there was an accident in which he was badly injured.

Decision: the reference on the ticket to conditions was received too late for the conditions to be included as contractual terms. At any rate, it was unreasonable for a term disclaiming liability for personal injury to be presented so obscurely. Note that since the Unfair Contracts Terms Act 1977 the personal injury clause would be unenforceable anyway.

An exception to the rule that there should be prior notice of the terms is where the parties have had **consistent dealings** with each other in the past, and the documents used then contained similar terms.

J Spurling Ltd v Bradshaw 1956
The facts: having dealt with a company of warehousemen for many years, the defendant gave it eight barrels of orange juice for storage. A document he received a few days later acknowledged receipt and contained a clause excluding liability for damage caused by negligence. When he collected the barrels they were empty and he refused to pay.

Decision: it was a valid clause as it had also been present in the course of previous dealings, even though he had never read it.

If the parties have had previous dealings (not on a consistent basis) then the person to be bound by the term must be **sufficiently aware** of it at the time of making the latest contract.

Hollier v Rambler Motors 1972
The facts: on three or four occasions over a period of five years the claimant had had repairs done at a garage. On each occasion he had signed a form by which the garage disclaimed liability for damage caused by fire to customers' cars. The car was damaged by fire caused by negligence of garage employees. The garage contended that the disclaimer had by course of dealing become an established term of any contract made between them and the claimant.

Decision: the garage was liable. There was no evidence to show that the claimant knew of and agreed to the condition as a continuing term of his contracts with the garage.

> ### Activity 5 (5 minutes)
>
> Customers of a self-service shop take goods from the shelves and then walk down a corridor to a till. A conspicuous notice is hung across this corridor incorporating an exclusion clause into contracts for the purchase of goods from the shop. Could a customer claim that the exclusion clause was invalid because he had selected goods before seeing the notice? Why is this so?

> ### Activity 6 (5 minutes)
>
> A road haulage company's standard conditions exclude liability for delays caused by factors beyond the company's control. Would this exclusion be interpreted to cover a delay due to a driver choosing to use minor roads because he found motorway driving boring, given that it is the company's policy never to interfere with drivers' choices of routes? Why?

Onerous terms

Where a term is particularly unusual and onerous it should be highlighted (although it is doubtful whether this applies to signed contracts). Failure to do so may mean that it does not become incorporated into the contract.

> *Interfoto Picture Library Ltd v Stiletto Visual Programmes Ltd 1988*
> *The facts*: 47 photographic transparencies were delivered to the defendant together with a delivery note with conditions on the back. Included in small type was a clause stating that for every day late each transparency was held a 'holding fee' of £5 plus VAT would be charged. They were returned fourteen days late. The claimants sued for the full amount.
>
> *Decision*: the term was onerous and had not been sufficiently brought to the attention of the defendant. The court reduced the fee to one tenth of the contractual figure to reflect more fairly the loss caused to the claimants by the delay.

Activity 7 **(5 minutes)**

Natasha hires a care from a car rental company. On arrival at their office she is given a form, which includes terms and conditions in small print on the back, and asked to sign it. She does so and pays the hire charge. When she gets into the car, she happens to look in the glove compartment and sees a document headed 'Limitation of Liability'. This states that the hire company will not be liable for any injury caused by a defect in the car unless this is as a result of the company's negligence. While Natasha is driving on the motorway, the airbag inflates and causes her to crash. She is badly injured. Assuming that negligence is not claimed, what is the status of the exclusion clause?

5.2 Interpretation of exclusion clauses

In deciding what an exclusion clause means, the courts interpret any ambiguity against the person at fault who relies on the exclusion. This is known as the ***contra proferentem* rule**. Liability can only be excluded or restricted by clear words.

In the *Hollier* case above, the court decided that as a matter of interpretation the disclaimer of liability could be interpreted to apply:

- Only to accidental fire damage, or
- To fire damage caused in any way including negligence.

It should therefore be interpreted against the garage in the **narrower sense** of (a) so that it did not give exemption from fire damage due to negligence. If a person wishes successfully to exclude or limit liability for loss caused by **negligence** the courts require that the word 'negligence', or an accepted synonym for it, should be included in the clause.

> *Alderslade v Hendon Laundry 1945*
> *The facts*: the conditions of contracts made by a laundry with its customers excluded liability for loss of or damage to customers' clothing in the possession of the laundry. By its negligence the laundry lost the claimant's handkerchief.

Decision: the exclusion clause would have no meaning unless it covered loss or damage due to negligence. It did therefore cover loss by negligence.

The 'main purpose' rule

When construing an exclusion clause the court will also consider the **main purpose rule**. By this, the court presumes that the clause was not intended to defeat the main purpose of the contract.

Fundamental breach

There is no doubt that at common law a **properly drafted** exclusion clause can cover any breach of contract.

> *Photo Productions v Securicor Transport 1980*
> *The facts*: the defendants agreed to guard the claimants' factory under a contract by which the defendant were excluded from liability for damage caused by any of their employees. One of the guards deliberately started a small fire which destroyed the factory and contents. It was contended that Securicor had entirely failed to perform their contract and so they could not rely on any exclusion clause in the contract.
>
> *Decision*: there is no principle that total failure to perform a contract deprives the party at fault of any exclusion from liability provided by the contract. In this case the exclusion clause was drawn widely enough to cover the damage which had happened. As the fire occurred before the UCTA was in force, the Act could not apply here. But if it had done it would have been necessary to consider whether the exclusion clause was reasonable.

6 THE UNFAIR CONTRACT TERMS ACT 1977

When considering the **validity** of exclusion clauses the courts have had to strike a balance between:

- The principle that parties should have complete **freedom to contract** on whatever terms they wish, and

- The need to **protect the public** from unfair exclusion clauses.

Exclusion clauses do have a proper place in business. They can be used to allocate contractual risk, and thus to determine in advance who is to insure against that risk. Between businessmen with similar bargaining power exclusion clauses are a legitimate device. The main limitations are now contained in the Unfair Contract Terms Act 1977.

Before we consider the specific terms of UCTA, it is necessary to describe how its scope is restricted.

(a) In general the Act only applies to clauses inserted into agreements by **commercial concerns or businesses**. In principle private persons may restrict liability as much as they wish.

(b) The Act does not apply to some contracts, for example contracts of insurance or contracts relating to the transfer of an interest in land.

(c)   Specifically, the Act applies to:

    (i)   Clauses that attempt to limit liability for negligence;

    (ii)   Clauses that attempt to limit liability for breach of contract.

The Act uses two techniques for controlling exclusion clauses – some types of clauses are **void,** whereas others are subject to a **test of reasonableness**.

The main provisions can be summarised as follows.

(a)   Any clause that attempts to restrict liability for death or personal injury arising from negligence is **void**.

(b)   Any clause that attempts to restrict liability for other loss or damage arising from negligence is void unless it can be shown to be **reasonable**.

(c)   Any clause that attempts to limit liability for breach of contract, where the contract is based on standard terms or conditions, or where one of the parties is a consumer, is void unless it can be shown to be **reasonable**.

6.1   Clauses which are void

If an exclusion clause is made **void by statute** it is unnecessary to consider how other legal rules might affect it. There is simply no need to assess whether it is reasonable.

A clause is void by statute in the following circumstances.

- A clause which purports to exclude or limit liability for **death or personal injury** resulting from negligence is void: s 2(1) UCTA.

- A guarantee clause which purports to exclude or limit liability for loss or damage caused by a **defect** of the goods in **consumer use** is void: s 5 UCTA.

- In a contract for the sale or hire purchase of goods, a clause that purports to exclude the condition that the seller has a **right to sell** the goods is void: s 6(1) UCTA.

- In a contract for the sale of goods, hire purchase, supply of work or materials or exchange *with a consumer*, a clause that purports to exclude or limit liability for breach of the conditions relating to description, quality, fitness and sample implied by the Sale of Goods Act 1979 is void: s 6(2) and 7(2) UCTA.

The first of these circumstances, as set down in S2(1) UCTA, is the most important one to be aware of.

6.2   Clauses which are subject to a test of reasonableness

If a clause is not automatically void, it is subject to a test of reasonableness. The main provisions of the Act that refer to this type of clause are set out in sections 2, 3, 6 and 7 of the Act.

6.3   Exclusion of liability for negligence (s 2)

As we saw above, a person acting in the course of a business cannot, by reference to any contract term, restrict his liability for **death or personal injury** resulting from negligence. The clause containing the term is simply void. In the case of **other loss or**

damage, a person cannot introduce a clause restricting his liability for negligence unless the term is **reasonable**.

6.4   Standard term contracts and consumer contracts (s 3)

The person who uses a standard-term contract in dealing with a **consumer** cannot, unless the term is **reasonable**, restrict liability for his own breach.

> *George Mitchell Ltd v Finney Lock Seeds Ltd 1983*
> *The facts*: the claimant ordered 30 pounds of Dutch winter cabbage seeds from the defendants. The defendant's standard term contract included an exclusion clause that limited their liability to a refund of the amount paid by the claimant. The wrong type of cabbage seed was delivered. The seed was planted over 63 acres, but when the crop came up it was not fit for human consumption. The claimant claimed £61,500 damages plus £30,000 interest.
>
> *Decision*: at common law the exclusion clause would have protected the defendant, but the court decided in favour of the claimant, relying exclusively on the statutory ground of reasonableness.

Consumers

Where a business engages in an activity which is merely incidental to the business, the activity will not be in the course of the business unless it is an integral part and carried on with a degree of regularity.

> *R & B Customs Brokers Ltd v United Dominions Trust Ltd 1988*
> *The facts*: the claimants, a company owned by Mr and Mrs Bell and operating as a shipping broker, bought a second-hand Colt Shogun. The car was to be used partly for business and partly for private use.
>
> *Decision*: this was a consumer sale, since the company was not in the business of buying cars.

6.5   Sale and supply of goods (ss 6 to 7)

Any contract (that is, consumer or non-consumer) for the sale or hire purchase of goods cannot exclude the implied condition that the seller has a **right to sell** the goods.

As we saw earlier when looking at clauses that are automatically void, a **consumer** contract for the sale of goods, hire purchase, supply of work or materials or exchange of goods cannot exclude or restrict liability for breach of the conditions relating to description, quality, fitness and sample implied by the Sale of Goods Act 1979 and the Supply of Goods and Services Act 1982. For a non-consumer contract, such exclusions are subject to a **reasonableness** test. The rules are set out in the following table.

Exemption clauses in contracts for the sale of goods or supply of work or materials		Consumer transaction	Non-consumer transaction
Implied terms	**Title**	Void	Void
	Description	Void	Subject to reasonableness test
	Quality and suitability	Void	Subject to reasonableness test
	Sample	Void	Subject to reasonableness test

Activity 8 **(5 minutes)**

A contract for the sale of a washing machine to a consumer contains the following clause: 'The seller undertakes to repair any defects arising within the first twelve months free of charge, and the buyer shall accordingly not be permitted to return the machine if it does not work at the time of sale'. A consumer would normally have a statutory right to return the machine if it did not work at the time of sale. Consider whether this right has effectively been excluded by the clause.

6.6 The statutory test of reasonableness (s 11)

The term must be **fair and reasonable** having regard to all the circumstances which were, or which ought to have been, known to the parties when the contract was made. The burden of proving reasonableness lies on the person seeking to rely on the clause. Statutory guidelines have been included in the Act to assist the determination of reasonableness. For instance, the court will consider the following.

- The relative **strength** of the parties' bargaining positions.

- Whether any **inducement** (for example, a reduced price) was offered to the customer to persuade him to accept limitation of his rights.

- Whether the customer **knew or ought to have known** of the existence and extent of the exclusion clause.

- If failure to comply with a condition (for example, failure to give notice of a defect within a short period) excludes or restricts the customer's rights, whether it was reasonable to expect when the contract was made that compliance with the condition would be practicable.

- Whether the goods were made, processed or adapted to the **special order** of the customer (UCTA Sch 2).

Smith v Eric S Bush 1989
The facts: a surveyor prepared a report on a property which contained a clause disclaiming liability for the accuracy and validity of the report. In fact the survey was negligently done and the claimant had to make good a lot of defects once the property was purchased.

Decision: in the absence of special difficulties, it was unreasonable for the surveyor to disclaim liability given the cost of the report, his profession and his knowledge that it would be relied upon to make a major purchase.

St Albans City and District Council v International Computers Ltd 1994
The facts: the defendants had been hired to assess population figures on which to base community charges (local government taxation). Their standard contract contained a clause restricting liability to £100,000. The database which they supplied to the claimants was seriously inaccurate and the latter sustained a loss of £1.3 million.

Decision: the clause was unreasonable. The defendants could not justify this limitation, which was very low in relation to the potential loss. In addition, they had aggregate insurance of £50 million. The defendants had to pay full damages.

BPP
LEARNING MEDIA

> **Activity 9**   **(10 minutes)**
>
> A contract under which a consumer buys a 20-volume encyclopaedia contains a clause excluding liability for defects not notified within a week of delivery. Two weeks after delivery, the buyer finds that several pages which should have been printed are blank. Will the seller be able to rely on the exclusion clause?
>
> What is the reason for your answer?

7 THE UNFAIR TERMS IN CONSUMER CONTRACTS REGULATIONS 1999

These Regulations implemented an EU Directive on unfair contract terms. UCTA 1977 continues to apply. There are now three layers of relevant law.

- The **common law,** which applies to all contracts, regardless of whether or not one party is a consumer

- **UCTA 1977,** which applies to all contracts and which has specific provisions for consumer contracts

- **The Regulations** (**UTCCR 1999**), which only apply to consumer contracts and to terms which have not been individually negotiated

The new Regulations apply to contracts for the supply of goods or services.

- They apply to terms in **consumer contracts**.

Definition

> A **consumer** is defined as 'a natural person who, in making a contract to which these regulations apply, is acting for purposes which are outside his business'.

- They apply to contractual terms which have **not** been **individually negotiated**.

- There are a number of **exceptions** including contracts relating to family law or to the incorporation or organisation of companies and partnerships and employment contracts.

A key aspect of the regulations is the definition of an unfair term.

Definition

> An **unfair term** is any term which causes a significant imbalance in the parties' rights and obligations under the contract to the detriment of the consumer.

In making an assessment of good faith, the courts will have regard to the following.

- The strength of the bargaining positions of the parties

- Whether the consumer had an inducement to agree to the term

- Whether the goods or services were sold or supplied to the special order of the consumer

- The extent to which the seller or supplier has dealt fairly and equitably with the consumer

The **effect** of the regulations is to render certain terms in consumer contracts unfair.

- Excluding or limiting liability of the seller when the consumer dies or is injured, where this results from an act or omission of the seller

- Excluding or limiting liability where there is partial or incomplete performance of a contract by the seller

- Making a contract binding on the consumer where the seller can still avoid performing the contract

Two forms of **redress** are available.

- A consumer who has concluded a contract containing an unfair term can ask the court to find that the unfair term should not be binding.

- A complaint, for example by an individual, a consumer group or a trading standards department can be made to the Director General of Fair Trading.

Activity 10   **(30 minutes)**

Find a business contract relating to your own responsibilities at work (eg for the purchase of office supplies, or a copy of your company's standard order form) or your homelife (eg your electricity supply contract). Examine it in detail and consider:

- Who drafted it?

- Is it a standard form contract?

- Why it is drafted the way it is.

- Whether you think any exclusion clauses would be effective.

NOTES

Chapter roundup

- If a purported contract omits an essential term, and gives no means for settling that term, there is no contract.

- Statements made in the course of negotiations may not become terms of a contract at all. They may only amount to representations.

- A condition is a term which is vital to a contract, and its breach allows the party not in breach to treat the contract as discharged. Breach of a warranty, on the other hand, only entitles the injured party to damages.

- Innominate terms can only be classified as conditions or warranties once the effects of their breach can be assessed.

- Some terms may be implied by law whereas others are so obvious that they are implied under the 'officious bystander' test.

- A force majeure clause can try to pre-empt the effect of a problem cropping up in the contract.

- *Force majeure* clauses are common in the building and engineering industries.

- Price variation clauses may be valid where the contract provides for it, but not often in consumer contracts.

- Retention of title means that in some circumstances the seller of goods can retain ownership of them until they have been paid for by the purchaser.

- Liquidated damages are calculated by reference to a pre-agreed formula included in the contract. If these are regarded as penalty clauses they are void and unenforceable.

- Exclusion clauses are not automatically illegal, but some such clauses are ruled out to prevent abuses of economic power by one party.

- Exclusion clauses must be properly incorporated into a contract at or before the time of acceptance, and must not be presented in a misleading manner.

- Exclusion clauses are interpreted strictly, against the person seeking to rely on them.

- The Unfair Contract Terms Act 1977 makes certain exclusion clauses void, and others void unless they are reasonable, especially in relation to consumers.

- The UTCCR 1999 defines what is meant by an unfair term.

Quick quiz

1   What is the difference between a representation and a contract term?

2   What is the difference between a condition and a warranty?

3   Explain the significance of an innominate term.

4   In what circumstances may additional terms, not expressed in the contract, nonetheless be implied as part of it?

5   When will a court treat an exclusion clause as void because the affected party was not properly informed?

6   What effect does the fact that parties have had previous dealings have on an exclusion clause?

7   If there is ambiguity in an exclusion clause, how does the court interpret the clause?

8   When may liability for negligence never be excluded?

9   What tests are applied to determine the reasonableness of an exclusion clause?

10   How does UCTA 1977 define a consumer?

Answers to quick quiz

1   A representation is something said before the contract. A term is something incorporated within the contract. (see Section 1)

2   Condition: central to the contract so a breach causes the contract to fail.
    Warranty: less important, so a breach does not cause the contract to fail. (para 2.1)

3   It can be interpreted as either a condition or a warranty, depending on the effects of the breach. (para 2.3)

4   By custom
    By statute
    By the courts (Section 3)

5   Where it was not properly incorporated in the contractual documents. (para 5.1)

6   If the previous dealings were consistent, the exclusion clause may be upheld. (para 5.1)

7   Against the person trying to enforce the exclusion clause. (para 5.2)

8   In cases of death or personal injury. (para 6.1)

9   Relative strength of bargaining positions
    Inducements offered
    Knowledge of the exclusion clause
    Failure to observe a condition
    Special treatment of the goods (para 6.2)

10   The consumer

   –   Is not acting in the course of a business
   –   The other party is acting in the course of a business
   –   The goods would normally be supplied for private use (Section 7)

Answers to activities

1   No: if there is no agreement, a definite price (£50,000) is automatically fixed.

2   (a)   A warranty
    (b)   A condition

    In the latter situation the buyer is being deprived of the whole benefit of the contract. In part (a) it is not an insurmountable problem.

3   No: it is an implied term that a qualified accountant can prepare a tax return in any form required by Her Majesty's Revenue and Customers (HMRC).

4   No: Q has not been misled.

5   No: the exclusion clause was notified before the contract was made at the till.

6   No: the company could choose to control its drivers' choices of routes.

7   There must be prior notice of the presence of an exclusion clause. The answer here will depend on whether this exclusion was included in the original terms and conditions (and therefore merely reinforced by the later document) or not. The hire company's only other possible defence will be to show a consistent course of dealings with Natasha.

8   No: a consumer contract cannot exclude the statutory term that goods are fit for their purpose.

9   No: it is not reasonable to expect a consumer to find all printing defects in a 20-volume work within the first two weeks of use.

10   There is no specific answer to this activity.

Chapter 8:

VITIATING FACTORS IN CONTRACT

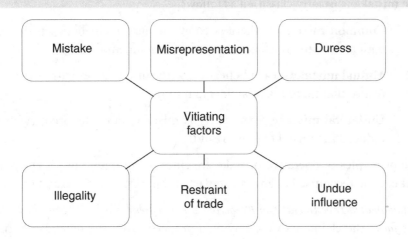

Introduction

Even if the essential elements of a contract can be shown, the contract may not necessarily be valid (it may be 'vitiated'). Validity may be affected by one of a number of vitiating factors.

Your objectives

In this chapter you will learn about the following.

(a) Different types of operative mistake and their effect on a purported contract

(b) Types of misrepresentation and the available remedies

(c) The effect on a contract if duress or undue influence can be shown

(d) Contracts in restraint of trade

(e) Illegal contracts

1 MISTAKE

There are many types of mistake in contract law, and it is important that you understand each of them.

1.1 Operative mistake

Operative mistake is usually classified as follows.

(a) **Common mistake** – there is complete agreement between the parties but both are equally mistaken as to some fundamental point.

(b) **Mutual mistake** – each believes that the other agrees with him and does not realise that there is a misunderstanding.

(c) **Unilateral mistake** – one party is mistaken and the other (who may have induced the mistake) is aware of it.

The basic principles of operative mistake are rules of common law. A key point is that the mistake, to be recognised at law, must exist at the time that the contract is formed.

> *Amalgamated Investments and Property Co Ltd v John Walker & Sons Ltd 1976*
>
> *The facts*: the claimants were buying a property from the defendants. In response to pre-contract enquiries, the defendants replied on 14 August that the property was not designated as a building of special historical interest. Neither party was aware that the Department of the Environment was planning to list the building. On 25 September a contract was signed. On 26 September the defendants were informed that the building was to be listed; this took effect from 27 September. The result was that the building was worth £210,000 instead of the contract price of £1.71 million. The claimants sought rescission of the contract on the grounds of common mistake.
>
> *Held*: the critical date was the date of the contract. At that date there was no mistake.

Common mistake

(a) *Res extincta*

If the parties make a contract relating to subject matter which, unknown to them both, does not exist, or which has ceased to exist, there is no contract between them.

> *Couturier v Hastie 1852*
>
> *The facts*: a contract was made in London for the sale of a cargo of corn thought to have been shipped from Salonika. Unknown to the parties the cargo had already been sold by the master of the ship at Tunis since it had begun to rot. The London purchaser repudiated the contract and the agent who had sold the corn to him was sued.
>
> *Held*: the claim against the agent failed. The corn was not in existence when the contract was made.

(b)   *Res sua*

The rule on non-existent subject matter (*res extincta*) has been extended to the infrequent cases where a person buys what already belongs to him (*res sua*).

Cochrane v Willis 1865
The facts: under a family settlement A would inherit property on the death of his brother B. B had become bankrupt in Calcutta and, to save the property from sale to a third party, A agreed with B's trustee in bankruptcy in England, to purchase the property from B's bankrupt estate. Unknown to A and B's trustee, B had already died in Calcutta and so the property had passed to A by inheritance before he bought it.

Held: the contract was void and A was not liable to pay the agreed contract price.

The **leading case on both parties being equally mistaken** on some fundamental point left open the question as to whether common mistake could be extended any further.

Bell v Lever Bros 1932
The facts: L, the controlling shareholder of a Nigerian company, appointed B to be the managing director. Before five years had elapsed, B became redundant owing to a merger and L negotiated with B for the cancellation of his service agreement on payment to B of £30,000. Later L discovered that while serving as managing director, B had used inside information to trade in cocoa on his own account. This was serious misconduct for which B might have been summarily dismissed. B was said to have forgotten the significance of his past conduct in negotiating the cancellation of his service agreement and it was treated as a case of common mistake. L's claim to recover £30,000 from B was that the service agreement for which L had paid £30,000 was in fact valueless to B, since he could have been dismissed without compensation.

Decision: L's claim may have been correct in its theoretical basis but there was not a sufficiently fundamental mistake as to the 'quality' of the subject matter.

Common mistake resulting in **a contract being void from the beginning** was upheld in the following case.

Associated Japanese Bank (International) v Credit du Nord SA 1988
The facts: a rogue entered into a sale and leaseback agreement with the claimant to fund the purchase of four machines. The defendant guaranteed the transaction as a leasing agreement. The claimant advanced £1m to the rogue, who made one quarterly repayment before being arrested for fraud, and adjudged bankrupt. The machines did not exist, and so the claimant sued to enforce the guarantee. The defendant claimed the contract was void for common or mutual mistake since the non-existence of the machines made the subject of the contract essentially different.

Held: the non-existence of the machines in the principal contract (the lease) on which the secondary contract (the guarantee) relied was so fundamental as to render the subject-matter essentially different. Hence there was common mistake – the guarantee was void and could not be enforced.

Mutual mistake

If the parties are at cross-purposes without either realising it, the **terms of the contract** usually resolve the misunderstanding in favour of one or the other.

> *Tamplin v James 1880*
>
> *The facts*: J went to an auction to bid for a public house. J believed that the property for sale included a field which had been occupied by the publican. The sale particulars, which J did not inspect, made it clear that the field was not included. J was the successful bidder but when he realised his mistake refused to proceed with the purchase.
>
> *Held*: J was bound to pay the price which he had bid for the property described in the particulars of sale. The contract was quite clear and his mistake did not invalidate it.

The parties may have failed to reach any agreement at all if the terms of the contract fail to identify the subject matter. Such a mistake renders the contract void.

> *Raffles v Wichelhaus 1864*
>
> *The facts*: A and B agreed in London on the sale from A to B of a cargo of cotton to arrive 'Ex *Peerless* from Bombay'. There were in fact two ships named *Peerless* with a cargo of cotton from Bombay; one sailed in October and the other in December. B intended the contract to refer to the October sailing and A to the December one.
>
> *Held*: as a preliminary point B could show that there was an ambiguity and that he intended to refer to the October shipment. If the case had gone further the contract would have been void.

If each party is unaware that the other intends subject matter of a different quality he may perform his side of the contract according to his intention.

> *Smith v Hughes 1871*
>
> *The facts*: oats were bought by sample. The buyer believed that they were old oats. The seller (who was unaware of the buyer's impression) was selling new oats which are less valuable. On discovering that they were new oats the buyer refused to complete the sale.
>
> *Held*: the contract was for the sale of 'oats' and the buyer's mistake as to a quality did not render the contract void. The seller was entitled to deliver and to receive payment for his oats.

> *Scriven Bros v Hindley & Co 1913*
>
> *The facts*: at an auction a buyer bid for two lots believing both to be hemp. In fact one lot was a mixed batch of hemp and tow. It was not normal practice to sell hemp and tow together and the sale particulars were confusing.
>
> *Held*: in the circumstances there was no agreement by which the buyer was bound to accept the mixed hemp and tow. The contract was therefore not binding.

Unilateral mistake

A **unilateral mistake** is usually the result of misrepresentation by one party. The party misled is entitled to rescind the contract for misrepresentation but it may then be too late to recover the goods. If, on the other hand, the contract is void for mistake at the outset, no title passes to the dishonest party and it may be possible for the party misled to recover his goods.

Most of the case law on this type of mistake is concerned with **mistake of identity**. A contract is only void for mistake by the seller about the buyer's identity if the seller intended to sell to someone different from the actual buyer.

The parties may negotiate the contract by correspondence without meeting face to face. If the buyer fraudulently adopts the identity of another person known to the seller the sale to the actual buyer is void.

Cundy v Lindsay 1878
The facts: Blenkarn wrote to C to order goods and signed the letter so that his name appeared to be 'Blenkiron & Co', a respectable firm known to C. The goods were consigned to Blenkiron & Co and Blenkarn re-sold the goods to L. C sued L for conversion to recover the value of the goods.

Held: C intended to sell only to B & Co, and no title passed to Blenkarn. L was liable to C for the value of the goods.

But if the buyer fraudulently adopts the alias of a non-existent person who could not have been known to the seller, the contract is only voidable for misrepresentation.

King's Norton Metal Co v Edridge Merrett & Co 1897
The facts: the claimants received an order for goods from 'Hallam & Co', an alias assumed by a rogue called Wallis. The claimants had not heard of H & Co. On receiving the goods (consigned to H & Co), W re-sold them to the defendants and the claimants sued the defendants for the value of the goods.

Held: the claimants intended to sell to the writer of the letter, who was W trading as H & Co. There was a mistake as to the quality of creditworthiness, not as to identity. W acquired title to the goods and the defendants in turn acquired title before the contract between the claimants and W was rescinded by the claimants. The defendants were not accountable for the value of the goods.

Unilateral mistake: face-to-face transactions

When the parties meet face to face it is generally inferred that the seller intends to sell to the person whom he meets.

Phillips v Brooks 1919
The facts: a rogue entered a jeweller's shop, selected various items and proposed to pay by cheque. The jeweller replied that delivery must be delayed until the cheque had been cleared. The rogue then said that he was Sir George Bullough and the jeweller checked that the real Sir G. B. lived at the address given by the rogue. The rogue then asked to take a ring away with him and the jeweller accepted his cheque and allowed him to have it. The rogue pledged the ring to a pawnbroker, who was sued by the jeweller.

Held: the action must fail. The jeweller had intended to contract with the person in the shop. There was no mistake of identity which made the contract void but only a mistake as to the creditworthiness of the buyer. Good title had passed to the rogue until the contract was avoided.

Lewis v Averay 1971
The facts: Lewis agreed to sell his car to a rogue who gave the impression that he was the actor Richard Greene. The rogue paid with a bad cheque signed in the name R A Green and was allowed to take the car and documents when he produced a pass for Pinewood Studios with an official stamp.

Held: Lewis had contracted to sell the car to a rogue. The contract might be voidable for fraud but it was not void for mistake. Perusal of a pass was insufficient to demonstrate that he only wished to contract with the actor.

Mistakes over documents – non est factum

The law recognises the problems of a blind or illiterate person who signs a document which he cannot read. If it is not what he supposes he may be able to repudiate it as not his deed (*non est factum*). The relief will not ordinarily be given to a person who merely failed to read what it was within his capacity to read and understand.

In the Saunders case described below the following conditions were laid down which must be satisfied in repudiating a signed document as *non est factum*:

(a) There must be a **fundamental difference** between the legal effect of the document signed and that which the person who signed it believed it to have, and

(b) The mistake must have been made **without carelessness** on the part of the person who signs.

Saunders v Anglia Building Society 1971 (also known as Gallie v Lee)
The facts: Mrs Gallie agreed to help her nephew, Parkin, to raise money on the security of her house provided that she might continue to live in it until her death. Parkin arranged that Lee, a solicitor's clerk, should prepare the mortgage. Lee produced a document which was in fact a transfer of the house on sale to Lee. However, Lee told Mrs Gallie that the document was a deed of gift to Parkin and she signed it at a time when her spectacles were broken and she could not read. Lee paid nothing to Mrs Gallie or to Parkin. Mrs Gallie sought to repudiate the document as *non est factum*.

Held: Mrs Gallie knew that she was transferring her house and her act in signing the document during a temporary inability to read amounted to carelessness. The claim to repudiate the transfer failed.

Foster v Mackinnon 1869
The facts: An elderly man of feeble sight was asked to sign a guarantee. He had done so before. The document put before him to sign was in fact a bill of exchange which he signed as acceptor. He repudiated it as *non est factum*.

Held: the document signed was so different from what it was believed to be that a defence of *non est factum* could be available.

Lloyds Bank plc v Waterhouse 1990
The facts: the bank obtained a guarantee from a father as security for a loan to his son to buy a farm. It also took a charge over the farm. The father did not read the guarantee because he was illiterate (which he did not tell the bank) but he did enquire of the bank about the guarantee's terms. As a result he believed that he was guaranteeing only the loan for the farm. In fact he signed a guarantee securing

all the son's indebtedness to the bank. The son defaulted and the bank called on the father's guarantee for that amount of the son's debts which was not repaid following the farm's sale.

Held: the father had made adequate attempts to discover his liability by questioning the bank's employees. They had caused him to believe he was signing something other than he believed. This was a case of both *non est factum* and negligent misrepresentation.

1.2 Equitable reliefs for mistakes

Rescission

As you have seen, this is an equitable remedy which is available when a contract is voidable. A different type of relief – **rectification** – may be claimed when the document does not correctly express the common intention of the parties.

> *Joscelyne v Nissen 1970*
> *The facts*: J lived in the same house with his married daughter N. J agreed to transfer his car hire business to N and N undertook as part of the bargain to pay all the household expenses including the electricity, gas and coal bills due in respect of the part of the house occupied by J. The bargain, not amounting at that stage to a contract, was then expressed in a written agreement which made no reference to N's liability to pay the household bills.
>
> *Held*: J was entitled to have the written agreement rectified.

Definition

> **Rectification** can be defined as an equitable remedy whereby a court may correct a written document, which, by mistake, does not represent the real intentions of the parties.

Non-operative mistakes

Unless it is unfair, a party who has made a non-operative mistake must abide by his contract.

Equity will sometimes impose a compromise on the parties:

> *Solle v Butcher 1950*
> *The facts*: extensive improvements were made to what had been a rent-controlled flat. Both landlord and tenant believed that the flat had therefore ceased to be subject to rent control. It was let at a rent of £250 per annum. It was discovered that the flat was still subject to rent control. The tenant sought to recover the excess rent and the landlord to rescind the lease.
>
> *Held*: the tenant should have the choice between a surrender of the lease and accepting a new lease at a controlled rent increased to make allowance for the landlord's improvements.

If A was aware of B's mistake but did not bring it about by misrepresentation, the court may refuse an order for specific performance since A is seeking to take unfair advantage of a mistake of the other party.

Webster v Cecil 1861

The facts: A was negotiating the purchase of property from B. A knew that B had refused an offer of £2,000. B however, wrote a letter to A offering to sell the property for £1,250. The court concluded that A knew that B wished to offer it at a price of £2,250. A sued for specific performance of the contract to purchase the land.

Held: the order for specific performance would not be made (for the reasons indicated above).

2 MISREPRESENTATION

A statement made in the course of contract negotiations may become a term of the contract. If it is a term of the contract and proves to be untrue, the party who has been misinformed may claim damages for breach of contract. If, however, the statement does not become a term of the contract and it is untrue, the party misled may be able to treat it as a **misrepresentation** and rescind (cancel) the contract, or in some cases, recover damages. The contract is voidable for misrepresentation.

2.1 Definition

A **misrepresentation** is:

- A statement of fact which is untrue.
- Made by one party to the other before the contract is made.
- An inducement to the party misled actually to enter into the contract.

In order to analyse whether a statement may be a misrepresentation, it is first of all necessary to decide whether it could have been a representation at all.

- A statement of fact is a representation.

- A statement of law, intention, opinion or mere sales talk is not a represent-ation.

- Silence is not usually a representation.

If a statement is not a representation, it cannot by definition become a misrepresent-tation.

Statement of opinion

A statement of opinion or intention is a statement that the opinion or intention exists, but not that it is a correct opinion or an intention which will be realised. In deciding whether a statement is a statement of fact or of opinion, the extent of the speaker's knowledge as much as the words he uses determines the category to which the statement belongs.

Bisset v Wilkinson 1927

The facts: a vendor of land which both parties knew had not previously been grazed by sheep stated that it would support about 2,000 sheep. This proved to be untrue.

Held: in the circumstances this was an honest statement of opinion as to the capacity of the farm, not a statement of fact.

Smith v Land and House Property Corporation 1884

The facts: a vendor of property described it as 'let to F (a most desirable tenant) at a rent of £400 per annum for two years thus offering a first class investment'. In fact F had only paid part of the rent due in the previous six months by instalments after the due date and he had failed altogether to pay the most recent quarter's rent.

Held: the description of F as a 'desirable tenant' was not a mere opinion but an implied assertion that nothing had occurred which could make F an undesirable tenant. As a statement of fact this was untrue.

Statement of intention

A statement of intention, or a statement as to future conduct, is not actionable. An affirmation of the truth of a fact (a representation) is different from a promise to do something in the future. If a person enters into a contract or takes steps relying on a representation, the fact that the representation is false entitles him to remedies at law. However, if he sues on a statement of intention – a promise – he must show that that promise forms part of a valid contract if he is to gain any remedy.

Maddison v Alderson 1883

The facts: the claimant had been the defendant's housekeeper for ten years. She had received no wages in this period. She announced that she wished to leave and get married. She alleged that the defendant had promised that, if she stayed with him, he would leave her in his will a life interest in his farm. She agreed to remain with him until he died. He left a will which included this promise, but because it had not been witnessed it was void. She claimed that the promise to make a will in her favour was a representation.

Held: 'the doctrine of estoppel by representation is applicable only to representations as to some state of facts alleged to be at the time actually in existence, and not to promises *de futuro* which, if binding at all, must be binding as contracts'

Statement of the law

A statement of the law is not a representation and hence no remedy is available if it is untrue. However, most representations on law are statements of the speaker's opinion of what the law is; if he does not in fact hold this opinion then there is a misrepresentation of his state of mind and hence a remedy may be available.

Activity 1   **(10 minutes)**

P sells a car to Q. Which of the following statements by P to Q could be misrepresentations?

(a) 'The car can do 120 mph.'
(b) 'I have enjoyed driving the car.'
(c) 'You should get the brakes checked before you agree to buy the car.'

Silence

As a general rule neither party is under any duty to disclose what he knows. If he keeps silent that is not a representation, so silence cannot be a misrepresentation. But there is a duty to disclose information in the following cases.

(a)   What is said must be complete enough to avoid giving a misleading impression. A half truth can be false.

R v Kylsant 1931
The facts: when inviting the public to subscribe for its shares, a company stated that it had paid a regular dividend throughout the years of the depression. This clearly implied that the company had made a profit during those years. This was not the case since the dividends had been paid out of the accumulated profits of the pre-depression years.

Held: the silence as to the source of the dividends was a misrepresentation since it distorted the true statement that dividends had been paid.

(b)   There is a duty to correct an earlier statement which was true when made but which may become untrue before the contract is completed.

With v O'Flanagan 1936
The facts: a contract was made for the sale of a medical practice. In the intervening period before completion, the profits fell substantially. The failure of the seller to tell the buyer of this was a misrepresentation, and the contract could be avoided.

(c)   In contracts of 'utmost good faith' (*uberrimae fidei*) there is a duty to disclose the material facts which one knows. Contracts of insurance fall into this category.

The person to whom a representation is made is entitled to rely on it without investigation, even if he is invited to make enquiries.

Redgrave v Hurd 1881
The facts: R told H that the income of his business was £300 per annum and produced to H papers which disclosed an income of £200 per annum. H queried the figure of £300 and R produced additional papers which R stated showed how the additional £100 per annum was obtained. H did not examine these papers which in fact showed only a very small amount of additional income. H entered into the contract but later discovered the true facts and he refused to complete the contract.

Held: H relied on R's statement and not on his own investigation. H had no duty to investigate the accuracy of R's statement and might rescind the contract.

Statement made by one party to another

Although in general a misrepresentation must have been made by the misrepresentor to the misrepresentee, there are two exceptions to the rule.

(a)   A misrepresentation can be made to the public in general, as where an advertisement contains a misleading representation.

(b) The misrepresentation need not be made directly on a one-to-one basis. It is sufficient that the misrepresentor knows that the misrepresentation would be passed on to the relevant person.

Pilmore v Hood 1873
The facts: H fraudulently misrepresented the turnover of his pub so as to sell it to X. X had insufficient funds and so repeated the representations, with H's knowledge, to P. On the basis of this P purchased the pub.

Held: H was liable for fraudulent misrepresentation even though he had not himself misrepresented the facts to P.

Inducement to enter into the contract

If the claimant was not aware of the misrepresentation, his action will fail.

Horsfall v Thomas 1862
The facts: H made a gun to be sold to T and, in making it, concealed a defect in the breech by inserting a metal plug. T bought the gun without inspecting it. The gun exploded and T claimed that he had been misled into purchasing it by a misrepresentation (the metal plug) that it was sound.

Held: T had not inspected the gun at the time of purchase. Therefore the metal plug could not have been a misleading inducement because he was unaware of it, and did not rely on it when he entered into the contract.

Since to be actionable a representation must have induced the person to enter into the contract, it follows that he must have known of its existence, allowed it to affect his judgement and been unaware of its untruth.

Activity 2 **(10 minutes)**

R sells some farmland to S. Before the contract is made, R states that the land is good for grazing. In fact it is good for grazing sheep, but not cattle. R also suggests that S might like to get an independent opinion on the quality of the land. Has R made a misrepresentation to S?

2.2 Types of misrepresentation

Misrepresentation is classified (for the purpose of determining what remedies are available) as:

(a) **Fraudulent misrepresentation**: a statement made with knowledge that it is untrue, or without believing it to be true, or recklessly careless whether it be true or false.

(b) **Negligent misrepresentation**: a statement made in the belief that it is true but without reasonable grounds for that belief.

(c) **Innocent misrepresentation**: a statement made in the belief that it is true and with reasonable grounds for that belief.

Fraudulent misrepresentation

There must be an absence of honest belief that the statement is true.

> *Derry v Peek 1889*
> *The facts*: D and other directors of a company published a prospectus inviting the public to apply for shares. The prospectus stated that the company (formed under a special Act of Parliament) had statutory powers to operate trams in Plymouth, drawn by horses or driven by steam power. The Act required that the company should obtain a licence from the Board of Trade for the operation of steam trams. The directors assumed that the licence would be granted whenever they might apply for it, but it was later refused.
>
> *Held*: the directors honestly believed that the statement made was true and so this was not a fraudulent misrepresentation. The false representation was not made knowingly, without belief in its truth or recklessly, and so the directors escaped liability.

Negligent misrepresentation

This is effectively a reckless statement. Negligent misrepresentation is possible under both common law and statute, the Misrepresentation Act 1967.

> *Hedley Byrne & Co Ltd v Heller & Partners Ltd 1963*
> *The facts*: The claimants were advertising agents acting for a new client E. If E defaulted on payment, the claimants would themselves be liable. They checked E's financial position by asking their bank to make enquiries of E's bank (the defendants). Relying on the replies they placed orders and suffered substantial losses when E went into liquidation.
>
> *Held*: the action failed because the defendants were able to rely on a disclaimer. However, had it not been for this, an action for negligence under common law would have succeeded. Liability for negligent statements depends upon the existence of a 'special relationship'; the defendants knew what the information was to be used for.

Under the Misrepresentation Act 1967 s 2(1) where a person has entered into a contract after a misrepresentation has been made to him by another party to the contract and has as a result suffered loss, then, if the person making the misrepresentation would be liable to damages if the misrepresentation had been made fraudulently, he will be liable to damages notwithstanding that the misrepresentation was not made fraudulently. He will escape liability if he can prove that he had reasonable grounds to believe, and did believe, up to the time the contract was made, that the facts represented were true.

This puts the burden of proof on the person making the representation. He will be deemed negligent and liable to pay damages unless he can disprove negligence. It is more advantageous for a claimant to bring a claim under the Act than at common law.

Innocent misrepresentation

Following the creation of the two categories of negligent misrepresentation, an innocent misrepresentation is any misrepresentation made without fault. (Before this, an innocent misrepresentation was any non-fraudulent misrepresentation.)

2.3 Remedies

One of the main remedies for misrepresentation, regardless of the type, is rescission. This entails setting the contract aside as if it had never been made. The principle seeks to ensure that the parties are restored to their original position, as it was before the contract was made.

Fraudulent misrepresentation

In a case of fraudulent misrepresentation the party misled may, under common law, rescind the contract (since it is voidable), refuse to perform his part of it and/or recover damages for any loss by a common law action for deceit (which is a tort).

Negligent misrepresentation

In a case of negligent misrepresentation the party misled may, under equitable principles, rescind the contract and refuse to perform his part under it. In order to gain a remedy, the claimant must show that the misrepresentation was in breach of a duty of care which arose out of a special relationship.

> *Esso Petroleum Co Ltd v Mardon 1976*
> *The facts*: E negligently told M that a filling station, the tenancy for which they were negotiating, had an annual turnover of 200,000 gallons. This induced M to take the tenancy, but in fact the turnover never rose to more than 86,000 gallons.
>
> *Held*: E owed a special duty of care and was in breach. Damages were awarded to M.

Innocent misrepresentation

In a case of innocent misrepresentation the party misled may also, in equity, rescind the contract and refuse to perform his part of it. He is not ordinarily entitled to claim damages for any additional loss.

Under the Misrepresentation Act 1967 a victim of negligent misrepresentation can claim damages for any actual loss caused by the misrepresentation. It is then up to the party who made the statement to prove, if he can, that he had reasonable grounds for making it and that it was not in fact negligent. As noted above, this placing of the burden of proof on the maker of the statement makes an action under the Act easier for the victim to win than an action at common law.

Under s 2(2) of the Act the court may in the case of non-fraudulent (negligent or innocent) misrepresentation award damages instead of rescission. This may be a fairer solution in some cases. But damages may only be awarded instead of rescission if the right to rescind has not been lost.

NOTES

> ### Activity 3 (10 minutes)
>
> X negotiates to sell some paper to Y. X tells Y that the paper is suitable for colour printing, whereas in fact it is only suitable for black and white printing. In making the statement to Y, X relies on statements made to him by the (reputable) paper merchant who supplied the paper to him, and on the independent opinion of a printer who had inspected the paper. However, two days before the contract is made (but after X makes his statement to Y), the printer tells X that he made a mistake and that the paper is not suitable for colour printing. Could X's misrepresentation to Y be treated as negligent?

Loss of the right to rescind

The principle of rescission is that the parties should be restored to their position as it was before the contract was made. The right to rescind is lost in any of the following circumstances.

(a) If the party misled affirms the contract (that is, continues to act according to the contract) after discovering the true facts he may not afterwards rescind.

(b) If the parties can no longer be restored to substantially the pre-contract position, the right to rescind is lost.

(c) If the rights of third parties, such as creditors of an insolvent company, would be prejudiced by rescission, it is too late to rescind.

(d) Lapse of time may bar rescission where the misrepresentation is innocent.

> ### Activity 4 (10 minutes)
>
> Nigel enters a contract with Megapru plc to insure his car. He does not disclose to Megapru that he has tunnel vision in both eyes. What effect do you think that this would have on the contract of insurance?

3 DURESS

A person who has been induced to enter into a contract by duress or undue influence is entitled to avoid it at common law – the contract is *voidable* at his option, because he has not given his genuine consent to its terms.

Duress is fundamentally a threat. This may be **physical duress** – of **physical violence**, imprisonment or damage to people or to goods or business – or it may be **economic duress,** when one party threatens to breach a contract if the other party does not submit. The threat may be translated to actual violence etc, but duress may still be implied merely from the threat.

Cumming v Ince 1847

The facts: an elderly lady was induced to make a settlement of her property in favour of a relative by a threat of unlawful imprisonment in a mental home.

Held: the settlement would be set aside on account of duress. (Note that the principles of duress and undue influence are applied to gifts (as in this case) as well as to contracts).

The Atlantic Baron 1979

The facts: the parties had reached agreement on the purchase price of a ship. There was then a currency devaluation and the vendor claimed a 10% increase in price. The purchaser refused to pay. The vendor then stated that if the extra was not paid he would terminate the contract and amicable business relations would not continue. The purchaser then agreed to pay the increased price.

Held: the threat to terminate the contract and discontinue amicable business relations amounted to economic duress. The contract was therefore voidable.

Atlas Express Ltd v Kafco (Exporters and Distributors) Ltd 1989

The facts: K had a big order to fulfil with W for a supply of baskets. K negotiated with A that deliveries should be made at £7.50 each. This was confirmed by telex. Later A decided that £7.50 was not enough and drew up an updated 'agreement'. A's driver arrived at K's depot with the update and said that he would not collect goods unless K signed the update. K protested but was unable to speak to someone in charge at A. Being bound to supply to W, K signed under protest and continued to pay only the original agreed amount.

Held: A could not enforce the higher payment since consent had been obtained by economic duress – K would have suffered dire consequences if it had been unable to supply W.

Such threats can be termed 'illegitimate pressure'. Whether it is or not depends on the circumstances, but much depends on whether the person's will has been overcome to such an extent as to invalidate his consent. Obviously the doctrine does not prevent businessmen from taking a negotiating position – the courts must distinguish between usual commercial behaviour and unacceptable duress.

The courts have shown themselves unwilling to introduce a concept of 'lawful act duress'.

CTN Cash and Carry Ltd v Gallaher Ltd 1994

The facts: the claimants purchased cigarettes wholesale from the defendants. The defendants made a delivery to the wrong warehouse (although this belonged to the claimants). They agreed to collect the consignment and re-deliver it, but the goods were stolen before this was possible. Each purchase constituted a separate sale under a separate credit contract. The defendants had a contractual right to withdraw the credit facilities, which they provided, at any time and for any reason. When the goods were stolen, they threatened to withdraw all credit facilities unless the claimants made full payment for the goods. The claimants paid, but later reclaimed the money arguing that they had paid under duress.

Held: although the method of obtaining payment was questionable and 'unattractive', it did not amount to duress. The court was unwilling to introduce a concept of 'lawful act duress'.

Duress cases often arise where two parties have a contractual relationship and one of them obtains a promise of an additional payment of money from the other. The validity of this promise is determined according to whether or not duress was present, not according to whether consideration passed: *Williams v Roffey Bros & Nicholls (Contractors) Ltd 1990.*

4 UNDUE INFLUENCE

A contract (or a gift) is *voidable* if the party who made the contract or gift did so under the undue influence of another person (usually the other party to the transaction). It is where free will to bargain is not possible.

To succeed in a claim for undue influence, the following must be shown.

(a) A relationship of trust and confidence existed (in some cases this is assumed).

(b) The weaker party did not exercise free judgement in making the contract.

(c) The resulting contract is to the manifest disadvantage of the weaker party and the obvious benefit of the stronger.

(d) The weaker party has sought to avoid the contract as soon as the undue influence ceased to affect him or her.

4.1 Presumed undue influence

When the parties stand in certain relationships the law presumes that one has undue influence over the other. These relationships include the following in which the stronger party is mentioned first (this is not an exhaustive list).

(a) Parent and minor child (*sometimes* even if the child is an adult)
(b) Guardian and ward
(c) Trustee and beneficiary under the trust
(d) Religious adviser and disciple
(e) Doctor and patient
(f) Solicitor and client

Note that the following relationships are not presumed to be ones in which undue influence is exerted – although this assumption may of course be rebutted.

(a) Bank and customer
(b) Husband and wife
(c) Employer and employee

It is possible to argue that any other relationship in which one person places trust and confidence in another has given the latter the opportunity for undue influence. The courts will look at all the facts in ascertaining whether in a particular case undue influence has in fact been exercised.

Hodgson v Marks 1970
The facts: an elderly lady transferred her house to her lodger and allowed him to manage her affairs. He later sold the house.

Held: undue influence was to be inferred from the relationship and the benefits obtained by the lodger.

Williams v Bayley 1866

The facts: a bank official told an elderly man that the bank might prosecute his son for forgery and to avoid such action the father mortgaged property to the bank.

Held: there is no presumption of undue influence in the relation of the bank and customer but it could be proved to exist (as it did in this case) by the relevant facts.

It is perfectly possible for a relationship to exist where one person places trust and confidence in another without a resulting contract being voidable for undue influence. It is only where the stronger person steps outside a fair and businesslike relationship and obtains a benefit from the abuse of trust that undue influence arises: *National Westminster Bank v Morgan 1985*.

4.2 Actual undue influence

An innocent party may also seek to have a contract set aside for undue influence where there is no presumption at all of undue influence, but there is evidence that power was unbalanced at the time the contract was formed.

4.3 Free judgement

If it appears that there is undue influence, the party who is deemed to have the influence may resist the attempt to set aside the contract by showing that the weaker party did in fact exercise a free judgement in making the contract. A person who has undue influence is presumed to have used it but this is rebuttable. In rebuttal it is usually necessary to show that the person, otherwise subject to undue influence, was advised by an independent adviser to whom the material facts were fully disclosed and that adequate consideration was given: *Inche Noriah v Shaik Ali bin Omar 1929*.

Lloyds Bank v Bundy 1975

The facts: on facts very like those of *Williams v Bayley* above (except that the son was in financial difficulty and the bank required additional security for its loan to him) a customer gave the bank a charge over his house.

Held: the bank could not itself give independent financial advice to a customer on a matter in which the bank was interested as a creditor. Since the bank had not arranged for the customer to have independent advice the charge in favour of the bank would be set aside.

However, there may be undue influence even where the defendant tries to rebut the presumption by showing that the claimant has refused independent advice.

Goldsworthy v Brickell 1987

The facts: G, an 85-year old man entered into an agreement to give tenancy of a farm to B, who had been helping him run it. The terms were highly favourable to B, but G had rejected opportunities to consult a solicitor. G sought for the agreement to be rescinded.

Held: although there had been no domination (see *Morgan's* case below), the fact that the agreement's terms were clearly unfair and that G placed trust in B meant that the presumption could not be rebutted by showing that free exercise of judgement was allowed. G could rescind.

4.4 Manifest disadvantage

A transaction will not be set aside on the ground of undue influence unless it can be shown that the transaction is to the *manifest disadvantage* of the person subjected to undue influence. The case below also demonstrates that a presumption of undue influence will not arise merely because a confidential relationship exists, provided that the person in whom confidence is placed keeps within the boundaries of a normal business relationship.

> *National Westminster Bank v Morgan 1985*
> *The facts*: a wife (W) signed a re-mortgage of the family home (owned jointly with her husband H) in favour of the bank, to prevent the original mortgagee from continuing with proceedings to repossess the home. The bank manager told her in good faith, but incorrectly, that the mortgage only secured liabilities in respect of the home. In fact, it covered all H's debts to the bank. W signed the mortgage at home, in the presence of the manager, and without taking independent advice. H and W fell into arrears with the payments and soon afterwards H died. At the time of his death, nothing was owed to the bank in respect of H's business liabilities. The bank sought possession, but W contended that she had only signed the mortgage because of undue influence from the bank and, therefore, it should be set aside.
>
> *Held*: The House of Lords, reversing the Court of Appeal's decision, held that the manager had not crossed the line between explaining an ordinary business transaction and entering into a relationship in which he had a dominant influence. Furthermore, the transaction was not unfair to W. Therefore, the bank was not under a duty to ensure that W took independent advice. The order for possession was granted.

Despite the words 'dominant influence' in Lord Scarman's judgement in the *Morgan* case, the Court of Appeal has stated subsequently in *Goldsworthy v Brickell 1987* (see above), in an apparent move away from the House of Lords position, that an influence stopping short of a dominant one may be sufficient to allow the court to set the contract aside on the basis of undue influence. Once trust has been shown to have existed, it is then necessary to demonstrate manifest disadvantage rather than that the position of trust has been abused and exercised as a dominating influence: *Woodstead Finance Ltd v Petrou 1986*.

The case below identifies what is and is not manifest disadvantage.

> *Bank of Credit and Commerce International v Aboody 1988*
> *The facts*: Mrs A purchased the family home in 1949 and it was registered in her sole name. Mr A ran a business in which his wife took no interest but in 1959 she became a director of his company on the understanding that she would have to do nothing. Between 1976 and 1980 she signed three guarantees and three mortgages over her house. Mr A deliberately concealed matters from his wife. The company collapsed due to Mr A's fraud and the bank sought to enforce the guarantees against Mr and Mrs A.
>
> *Held*: there had been actual undue influence over his wife by Mr A but Mrs A had suffered no manifest disadvantage since, at the time she signed the documents, her husband's business was comfortably supporting her and there was no indication that it would not continue to do so. She had benefited from the business which she secured and could not be said to have suffered manifest disadvantage in that sense.

4.5 Rescission

The right to rescind the contract (or gift) for undue influence is lost if there is delay in taking action after the influence has ceased to have effect.

> *Allcard v Skinner 1887*
> *The facts*: under the influence of a clergyman, A entered a Protestant convent and in compliance with a vow of poverty transferred property worth about £7,000 to the order. After ten years A left the order and became a Roman Catholic. Six years later she demanded the return of the unexpended balance of her gift.
>
> *Held*: it was a clear case of undue influence since, among other things, the rules of the order forbade its members to seek advice from any outsider. But A's delay of six years (after leaving the order) in making her claim, debarred her from setting aside the gift and recovering her property. (This is an example of the equitable doctrine of 'laches' or delay).

The right to rescission is also lost if the party affirms the contract by performing obligations without protest, or if an innocent third party has acquired rights.

5 RESTRAINT OF TRADE

To complete this chapter on vitiating factors, we look at a specific type of term which is often encountered in two different situations:

(a) The contract of employment, and
(b) The contract for sale and purchase of a business.

A **restraint of trade** clause seeks to limit a person's freedom to carry on a trade or business.

If a contract includes a restraint of trade clause, the restraint may be void and unenforceable but the rest of the contract is usually valid. As explained below the **general policy of the law is against upholding any restrictions on a person's freedom to work** or carry on a trade. But there are some exceptions.

Definition

> Any restriction on a person's normal freedom to carry on a trade, business or profession in such a way and with such persons as he chooses is a **restraint of trade**.

A restraint of trade is treated as contrary to public policy and therefore **void** on the ground of illegality unless it can be justified under the principles explained below. If a restraint is void the remainder of the contract by which the restraint is imposed is usually valid and binding – it is merely the restraint which is struck out as invalid.

The objection to a restraint of trade is that it denies to a community useful services which would otherwise be available. On the other hand, it is recognised that a restraint may be needed to **protect legitimate interests**. A restraint of trade **may** therefore **be justified** and be **enforceable** in the following circumstances.

- The person who imposes it has a **legitimate interest** to protect

- The restraint is **reasonable between the parties** as a protection of that interest

- It is also **reasonable from the standpoint of the community**

In principle any restraint of trade may be subject to scrutiny by reference to the tests set out in the previous paragraph. But where the parties have agreed upon it in the normal course of business and on the basis of **equal bargaining strength**, it is accepted that the restraint is justifiable and valid without detailed examination. **In practice, the doctrine of restraint of trade is applicable only in two areas.**

5.1 Restraints on employees

An employer may (in consideration of the payment of wages) insist that the employee's services shall be given only to him while the employment continues. But any restraint imposed on the employee's freedom to take up other employment (or to carry on business on his own account) **after** leaving the employer's service is **void** unless it can be **justified**.

Justifying a restraint

To justify a restraint the employer must show:

- That he has an interest to protect (eg business connections, trade secrets),
- That the restraint is reasonable, and
- That the restraint does not run counter to the public interest

Protecting an interest

An employee who has access to **trade secrets** such as manufacturing processes or even financial and commercial information which is confidential, may therefore be restricted to prevent his using it after leaving his present job.

In contrast to trade secrets the employer has no right to restrain an employee from exercising a **personal skill** acquired in the employer's service.

> *Forster & Sons v Suggett 1918*
> *The facts*: as works manager S had access to technical know-how of his employer's business of making glass bottles. His contract of employment provided that for five years after leaving his employer's service he would not carry on or be interested in the manufacture of glass bottles in the UK or other glass-making similar to that of his employer's business.
>
> *Decision*: it must be shown (and in this case it had been) that the employee had access to secret manufacturing processes. The restraint was valid.

> *Morris v Saxelby 1916*
> *The facts*: S worked for M as an apprentice and rose to become head of a department. He had some limited knowledge of the employer's technical secrets but essentially he became a skilled draftsman in engineering design work. He undertook that for seven years after leaving his employment he would not engage in any similar business in the UK.

Decision: this was a restraint on the use by S of technical skill and knowledge acquired in the service of M. M had no right to be protected from the competition of a former employee using his own skills.

If the employer imposes the restraint to protect his **connection** with his customers or clients, he must show that the employee had something **more than a routine contact** with them.

The restraint is **only valid** if the **nature** of the employee's duties gives him an **intimate knowledge** of the affairs or requirements of customers such that, if he leaves to take up other work, they might follow him because of his knowledge (as distinct from his personal skill).

> *Fitch v Dewes 1921*
> *The facts*: D was successively an articled clerk and a managing clerk in the employment of F, a solicitor. D undertook never to practice as a solicitor (after leaving F) within seven miles of F's practice.
>
> *Decision*: the restraint was valid since D's knowledge of the affairs of F's clients should not be used to the detriment of F. (In modern practice a restriction unlimited in time will probably be treated as excessive.)

> *S W Strange v Mann 1965*
> *The facts*: a bookmaker employed M to conduct business, mainly by telephone, with his clients. M's contract of service restricted his freedom to take similar employment.
>
> *Decision*: the contact between M and his employer's clients was too remote to give him the required influence over them. The restraint was void.

Reasonableness of the restraint

If the employer can show that the restraint is imposed to protect his legitimate interest he must next show that it is **reasonable** between parties – **no more than is necessary to protect his interest**. Many restraints have been held void because they:

- Prohibited the employee from working in a wider area than the catchment area of the employer's business (*Mason Provident Clothing & Supply Co Ltd 1973*), or

- Restricted him for an excessively long time, more than was necessary to eliminate his influence

The reasonableness of the geographical extent or time limit of restraint of trade clauses will depend on the circumstances of each case. In the *Dewes* case, above, the area was predominantly rural and there was therefore a limited number of clients in the seven-mile restriction area. In the *Office Angels* case, below, in heavily populated London, a three-kilometre restriction was unreasonable.

Note that in *Dewes* case above a lifelong restraint was held valid – it depends on the nature of the employer's interest to be protected.

The modern practice is generally to restrain an employee only for a short time within an area related to the employer's business or to prohibit him only from soliciting or doing business with customers known to him.

If the restraint is too wide the entire restriction is usually void and not merely the excess which is unreasonable. The court will not rewrite an excessive restraint by limiting it to that part which might be reasonable.

> *Office Angels Ltd v Rainer-Thomas and O'Connor 1991*
>
> *The facts*: the defendants' contracts of employment included clauses stating that, for a period of six months after leaving the claimant's employ, they would neither solicit clients of the business nor engage in similar business within a radius of three kilometres of the branch in the City of London. The defendants left and set up their own business in a nearby location. An injunction was obtained preventing this in the High Court. The defendants appealed.
>
> *Decision*: the restraint on the poaching of clients was reasonable, but the area of restraint was not. The whole restraint clause was void.

The blue pencil rule

In some cases however, the court has concluded that the **parties did not intend** by the words used **to adopt as wide a restraint** as the words might impose and have **struck out the words which are too wide**. This is the '**blue pencil**' rule of **simple deletion**.

> *Home Counties Dairies v Skilton 1970*
>
> *The facts*: a milk roundsman's contract of employment prohibited him, for one year after leaving his employment, from selling milk or dairy produce to customers of the employer to whom the roundsman had supplied his employer's goods during the final six months of his employment.
>
> *Decision*: the words 'or dairy produce' were excessive since they would prevent the employee from engaging in a different trade, such as a grocery shop. As the object of the restraint was to protect the employer's connection with customers who purchased their milk, the restraint would be upheld in respect of milk supplied only.

The public interest

A restraint (in a contract of service) which is reasonable between the parties is not, by definition, prejudicial to the public interest.

In recent years a subtle form of restriction has become popular with employers: the **'garden leave' clause,** whereby the employer insists that the employee serves out a long period of notice at home. However, if the employer does not keep up salaries and benefits, he risks a claim for breach of contract.

5.2 Restraints on vendors of businesses

A purchaser of the goodwill of a business has a right to protect what he has bought by imposing restrictions to prevent the vendor doing business with his old customers or clients. The restraint must **protect** the business sold and it **must not be excessive**.

> *British Reinforced Concrete Engineering Co v Schelff 1921*
>
> *The facts*: S carried on a small local business of making one type of road reinforcement. He sold his business to BC which carried on business throughout the UK in making a range of road reinforcements. S undertook not to compete with BC in the sale or manufacture of road reinforcements.

Decision: the restraint was void since it was widely drawn to protect BC from any competition by S. In buying the business of S, BC was only entitled to protect what they bought – a local business making one type of product and not the entire range produced by BC in the UK.

Allied Dunbar (Frank Weisinger) Ltd v Frank Weisinger 1987
The facts: the defendant had sold his business to A, for a sum which included £386,000 as consideration for F, a financial consultant who had built up his successful business from scratch, not to be employed in a similar capacity for two years.

Decision: the restraint was valid, since it was agreed after equal negotiation, paid for and reasonable in itself.

For goodwill to be protected it must actually exist. The courts will not allow 'protection of goodwill' to be a smokescreen for barefaced restraint of competition.

Vancouver Malt & Sake Brewing Co Ltd v Vancouver Breweries Ltd 1934
The facts: the defendant was licensed to brew beer but in fact only produced sake. It sold its business and agreed to a term restraining it from brewing beer for 15 years. It later began to produce beer and the purchaser sought to enforce the restraint.

Decision: since the seller did not, at the time of sale, produce beer the purchaser only paid for tangible assets because there was no beer-brewing goodwill to sell. The purchaser had not provided consideration for the promise not to produce beer and so he could not enforce it.

6 ILLEGALITY

Some types of contract cannot be enforced in a court of law because they are unlawful in themselves or disapproved as contrary to public policy. The following categories may be distinguished.

(a) **Contracts which are void at common law on the grounds of public policy,** of which the most important are contracts in restraint of trade.

(b) **Contracts which are illegal and void at common law as contrary to public morals or the interests of the state,** including agreements to commit a crime or tort (such as assault or defrauding HM Revenue and Customs), contracts to promote sexual immorality or contracts to promote corruption in public life.

(c) **Contracts void by statute,** including restrictive trading agreements and resale price maintenance agreements.

(d) **Contracts which are illegal, void and prohibited by statute,** such as cartel agreements.

Since all such contracts are **void,** neither party can enforce them by legal action. In general, money paid or property transferred under a contract which is merely void may be recovered. If the void part can be separated from the other terms without rendering the agreement meaningless, then the remainder may be valid. But if the contract is also illegal the courts will not (subject to some exceptions) assist a party to recover his money or property. The rules on the consequences of illegal contracts are very involved and what follows is an outline only.

Effects of an illegal contract

If the contract is obviously illegal in its inception or if the contract appears to be legal but both parties intend to accomplish an illegal purpose by it, neither has an enforceable right at law against the other.

> *Pearce v Brooks 1866*
> *The facts*: the claimants, who were coachbuilders, let a carriage described as 'of a somewhat intriguing nature' to a prostitute. They knew that she was a prostitute and the jury found (although they denied it) that they also knew that she intended to parade along the streets in the carriage as a means of soliciting clients and would pay for the carriage out of her immoral earnings. She failed to pay the agreed amount and they sued to recover it.
>
> *Held*: although the letting of a carriage is not obviously unlawful, to do so to facilitate known immoral purposes is an illegal contract which will not be enforced.

If the contract is legal at its inception and one party later performs his side of it for illegal purposes, the other innocent party may recover money paid or property transferred or payment for services rendered (while in ignorance of the illegality).

> *Clay v Yates 1856*
> *The facts*: a printer agreed with an author to print copies of the author's book. The printer was unaware that the book contained libellous material. He discovered the libel after he had printed part of the book and refused to do any more. He claimed the value of work done (*quantum meruit*), but the author refused to pay for incomplete performance.
>
> *Held*: the printer was justified in ceasing work on the book and might recover payment for work done.

6.1 Contracts void at common law

As stated above, contracts in restraint of trade, described in the previous section, are by far the most important examples of this type of void agreement. However, two other categories should not be forgotten.

Contracts prejudicial to the state of marriage include any agreement which restricts a person's freedom to marry. Hence an agreement not to marry someone, or to marry only one person or one from a set of persons, is void. Similarly, a 'brokerage' contract is void, whereby one person agrees for a money payment to procure a marriage. It used to be the case that a promise from A to marry B (a woman) was enforceable in the courts. Although this is no longer the law, it is still public policy to protect freedom of marriage.

Contracts to oust the court's jurisdiction are those whereby the parties agree not to apply to the courts no matter what may happen. For example, a separated husband and wife may draw up a contract whereby one agrees to pay maintenance to the other. Any clause in it that the recipient should not seek to enforce the contract in court is void as it seeks to oust the court's role. Note that it is perfectly allowable for parties to agree in a contract that disputes should be referred to arbitration rather than to the courts, because arbitration is an effective and independent alternative to the court. What is avoided by the common law is an attempt to agree that a path of recourse to the law which is there as of right should be closed off.

6.2 Contracts void by statute

Since restraints of trade are seen as contrary to public policy, they are void for the most part under common law. However, such a restriction on a clause in restraint of trade is only then enforced if the courts become involved. In order to regulate commercial agreements more effectively by statute, the Competition Act exists to make such agreements void by statute.

Chapter roundup

- The general rule is that a party to a contract is not discharged from his obligations because he is mistaken as to the terms of the contract or the relevant circumstances. There are a number of exceptional circumstances in which 'operative mistake' may render the contract void.

  - Common mistake occurs where the parties are both mistaken as to some fundamental point, for example the existence of the subject matter of the contract.

  - Mutual mistake occurs where the parties, without realising it, are at cross-purposes.

  - Unilateral mistake arises where one party is mistaken and the other is aware of it.

- A representation is a statement made in pre-contract negotiations, intended to induce the other party to enter into the agreement; it may or may not subsequently become a contract term.

- A contract entered into following a misrepresentation is voidable by the person to whom the misrepresentation was made. A misrepresentation is a statement of fact which is untrue, made by one party to the other in order to induce the latter to enter into the agreement, and a matter of some importance actually relied upon by the person misled.

- Fraudulent misrepresentation is a statement made knowing it to be untrue, not believing it to be true or recklessly, careless whether it be true or false. Remedies are rescission, refusal to perform and damages for loss in the tort of deceit.

- Negligent misrepresentation is a statement made in the belief that it is true but without reasonable grounds for that belief. Remedies are rescission under the common law, refusal to perform, damages for loss under the Misrepresentation Act 1967 and damages instead of rescission.

- Innocent misrepresentation, the residual category, is any statement made in the belief that it is true and with reasonable grounds for that belief. Remedies are rescission, refusal to perform and damages instead of rescission.

NOTES

Chapter roundup (cont'd)

- Duress (physical or economic) is fundamentally a threat. A person who has been induced to enter into a contract by duress is entitled to avoid it at common law. The contract is voidable at his option, because he has not given his genuine consent to its terms.

- Undue influence may arise either where a relationship of trust and confidence exists (which gives rise to presumed undue influence) and one party exerts influence on the other party to a contract to the disadvantage of the weaker party or where there is actual wider influence. The contract is voidable at the option of the weaker party.

- In addition to contracts in restraint of trade, certain other categories of contract cannot be enforced in a court of law because they are unlawful in themselves or disapproved as contrary to public policy. All such contracts are void; some are also illegal.

- Any restriction on a person's normal freedom to carry on a trade, business or profession in such a way and with such persons as he chooses is a restraint of trade.

Quick quiz

1   What is *res sua*?

2   What is the effect of a mistake concerning the qualities of the subject matter of a contract?

3   What is a misrepresentation?

4   What are the two categories of negligent misrepresentation?

5   How may the representee affirm a contract following a misrepresentation?

6   List four situations in which the right to rescind is lost.

7   What actions may constitute duress?

8   What four conditions must be demonstrated for a claim for undue influence to succeed?

9   Give three examples of relationships where a relationship of trust and confidence is assumed to exist.

Answers to quick quiz

1   When a person unwittingly buys something which already belongs to him. (see para 1.1)

2   The contract would remain valid. (para 1.1)

3   A false statement of fact made by one party to the other, before the contract is made, inducing the party misled to enter the contract. (para 2.1)

4   Negligent (ie reckless) and innocent (ie without fault). (para 2.2)

5   By continuing to act under the contract after he is aware of the misrepresentation. (para 2.2)

6   Party misled affirms the contract

    Pre-contractual position cannot be restored
    Rights of third parties prejudiced
    Lapse of time (para 2.3)

7   A threat of physical violence, imprisonment, damage to goods or a business or intention of breach of contract. (para 3)

8   (a)   A relationship of trust and confidence existed

    (b)   The weaker party did not exercise free judgement in making the contract

    (c)   The resulting contract is to the manifest disadvantage of the weaker party

    (d)   The weaker party sought to avoid the contract as soon as he was free of the undue influence. (para 4)

9   (a)   Parent and minor child
    (b)   Guardian and ward
    (c)   Trustee and beneficiary
    (d)   Religious advisor and follower
    (e)   Doctor and patient
    (f)   Solicitor and client (para 4.1)

Answers to activities

1   (a) and (b). Both are statements of fact.

2   Yes, he was not sufficiently specific.

3   Yes, when the contract was made, X had lost his reasonable grounds for believing that his representation was true.

4   It would render it invalid, as Nigel has not acted *uberrimae fidei*.

Chapter 9:
DISCHARGE OF CONTRACT AND REMEDIES

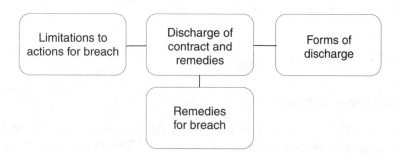

Introduction

A party who is subject to the obligations of a contract may be discharged from those obligations in one of four ways. The four ways are **performance, agreement, frustration** and **breach**. These are discussed in the first half of this chapter.

Most business contracts are discharged by performance as the parties intended. However, if it is discharged by breach, the injured party will be able to seek remedies. There are a number of available remedies.

- **Damages** are a form of compensation for loss caused by the breach.

- An **action for the price** may be commenced where the breach is failure to pay.

- A *quantum meruit* is payment to the claimant for the value of what he has done.

- **Specific performance**, an equitable remedy, is a court order to the defendant to perform the contract.

- An **injunction** is a court order for the other party to observe negative restrictions.

- **Rescission** means that the contract is cancelled or rejected and the parties restored to their pre-contract positions. It is usually applied when a contract is voidable because of circumstances such as a misrepresentation.

Damages and action for the price are **common law remedies** and are most frequently sought when a remedy is needed for breach of contract, since they arise as of right. The other types of remedy are **equitable remedies** which are only appropriate in specialised circumstances.

Your objectives

In this chapter you will learn about the following.

(a)   The different forms of discharge of a contract

(b)   The remedies which may be awarded for breach of contract, both at common law and under equity

(c)   The importance of distinguishing between liquidated damages and penalty clauses

(d)   Limitations to actions for breach

1   FORMS OF DISCHARGE

1.1   Performance of the contract

Most business contracts are duly discharged in the way that the parties intended when establishing their respective contractual obligations. The obligations of each party are usually **discharged** by **performance**.

Performance is the normal method of discharge. Each party fulfils or performs his contractual obligations and the agreement is then ended. As a general rule contractual obligations are discharged only by **complete and exact performance**.

> *Cutter v Powell 1795*
> *The facts*: the defendant employed C as second mate of a ship sailing from Jamaica to Liverpool at a wage for the complete voyage of 30 guineas. The voyage began on 2 August, and C died at sea on 20 September, when the ship was still nineteen days from Liverpool. C's widow sued for a proportionate part of the agreed sum.
>
> *Decision*: C was entitled to nothing unless he completed the voyage.

> *Bolton v Mahadeva 1972*
> *The facts*: the claimant agreed to install a central heating system in the defendant's home for £800. The work was defective: the system did not heat adequately and it gave off fumes. The defendant refused to pay for it.
>
> *Decision*: the claimant could recover nothing.

In each of these cases the defendant might appear to have profited since he obtained part of what the claimant contracted to deliver without himself having to pay anything. The courts have developed a number of exceptions to the rule to ensure that the interests of both parties are protected. The exceptions are as follows.

- The doctrine of substantial performance
- Where the promisee accepts partial performance
- Where the promisee prevents performance
- Where time is not of the essence
- Severable contracts

Substantial performance

The doctrine of substantial performance may be applied, especially in contracts for building work. If the building contractor has completed a very large part of the essential work, he may claim the contract price less a deduction for the minor work outstanding.

> *Sumpter v Hedges 1898*
>
> *The facts*: the claimant undertook to erect buildings on the land of the defendant for a price of £565. He partially erected the buildings, then abandoned the work when it was only completed to the value of £333. The defendant completed the work using materials left on his land. The claimant sued for the value of his materials used by the defendant and for the value of his work.
>
> *Decision*: the defendant must pay for the materials since he had elected to use them but he had no obligation to pay the unpaid balance of the charges for work done by the claimant before abandoning it. It was not a case of substantial performance of the contract.

> *Hoenig v Isaacs 1952*
>
> *The facts*: the defendant employed the claimant to decorate and furnish his flat at a total price of £750. There were defects in the furniture which could be put right at a cost of £56. The defendant argued that the claimant was only entitled to reasonable remuneration.
>
> *Decision*: the defendant must pay the balance owing of the total price of £750 less an allowance of £56, as the claimant had substantially completed the contract.

Partial performance

The promisee may accept partial performance and must then pay for it. The principle here is that although the promisor has only partially fulfilled his contractual obligations, it may sometimes be possible to infer the existence of a fresh agreement by which it is agreed that payment will be made for work already done or goods already supplied. Mere performance by the promisor is not enough; it must be open to the promisee either to accept or reject the benefit of the contract.

Prevention of performance

The promisee may **prevent performance**. In that case the offer of performance is sufficient discharge.

If one party is prevented by the other from performing the contract completely he may sue for damages for breach of contract, or alternatively bring a *quantum meruit* action to claim for the amount of work done.

> *Planché v Colburn 1831*
>
> *The facts*: the claimant had agreed to write a book on costumes and armour for the defendants' 'Juvenile Library' series. He was to receive £100 on completion. He did some research and wrote part of the book. The defendants then abandoned the series.
>
> *Decision*: the claimant was entitled to 50 guineas as reasonable remuneration on a *quantum meruit* basis.

Time of performance

If one party fails to perform at the agreed time he may perform the contract later – the contract continues in force, unless **time is of the essence**. In that case the injured party may refuse late performance and treat the contract as discharged by breach.

If the parties expressly agree that time is of the essence and so prompt performance is to be a condition, conclusive and late performance does not discharge obligations. If they make no such express stipulation the following rules apply.

(a) In a commercial contract, time of performance is usually treated as an essential condition.

(b) In a contract for the sale of land equity may permit the claimant to have an order for specific performance even if he is late.

(c) If time was not originally of the essence, either party may make it so by serving on the other a notice to complete within a reasonable time.

Severable contracts

The contract may provide for performance by instalments with separate payment for each of them (a **divisible** or **severable** contract).

Taylor v Laird 1856
The facts: the claimant agreed to captain a ship up the River Niger at a rate of £50 per month. He abandoned the job before it was completed. He claimed his pay for the months completed.

Decision: he was entitled to £50 for each complete month. Effectively this was a contract that provided for performance and payment in monthly instalments.

Sale of Goods Act 1979

As indicated above, acceptance of goods, or part of them (unless the contract is severable), deprives the buyer of his right to treat the contract as discharged by breach of condition on the part of the seller. But he may claim damages.

The buyer must have a reasonable opportunity to examine the goods before accepting them: s 34.

Situations when the buyer loses his right to reject goods

- He waives the breached condition
- He elects to treat the breach of condition as a breach of warranty
- He has accepted the goods
- He is unable to return the goods

1.2 Agreement

Instead of performing the contract, **the parties may agree to cancel the contract before it has been completely performed** on both sides. If there are unperformed obligations of the original contract on both sides, each party provides consideration for his own release by agreeing to release the other (**bilateral discharge**). Each party surrenders something of value.

But if one party has completely performed his obligations, his agreement to release the other from his obligations (**unilateral discharge**) requires consideration, such as payment of a cancellation fee (this is called **accord and satisfaction**).

If the parties enter into a new contract to replace the unperformed contract, the new contract provides any necessary consideration. This is called **novation** of the old contract – it is replaced by a new one.

A contract may include provision for its own discharge by imposing a **condition precedent,** which prevents the contract from coming into operation unless the condition is satisfied. Alternatively, it may impose a **condition subsequent** by which the contract is discharged on the later happening of an event; a simple example of the latter is provision for termination by notice given by one party to the other. Effectively these are contracts whereby discharge may arise through agreement.

1.3 Frustration

If it is **impossible** to perform the contract when it is made, there is usually no contract at all. In addition, the parties are free to negotiate escape clauses or *force majeure* clauses covering impossibility which arises after the contract has been made. If they fail to do so, they are, as a general rule, in **breach** of contract if they find themselves unable to do what they have agreed to do.

The rigour of this principle is modified by the doctrine that in certain circumstances a contract may be discharged by **frustration**. If it appears that the parties assumed that certain underlying conditions would continue, the contract may be frustrated if their assumption proves to be false.

Definition

'The term **frustration** refers to the discharge of a contract by some outside event for which neither party is responsible which makes further performance impossible. It must be some fundamental change in circumstances such as the accidental destruction of the subject-matter upon which the contract depends. The contract is thereby brought to an end and the rights and obligations of the parties will, in many cases, be adjusted by the application of the Law Reform (Frustrated Contracts) Act 1943.'

Destruction of the subject matter

In the case which gave rise to the doctrine of frustration, the **subject matter** of the contract was destroyed before performance fell due.

> *Taylor v Caldwell 1863*
> *The facts*: a hall was let to the claimant for a series of concerts on specified dates. Before the date of the first concert the hall was accidentally destroyed by fire. The claimant sued the owner of the hall for damages for failure to let him have the use of the hall as agreed.
>
> *Decision*: destruction of the subject matter rendered the contract impossible to perform and discharged the defendant from his obligations under the contract.

Personal incapacity to perform a contract of personal service

The principle that a physical thing must be available applies equally to a person, if that person's presence is a fundamental requirement. Not every illness will discharge a contract of personal service – personal incapacity must be established.

> *Condor v Barron Knights 1966*
> *The facts*: the claimant, aged sixteen, contracted to perform as drummer in a pop group. His duties, when the group had work, were to play on every night of the week. He fell ill and his doctor advised that he should restrict his performances to four nights per week. The group terminated his contract.
>
> *Decision*: a contract of personal service is based on the assumption that the employee's health will permit him to perform his duties. If that is not so the contract is discharged by frustration.

Government intervention

Government intervention is a common cause of frustration, particularly in time of war. If maintenance of the contract would impose upon the parties a contract fundamentally different from that which they made, the contract is discharged.

> *Metropolitan Water Board v Dick, Kerr & Co 1918*
> *The facts*: the defendants contracted in July 1914 to build a reservoir for the claimants within six years, subject to a proviso that the time should be extended if delays were caused by difficulties, impediments or obstructions. In February 1916 the Minister of Munitions ordered the defendants to cease work and sell all their plant.
>
> *Decision*: the proviso in the contract did not cover such a substantial interference with the contract. The interruption was likely to cause the contract, if resumed, to be radically different from that contemplated by the parties. The contract was discharged.

Supervening illegality

In many cases of government intervention, further performance of the contract becomes **illegal** due to 'supervening illegality'. This may be the case when war breaks out.

> *Avery v Bowden 1855*
> *The facts*: the defendant entered into a contract to charter a ship from the claimant to load grain at Odessa within a period of 45 days. The ship arrived at Odessa and the charterer told the claimant that he did not propose to load a cargo. The master remained at Odessa hoping the charterer would change his. Before the 45 days (for loading cargo) had expired, the outbreak of the Crimean War discharged the contract by frustration.
>
> *Decision*: the contract was discharged by frustration (the outbreak of war) without liability for either party.

Non-occurrence of an event if it is the sole purpose of the contract

Two contrasting examples of this application of the doctrine are given by the so-called coronation cases.

Krell v Henry 1903

The facts: a room belonging to the claimant and overlooking the route of the coronation procession of Edward VII was let for the day of the coronation for the purpose of viewing the procession. The coronation was postponed owing to the illness of the King. The owner of the rooms sued for the agreed fee, which was payable on the day of the coronation.

Decision: the contract was made for the sole purpose of viewing the procession. As that event did not occur the contract was frustrated.

Herne Bay Steamboat Co v Hutton 1903

The facts: a steamboat was hired for two days to carry passengers, for the purpose of viewing the naval review (at Spithead) and for a day's cruise round the fleet. The review had been arranged as part of the coronation celebrations. The naval review was cancelled owing to the King's illness but the steamboat could have taken passengers for a trip round the assembled fleet, which remained at Spithead.

Decision: the royal review of the fleet was not the sole occasion of the contract, and the contract was not discharged. The owner of the steamboat was entitled to the agreed hire charge less what he had earned from the normal use of the vessel over the two-day period.

Exceptions

A contract is not discharged by frustration in the following circumstances.

(a)   If an **alternative mode of performance** is still possible.

   Tsakiroglou & Co v Noblee and Thorl GmbH 1962

   The facts: in October 1956 the sellers contracted to sell 300 tons of Sudanese groundnuts and transport them to Hamburg. The normal and intended method of shipment from Port Sudan (on the Red Sea coast) was by a ship routed through the Suez Canal to Hamburg. Before shipment the Suez Canal was closed; the sellers refused to ship the cargo arguing that it was an implied term that shipment should be via Suez or alternatively that shipment via the Cape of Good Hope would make the contract 'commercially and fundamentally' different, so that it was discharged by frustration.

   Decision: both arguments failed. There was no evidence to support the implied term argument nor was the use of a different (although more expensive) route an alteration of the fundamental nature of the contract sufficient to discharge it by frustration.

(b)   If performance becomes suddenly more **expensive**.

(c)   If one party **has accepted the risk** that he will be unable to perform.

(d)   If one party **has induced frustration** by his own choice between alternatives.

The Law Reform (Frustrated Contracts) Act 1943

Where a contract is frustrated, the common law rule provides that the occurrence of the frustrating event brings the contract automatically to an end forthwith. At common law, the consequences of this can be harsh.

> *Chandler v Webster 1904*
> *The facts*: the defendant agreed to let the claimant have a room for £141.15s for the purpose of viewing the coronation procession of Edward VII. The contract provided that the money was payable immediately. The coronation was postponed owing to the illness of the King. The claimant sued for the return of his £100 and the defendant counterclaimed for the unpaid amount of £41.15s.
>
> *Decision*: the obligation to pay rent had fallen due before the frustrating event. The claimant's action failed and the defendant's claim was upheld.

This case can be contrasted with *Krell v Henry 1903*, where the contract stipulated that payment was due on the day of the procession. Only in 1942 was the doctrine modified, so that, where there is a complete failure of consideration, the contract can be held void *ab initio*.

> *Fibrosa v Fairbairn 1942*
> *The facts*: the claimant placed an order for machinery to be delivered in Poland. He paid £1,000 of the contract price of £4,800 with his order. Shortly afterwards the outbreak of the Second World War frustrated the contract since the German army occupied Poland. The claimant sued to recover the £1,000 which had been paid.
>
> *Decision*: the deposit was repayable since the claimant had received absolutely nothing for it – there had been a total failure of consideration.

In most cases now the rights and liabilities of parties to a contract discharged by frustration are regulated by the Law Reform (Frustrated Contracts) Act 1943 as follows.

(a)   Any money paid under the contract by one party to the other is to be repaid. Any sums due for payment under the contract then or later cease to be payable.

(b)   If a person has to repay money under (a), or if he must forego payment earned, he may be able to recover or set off expenses incurred up to the time the contract was frustrated.

(c)   If either party has obtained a valuable benefit (other than payment of money) under the contract before it is discharged, the court may in its discretion order him to pay to the other party all or part of that value.

> *BP Exploration Co (Libya) Ltd v Hunt (No 2) 1982*
> *The facts*: Hunt owned an oil concession in Libya, BP was contracted to explore and exploit the potential oil fields in return for a share of the concession if successful. BP's investigation revealed a large oil field and pipelines were laid. The Libyan government then cancelled the concession, thus frustrating the contract.
>
> *Decision*: the court held that Hunt had received a valuable benefit of around $85m in terms of the increased value of his concession as a result of discovering oil. The court awarded a 'just sum' of around $35m to represent this valuable benefit. It took into account all the circumstances, namely the value of the oil already removed, the potential claim for compensation against the Libyan Government and the allocation of risk expressed in the contract.

1.4 Breach of contract

A party is said to be in breach of contract where, without lawful excuse, he does not perform his contractual obligations precisely. A person sometimes has a **lawful excuse** not to perform contractual obligations.

- Performance is **impossible**, perhaps because of some unforeseeable event.
- He has tendered performance but this has been **rejected**.
- The **other party** has made it **impossible** for him to perform.
- The contract has been discharged through **frustration**.
- The parties have by **agreement** permitted **non-performance**.

Breach of contract gives rise to a secondary obligation to pay **damages** to the other party but, the **primary obligation to perform the contract's terms remains** unless breach falls into one of two categories.

(a) Where the party in default has **repudiated** the contract, either before performance is due or before the contract has been fully performed.

(b) Where the party in default has committed a **fundamental breach**.

Definition

> **Repudiation** can be defined as 'a rejection to avoid a contract or to bring a contract to an end for breach of condition. The term may also be applied to a situation where a party renounces his/her contractual obligations in advance of the date for performance'.

Repudiatory breach

A **repudiatory breach** occurs where a party indicates, either by words or by conduct, that he does not intend to honour his contractual obligations. A repudiatory breach is a serious actual breach of contract. It does not automatically discharge the contract – indeed the injured party has a choice.

(a) He can elect to treat the contract as repudiated by the other, recover damages and treat himself as being discharged from his primary obligations under the contract.

(b) He can elect to affirm the contract.

Types of repudiatory breach

Repudiatory breach giving rise to a right either to terminate or to affirm arises in the following circumstances.

(a) **Refusal to perform (renunciation).** One party renounces his contractual obligations by showing that he has no intention to perform them: *Hochster v De la Tour 1853*. (See below.)

(b) **Failure to perform an entire obligation.** An entire obligation is said to be one where complete and precise performance of it is a precondition of the other party's performance.

(c) **Incapacitation**. Where a party prevents himself from performing his contractual obligations he is treated as if he refused to perform them. For instance, where A sells a thing to C even though he promised to sell it to B he is in repudiatory breach of his contract with B.

(d) Breach of a condition or an innominate term. (See Chapter 7.)

Genuine mistakes, even to one party's detriment, will not necessarily repudiate a contract. This was the decision in *Vaswani Motors (Sales and Services) Ltd 1996*. A seller of a motor vehicle, acting in good faith, mistakenly demanded a higher price than that specified in the contract. However, the buyer could not evade his responsibilities under the contract, since he could have offered to pay the original price.

Anticipatory breach

Repudiation may be **explicit** or **implicit**. A party may break a condition of the contract merely by declaring in advance that he will not perform it, or by some other action which makes future performance impossible. The other party may treat this as **anticipatory breach**.

- Treat the contract as discharged forthwith

- At his option may allow the contract to continue until there is an actual breach

Hochster v De La Tour 1853
The facts: the defendant engaged the claimant as a courier to accompany him on a European tour commencing on 1 June. On 11 May he wrote to the claimant to say that he no longer required his services. On 22 May the claimant commenced legal proceedings for anticipatory breach of contract. The defendant objected that there was no actionable breach until 1 June.

Decision: the claimant was entitled to sue as soon as the anticipatory breach occurred on 11 May.

Where the injured party allows the contract to continue, it may happen that the parties are discharged from their obligations without liability if the contract is later frustrated: *Avery v Bowden 1855* (detailed in Section 3).

If the innocent party elects to treat the contract as still in force the former may continue with his preparations for performance and **recover the agreed price** for his services. Any claim for damages will be assessed on the basis of what the claimant has really lost.

White & Carter (Councils) v McGregor 1961
The facts: the claimants supplied litter bins to local councils, and were paid not by the councils but by traders who hired advertising space on the bins. The defendant contracted with them for advertising of his business. He then wrote to cancel the contract but the claimants elected to advertise as agreed, even though they had at the time of cancellation taken no steps to perform the contract. They performed the contract and claimed the agreed payment.

Decision: the contract continued in force and they were entitled to recover the agreed price for their services. Repudiation does not, of itself, bring the contract to an end. It gives the innocent party the choice of affirmation or rejection.

The Mihalis Angelos 1971

The facts: the parties entered into an agreement for the charter of a ship to be 'ready to load at Haiphong' (in Vietnam) on 1 July 1965. The charterers had the option to cancel if the ship was not ready to load by 20 July. On 17 July the charterers repudiated the contract believing (wrongly) that they were entitled to do so. The shipowners accepted the repudiation and claimed damages. On 17 July the ship was still in Hong Kong and could not have reached Haiphong by 20 July.

Decision: the shipowners were entitled only to nominal damages since they would have been unable to perform the contract and the charterers could have cancelled it without liability on 20 July.

Termination for repudiatory breach

To terminate for repudiatory breach the innocent party must notify the other of his decision. This may be by way of refusal to accept defects in performance, refusal to accept further performance or refusal to perform his own obligations.

(a) He is not bound by his future or continuing contractual obligations, and cannot be sued on them.

(b) He need not accept nor pay for further performance.

(c) He can refuse to pay for partial or defective performance already received.

(d) He can reclaim money paid to a defaulter if he can and does reject defective performance.

(e) He is not discharged from the contractual obligations which were due at the time of termination.

The innocent party can also claim damages from the defaulter. An innocent party who began to perform his contractual obligations but who was prevented from completing them by the defaulter can claim reasonable remuneration on a *quantum meruit* basis (see Section 2).

Affirmation after repudiatory breach

If a person is aware of the other party's repudiatory breach and of his own right to terminate the contract as a result but still decides to treat the contract as being in existence he is said to have **affirmed the contract**. The contract remains fully in force.

Activity 1 **(30 minutes)**

Rodney and Horatio have entered into a contract whereby Rodney is to provide a ship to load waste at Palermo within 30 days of the ship's arrival. The ship arrives at Palermo but because the waste is unsafe, Horatio does not load it. The ship remains at Palermo but after 28 days the Italian government passes a law banning the transportation of unsafe waste by sea.

Analyse the legal position.

2 REMEDIES FOR BREACH

2.1 Damages

Definition

> **Damages** are a common law remedy and are primarily intended to **restore the party who has suffered loss to the same position he would have been in if the contract had been performed**.

In a claim for damages the first issue is **remoteness of damage**. Here the courts consider how far down the sequence of cause and effect the consequences of breach should be traced before they should be ignored. Secondly, the court must decide how much money to award in respect of the breach and its relevant consequences. This is the **measure of damages**.

Remoteness of damage

Under the rule in *Hadley v Baxendale* damages may only be awarded in respect of loss as follows.

(a)   (i)   The loss must arise naturally from the breach.

        (ii)   The loss must arise **in a manner which the parties may reasonably be supposed to have contemplated**, in making the contract, as the probable result of the breach of it.

(b)   A loss outside the natural course of events will only be compensated if the exceptional circumstances are within the defendant's knowledge when he made the contract.

Hadley v Baxendale 1854

The facts: the claimants owned a mill at Gloucester whose main crank shaft had broken. They made a contract with the defendant for the transport of the broken shaft to Greenwich to serve as a pattern for making a new shaft. Owing to neglect by the defendant delivery was delayed and the mill was out of action for a longer period. The defendant did not know that the mill would be idle during this interval. He was merely aware that he had to transport a broken millshaft. The claimants claimed for loss of profits of the mill during the period of delay.

Decision: although the failure of the carrier to perform the contract promptly was the direct cause of the stoppage of the mill for an unnecessarily long time, the claim must fail since the defendant did not know that the mill would be idle until the new shaft was delivered. Moreover it was not a natural consequence of delay in transport of a broken shaft that the mill would be out of action. The miller might have a spare.

The defendant is liable only if he knew of the special circumstances from which the abnormal consequence of breach could arise.

Victoria Laundry (Windsor) v Newman Industries 1949

The facts: the defendants contracted to sell a large boiler to the claimants 'for immediate use' in their business of launderers and dyers. Owing to an accident in dismantling the boiler at its previous site delivery was delayed. The defendants were aware of the nature of the claimants' business and had been informed that the claimants were most anxious to put the boiler into use in the shortest possible space of time. The claimants claimed damages for normal loss of profits for the period of delay and for loss of abnormal profits from losing 'highly lucrative' dyeing contracts to be undertaken if the boiler had been delivered on time.

Decision: damages for loss of normal profits were recoverable since in the circumstances failure to deliver major industrial equipment ordered for immediate use would be expected to prevent operation of the plant. The claim for loss of special profits failed because the defendants had no knowledge of the dyeing contracts.

Contrast this ruling with the case below.

The Heron II 1969

The facts: K entered into a contract with C for the shipment of a cargo of sugar belonging to C to Basra. He was aware that C were sugar merchants but he did not know that C intended to sell the cargo as soon as it reached Basra. The ship arrived nine days late and in that time the price of sugar on the market in Basra had fallen. C claimed damages for the loss due to the fall in market value.

Decision: the claim succeeded. It is common knowledge that market values of commodities fluctuate so that delay might cause loss.

If the type of loss caused is not too remote the defendant may be liable for serious consequences.

H Parsons (Livestock) v Uttley Ingham 1978

The facts: there was a contract for the supply and installation of a large storage hopper to hold pig foods. Owing to negligence of the defendant supplier the ventilation cowl was left closed. The pig food went mouldy. Young pigs contracted a rare intestinal disease, from which 254 died. The pig farmer claimed damages for the value of the dead pigs and loss of profits from selling the pigs when mature.

Decision: some degree of illness of the pigs was to be expected as a natural consequence. Since illness was to be expected, death from illness was not too remote.

Measure of damages

As a general rule the amount awarded as damages is what is needed to put the claimant in the position he would have achieved if the contract had been performed. This is sometimes referred to as protecting the **expectation interest** of the claimant.

A claimant may alternatively seek to have his **reliance interest** protected; this refers to the position he would have been in had he not relied on the contract. This compensates for wasted expenditure.

The onus is on the defendant to show that the expenditure would not have been recovered if the contract had been performed.

C & P Haulage v Middleton 1983
The facts: the claimants granted to the defendant a six-month renewable licence to occupy premises as an engineering workshop. He incurred expenditure in doing up the premises, although the contract provided that he could not remove any fixtures he installed. He was ejected in breach of the licence agreement ten weeks before the end of a six-month term. He sued for damages.

Decision: the defendant could only recover nominal damages. He could not recover the cost of equipping the premises (as reliance loss) as he would not have been able to do so if the contract had been lawfully terminated.

However, if a contract is speculative, it may be unclear what profit might result.

Anglia Television Ltd v Reed 1972
The facts: the claimants engaged an actor to appear in a film they were making for television. He pulled out at the last moment and the project was abandoned. The claimants claimed the preparatory expenditure, such as hiring other actors and researching suitable locations.

Decision: damages were awarded as claimed. It is impossible to tell whether an unmade film will be a success or a failure and, had the claimants claimed for loss of profits, they would not have succeeded.

The general principle is to compensate for **actual financial loss**.

Thompson Ltd v Robinson (Gunmakers) Ltd 1955
The facts: the defendants contracted to buy a Vanguard car from the claimants. They refused to take delivery and the claimants sued for loss of profit on the transaction. There was at the time a considerable excess of supply of such cars over demand for them and the claimants were unable to sell the car.

Decision: the market price rule, which the defendants argued should be applied, was inappropriate in the current market. The seller had lost a sale and was entitled to the profit.

Charter v Sullivan 1957
The facts: the facts were the same as in the previous case, except that the sellers were able to sell every car obtained from the manufacturers.

Decision: only nominal damages were payable.

Market price rule

The measure of damages for breaches of contract for the sale of goods is usually made in relation to the **market price** of the goods. Where a seller fails to sell the goods, the buyer can go into the market and purchase **equivalent goods** instead. The seller would have to compensate the buyer for any additional cost the buyer incurred over the contract cost. The situation is reversed when the buyer fails to purchase the goods. The seller can sell the goods on the **open market** and recover any **loss of income** he incurred by having to sell the goods at a lower price than that to which he contracted.

Non-financial loss

In some recent cases damages have been recovered for mental distress where that is the main result of the breach. It is uncertain how far the courts will develop this concept. Contrast the cases below.

> *Jarvis v Swan Tours 1973*
> *The facts*: the claimant entered into a contract for holiday accommodation at a winter sports centre. What was provided was much inferior to the description given in the defendant's brochure. Damages on the basis of financial loss only were assessed at £32.
>
> *Decision*: the damages should be increased to £125 to compensate for disappointment and distress because this was a contract the principle purpose of which was the giving of pleasure.
>
> *Alexander v Rolls Royce Motor Cars Ltd 1995*
> *The facts*: the claimant sued for breach of contract to repair his Rolls Royce motor car and claimed damages for distress and inconvenience or loss of enjoyment of the car.
>
> *Decision*: breach of contract to repair a car did not give rise to any liability for damages for distress, inconvenience or loss of enjoyment.

Cost of cure

Where there has been a breach and the claimant is seeking to be put in the position he would have been in if the contract had been performed, by seeking a sum of money to 'cure' the defect which constituted the breach, he may be denied the cost of cure if it is **wholly disproportionate** to the breach.

> *Ruxley Electronics and Construction Ltd v Forsyth 1995*
> *The facts*: a householder discovered that the swimming pool he had ordered to be built was shallower than specified. He sued the builder for damages, including the cost of demolition of the pool and construction of a new one. Despite its shortcomings, the pool as built was perfectly serviceable and safe to dive into.
>
> *Decision*: the expenditure involved in rectifying the breach was out of all proportion to the benefit of such rectification. The claimant was awarded a small sum to cover loss of amenity.

Mitigation of loss

In assessing the amount of damages it is assumed that the claimant will take any reasonable steps to reduce or **mitigate** his loss. The burden of proof is on the defendant to show that the claimant failed to take a reasonable opportunity of mitigation.

> *Payzu Ltd v Saunders 1919*
> *The facts*: the parties had entered into a contract for the supply of goods to be delivered and paid for by instalments. The claimants failed to pay for the first instalment when due, one month after delivery. The defendants declined to make further deliveries unless the claimants paid cash in advance with their orders. The claimants refused to accept delivery on those terms. The price of the goods rose, and they sued for breach of contract.

Decision: the seller had no right to repudiate the original contract. But the claimants should have mitigated their loss by accepting the seller's offer of delivery against cash payment. Damages were limited to the amount of their assumed loss if they had paid in advance, which was interest over the period of pre-payment.

The injured party is not required to take **discreditable** or **risky measures** to reduce his loss since these are not 'reasonable'.

Pilkington v Wood 1953
The facts: the claimant bought a house in Hampshire, having been advised by his solicitor that title was good. The following year, he decided to sell it. A purchaser was found but it was discovered that the house was not saleable at the agreed price, as the title was not good. The defendant was negligent in his investigation of title and was liable to pay damages of £2,000, being the difference between the market value of the house with good title and its market value with defective title. The defendant argued that the claimant should have mitigated his loss by taking action against the previous vendor for conveying a defective title.

Decision: this would have involved complicated litigation and it was not clear that he would have succeeded. The claimant was under no duty to embark on such a hazardous venture 'to protect his solicitor from the consequences of his own carelessness'.

Liquidated damages and penalty clauses

To avoid later complicated calculations of loss, or disputes over damages payable, as we have seen the parties may include up-front in their contract a formula (**liquidated damages**) for determining the damages payable for breach. These may be upheld in commercial contracts if they are reasonable; if they are regarded as penalty clauses they will not. (See Chapter 7.)

2.2 Other common law remedies

Action for the price

If the breach of contract arises out of one party's failure to pay the contractually agreed price due under the contract, the creditor should bring a personal action against the debtor to recover that sum. This is a fairly straightforward procedure but is subject to two specific limitations.

The first is that an **action for the price** under a contract for the sale of goods may only be brought if property has passed to the buyer, unless the price has been agreed to be payable on a specific date: s 49 Sale of Goods Act 1979.

Secondly, whilst the injured party may recover an agreed sum due at the time of an anticipatory breach, sums which become due after the anticipatory breach may not be recovered unless he affirms the contract.

Quantum meruit

In particular situations, a claim may be made on a *quantum meruit* basis as an alternative to an action for damages for breach of contract.

The phrase *quantum meruit* literally means '**how much it is worth**'. It is a measure of the value of contractual work which has been performed. The aim of such an award is to restore the claimant to the position he would have been in if the contract had never been made, and is therefore known as a **restitutory** award.

Quantum meruit is likely to be sought where one party has already performed part of his obligations and the other party then repudiates the contract.

> *De Barnardy v Harding 1853*
> *The facts*: the claimant agreed to advertise and sell tickets for the defendant, who was erecting stands for spectators to view the funeral of the Duke of Wellington. The defendant cancelled the arrangement without justification.
>
> *Decision*: the claimant might recover the value of services rendered.

In most cases, a *quantum meruit* claim is needed because the other party has unjustifiably prevented performance: *Planché v Colburn 1831*.

Because it is restitutory, a *quantum meruit* award is usually for a smaller amount than an award of damages. However where only nominal damages would be awarded (say because the claimant would not have been able to perform the contract anyway) a *quantum meruit* claim would still be available and would yield a higher amount.

2.3 Equitable remedies

Specific performance

The court may at its discretion give an equitable remedy by ordering the defendant to perform his part of the contract instead of letting him 'buy himself out of it' by paying damages for breach.

Definition

> **Specific performance** can be defined as 'an order of the court directing a person to perform an obligation. It is an equitable remedy awarded at the discretion of the court when damages would not be an adequate remedy. Its principal use is in contracts for the sale of land but may also be used to compel a sale of shares or debentures. It will never be used in the case of employment or other contracts involving personal services'.

An order will be made for specific performance of a contract for the sale of land since the claimant may need the land for a particular purpose and would not be adequately compensated by damages for the loss of his bargain. However, for items with no special features, specific performance will not be given, as damages would be a sufficient remedy.

The order will not be made if it would require performance over a period of time and the court could not ensure that the defendant did comply fully with the order. Therefore specific performance is not ordered for contracts of employment or personal service nor usually for building contracts.

Injunction

Definition

> An **injunction** is a discretionary court order and an equitable remedy, requiring the defendant to do, or not do, something.

An injunction may be made to enforce a contract of personal service. This would be achieved by preventing a person from taking a course of action which would breach the contract.

Warner Bros Pictures Inc v Nelson 1937
The facts: the defendant (the film star Bette Davis) agreed to work for a year for the claimants and not during the year to work for any other producer nor 'to engage in any other occupation' without the consent of the claimants. She came to England during the year to work for a British film producer. The claimants sued for an injunction to restrain her from this work and she resisted arguing that if the restriction were enforced she must either work for them or abandon her livelihood.

Decision: the court would not make an injunction if it would have the result suggested by the defendant. But the claimants merely asked for an injunction to restrain her from working for a British film producer. This was one part of the restriction accepted by her under her contract and it was fair to hold her to it to that extent.

An injunction may **enforce contract terms** which are in substance negative restraints.

Metropolitan Electric Supply Co v Ginder 1901
The facts: the defendant contracted to take all the electricity which he required from the claimants. They sued for an injunction to restrain him from obtaining electricity from another supplier.

Decision: the contract term (electricity only from the one supplier) implied a negative restriction (no supplies from any other source) and to that extent it could be enforced by injunction.

An injunction would **not** be made merely to **restrain** the defendant from acts inconsistent with his positive obligations.

Whitwood Chemical Co v Hardman 1891
The facts: the defendant agreed to give the whole of his time to his employers, the claimants. In fact he occasionally worked for others. The employers sued for an injunction to restrain him.

Decision: by his contract he merely stated what he would do. This did not imply an undertaking to abstain from doing other things.

There are three types of injunction that can be granted in the court's discretion.

- A **mandatory injunction** which is restorative in its effect. It directs the defendant to take **positive** steps to undo something he has already done in breach of contract, for example to demolish a building that he has erected in breach of contract. This is a relatively rare remedy and will only be granted where it will produce a fair result in all the circumstances.

- A **prohibitory injunction** which requires the defendant to observe a **negative** promise in a contract.

  Note that where a person enters into a contract to perform personal services for A and not to perform them for B, an injunction may be given to enforce the negative promise, even though an order of specific performance of the positive promise would be refused.

- An **asset-freezing injunction** prevents the defendant from dealing with assets where the claimant can convince the court that he has a good case and that there is a danger of the defendant's assets being exported or dissipated.

Rescission

Strictly speaking the equitable right to **rescind** an agreement is not a remedy for breach of contract – it is a right which exists in certain circumstances, such as where a contract is **voidable** for misrepresentation.

Rescinding a contract means that it is cancelled or rejected and the parties are restored to their pre-contract condition. Four conditions must be met.

(a) It must be possible for each party to be returned to the pre-contract condition *(restitutio in integrum)*.

(b) An innocent third party who has acquired rights in the subject matter of the contract will prevent the original transaction being rescinded.

(c) The right to rescission must be exercised within a reasonable time of it arising.

(d) Where a person affirms a contract expressly or by conduct it may not then be rescinded.

Activity 2   **(30 minutes)**

Harriet and Mark had entered into an agreement for the supply of goods to be delivered and paid for by instalments. Mark failed to pay the first instalment when it was due. Harriet refused to make further deliveries unless Mark paid cash on delivery. Mark refused to accept delivery on those terms. The price of the goods rose and Mark sued for breach of contract.

What is the contract position?

---

3   LIMITATIONS TO ACTIONS FOR BREACH

The right to sue for breach of contract becomes statute-barred after six years from the date on which the cause of action accrued: s 5 Limitation Act 1980. The period is twelve years if the contract is by deed.

In three situations the six-year period begins not at the date of the breach but later.

(a) If the claimant is a minor or under some other contractual disability (eg of unsound mind) at the time of the breach of contract, the six year period begins to run only when his disability ceases or he dies.

(b) If the defendant or his agent conceals the right of action by fraud or if the action is for relief from the results of a mistake, the six-year period begins to run only when the claimant discovered or could by reasonable diligence have discovered the fraud, concealment or mistake: s 32 Limitation Act 1980. An innocent third party who acquired property which is affected by these rules is protected against any action in respect of them: s 32(4).

(c) The normal period of six years can be extended where information relevant to the possible claims is deliberately concealed after the period of six years has started to run.

Where the claim can only be for specific performance or injunction, the Limitation Act 1980 does not apply. Instead, the claim may be limited by the equitable doctrine of delay or 'laches'.

Allcard v Skinner 1887

The facts: the claimant entered a Protestant convent in 1868 and, in compliance with a vow of poverty, transferred property worth about £7,000 to the Order by 1878. In 1879 she left the order and became a Roman Catholic. Six years later she demanded the return of the balance of her gift, claiming undue influence by the defendant, the Lady Superior of the Protestant sisterhood.

Decision: this was a case of undue influence for which a right of rescission may be available, since the rule of the Order forbade its members from seeking the advice of outsiders. But the claimant's delay in making her claim debarred her from recovering her property.

Extension of the limitation period

The limitation period may be extended if the debt, or any other certain monetary amount, is either acknowledged or paid in part before the original six (or twelve) years has expired: s 29. Hence if a debt accrues on 1.1.08, the original limitation period expires on 31.12.13. But if part-payment is received on 1.1.10, the debt is reinstated and does not then become 'statute-barred' until 31.12.15.

(a) The claim must be acknowledged as existing, not just as possible, but it need not be quantified. It must be in writing, signed by the debtor and addressed to the creditor: s 30.

(b) To be effective, the part payment must be identifiable with the particular debt, not just a payment on a running account.

Chapter roundup

- The normal method of discharge is performance. Obligations of the parties in the vast majority of commercial contracts are discharged by performance. Performance must be complete and exact. There is no right to receive payment proportionate to partially completed work unless one of the recognised exceptions applies.

- The obligations of the parties may also be discharged by agreement.

- If the parties to the contract assumed, at the time of the agreement, that certain underlying conditions would continue, the contract is discharged by frustration if these assumptions prove to be false. The contract is then fundamentally different in nature from the original agreement.

- The common law consequences of frustration are modified by the Law Reform (Frustrated Contracts) Act 1943, which regulates the rights and obligations of the parties to a contract discharged by frustration.

- Breach of a condition in a contract may lead to the entire agreement being discharged by fundamental breach, unless the injured party elects to treat the contract as continuing and merely claim damages for his loss.

- If there is anticipatory breach (one party declares in advance that he will not perform his side of the bargain when the time for performance arrives) the other party may treat the contract as discharged forthwith, or continue with his obligations until actual breach occurs. His claim for damages will then depend upon what he has actually lost.

- Damages are a common law remedy intended to restore the party who has suffered loss to the position he would have been in had the contract been performed. The two tests applied to a claim for damages relate to remoteness of damage and measure of damages.

- Remoteness of damage is tested by the two limbs of the rule in *Hadley v Baxendale 1854*.

- The first part of the rule states that the loss must arise either naturally, according to the usual course of things, from the breach or in a manner which the parties may reasonably be supposed to have contemplated, in making the contract, as a probable result of its breach.

  - The second part of the rule provides that a loss outside the usual course of events will only be compensated if the exceptional circumstances which caused it were within the defendant's actual or constructive knowledge when he made the contract.

  - The measure of damages is that which will compensate for the loss incurred. It is not intended that the injured party should profit from a claim.

- A simple action for the price to recover the agreed sum should be brought if breach of contract is failure to pay the price. But property must have passed from seller to buyer, and complications arise where there is anticipatory breach.

Chapter roundup (cont'd)

- A *quantum meruit* is a claim which is available as an alternative to damages. The injured party in a breach of a contract may claim the value of his work. The aim of such an award is to restore the claimant to the position he would have been in had the contract never been made. It is a restitutory award.

- An order for specific performance is an equitable remedy. The party in breach is ordered to perform his side of the contract. Such an order is only made where damages are inadequate compensation, such as in a sale of land, and where actual consideration has passed.

- An injunction is an equitable remedy which requires someone to do, or not do, something. There are three types: mandatory, prohibitory and asset-freezing.

Quick quiz

1   In a building contract, explain what option is open to a builder who has completed most of the work but who has not been paid.

2   What is novation?

3   When anticipatory breach occurs, the injured party has two options. What are they?

4   In the event of a breach of contract, if the innocent party elects to treat the contract as still in force, may he continue with his preparations for performance and recover the agreed price for his services?

5   What is frustration?

6   In the event of contract frustration, how are the rights and liabilities of the parties determined?

7   State the rule in *Hadley v Baxendale*.

Answers to quick quiz

1   Under the doctrine of substantial performance, he may claim the contract price less a deduction for the work outstanding. (see para 1)

2   The replacement of an unperformed contract by a new one, the new contract itself forming the consideration for agreement to cancel the old one. (para 1)

3   He may treat the contract as discharged forthwith or alternatively he may allow the contract to continue until there is an actual breach. (para 1.4)

4   Yes. (para 1.4)

5   A fundamental change in circumstances such as the destruction of the subject matter of the contract, such that performance is rendered impossible and the contract bought to an end. (para 1.3)

6   In most cases now the rights and liabilities of parties to a contract discharged by frustration are regulated by the Law Reform (Frustrated Contracts) Act 1943 as follows.

   (a) Any money paid under the contract by one party to the other is to be repaid. Any sums due for payment under the contract then or later cease to be payable.

   (b) If a person has to repay money under (a), or if he must forego payment earned, he may be able to recover or set off expenses incurred up to the time the contract was frustrated.

   (c) If either party has obtained a valuable benefit (other than payment of money) under the contract before it is discharged, the court may in its discretion order him to pay to the other party all or part of that value. (para 1.3)

7   Under the rule in *Hadley v Baxendale* damages may only be awarded in respect of loss as follows.

   (a) (i)   The loss must arise naturally from the breach.

        (ii) The loss must arise **in a manner which the parties may reasonably be supposed to have contemplated**, in making the contract, as the probable result of the breach of it.

   (b) A loss outside the natural course of events will only be compensated if the exceptional circumstances are within the defendant's knowledge when he made the contract. (para 2.1)

Answers to activities

1   Horatio was within the terms of the contract in not loading the waste in the first 28 days. Had he informed Rodney that he had no intention of loading, that would have constituted anticipatory breach. However, as Rodney had taken no action against him, the frustrating event (supervening illegality) would have overridden a breach. The contract has been frustrated.

2   Mark is entitled to sue for breach of contract due to non-delivery. He will only recover limited damages as he should have accepted COD when this was offered. (This is a similar scenario to the case of *Payzu v Saunders*.)

PART C

EMPLOYMENT LAW

Chapter 10:
THE CONTRACT OF EMPLOYMENT

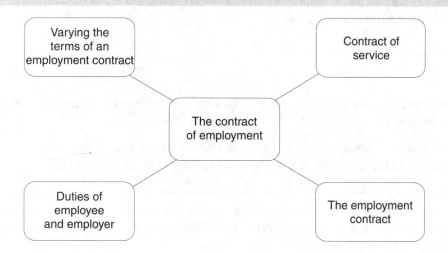

Introduction

We begin our study of employment law by looking at the **distinction** between the **employed** and the **self-employed**. This distinction is very important as it has implications regarding employee **rights** and **liabilities**.

The chapter continues by examining the **contents** of an employment contract. Like any other contract it may include **express** and **implied terms** and you should be able to explain how these terms are included.

Employers and employees owe certain **duties** to one another; breach of these duties may result in legal action against the party who breached their duty. Learn these duties and the supporting case law as they are an important part of your syllabus.

Statutory references in this chapter are to the Employment Rights Act 1996 (ERA 1996) unless otherwise noted.

Your objectives

In this chapter you will learn about the following.

    (a)   The difference between employment and self-employment, and the importance of the difference

    (b)   The form of the employment contract

    (c)   Common law and statutory duties of employer and employee

    (d)   Changes in contract terms

1   CONTRACT OF SERVICE

A general rule is that an employee is someone who is employed under a **contract of service**, as distinguished from an independent contractor, who is someone who works under a **contract for services**.

However, it is important to note that some statutory provisions apply to 'workers' and this term is wider than 'employees' and includes those personally performing work or services unless truly self-employed.

Definitions

> **Employee**: 'an individual who has entered into or works under a contract of employment'. (ERA 1996)
>
> **Contract of employment**: 'a contract of service or apprenticeship, whether express or implied, and (if it is express) whether it is oral or in writing'.

In practice this distinction depends on many factors. As we will discuss in Section 2 it can be very important to know whether an individual is an employee or an independent contractor. The courts will apply a series of **tests**.

Primarily, the court will look at the **reality of the situation**. This may be in spite of the form of the arrangement.

> *Ferguson v John Dawson & Partners 1976*
> *The facts*: a builder's labourer was paid his wages without deduction of income tax or National Insurance contributions and worked as a self-employed contractor providing services. His 'employer' could dismiss him, decide on which site he would work, direct him as to the work he should do and also provided the tools which he used. He was injured in an accident and sued his employers on the basis that they owed him legal duties as his employer.
>
> *Decision*: on the facts taken as a whole, he was an employee working under a contract of employment.

Where there is some **doubt** as to the nature of the relationship the courts will then look at any **agreement between the parties**.

> *Massey v Crown Life Assurance 1978*
> *The facts*: the claimant was originally employed by an insurance company as a departmental manager; he also earned commission on business which he introduced. At his own request he changed to a self-employed basis. Tax and other payments were no longer deducted by the employers but he continued to perform the same duties. The employers terminated these arrangements and the claimant claimed compensation for unfair dismissal.
>
> *Decision*: as he had opted to become self-employed and his status in the organisation was consistent with that situation, his claim to be a dismissed employee failed.

1.1 Testing for the contract of service

It can still be unclear whether a person is an employee or an independent contractor. Historically, the tests of **control, integration** into the employer's organisation, and **economic reality** (or the multiple test) have been applied in such cases.

The fundamental prerequisite of a contract of employment is that there must be **mutual obligations** on the employer to provide, and the employee to perform, work.

The control test

The court will consider whether the employer has **control** over the way in which the employee performs his duties.

> *Mersey Docks & Harbour Board v Coggins & Griffiths (Liverpool) 1947*
> *The facts*: stevedores hired a crane with its driver from the harbour board under a contract which provided that the driver (appointed and paid by the harbour board) should be the employee of the stevedores. Owing to the driver's negligence a checker was injured. The case was concerned with whether the stevedores or the harbour board were vicariously liable as employers.
>
> *Decision*: in the House of Lords, that the issue must be settled on the facts and not on the terms of the contract. The stevedores could only be treated as employers of the driver if they could control in detail how he did his work. But although they could instruct him what to do, they could not control him in how he operated the crane. The harbour board (as 'general employer') was therefore still the driver's employer.

The integration test

The courts consider whether, if the employee is so skilled that he cannot be controlled in the performance of his duties, he was **integrated** into the employer's organisation.

> *Cassidy v Ministry of Health 1951*
> *The facts*: the full-time assistant medical officer at a hospital carried out a surgical operation in a negligent fashion. The patient sued the Ministry of Health as employer. The Ministry resisted the claim arguing that it had no control over the doctor in his medical work.
>
> *Decision*: in such circumstances the proper test was whether the employer appointed the employee, selected him for his task and so integrated him into the organisation. If the patient had chosen the doctor the Ministry would not have been liable as employer. But here the Ministry (the hospital management) made the choice and so it was liable.

The control and integration tests are important, but **no longer decisive** in determining whether a person is an employee.

The multiple (economic reality) test

They also consider whether the employee was **working on his own account** and this requires numerous factors to be taken into account.

Ready Mixed Concrete (South East) v Ministry of Pensions & National Insurance 1968
The facts: the driver of a special vehicle worked for one company only in the delivery of liquid concrete to building sites. He provided his own vehicle (obtained on hire purchase from the company) and was responsible for its maintenance and repair. He was free to provide a substitute driver. The vehicle was painted in the company's colours and the driver wore its uniform. He was paid gross amounts (no tax etc deducted) on the basis of mileage and quantity delivered as a self-employed contractor. The Ministry of Pensions claimed that he was in fact an employee for whom the company should make the employer's insurance contributions.

Decision: in such cases the most important test is whether the worker is working on his own account (the entrepreneurial test or multiple test). On these facts the driver was a self-employed transport contractor and not an employee.

In the above case, Mackenna J held that a contract of service existed where:

- There is **agreement** from the worker that they will provide work for their master in exchange for remuneration.

- The worker agrees either expressly or impliedly that their master can exercise **control** over their performance.

- There are other **factors** included in the contract that make it **consistent** with a contract for service.

The fact that the drivers could appoint a **replacement** for themselves was a major factor in the decision that found them as contractors rather than employees.

Agency workers

The status of agency workers has been the subject of numerous cases in recent years as the numbers employed under such contracts as increased. Two key cases have considered **length of service** of agency workers and **control** that the client of the agency has over the worker.

(a) **Length of service**

In *Franks v Reuters Ltd 2003*, the agency worker had been providing services to the client for some **six years** engaged in a variety of jobs, and was effectively so thoroughly integrated with the employer's organisation as to be **indistinguishable** from the employer's staff.

Mummery LJ, said that an

'implied contract of employment did not arise simply by virtue of the length of the employment, but it could well be a factor in applying the overall tests appropriate to establish (or otherwise) an employment status. The case was remitted to the tribunal for further consideration, but the length of an assignment of an agency worker clearly has implications for the development of other indications of an employment relationship, with those utilising the services of the worker forgetting the true nature of the relationship and behaving towards the work as if he or she was an employee. It may be that at this point the relevant approach also starts to involve the 'integration' test'.

(b) **Control over the worker**

Where the client of the agency has **sufficient control** over the employee provided by the agency, it could be held that they are in fact the true employer.

Motorola v Davidson and Melville Craig (2001)
The facts: Davidson was contracted with the Melville Craig agency and was assigned to work for Motorola. Both the agency and Motorola had agreed that Davidson could be sent back to the agency if his work was unacceptable. Following a disciplinary hearing Davidson was found unacceptable and returned to the agency. Davidson took Motorola to an employment tribunal for unfair dismissal.

Decision: Motorola had sufficient control over Davidson to make them the employer. It was held that the court should look beyond the pure legal situation and look at the practical control aspects in such cases as well.

Other relevant factors

Significant factors that you should consider when deciding whether or not a person is employed or self-employed are as follows.

- Does the employee use his **own tools and equipment** or does the employer provide them?

- Does the alleged employer have the power to **select or appoint** its employees, and may it dismiss them?

- **Payment of salary** is a fair indication of there being a contract of employment.

- **Working for a number of different people** is not necessarily a sign of self-employment. A number of assignments may be construed as 'a series of employments'.

In difficult cases, courts will consider whether the employee can **delegate** all his obligations, whether there is restriction as to place of work, whether there is a **mutual obligation** and whether holidays and hours of work are agreed.

O'Kelly v Trusthouse Forte plc 1983
The facts: the employee was a 'regular casual' working when required as a waiter. There was an understanding that he would accept work when offered and that the employer would give him preference over other casual employees. The employment tribunal held that there was no contract of employment because the employer had no obligation to provide work and the employee had no obligation to accept work when offered.

Decision: the Court of Appeal agreed with this finding. Whether there is a contract of employment is a question of law but it depends entirely on the facts of each case; here there was no 'mutuality of obligations' and hence no contract.

The decision whether to classify an individual as an employee or not is also influenced by **policy considerations**. For example, an employment tribunal might regard a person as an employee for the purpose of unfair dismissal despite the fact that the tax authorities treated him or her as self-employed.

Airfix Footwear Ltd v Cope 1978.
The facts: the EAT was concerned with a classic outworking arrangement under which the applicant (having been given training and thereafter supplied with the necessary tools and materials) generally worked five days a week making heels for shoes manufactured by the respondent company. She was paid on a piece work basis without deduction of income tax or NIC.

Decision: working for some seven years, generally for five days a week, resulted in the arrangement being properly classified as employment under a contract of employment.

1.2 The difference between employment and self-employment

The first thing that it is important to note is that much of the recent legislation which gives protection to employees **extends further than employees**. Much of it is drafted to cover 'workers' which has a wide definition to cover most people providing services to others outside of the course of (their own) business.

This has reduced the importance of the distinction between employee and independent contractor in this area.

However, there are several other **practical reasons** why the distinction between a contract of service and a contract for services is important.

SIGNIFICANCE OF THE DISTINCTION		
	Employed	**Self-employed**
Social security	Employers must pay secondary Class 1 contributions on behalf of employees Employees make primary Class 1 contributions There are also differences in statutory sick pay and levies for industrial training purposes	Independent contractors pay Class 2 and Class 4 contributions
Taxation	Deductions must be made by an employer for income tax under PAYE (Schedule E) from salary paid to employee	The self-employed are taxed under Schedule D and are directly responsible to the HM Revenue and Customs for tax due
Employment protection	There is legislation which confers protection and benefits upon employees under a contract of service, including • Minimum periods of notice • Remedies for unfair dismissal	Employment protection is not available for contractors
Tortious acts	Employer is generally vicariously liable for tortious acts of employees, committed in the course of employment	Liability of person hiring an independent contractor for contractors' acts severely limited unless there is strict liability

SIGNIFICANCE OF THE DISTINCTION

	Employed	Self-employed
Implied terms	There are rights and duties implied by statute for employers and employees This will affect things such as copyrights and patents	These implied rights and duties do not apply to such an extent to a contract for services
VAT	Employees do not have to register for or charge VAT	An independent contractor may have to register for, and charge VAT
Bankruptcy	In liquidation, an employee has preferential rights as a creditor for payment of outstanding salary and redundancy payments, up to certain limits	Contractors are treated as non-preferential creditors if their employer is liquidated
Health and safety	There is significant common law and regulation governing employers' duties to employees with regard to health and safety	The common law provisions and much of the regulation relating to employees also relates to independent contractors

2 THE EMPLOYMENT CONTRACT

The definition of an employment contract was given in Section 1. To recap, it is a contract of service which may be **express** or **implied**. If express, it can be either **oral** or **written**. In essence, then, an employment contract can be a simple, straightforward agreement. The contact must, of course, comply with the usual rules relating to the formation of a valid contract.

Activity 1 (10 minutes)

As with any other contract, agreements for employment require offer and acceptance, consideration and the intention to create legal relations. How are these three essential elements manifested in a contract of employment?

At the one extreme, an employment contract may be a **document** drawn up by solicitors and signed by both parties; at the other extreme it may consist of a **handshake** and a 'See you on Monday'. In such cases the court has to clarify the agreement by determining what the parties must be taken to have agreed.

Senior personnel may sign a contract specially drafted to include terms on **confidentiality** and **restraint of trade**. Other employees may sign a standard form contract, exchange letters with the new employer or simply agree terms orally at interview.

Each of these situations will form a valid contract of employment, subject to the requirements outlined below as to written particulars, as long as there is **agreement** on **essential terms** such as hours and wages. We will consider some of these essential terms in the following sections. Nor should it be forgotten that even prior to employment commencing the potential employer has legal obligations, for example not to discriminate in recruitment.

2.1 Implied terms

Implied terms usually arise out of **custom** and **practice** within a profession or industry. In *Henry v London General Transport Services Ltd (2001)* it was held that four requirements should be met before such terms can be read into a contract.

- The terms must be reasonable, certain and notorious

- They must represent the wishes of both parties

- Proof of the custom or practice must be provided by the party seeking to rely on the term

- A **distinction** must be made between implying terms that make **minor** and **fundamental** changes to the terms of the contract

2.2 Requirement for written particulars

Within two months of the beginning of the employment the employer must give to an employee a written **statement of prescribed particulars** of his employment: s 1.

The statement should identify the following.

- The names of **employer** and **employee**

- The **date** on which employment began

- Whether any service with a previous employer forms part of the employee's **continuous period** of employment

- **Pay** – scale or rate and intervals at which paid

- **Hours** of work (including any specified 'normal working hours')

- Any **holiday** and **holiday pay** entitlement

- **Sick leave** and **sick pay** entitlement

- **Pensions** and pension **schemes**

- Length of **notice** of termination to be given on either side

- The **title** of the job which the employee is employed to do (or a brief job description)

A 'principal statement', which must include the **first six items** above and the title of the job, must be provided, but other particulars may be given by way of separate documents.

If the employee has a **written contract of employment** covering these points and has been given a copy it is not necessary to provide him with separate written particulars.

The written particulars must also contain details of **disciplinary procedures** and **grievance procedures** or reference to where they can be found. S35 Employment Act 2002.

If the employer fails to comply with these requirements the employee may apply to an **employment tribunal** for a declaration of what the terms should be: s 11. S38 Employment Act 2002 allows a tribunal to award compensation to an employee claiming unfair dismissal if the particulars are incomplete.

Activity 2   **(10 minutes)**

Charles saw a sign advertising vacancies at a local building site. He contacted the foreman and was told that he would be required but that, because work depended on the weather conditions, he would not be given an employment contract – he would be accountable for his own income tax and National Insurance. The foreman added that he would be provided with tools and that at the beginning of each day he would be told which site he would work on that day. Lateness or theft of materials would lead to his dismissal.

Is Charles an employee?

---

3   DUTIES OF EMPLOYEE AND EMPLOYER

3.1   Employee's common law duties

The employee has a **fundamental duty of faithful service** to his employer. All other duties are features of this general duty.

> *Hivac Ltd v Park Royal Scientific Instruments Ltd 1946*
> *The facts*: in their spare time certain of the claimant's employees worked for the defendant company, which directly competed with the claimant.
>
> *Decision*: even though the employees had not passed on any confidential information, they were still in breach of their duty of fidelity to the claimants.

This duty also extends after the employment where **trade secrets** are concerned. Employees will be in breach of their duty if they disclose such secrets to their new employer. The **facts of the case** and the **nature of employment** should be considered when making a decision, for example customer lists of a chicken selling business was not considered a trade secret when a sales manager set up his own competing organisation (*Faccenda Chicken Ltd v Fowler (1986)*).

The **implied** duties of the employee include the following.

- **Reasonable competence** to do his job.

- **Obedience** to the employer's instructions unless they require him to do an unlawful act or to expose himself to personal danger (not inherent in his work) or are instructions outside the employee's contract.

> *Pepper v Webb (1969)*
> *The facts*: the defendant, a gardener refused to obey instructions from his employer regarding planting in the garden. He also swore at them.
>
> *Decision*: the gardener was in breach of his implied duty to obey as the instructions were lawful and reasonable.

- **Duty to account for all money and property** received during the course of his employment.

  Boston Deep Sea Fishing and Ice Co v Ansell (1888)

  The facts: the defendant, who was managing director of the claimant company, accepted personal commissions from suppliers on orders which he placed with them for goods supplied to the company. He was dismissed and the company sued to recover from him the commissions.

  Decision: the company was justified in dismissing the claimant and he must account to it for the commissions.

- **Reasonable care and skill** in the performance of his work: *Lister v Romford Ice and Cold Storage Co (1957)*. What is reasonable depends on the degree of skill and experience which the employee professes to have.

- **Personal service** – the contract of employment is a personal one and so the employee may not delegate his duties without the employer's express or implied consent.

3.2 Employer's common law duties

There is an overriding **duty of mutual trust and confidence** between the employer and the employee. Examples of where this duty have been breached include:

- A director calling his secretary 'an intolerable bitch on a Monday morning' – *Isle of Wight Tourist Board v Coombes (1976)*.

- Failure to investigate a sexual harassment claim – *Bracebridge Engineering v Darby (1990)*.

The employer usually also has the following duties at common law:

- To **pay remuneration** to employees. If there is no rate fixed by the parties, this duty is to pay **reasonable** remuneration. There is statutory provision for this, see Section 5.

- To **indemnify the employee** against expenses and losses incurred in the course of employment.

- To take care of the employees' **health and safety** at work. This is also provided for in statute.

- To **provide work**, where:

  - Employee is an apprentice

  - Employee is paid with reference to work done

  - The opportunity to work is the essence of the contract (for example, for actors)

  - There is work available to be done (subject to contractual terms to the contrary) **and** the relevant employee is a skilled worker who needs work to preserve his or her skills – *William Hill Organisation v Tucker (1998)*.

> – There is no breach of duty if there is **no work** available and the employer continues to pay its employees. However, if an employee was appointed to a **particular role** and no work was provided there may be a breach of duty to provide work if it denies the employee the opportunity to maintain his skills – *Collier v Sunday Referee Publishing Co Ltd (1940)*.

There is no duty to provide a **reference** when employees leave service. Employers may be liable under negligence for not taking reasonable care over accuracy and fairness if they do provide one *(Cox v Sun Alliance Life (2001))*.

The importance of these common law implied duties on both parties is that:

(a) **Breach of a legal duty**, if it is important enough, may entitle the injured party to treat the contract as **discharged** and to claim damages for breach of contract at common law; and

(b) In an employee's claim for compensation for unfair dismissal, the employee may argue that it was a case of **constructive dismissal** by the employer, or the employer may seek to justify his express dismissal of the employee by reference to his conduct. We shall discuss constructive dismissal in Chapter 11.

3.3 Employer statutory duties

Various matters are implied into contracts of employment by statute. Some of them build upon the **basic matters** covered by common law above. Most of the employment statutes in this area implement European Directives on employment law issues. The employer has statutory duties in the following areas:

- Pay
- Time off work
- Maternity rights and the 'work-life balance'
- Health and safety
- Working time

Pay

There are two key pieces of legislation in relation to pay. These are the **Equal Pay Act 1970** and the **National Minimum Wage Act 1998**.

Under the Equal Pay Act 1970, contractual **employment terms should be at least as favourable as those given to an employee of the opposite sex**. The Act covers terms such as sick pay, holiday pay and working hours, and it applies to all forms of full-time and part-time work.

> *Hayward v Cammell Laird Shipbuilders 1986*
> *The facts*: the House of Lords upheld the claim of a canteen cook to equal pay with painters, joiners and thermal insulation engineers employed in the same shipyard on the ground that her work was of equal value.
>
> *Decision*: overall the applicant was considered to be employed on work of equal value. Hayward's application was the first successful claim for equal pay for work of equal value.

A difference in pay which is connected with economic factors affecting the efficient carrying on of the employer's business or other activity may well be relevant: *Rainey v Greater Glasgow Health Board 1987*. Examples are as follows.

- Greater length of service is a material factor: *Capper Pass v Lawton 1977*.

- Working at different times of day is not a material factor: *Dugdale v Kraft Foods 1977*.

- A distinction in hourly pay between workers in London and those based in (the cheaper area of) Nottingham is based on a material factor: *NAAFI v Varley 1976*.

- 'Market forces' do not necessarily amount to a genuine material factor: *Ratcliffe & Others v North Yorkshire County Council 1995*.

A national minimum wage was introduced in the UK in The National Minimum Wage Act 1999. The current **hourly rate** (from October 2007) is £5.52. For persons between the ages of 18 and 21, the rate is £4.60 and for 16 to 17 year olds it is £3.40.

Employers are obliged to provide an itemised pay statement: s 8.

Time off work

In addition to the rights relating to maternity and parental leave discussed below, statute lists several occasions when an employee has a right to time off work.

(a) **Trade union officials** are entitled to time off on full pay at the employer's expense to enable them to carry out **trade union duties**: ss 168-169 Trade Union and Labour Relations (Consolidation) Act 1992.

(b) An employee who has been given notice of dismissal for **redundancy** may have time off to look for work or to arrange training for other work.

(c) A member of a recognised independent **trade union** may have time off work (without statutory right to pay) for **trade union activities**, for example, attending a branch meeting: s 170 TULRCA 1992.

(d) Employees also have a duty to allow an employee to have reasonable time off to carry out certain **public duties**, for example performing his duties as a magistrate. There is **no statutory provision** entitling an employee to time off for jury service, but prevention of a person from attending as a juror is contempt of court.

Maternity rights and the 'work-life balance'

A woman who is pregnant is given substantial rights under statute, including:

- A right to **time off work** for ante-natal care

- The right to **ordinary maternity leave**

- The right to **additional maternity leave**

- The right to **maternity pay**

- The right to **return to work** after maternity leave

- If dismissed, a claim for **unfair dismissal** (this will be discussed in Chapter 11)

Much recent employment legislation, including provisions introduced by the Employment Act 2002, has been concerned with the introduction of **family-friendly** employment policies. There has been a specific focus on the so-called 'work-life balance'. The law has developed as a result in the areas of:

- Maternity leave and pay
- Paternity leave
- Rights of adoptive parents
- A right to request flexible working

Ante-natal care

An employee has a right not to be unreasonably refused time off for ante-natal care during working hours. She is also entitled to pay during such an absence. There is **no minimum qualifying period**, ss 55 to 57 Employment Rights Act 1996.

Maternity leave

Every woman is given the right to **ordinary maternity leave** which is **twenty-six weeks** long, subject to her satisfying conditions for giving her employer notice of her intentions. A woman who has been continuously employed for 26 weeks has a right to **additional maternity leave,** which allows the employee a further period of **twenty-six weeks' leave**. This means that the total period of statutory maternity leave is 52 weeks.

An employee on **ordinary** maternity leave has the **right to return to work** in the job she had before her absence, with her seniority, pension and similar rights which she would have had if she had not been absent and on no less favourable terms than if she had not been absent: s 71.

An employee on **additional** maternity leave has the same rights, except if it is **not practicable** for her to return to the job she had before, she has the right to another job which is **suitable and appropriate** to her, on the same or better status, terms and conditions.

Maternity pay

Statutory maternity pay is paid during an employee's ordinary maternity leave. Additional maternity leave is unpaid. The employee must have at least 26 weeks of continuous employment and her average earnings must be above a certain level (otherwise she may be entitled to claim **maternity allowance** instead). SMP is paid at the following rate:

(a) For the first six weeks, 90% of salary,

(b) For the remainder of ordinary maternity leave, the lower of £100 per week or 90% of her average weekly earnings.

Paternity leave

New rights to **paternity leave** and pay are available to employees of children born on or after 6 April 2003. The employee claiming the right must:

- Be the biological father of the child or the mother's husband or partner;
- Have or expect to have responsibility for the child's upbringing;
- Have 26 weeks' continuous service.

Eligible employees will be entitled to take either **one week** or **two consecutive** weeks paid paternity leave. The leave must be completed within 56 days of the actual birth of the child.

Statutory Paternity Pay will be paid during the paternity leave. This will be paid at the lower of £100 per week or 90% of the employee's average weekly earnings. These rights are **in addition to** the existing parental leave provisions (see below) which allow up to thirteen weeks of **unpaid** paternity leave for each child under five years old, provided that the employee has one year's continuous service.

Adoptive parents

The family-friendly employment policies introduced by the Employment Act 2002 extend to adoptive parents, who now have similar rights to those provided under the maternity provisions. There is a right to **statutory adoption leave** (SAL) and **statutory adoption pay** (SAP). Statutory adoption leave may consist of 26 weeks of ordinary adoption leave and 26 weeks of additional adoption leave.

Adoptive parents' rights extend to one of the adopting couple but not to both. The adopting parent must have 26 weeks of continuous employment. Leave is not available in cases of step family adoption, adoption by existing step parents or extended family adoption.

Flexible working

Employees have the **right**:

- To apply for a change in terms and conditions of employment in respect of hours, time and place of work, and

- Not to be unreasonably refused.

To be **eligible** to apply for flexible working, the employee must:

- Have a child under six years of age (or under eighteen if the child is disabled)

- Have been continuously employed for 26 weeks at the date of the application

- Have, or expect to have, responsibility for the child's upbringing

- Be making the application in order to care for the child and

- Not have made another application for flexible working in the previous twelve months

There is a detailed set of procedures for the submission of an application, the provision of a response by the employer and, if necessary, any subsequent appeal by the employee.

If a request is granted, any changes are regarded as **permanent contract changes**. The employer may reasonably refuse a request on the grounds of:

- The burden of additional cost

- A detrimental effect on ability to meet customer demand

- An inability to re-organise the work amongst existing staff or to recruit additional staff

- A detrimental impact on quality or performance

- Insufficiency of work during the periods the employee proposes to work or

- Planned structural changes

The given business reasons may not be contested by the employee. The only grounds for complaint are either that the employer has **failed** to follow the procedures properly or that the decision to reject an application was based on incorrect facts. If the body to which a complaint is made (an employment tribunal or ACAS) upholds the complaint it may award **compensation** up to a maximum of eight weeks' pay but can not order the employer to implement the request for flexible working.

Parental leave

Any employee with a year's continuous service who has responsibility for a child is entitled to **unpaid parental leave** to care for that child: s 7 Employment Relations Act 1999.

The period allowed is thirteen weeks for each child born or adopted after 15 December 1999. The entitlement ceases after the child is five years old, or on the fifth anniversary of the child being adopted. If the child is disabled (entitled to disability allowance), the right ceases after the child's eighteenth birthday.

The leave may not be taken in periods of less than one week, unless the child is disabled.

Health and safety

The key legislation under which an employer has a duty to his employees with regard to **health and safety** is the Health and Safety at Work Act 1974, which has been augmented by subsequent regulations, notably the Health and Safety at Work Regulations 1999. This Act makes it the duty of every employer to ensure the health, safety and welfare of his employees, as far as is practicable.

This general duty includes the following issues.

- Provide and maintain plant and systems of work which are safe and without risk

- Make arrangements to ensure safe use, handling, storage and transport of articles/substances

- Provide adequate information, instruction, training and supervision

- Maintain safe places of work and ensure that there is adequate access in and out

- Provide a safe and healthy working environment

The contract of employment contains an implied right not to be subjected to detriment by the employer on grounds of health and safety: s 44(1). Specifically, the employee has a right not to be subjected to detriment on the ground that he intended to or did:

- Carry out activities designated to him in connection with preventing/reducing health and safety risks at work

- Perform duties as a representative of workers on issues of health and safety

- Take part in consultation with the employer under the Health and Safety (Consultation with Employees) Regulations 1996

- Leave his place of work or refused to work in circumstances which he reasonably believed to be serious or imminent and he could not reasonably be expected to avert

- Take appropriate steps to protect himself or others from circumstances of danger which he believed to be serious and imminent

Working time

The Working Time Regulations 1998 provide broadly that a worker's **average working time in a seventeen-week period,** (including overtime) shall **not exceed 48 hours for each seven-day period**, unless the worker has agreed in writing that this limit shall not apply.

The Regulations also give every worker the **right to paid annual leave**, which shall be a minimum of four weeks long. The employer may be able to specify when such holiday can or cannot be taken, but must give the employees notice of such occasions.

There are special rules relating to Sunday working.

4   VARYING THE TERMS OF AN EMPLOYMENT CONTRACT

It should be clear, from your earlier studies of general contract law, that a change in contract terms **can only be made with the consent of both parties** to the contract.

- Some terms are negotiated on a **collective** basis between employer and union(s).

- Some terms are negotiated **individually**.

- Some terms are implied by **statute**.

4.1   Varying terms without changing the contract

There may be circumstances in which an employer can vary the terms of an employment contract without actually needing to vary the contract itself. For example, there may be an **express term** in the contract which itself gives rights of variation, for example to allow a change in area of work.

Alternatively, an **implied term** may act to vary the contract.

(a)   A sales representative may be required to take responsibility for such area as his employer considers necessary in order to meet changing market conditions: *Burnett v F A Hughes.*

(b)   Terms may also be implied by custom, for example, where a steel erector is required at the request of his employer to change sites: *Stevenson v Teeside Bridge & Engineering Co Ltd 1971.*

4.2   Changing the existing contract

The existing contract can be changed by **consent**. Consent might be demonstrated by **oral agreement** to new terms, by the **signing** of a new statement of terms and conditions or by the employee showing acceptance by **working** under the new terms.

If an employer does not obtain **willing agreement** to a variation but the employer changes the contract anyway, the employee has a number of options.

- He may consent.

- He may stay in employment but make it clear by that he does not accept the variation.

- He may resign and claim constructive dismissal. (See Chapter 11.)

4.3   Signing a new contract

The third broad option open to the employer is to give contractual notice to the employee and then offer a new contract on the new terms. This opens the employer to a **potential claim** for unfair dismissal. It is generally best for the employer to obtain consent to vary the terms of an existing contract.

4.4   Continuous employment

You may have noticed references to 'continuous employment' in the previous sections. Most of the employment protection discussed here and in the following chapter is given to an employee who has one year's continuous service.

There are provisions in statute for how the year's continuous service should be calculated, and what counts as service and what does not. **The basic rule is that a year is twelve calendar months**.

Certain weeks might not be taken into account in calculating continuous service, but they do not break the period of continuous service. This might be the case if the employee takes place in a strike, or is absent due to service in the armed forces.

EXAMPLE

Illustration

If Ben was employed for eight months and then was given leave to do some service in the armed services for five months, on his return to the employer he would have been employed for thirteen calendar months.

However, until he completes another four months of service he will not be eligible for the employment protection given to those employees with a year's continuous service.

NOTES

Once he has completed those four months, the eight months prior and the four months subsequent to the armed service will count as continuous service, despite being split by a period away from the employer.

Transfer of undertakings

Another factor that impacts on continuous service is when a business or undertaking is transferred by one person to another. Where the business is transferred, so that an employee works for a new employer, this change represents **no break in the continuous service of the employee** (Transfer of Undertaking Regulations 1981).

Chapter roundup

- It is important to distinguish between a **contract of service** (employment) and a **contract for services** (independent contractor). Each type of contract has different rules for taxation, health and safety provisions, protection of contract and vicarious liability in tort and contract.

- A contract of service is **distinguished** from a contract for services usually because the parties **express** the agreement to be one of service. This does not always mean that an employee will not be treated as an independent contractor by the court, however; much depends on the three tests.

  - Control test
  - Integration test
  - Economic reality test

- The distinction between **employed** and **self-employed** is important as to whether certain **rights** are available to an individual and how they are treated for **tax purposes**.

- There are no particular legal rules relating to the commencement of employment – it is really **just like any other contract** in requiring offer and acceptance, consideration and intention to create legal relations.

- The **employer** has an implied **duty at common law** to take **reasonable care** of his employees; he must select proper staff, materials and provide a safe system of working.

- The **employee** has a duty to exercise **care and skill** in performance of his duties.

- **Statute** implies terms into employment contracts, which may not usually be overridden, regarding pay, maternity leave and work-life balance generally, time off, health and safety and working time.

- A contract of employment can only be **varied** if the contract **expressly** gives that right, or if all parties consent to the variation.

- Many rights given to employees under the **Employment Rights Act 1996** are only available if an employee has a specified period of **continuous employment**.

Quick quiz

1   What tests are applied by the courts to answer these questions?

 • Has the employer control over the way in which the employee performs his duties? (1) ………………..

 • Is the skilled employee part of the employer's organisation? (2) ………………..

 • Is the employee working on his own account? (3)………………..

2   Is working for a number of different people an automatic sign of self-employment?

True ☐

False ☐

3   Give five reasons why the distinction between employed and self-employed workers is important.

4   A 'principal statement' must include the following (tick all that apply).

 (a) Names of parties ☐

 (b) Job title ☐

 (c) Date employment began ☐

 (d) Notice details ☐

 (e) Details of continuous employment ☐

 (f) Pay details ☐

 (g) Pensions and pension scheme details ☐

 (h) Holiday entitlement ☐

5   What is an employee's fundamental duty?

6   Which of these options are open to an employer who wishes to vary the terms of an employment contract?

 (i)   Sign a wholly new contract
 (ii) Vary the terms without changing the contract
 (iii) Change the existing contract

 A   (iii) only
 B   (i) and (ii) only
 C   (ii) and (iii) only
 D   (i), (ii) and (iii)

Answers to quick quiz

1 (1) Control test
   (2) Integration test
   (3) Multiple (economic reality) test (see para 1.1)

2 False. Other facts will be considered. (para 1.1)

3 Social security
   Taxation
   Employment protection
   Tortious acts
   Health and safety
   (also implied terms, VAT, rights in bankruptcy) (para 1.2)

4 (a) (b) (c) (e) (f) (h) (para 2.2)

5 Faithful service to his employer (para 3.1)

6 D. All the options are available (Section 4)

Answers to activities

1 Generally the offer comes from the employer and acceptance from the employee, who may write a letter or simply turn up for work at an agreed time. Consideration comprises the promises each party gives to the other – a promise to work for a promise to pay. If there is no consideration, a deed must be executed for there to be a contract of employment. The intention to create legal relations is imputed from the fact that essentially employment is a commercial transaction.

2 Charles is an employee. Even though he does not receive an employment contract the facts indicate a contract of service since he is controlled by the employer in that the latter provides tools, tells him where to work and reserves the right to dismiss him.

Chapter 11:
TERMINATION OF EMPLOYMENT

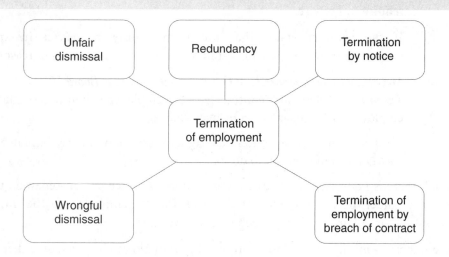

Introduction

Ending an employment contract can be a traumatic time for all involved and it can result in legal action. Both employees and employers must know their rights and obligations to minimise the risk of such action.

Statutory references in this chapter are to the Employment Rights Act 1996 unless otherwise noted.

Your objectives

In this chapter you will learn about the following.

    (a)   The ways in which a contract of employment can come to an end

    (b)   Giving notice of termination

    (c)   The effects of breaching an employment contract

    (d)   Wrongful and unfair dismissal

    (e)   Remedies for wrongful and unfair dismissal

    (f)   The rules surrounding redundancy

1   TERMINATION BY NOTICE

A contract of employment may be terminated by **notice**. The following rules apply.

(a)   The period of notice given must **not be less than the statutory minimum,** whatever the contract may specify.

(b)   It **may be given without specific reason** for so doing, unless the contract requires otherwise.

(c)   If the contract states that notice may **only be given in specific circumstances** then generally it may **not** be given for any other reason.

McClelland v Northern Ireland General Health Services Board 1957
The facts: the claimant's contract gave the employer a right to terminate his employment for misconduct or inefficiency.

Decision: there was no contractual right of termination for redundancy – it was a breach of contract to do so.

Although there is no breach of contract, termination by notice or non-renewal qualifies as 'dismissal' under the statutory code. This means that the employee may be entitled to compensation for unfair dismissal, which we shall see later.

Statute imposes a **minimum period of notice** of termination to be given on either side.

1.1   Minimum period of notice

If an employer terminates the contract of employment by giving notice, the **minimum period of notice** to be given is determined by the employee's length of continuous service in the employer's service as follows: s 86.

(a)   An employee who has been continuously employed for **one month or more** but less than one year is entitled to not less than **one week's** notice.

(b)   An employee who has been continuously employed for **two years or more** but less than twelve years is entitled to **one week's notice for each year of continuous employment**.

(c)   Any employee who has been employed for **twelve years** or more is entitled to not less than **twelve weeks'** notice.

If the **employee** gives notice, the minimum period required is **one week** if he has been employed for at least one month.

The notice must specify the **date of its expiry**. Either party may waive his entitlement to notice or accept a sum *in lieu* of notice.

The statutory rules on length of notice merely prescribe a **minimum**. If the contract provides for a longer period, notice must be given in accordance with the contract.

During the period of notice an employee is entitled to pay at a rate not less than the average of his earnings over the previous twelve weeks.

If the employee is **dismissed** in any way he may request his employer to give him a **written statement of the reasons** for his dismissal and **the employer must provide it** within fourteen days. The statement must contain at the least a simple summary of the reasons for dismissal and can be used as **admissible evidence** before an employment tribunal: s 92.

Dismissal is the word used to describe termination of an employment contract by the employer. This term is used in several ways, which we shall investigate through the rest of this chapter. Here are a few definitions relating to dismissal.

Definitions

> **Summary dismissal** is where the employer dismisses the employee without notice. He may do this if the employee has committed a serious breach of contract.
>
> **Constructive dismissal** is where the employer commits a breach of contract, thereby causing the employee to resign. By implication, this is also dismissal without notice.
>
> **Wrongful dismissal** is a common law concept arising in specific circum-stances (which are discussed in Section 3). It gives the employee an action for breach of contract.
>
> **Unfair dismissal** is a statutory concept introduced by employment protection legislation. As a rule, every employee has the right not to be unfairly dismissed: s 54.
>
> Correspondingly, **fair dismissal** is a statutory concept where a person has been dismissed as a result of a fair reason under legislation. (Fair and unfair dismissal will be discussed in Section 5.)

Note that the distinction between wrongful and unfair dismissal depends not so much upon the nature of the dismissal, as on the remedies available.

2 TERMINATION OF EMPLOYMENT BY BREACH OF CONTRACT

An employment contract is **terminated by breach in the following circumstances**.

- Summary dismissal
- Constructive dismissal
- Inability on the employer's behalf to continue
- Repudiation of the contract by the employee

The concepts of summary dismissal and constructive dismissal are both examples of dismissal without proper notice. A dismissal with proper notice is generally held to be lawful, unless it is shown to be wrongful or unfair.

However, under the ERA 1996, the reason for dismissal has to be determined in relation to both when the notice is given and when the employment is terminated.

2.1 Summary dismissal

Summary dismissal occurs where the employer dismisses the employee without notice. He may do this if the employee has committed a serious breach of contract and, if so, the employer incurs no liability.

If, however, he has **no sufficient justification** the employer is liable for **breach of contract** and the employee may claim a remedy for wrongful dismissal. Whether the employee's conduct justifies summary dismissal will vary according to the circumstances of the case.

Wilson v Racher 1974
The facts: a gardener swore at his employer using extreme obscenities.

Decision: his action for wrongful dismissal succeeded, as the employer's own conduct had provoked the outburst. This was a solitary outburst following a history of diligence and competence.

Contrast this with *Pepper v Webb (1969)* that we saw in the previous chapter. The decision in this case favoured the employer as the incident also included a refusal to obey a reasonable and lawful instruction by the employee.

2.2 Constructive dismissal

Constructive dismissal occurs where the employer, although willing to continue the employment, repudiates some **essential term** of the contract, for example by the imposition of a complete change in the employee's duties, and the employee resigns. The employer is liable for breach of contract.

Establishing constructive dismissal

To establish constructive dismissal, an **employee** must show that:

- His employer has committed a serious breach of contract (a repudiatory breach).

- He left because of the breach.

- He has not 'waived' the breach, thereby affirming the contract.

Examples of breaches of contract which have lead to claims of constructive dismissal include the following.

- A reduction in pay: *Industrial Rubber Products v Gillon (1977)*

- A complete change in the nature of the job: *Ford v Milthorn Toleman Ltd (1980)*

- A failure to follow the prescribed disciplinary procedure: *Post Office v Strange (1981)*

- A failure to provide a suitable working environment: *Waltons and Morse v Dorrington (1997)*

- A failure to implement a proper procedure: *WA Goold (Pearmak) Ltd v McConnell & Another (1995)*

The breach must be a serious one.

Western Excavating (ECC) Ltd v Sharp 1978
The facts: the defendant was suspended without pay for misconduct. This caused him financial difficulties, and so he applied for an advance against holiday pay but was refused. He then left and claimed for constructive dismissal.

Decision: the employers had not repudiated the contract and so there had been no dismissal.

2.3 Employer's inability to continue employment

If a personal employer dies, an employing firm of partners is dissolved, an employing company is compulsorily wound up, a receiver is appointed or the employee's place of employment is permanently closed, the employer may become unable to continue to employ the employee.

2.4 Repudiation of the contract by the employee

If the employee resigns or goes on strike or fails to perform the contract and to observe its conditions, that is breach of contract by him and the employer may dismiss him or treat the contract as discharged by the employee's breach.

3 WRONGFUL DISMISSAL

An action for wrongful dismissal, since it derives from the employee's **common law** rights in contract, must be brought in the county court or the High Court. Claimants must show that they were **dismissed in breach of contract**, for example with less than the statutory minimum period of notice and that they have **as a result suffered loss**.

As the action is taken for a breach of contract, the courts will usually only award damages for the loss of notice period. This was confirmed in *Johnson v Unisys Ltd (2001)* when the claimant was refused damages for breach of implied contractual terms that he alleged to have caused damage to his mental health.

A dismissal will not be wrongful if it is **justified**.

3.1 Justification of dismissal

The following have been taken as justifiable circumstances.

(a) **Wilful disobedience** of a lawful order suffices if it amounts to wilful and serious defiance of authority.

(b) **Misconduct,** in connection with the business or outside it if it is sufficiently grave. For example, acceptance of a secret commission, disclosure of confidential information, assault on a fellow employee or even financial embarrassment of an employee in a position of trust (*Pearce v Foster 1886* – stockbroker's clerk who incurred heavy gambling losses).

(c) **Dishonesty,** where the employee is in a position of particular trust.

(d) **Incompetence or neglect,** insofar as the employee lacks or fails to use skill which he professes to have.

(e) **Gross negligence,** depending on the nature of the job.

(f) **Immorality,** only if it is likely to affect performance of duties or the reputation of the business.

(g)   **Drunkenness,** only if it occurs in aggravated circumstances such as when driving a vehicle or a train, or is repeated: *Williams v Royal Institute of Chartered Surveyors 1997.*

3.2   Remedies for wrongful dismissal

As with any other case of compensation, the wronged party is expected to **mitigate** his loss by, say, seeking other employment.

Where breach of contract leaves the employer as the injured party, he may dismiss the employee and withhold wages. The employer may recover confidential papers, or apply for an injunction to enforce a valid restrictive covenant: *Thomas Marshall (Exporters) v Guinle 1978.*

Employment tribunals have jurisdiction to deal with wrongful dismissal cases, which formerly had to be heard in the civil courts.

4   UNFAIR DISMISSAL

Unfair dismissal is an extremely important element of employment protection legislation.

The remedies available following a successful action for **wrongful dismissal** are **limited to damages** compensating for the sum which would have been earned **if proper notice had been given**.

Legislation seeks to **widen the scope of protection** and **increase the range of remedies** available to an employee who has been unfairly dismissed. Under the terms of the **Employment Rights Act 1996,** the top rate of compensation for proven unfair dismissal is £60,600. This cap does not apply to those dismissed for 'whistleblowing', which falls under the Public Interest Disclosure Act 1998.

4.1   Scope of the unfair dismissal rules

Every **included employee who qualifies** under the criteria (a) and (b) below has a statutory right not to be unfairly dismissed: s 94. Certain categories of employee are **excluded** from the statutory unfair dismissal code.

- Persons employed to work **outside Great Britain**

- Employees dismissed while taking **unofficial strike** or other industrial action

- Other categories, including members of the police

In order to obtain compensation or other remedies for unfair dismissal the employee must satisfy several criteria.

(a)   Have been **continuously employed for one year** whether full-time or part-time.

(b)   Have been **dismissed**. This may have to be determined by the tribunal, for example if the employee resigned claiming constructive dismissal.

(c)   Have been **unfairly** dismissed. Dismissal may be unfair even though it is not a breach of contract by the employer.

There are some **exceptions** to the one year's continuous service qualification. These are:

- Where the matter concerns a **safety representative** being penalised for carrying out legitimate health and safety activities

- Where an employee is being **denied a statutory** right (for example an unlawful deduction from wages)

- Where the employee is **pregnant**

You should learn these exceptions to the continuous service rule.

The **effective date** of **dismissal** is reckoned as follows.

- Where there is termination by notice, the date on which the notice expires

- Where there is termination without notice, the date on which the termination takes effect

- Where an employee's fixed-term contract is not renewed, the date on which that term expires

4.2 Making an unfair dismissal claim

There are four steps to making a claim for **compensation** for unfair dismissal.

Step 1. The employee must apply to a tribunal within three months of dismissal

Step 2. The employee must show that he is a qualifying employee and that he has in fact been dismissed.

Step 3. Then the employer must demonstrate (prove):

    (a) What was the alleged **only or principal reason** for dismissal.

    (b) That it was one of the reasons listed in s 96 (discussed in Paragraph 4.4 below) or was otherwise a '**substantial reason** of a kind such as to be capable of justifying the dismissal of an employee' in this position.

Step 4. Then the tribunal must decide if the principal reason did in fact justify the dismissal and whether the employer acted reasonably in treating the reason as sufficient.

If the employer cannot show that the principal reason allegedly justifying the dismissal was one of the fair reasons given in statute (these are discussed in Section 6.1), the dismissal is unfair.

Dismissal may be identified in three separate circumstances.

    (a) **Actual dismissal** is usually fairly clear-cut and can be recognised from the words used by an employer.

    (b) **Constructive dismissal,** as described earlier, involves a fundamental breach of the employment contract by the employer.

    (c) **Expiry of a fixed-term contract** without renewal amounts to a dismissal.

The employee must show that he has in fact been dismissed. The courts often have to debate whether or not the use of abusive language by employers constitutes mere abuse or indicates dismissal.

4.3 The reason for dismissal

The fair reasons for dismissal are discussed in Para 4.4 below. As noted above, if the principal reason for dismissal is not one of those fair reasons, then dismissal will be deemed unfair.

However, even if the employer shows that he dismissed the employee for a reason which is recognised as capable of being sufficient, **a tribunal may still decide that the dismissal was unfair** if it considers that on the basis of **equity and the substantial merits** of the case **the employer acted unreasonably** in dismissing the employee: s 98.

Reasonableness of employer

The **employment tribunal** is required to review the circumstances and to decide whether it was reasonable to dismiss the employee for the reasons given.

Determining whether the employer has acted reasonably requires the tribunal to ask:

- Has the correct **procedure** been applied?
- Did the employer take all **circumstances** into consideration?
- What would any **reasonable employer** have done?

The employer does not act reasonably unless he **takes account of the relevant circumstances**. If an inexperienced employee is struggling to do his work, the employer is expected to help by advice or supervision in the hope that he may improve.

The emphasis placed on giving one or more warnings before dismissing is partly so that the employee may heed the warning and amend his conduct or his performance.

Disciplinary procedure

Since October 2004 there have been statutory rules for dealing with disciplinary and grievance procedures. These provisions form part of an employee's contract of employment.

The standard statutory procedure for dismissal (and disciplinary) cases sets out three steps.

Step 1. There must be a statement of the grounds for the action and an invitation to a meeting

Step 2. The nature of the meeting

Step 3. An appeal stage

Where dismissal has already taken place the employer must provide details of the grounds for the dismissal and permit the employee to appeal that decision.

These procedures (set out in the Employment Act 2002) have three general requirements.

- The timing and location of any meeting must be reasonable.

- The meeting must be conducted in such a way as to allow both the employer and the employee to explain their case.

- If there is more than one meeting the employer should, if reasonably practicable, be represented by a more senior person then at the first meeting.

All steps in the procedure should also be taken without unreasonable delay.

If either party fails to comply with the relevant procedures then neither party has to comply with the rest of the procedures. Under s 98A a dismissal will also be **automatically** unfair if the employer fails to comply with the procedures but the employer may still be able to prove the dismissal was reasonable if he can show he would have dismissed the employee even if the procedure had been followed.

Warnings

Except in the most flagrant cases it is **not reasonable for an employer to dismiss an employee without first warning him** that if he continues or repeats what has happened at least once he is likely to be dismissed.

> *Newman v T H White Motors 1972*
> *The facts*: an employee used foul language to a trainee. The employer asked him not to do so. When he persisted the employer dismissed him.
>
> *Decision*: this was an unreasonable and therefore unfair dismissal. The employer must make it clear to the employee that he risks dismissal if he persists.

Concluding on reasonableness

In reaching its conclusion on the issue of reasonableness, **the tribunal should not substitute what it would have done if placed in the employer's situation**. It is necessary to set the rights and interests of the employee against the interests of the employer's business and then decide whether **any reasonable employer could have come to a different conclusion**.

Unreasonableness and breach of contract by the employer must be distinguished. Some unreasonable conduct of the employer may be serious enough to amount to repudiation of the contract, and if the employee leaves he can claim for constructive dismissal by the employer.

If the employer acts unreasonably but in a manner which does not amount to repudiation of the contract, the employee who resigns terminates a contract by his own act and cannot claim constructive dismissal: *Western Excavating (ECC) Ltd v Sharp 1978*.

4.4 Unfair dismissal – justification of dismissal

Some reasons for dismissal are potentially fair, some are automatically fair, and some are automatically unfair.

Potentially fair reasons for dismissal

To be able to justify dismissal as fair dismissal the employer must show that his **principal reason** related to one of the following.

(a) The **capability or qualifications** of the employee for performing work of the kind which he was employed to do

(b) The **conduct** of the employee

(c) **Redundancy**

(d) **Legal prohibition** or restriction by which the employee could not lawfully continue to work in the position which he held (for example, if a doctor or a solicitor employed as such is struck off the relevant professional register or an employee loses his driving licence which he needs to be able to do his job)

(e) **Some other substantial reason** which justifies dismissal

Capability/qualifications

If the employer dismisses for want of capability on the part of the employee, the employer has to establish that fault.

- What does the contract require?

- What is the general standard of performance of his employees in this trade?

- What is the previous standard of performance of the dismissed employee himself?

If the employee is incompetent it must be of such a nature and quality as to justify dismissal – such as a shop manageress who left her shop dirty and untidy, who failed to maintain cash registers and who did not put stock away: *Lewis Shops Group Ltd v Wiggins 1973.*

'**Capability**' is to be assessed by reference to skills, aptitude, health or any other physical or mental quality. '**Qualification**' means any academic or technical qualifications relevant to the position that the employee holds': s 98(3).

'**Reasonableness**' on the part of the employer is required, for example:

- **Consultation** with employee to determine areas of difficulty
- Allowing a **reasonable time** for improvement
- Providing **training** if necessary
- Considering **all alternatives** to dismissal

If the employer relies on **ill health** as the grounds of incapability there must be **proper medical evidence**. The employer is entitled to consider his own business needs. A reasonable procedure involves cautions, confrontation with records and the granting of a period for improvement.

International Sports Ltd v Thomson 1980
The facts: the employee had been away from work for around 25% of the time, suffering from a number of complaints all of which were certified by medical certificates. She received a number of warnings. Following a final warning and prior to dismissal the company consulted their medical adviser. As the illnesses were unrelated and unverifiable, he did not consider an examination worthwhile. She was dismissed.

Decision: the dismissal was fair.

Misconduct

It is usual to apply the common law distinction between **gross misconduct** which justifies summary dismissal on the first occasion, for example, theft, and **ordinary misconduct** which is not usually sufficient grounds for dismissal unless it is persistent.

EXAMPLE

Assault on a fellow employee, conduct exposing others to danger (for example, smoking in an area prohibited for safety reasons), unpleasant behaviour towards customers and persistent absences from work have been treated as sufficient misconduct to justify dismissal.

Redundancy

If an employee is dismissed mainly or only on the ground of **redundancy**, he may claim remedies for unfair dismissal if he can show one of the following.

(a) There were one or more other employees in similar positions who might have been made redundant and that he was **selected for redundancy in breach of a customary arrangement or agreed procedure**.

(b) He was selected for a reason connected with **trade union membership**.

A redundancy selection procedure should be in conformity with **good industrial relations practice** which requires consultation and objective criteria of selection. The criteria set out by the EAT in *Williams v Compair Maxam Ltd 1982* have been accepted as standards of behaviour.

(a) The employer should give as much **warning** as possible of impending redundancies.

(b) The employer should **consult with the trade union** as to the best means of achieving the desired management result. In *Mugford v Midland Bank plc 1997* it was held that even when an employer has consulted a trade union over the selection criteria for redundancy, this does not release the employer from consulting the individual to be made redundant before a final decision is taken.

(c) It should be possible to check **criteria** for selection against such things as attendance records, efficiency at the job and length of service.

(d) The employer should ensure that the selection is made **fairly**.

(e) The employer should consider whether an **offer of alternative employment** can be made.

Redundancy is discussed further later.

Other substantial reason

The category of **other substantial reason** permits the employer to rely on some factor which is unusual and likely to affect him adversely. An employer has justified dismissal on specific grounds.

(a)   The employee was married to one of his competitors.

(b)   The employee refused to accept a reorganisation, for example, a change of shift working, made in the interests of the business and with the agreement of a large majority of other employees.

Automatically fair reasons for dismissal

Other reasons are designated as being **automatically fair** by legislation.

- Taking part in unofficial industrial action
- Being a threat to national security (to be certified by the government)

An employee who strikes or refuses to work normally may be fairly dismissed unless the industrial action has been **lawfully organised** under the protection conferred by the Employment Relations Act 1999. Where dismissal results from a lock-out or a strike, the tribunal cannot deal with it as a case of alleged unfair dismissal unless victimisation is established.

Automatically unfair reasons for dismissal

Some reasons are automatically unfair (known as '**inadmissible reasons**'). Examples include:

- Pregnancy or other maternity-related grounds

- A spent conviction under the Rehabilitation of Offenders Act 1974

- Trade union membership or activities

- Dismissal on transfer of an undertaking (unless there are 'economic, technical or organisational reasons' justifying the dismissal)

- Taking steps to avert danger to health and safety at work

- Seeking to enforce rights relating to the national minimum wage

- Exercising rights under the Working Time Regulations 1998

- Refusing or opting out of Sunday working (in the retail sector)

- Making a protected disclosure order under the Public Interest Disclosure Act 1998.

Dismissal on grounds of pregnancy or pregnancy-related illness is automatically unfair, **regardless of length of service** as it amounts to **gender discrimination**.

4.5   Proving what was the reason for dismissal

The employer may be required to give to the employee a **written statement** of the **reason for dismissal**: s 92.

If an employee is dismissed for trying to **enforce his employment rights**, by for example asking for a written statement of particulars or an itemised pay statement, he may claim unfair dismissal **regardless of the length of service** and hours worked.

Activity 1   **(10 minutes)**

What is the difference between wrongful dismissal and unfair dismissal?

4.6 Remedies for unfair dismissal

An employee who alleges unfair dismissal must present his complaint to an **employment tribunal** within three months of the effective date of termination. The dispute is referred to a Conciliation Officer and only comes before the tribunal if his efforts to promote a settlement fail.

Reinstatement

If unfair dismissal is established, the tribunal first considers the possibility of making an order for reinstatement.

Definition

Reinstatement is return to the same job without any break of continuity: s 114.

Re-engagement

The tribunal may alternatively order **re-engagement**. The new employment must be comparable with the old or otherwise suitable.

Definition

Re-engagement means that the employee is given new employment with the employer (or his successor or associate) on terms specified in the order.

In deciding whether to exercise these powers, the tribunal must take into account whether the complainant wishes to be reinstated and, whether it is practicable and just for the employer to comply. **Such orders are in fact very infrequent**.

The Employment Appeal Tribunal has ruled that an order for re-engagement should not be made if there has been a breakdown in confidence between the parties: *Wood Group Heavy Industrial Turbines Ltd v Crossan 1998* (employee dismissed following allegations of drug dealing on company premises and time-keeping offences).

Compensation

If the tribunal does not order reinstatement or re-engagement the tribunal may award **compensation,** which may be made in three stages as follows.

(a) A **basic award** calculated as follows. Those aged 41 and over receive one and a half weeks' pay (up to a current (from February 2007) maximum of £310 gross per week) for each year of service up to a maximum of twenty years. In other age groups the same provisions apply, except that the 22 to 40 age group receive one week's pay per year and the under 22-age group receive half a week's pay.

(b) A **compensatory award** (taking account of the basic award) for any additional loss of earnings, expenses and benefits on common law principles of damages for breach of contract: s 124. This is limited to £60,600 by the Employment Rights Act 1996.

(c) If the employer does not comply with an order for reinstatement or re-engagement and does not show that it was impracticable to do so a **punitive additional award** is made of between 26 and 52 weeks' pay (again subject to the £310 per week maximum).

The tribunal may reduce the amount of the award in any of the following circumstances.

• If the employee **contributed** in some way to his own dismissal: s 123(6)

• If he has **unreasonably refused** an offer of reinstatement

• If it is **just and equitable** to reduce the basic award by reason of some matter which occurred before dismissal: s 123(1)

Activity 2 (10 minutes)

Nick commences employment under a three-year contract with Equis Ltd on 1 August 20X6. On 30 June 20X9 he is given notice that the contract is not to be renewed. Assuming that he has a case, what claims may he bring against Equis Ltd?

5 REDUNDANCY

An employee may claim a redundancy payment where he is

• Dismissed by his employer by reason of redundancy
• Laid off or kept on short time

5.1 What is redundancy?

Definition

> A dismissal is treated as caused by **redundancy** if the only or main reason is that:
>
> • The employer has ceased, or intends to cease, to carry on the business (or the local establishment of the business) in which the employee has been employed.
>
> • The requirements of that business for employees to carry on the work done by the employee have ceased or diminished (or are expected to): s 139 (1).

If the employee's contract requires him to work at other places than his present place of employment, and the employer **under the terms of the contract** requires him to move to a different place of work because there is no longer work at his present place of employment, that is not a case of redundancy, although in some cases it might be constructive dismissal.

The Court of Appeal has decided that the proper test for determining whether or not an employee is redundant is to see whether there has been a reduction of the employers' requirements for employees to work **at the place where the person concerned is employed**.

> *High Table Ltd v Horst and Others 1997*
>
> *The facts*: High Table Ltd, contract caterers, employed waitresses who had worked for several years at one company. The client company told High Table that the waitresses were no longer required, so they were dismissed by High Table on the grounds of redundancy. The waitresses, who had mobility clauses in their contracts, alleged unfair dismissal since High Table had not tried to re-employ them somewhere else.
>
> *Decision*: The Court of Appeal ruled against them, saying that the place of work was at the client company premises and the dismissals were for genuine redundancy.

In considering whether the requirements of the business for staff have diminished, it is the *overall* position which must be considered. If for example A's job is abolished and A is moved into B's job and B is dismissed, that is a case of redundancy although B's job continues.

In *British Broadcasting Corporation v Farnworth 1998* a radio producer's fixed-term contract was not renewed and the employer advertised for a radio producer with more experience. It was held by the EAT that the less experienced radio producer was indeed redundant as the requirement for her level of services had diminished.

If the employer reorganises his business or alters his methods so that the same work has to be done by different means which are beyond the capacity of the employee, that is not redundancy.

217

North Riding Garages v Butterwick 1967
The facts: a garage reorganised its working arrangements so that the workshop manager's duties included more administrative work . He was dismissed when it was found he could not perform these duties.

Decision: his claim for redundancy pay must fail since it was not a case of redundancy.

Vaux and Associated Breweries v Ward 1969
The facts: the owners of a public house renovated their premises and as part of the new image they dismissed the middle-aged barmaid and replaced her with a younger employee.

Decision: the claim for redundancy pay must fail since the same job still existed.

You should link your studies on redundancy and unfair dismissal to the material on remedies.

5.2 Calculation of redundancy pay

Redundancy pay is calculated on the same basis as the basic compensation for unfair dismissal.

5.3 Exceptions to the right to redundancy payment

A person is excluded from having a right to redundancy payment where:

- They do not fit the **definition** of 'employee' given in statute
- They have not been **continuously employed** for **two** years
- They have been or could be dismissed for **misconduct**
- An offer to **renew the contract** is unreasonably **refused**
- Claim is made **out of time** (after six months)
- The **employee leaves** before **being** made redundant having been notified of the possibility of redundancies

Misconduct of the employee

An employee who is dismissed for **misconduct** is **not entitled to redundancy pay** even though he may become redundant.

Sanders v Neale 1974
The facts: in the course of a dispute employees refused to work normally. The employer dismissed them and closed down his business. The employees claimed redundancy pay.

Decision: the claim must be dismissed since the employees had repudiated the contract before the employer's decision to close down made them redundant.

An employee can be dismissed for misconduct but still claim redundancy pay in the event of a strike:

- After receiving notice of termination of the contract from the employer

- After the employee has given notice claiming redundancy pay on account of lay-off or short time

Offer of further employment

The employer may offer a redundant employee alternative employment for the future. If the employee then unreasonably refuses the offer, he loses his entitlement to redundancy pay: s 141.

The offer must be of alternative employment **in the same capacity,** at the same place and on the same terms and conditions as the previous employment. It should not be perceived as being lower in status: *Cambridge District Co-operative Society v Ruse 1993.*

When there is a difference between the terms and conditions of a new contract and the previous contract, the employee is entitled to a **four-week trial** period in the new employment. If either party terminates the new contract during the trial period, it is treated as a case of dismissal for redundancy at the expiry date of the previous employment. The employee can also still bring claims for unfair dismissal: *Trafalgar House Services Ltd v Carder 1997.*

5.4 Lay-off and short time

An employee's exact remuneration may depend on the employer providing work. He is 'laid off' in any week in which he earns nothing by reason of lack of work or he is 'kept on short time', which is any week in which he earns less than half a normal week's pay: s 86.

When an employee is **laid off** or **kept on short time** for four or more consecutive weeks, or six weeks in a period of thirteen weeks he **may claim redundancy** pay by giving notice to the employer of his intention to claim.

In addition to his notice of claim the employee must also give notice to the employer to terminate the contract of employment: s 150(1).

5.5 Strike action

Employees involved in **strike action after** redundancy notice is served **will** be entitled to redundancy payments. However, if they are **on strike** when the notice is served they will **not** be eligible for the payment.

Chapter roundup

- When an employment contract is terminated by notice there is **no** breach of contract unless the **contents** of the notice (such as notice period) are themselves in breach.

- Where employment is **terminated by notice** the period given must **not be less** than the **statutory minimum**.

- **Breach of the employment contract** occurs where there is **summary dismissal**, **constructive dismissal**, **inability** on the employer's side to **continue employment**, or **repudiation** of the contract by the employee.

- Where the employer has **summarily dismissed** an employee without notice (as where the employer becomes insolvent), there may be a claim for **damages** at common law for **wrongful dismissal**.

- Generally, the only **effective remedy** available to a **wrongfully dismissed** employee is a claim for **damages** based on **the loss of earnings**. The measure of damages is usually the sum that would have been earned if **proper notice** had been given.

- Certain employees have a right not to be **unfairly dismissed**. Breach of that right allows an employee to claim compensation from a tribunal. To claim for unfair dismissal, the employee must satisfy certain criteria.

- Dismissal must be **justified** if it related to the employee's capability or qualifications, the employee's conduct, redundancy, legal prohibition or restriction on the employee's continued employment or some other substantial reason.

- Dismissal is **automatically unfair** if it is on the grounds of trade union membership or activities, refusal to join a trade union, pregnancy, redundancy when others are retained, a criminal conviction which is 'spent' under the Rehabilitation of Offenders Act 1974 or race or sex.

- Remedies for **unfair dismissal** include:
  - **Reinstatement**
  - **Re-engagement**
  - **Compensation**

- Dismissal is caused by **redundancy** when the employer has ceased to carry on the business in which the employee has been employed or the business no longer needs employees to carry on that work. In these circumstances, dismissal is **presumed** by the courts to be by redundancy unless otherwise demonstrated.

Quick quiz

1   To how much notice is an employee with five years' continuous service entitled?

2   Is summary dismissal ever justified? If so, when?

3   If an employer cannot continue with the employment contract because the company has gone into liquidation, does that constitute breach of contract?

Yes ☐

No ☐

4   **Fill in the blanks** below, using the words in the box.

To claim (1) .... for unfair dismissal, three issues have to be considered.

* The employee must show that he is a (2) .... employee and that he has been (3) ....

* The (4) .... must show what was the (5) .... for dismissal

* Application has to be made to the (6) .... within (7) .... months of the dismissal

• qualifying	• dismissed	• employer
• reason	• three	• compensation
• employment tribunal		

5   Expiry of a fixed-term contract without renewal amounts to a dismissal.

True ☐

False ☐

6   Which of the following is *not* a question that a tribunal, when considering an employer's reasonableness in an unfair dismissal claim, will want to answer?

A   What would a reasonable employer have done?
B   Has the correct procedure been applied?
C   Has any employee been dismissed in this way before?
D   Did the employer take all circumstances into consideration?

7   Give an automatically fair reason for dismissal.

8   Which is the most frequent remedy awarded for unfair dismissal?

A   Compensation
B   Re-engagement
C   Re-instalment

9   An employee is not entitled to redundancy pay if he resigns voluntarily.

True ☐

False ☐

Answers to quick quiz

1   Five weeks (one week for each year's continuous service). (see para 1.1)

2   Yes, in cases of serious breach of contract by the employee. (para 2.1)

3   Yes, the contract is effectively repudiated. (para 2.3)

4   (1) compensation (2) qualifying (3) dismissed (4) employer (5) reason (6) employment tribunal (7) three (para 4.1)

5   True. Non-renewal constitutes dismissal. (para 4.1)

6   C. The question is irrelevant to the employee's situation. (para 4.3)

7   Being a threat to national security (alternatively, taking part in unofficial industrial action). (para 4.4)

8   Compensation, as in most cases the working relationship would have been irrevocably damaged. (para 4.6)

9   True, as he is not being made redundant. (para 5.3)

Answers to activities

1   **Wrongful dismissal** is a common law concept arising in specific circumstances and which gives the employee an action for breach of contract, for example where insufficient notice has been given.

   Unfair dismissal is a statutory concept introduced by employment protection legislation. As a rule, every employee has the right not to be unfairly dismissed: s 54. Note that the distinction between wrongful and unfair dismissal depends not so much upon the nature of the dismissal, as on the remedies available.

2   For the purposes of the Act, dismissal occurs when a fixed term contract is not renewed even though such an eventuality is implicit in the fact that the agreement has a fixed term. Nick is therefore entitled to claim for redundancy pay and/or compensation for unfair dismissal if he can prove the requisite facts. However, non-renewal cannot give rise to a claim for wrongful dismissal, which is only possible when there has been summary dismissal or dismissal with less than the required period of notice.

PART D

THE LAW OF TORT

224

Chapter 12:

INTRODUCTION TO TYPES OF TORT

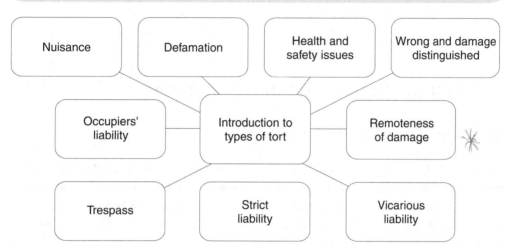

Introduction

There is no entirely satisfactory definition of tort. The principle is that the law gives various rights to persons, such as the right of a person in possession of land to occupy it without interference or invasion by trespassers. When such a right is infringed the wrongdoer is liable in tort. The law of tort is concerned really with a person's responsibility to others. It applies to both individuals and companies.

There is therefore a duty imposed by law to respect the legal rights of others. When a tort is committed the remedy is an action at common law for unliquidated damages (ie damages not established by a formula in a contract), which represent such compensation as the court may see fit to award. The principles of tort are based on rights, the related duty to respect them and compensation for infringement.

Tort is distinguished from other legal wrongs.

(a) A **crime** is an offence prohibited by law. The state **prosecutes** the offender and **punishment** is by fine or imprisonment. A tort is a **civil wrong** and the person wronged **sues** in a civil court for compensation (or for an injunction against repetition).

(b) **Breach of contract** and breach of trust are **civil wrongs**. It must be shown that the defendant was subject to the obligations of a contract or a trust and did not perform or observe those obligations. In tort no previous transaction or relationship need exist: the parties may be complete strangers.

Your objectives

In this chapter you will learn about the following.

    (a)   The significance of both wrong and damage

    (b)   How damage is assessed for remoteness

    (c)   When an employer may be responsible for a tort committed by an employee

    (d)   The rule in *Rylands v Fletcher*

    (e)   Trespass and occupiers' liability

    (f)   Health and safety issues

1   WRONG AND DAMAGE DISTINGUISHED

1.1   Wrong (*injuria*) and damage (*damnum*)

When a claimant sues in tort claiming damages as compensation for loss, he must normally prove his loss. But the necessary basis of his claim is that he has suffered a wrong. If there is no wrong (*injuria*) for which the law gives a remedy, no amount of damage (*damnum*) caused by the defendant can make him liable. *Damnum sine injuria* (loss not caused by wrong) is not actionable.

> *Electrochrome v Welsh Plastics 1968*
> *The facts*: the defendant's lorry, driven carelessly, crashed into a fire hydrant. As a result the water supply to the claimant's factory nearby was cut off. The factory had to close until the supply was restored. The claimant claimed damages for his loss.
>
> *Held*: the fire hydrant was not the claimant's property and so, in spite of his loss, no legal wrong had been done to him for which he could hold the defendant liable.

In some torts it is necessary to establish both wrong and loss resulting from it; this is the rule in the tort of negligence. But in other cases, for example, trespass or libel, it is enough to prove that a legal wrong has been done and damages (possibly nominal in amount) may be recovered without proof of any loss (*injuria sine damno*). Substantial damages may be awarded where the loss is serious, but difficult to quantify in money terms, as in cases of damage to reputation by defamation.

Negligence will be covered in the next chapter.

1.2   Motive

In tort, unlike crime, it is not usually necessary to prove anything about the defendant's state of mind. A good motive will not excuse a tortious act and a bad motive (*malice*) will not turn an innocent act into a tortious one. (There are a few exceptions such as the tort of **malicious prosecution** where there must be evidence of malice.)

> *Mayor of Bradford v Pickles 1895*
> *The facts*: P wished the Bradford Corporation to buy his land, adjoining the corporation's water reservoir, at a very high price. He sank a shaft on his

land to divert the flow of subterranean water through it (as he was legally entitled to do). As a result less water flowed into the reservoir and it was discoloured. The corporation sued for an injunction, a court order to P to desist.

Decision: the action must fail. P was exercising his rights as a landowner and was not infringing any rights of the corporation. It was immaterial that the corporation had suffered loss and that P's express motive was to inflict loss.

Activity 1   **(10 minutes)**

Tony plants trees in his garden. The roots remain on his land, but the trees soak up water from Peter's garden next door, thereby causing Peter's plants to wither. Is there *injuria*? Is there *damnum*?

2   REMOTENESS OF DAMAGE

When a person commits a tort with the intention of causing loss or harm which in fact results from the wrongful act, that loss or harm can never be too remote a consequence. Damages will be awarded for it.

2.1   *Novus actus interveniens*

However, if the sequence of cause and effect includes a new act (called a *novus actus interveniens*) of a third party or of the claimant, it may terminate the defendant's liability at that point: further consequences are too remote and he is not required to pay compensation for them. But where the intervening act is that of a third party who could be expected to behave as he did in the situation arising from the defendant's original wrongful act, the intervening act does not break the chain of liability.

> *Scott v Shepherd 1773*
> *The facts*: A threw a lighted firework cracker into a crowded market. It landed on the stall of B who threw it away. It then landed on the stall of C who threw it away and it then hit D in the face and blinded him in one eye. D sued A.
>
> *Held*: there was no break in the chain of causation from A's intentional wrongful act despite the fact that it was C who actually threw it so it hit D. A was liable to D.

Courts will only impart liability where there is a cause of events that are a **probable** result of the defendant's actions. Defendants will not be liable for damage when the chain of events is broken. There are **three types** of intervening act that will break the chain of causation.

Act of the claimant

The actions of the claimant themselves may **break** the chain of causation. The rule is that where the act is **reasonable** and in the **ordinary course of things** an act by the claimant will not break the chain.

McKew v Holland, Hannen and Cubbitts (Scotland) Ltd (1969)
The facts: the claimant had a leg injury which was prone to causing his leg to give way from time to time. While at work he failed to ask for assistance when negotiating a flight of stairs. He fell and was injured as a result.

Decision: the fact that the claimant failed to seek assistance was unreasonable and was sufficient to break the chain of causality.

Act of a third party

Where a **third party** intervenes in the course of events the defendant will normally only be liable for damage **until** the intervention.

2.2 Reasonable foresight

If the intervening act is that of the claimant himself and he acts unreasonably, for example, by taking an avoidable and foreseeable risk of injury to himself, that breaks the chain (or if it does not it may reduce his claim for loss because of his contributory negligence).

When there is a sequence of physical cause and effect without human intervention, the ultimate loss is too remote (so that damages cannot be recovered for it) unless it could have been reasonably foreseen that some loss of that kind might occur as a consequence of the wrong.

The Wagon Mound 1961
The facts: a ship (the *Wagon Mound*) was taking on furnace oil in Sydney harbour. By negligence oil was spilled onto the water and it drifted to a wharf 200 yards away where welding equipment was being used to repair another ship. The owner of the wharf at first stopped work because of the fire risk but later resumed working because he was advised that sparks from a welding torch were unlikely to set fire to furnace oil. Safety precautions were taken. A spark fell onto a piece of cotton waste floating in the oil and this served as a wick, thereby starting a fire which caused damage to the wharf. The owners of the wharf sued the charterers of the *Wagon Mound*, basing their claim on an earlier decision that damage caused by a direct and uninterrupted sequence of physical events is never too remote even though it could not reasonably be foreseen.

Decision: the claim must fail. The earlier decision was overruled and the reasonable foresight test was laid down. Pollution was the foreseeable risk: fire was not. This was a decision of the Privy Council on appeal from Australia and as such only a persuasive precedent for English courts. But as it was a decision of the most senior English judges, it is always applied in cases where the claim is for negligence.

Hughes v Lord Advocate 1963
The facts: workmen left lighted paraffin lamps as a warning sign of an open manhole in the street. Two small boys took one of the lamps as a light and went down the manhole. As they clambered out the lamp fell into the hole and caused an explosion in which the boys were injured. Evidence was given that a fire might have been foreseen but an explosion was improbable.

Decision: the defendants were liable for negligence in leaving the lamps where they did. A risk of fire was foreseeable and the explosion must be regarded as 'an unexpected manifestation of the apprehended physical dangers'. It was not (as it was in the *Wagon Mound* case) damage of an entirely different kind.

Doughty v Turner Manufacturing Co 1964
The facts: an asbestos cement lid accidentally fell into a cauldron of sodium cyanide at a temperature of 800 degrees Centigrade. The intense heat caused a chemical change in the asbestos lid as a result of which there was an explosion. The claimant was injured by the eruption of molten liquid. The chemical reaction leading to the explosion was previously unknown to science.

Decision: a splash of sodium cyanide was foreseeable but a violent explosion was not. The result was unforeseeable as no one knew it could happen and therefore too remote.

The House of Lords decided in the case of *Jolley v London Borough of Sutton (2000)* that the remoteness test can be passed if *some* harm is foreseeable even if the exact nature of the injuries could not be.

Jolley v London Borough of Sutton (2000)
The facts: the defendants should have removed a boat which had been dumped two years previously. A teenage boy was injured while attempting to repair it.

Decision: even though the precise incident was not foreseeable, the authority should have foreseen that some harm could be caused since they knew children regularly played on the abandoned boat.

In cases of physical injury which is more serious than would normally be expected because the claimant proves to be abnormally vulnerable, the defendant is liable for the full amount of injury done. This is the thin skull (or 'eggshell skull') principle: if A taps B on the head and cracks B's skull because it is abnormally thin, A is liable for the fracture.

Smith v Leech Braine & Co 1962
The facts: a workman was near a tank of molten zinc in which metal articles were dipped to galvanise them. One article was allowed to slip and the workman was burnt on the lip by a drop of molten zinc. The burn activated latent cancer from which he died three years later. His widow sued for damages.

Decision: damages for a fatal accident would be awarded. Some physical injury (the burn on the lip) was a foreseeable consequence. The defendants must accept liability for the much more serious physical injury (cancer) caused by their negligence.

If the claimant suffers avoidable loss because his lack of resources prevents him from taking costly measures to reduce his loss, he may still recover damages for it: *Martindale v Duncan 1973*.

Activity 2   **(10 minutes)**

A factory owner noticed that a machine was not running smoothly. She had heard of similar cases in which the increased vibration had led to small parts flying off and causing minor injuries, so she warned the workers to check that all such parts were secure and instructed them to carry on using the machine. The motor disintegrated and part of it broke through the casing and badly injured a worker, who then sued the factory owner. Why would the factory owner be unlikely to be able to rely on either *The Wagon Mound 1961* or *Doughty v Turner Manufacturing Co 1964* in her defence?

3   VICARIOUS LIABILITY

Definitions

> **Tortfeasor**: a person who commits a tort.
>
> **Joint and several liability**. Where one person commits a tort, another person may be liable jointly with the tortfeasor, or even separately on his own if the tortfeasor has disappeared.

A tortfeasor is always liable for his wrong. Others may be jointly and severally liable with him under the principle of **vicarious liability**. If, for example, a partner commits a tort either with the authority of the other partners or in the ordinary course of the firm's business, the other partners are liable with him.

The most important application of the principle of vicarious liability is to the **relationship of employer and employee**. It is often not worthwhile to sue the individual employee for damages since he is unable to pay them. The employer however has greater resources and may also have insurance cover.

To make the employer liable for a tort of the employee it is necessary that:

(a)   there is the relationship between them of **employer and employee**; and

(b)   the employee's tort is **committed in the course of his employment**.

The employee remains liable as a joint tortfeasor and has an obligation to indemnify his employer where the latter has to pay damages. The employers liability is 'strict', ie does not depend on proof of fault on his part.

3.1   Relationship of employer and employee

The existence of the employer/employee relationship is usually fairly obvious. It is characterised by such features as a contract of service and the deduction by the employer of PAYE and national insurance from the employee's gross pay. However in certain cases it is not clear whether a person is an employee or an independent contractor, and the courts have devised certain tests to establish whether the employer/employee relationship exists in such situations. The distinction is important because, if it does not, there is no vicarious liability except in certain special cases.

The parties therefore are obliged to reach an express understanding as to whether or not there is a contract of employment. But their expressed intentions do not necessarily prevail.

Ferguson v John Dawson & Partners 1976

The facts: a builder's labourer worked 'on the lump' – he was paid his wages without deduction of income tax or National Insurance contributions and worked as a self-employed contractor providing services. But his 'employer' could dismiss him, decide on which site he would work, direct him as to the work he should do and also provided the tools which he used. He was injured in an accident and sued his employers on the basis that they owed him legal duties as their employee.

Held: on the facts taken as a whole, he was an employee working under a contract of employment.

Massey v Crown Life Assurance 1978

The facts: M was originally employed by an insurance company as a departmental manager; he also earned commission on business which he introduced. At his own request he changed to a self-employed basis. Tax etc was no longer deducted by the employers but he continued to perform the same duties. The employers terminated these arrangements and M claimed compensation for unfair dismissal on the basis that he had continued to be an employee.

Held: as he had opted to become self-employed and his status in the organisation was consistent with that situation, he must abide by his decision. His claim to be a dismissed employee failed.

3.2 Tests applied by the courts

In borderline cases such as these it can be unclear whether a person is an employee or an independent contractor. The tests of **control**, **integration** into the employer's organisation, and **economic reality** (or the multiple test) are applied in such cases.

The control test

Has the employer *control* over the way in which the employee performs his duties?

Mersey Docks & Harbour Board v Coggins & Griffiths (Liverpool) 1947

The facts: stevedores hired a crane with its driver from the harbour board under a contract which provided that the driver (appointed and paid by the harbour board) should be the employee of the stevedores. Owing to the driver's negligence a checker was injured. The case was concerned with whether the stevedores or the harbour board were vicariously liable as employers.

Held: in the House of Lords, that the issue must be settled on the facts and not on the terms of the contract. The stevedores could only be treated as employers of the driver if they could control in detail how he did his work. But although they could instruct him what to do, they could not control him in how he operated the crane. The harbour board (as 'general employer') was therefore still the driver's employer.

The integration test

If the employee is so skilled that he cannot be controlled in the performance of his duties, was he appointed and assigned to his duties by the employer – was he **integrated** into the employer's organisation?

Cassidy v Ministry of Health 1951

The facts: the full-time assistant medical officer at a hospital carried out a surgical operation in a negligent fashion. The patient sued the Ministry of Health as employer. The Ministry resisted the claim arguing that it had no control over the doctor in his medical work.

Decision: in such circumstances the proper test was whether the employer appointed the employee, selected him for his task and so integrated him into the organisation. If the patient had chosen the doctor the Ministry would not have been liable as employer. But here the Ministry (the hospital management) made the choice and so it was liable.

The multiple test

Is the employee working **on his own account**?

Ready Mixed Concrete (South East) v Ministry of Pensions & National Insurance 1968

The facts: the driver of a special vehicle worked for one company only in the delivery of liquid concrete to building sites. He provided his own vehicle (obtained on hire purchase from the company) and was responsible for its maintenance and repair. He was free to provide a substitute driver. The vehicle was painted in the company's colours and the driver wore its uniform. He was paid gross amounts (no tax etc deducted) on the basis of mileage and quantity delivered as a self-employed contractor. The Ministry of Pensions claimed that he was in fact an employee for whom the company should make the employer's insurance contributions.

Decision: in such cases the most important test is whether the worker is working on his own account (the **entrepreneurial** test or **multiple** test). On these facts the driver was a self-employed transport contractor and not an employee.

Other factors

Other significant factors are as follows.

(a) Does the employee use his own **tools and equipment** or does the employer provide them?

(b) Does the alleged employer have the power to **select or appoint its employees**, and may it dismiss them?

(c) **Payment of salary** is, as mentioned above, a fair indication of there being a contract of employment. But there are exceptions. A person may still be an employee if he is paid no salary but derives his income solely from commission or tips. A person may receive a salary but not be an employee – for instance, Members of Parliament.

(d) Working for a number of different people is not necessarily a sign of self-employment. A number of assignments may be construed as a series of employments: *Hull v Lorimer 1994*.

In difficult cases, the court will also consider whether the 'employee' can **delegate** all his obligations (in which case, there is no contract of employment), whether there is restriction as to place of work, whether there is an obligation to work and whether holidays and hours of work are agreed.

> *O'Kelly v Trusthouse Forte Plc 1983*
> *The facts*: the employee was a 'regular casual' working when required as a waiter in the banqueting department of the Grosvenor Hotel. There was an understanding that he would accept work when offered and that the employer would give him preference over other more 'casual' employees, though they were all paid at the same rate. The industrial tribunal held that there was no contract of employment because the employer had no obligation to provide work and the employee had no obligation to accept work when offered. The Employment Appeal Tribunal however held that there had been a sequence of contracts of employment on each occasion.
>
> *Decision*: the Court of Appeal reinstated the finding of the industrial tribunal since it was a reasonable conclusion drawn from the particular facts. Whether there is a contract of employment is a question of law but it depends entirely on the facts of each case; here there was no 'mutuality of obligations' and hence no contract.

3.3 Torts committed in the course of employment

The employer is only liable for the employee's torts committed **in the course of employment**. Otherwise you could have the silly situation of an employer being liable for an employee's motorcycle accident while driving a private bike on holiday.

The law relating to whether an employee was acting in the course of his employment has recently been revised considerably by the following case.

> *Lister and ors v Hesley Hall Ltd 2001*
> *The facts*: the warden of a boarding school was found guilty of sexually abusing children resident there.
>
> *Decision*: the school was vicariously liable. The nature of the warden's work created a sufficient connection between the acts of abuse which he had committed and the work which he was employed to do.

Obviously, in this case, the school did not employ the warden for the purposes of abusing the children. In that sense, he was not acting in the course of his employment when he carried out the abuse. However, the House of Lords concluded that the acts that he carried out were so closely connected with the nature of his work, that it was fair and just to hold employer liable. In other words, he was employed to look after the children, and the torts committed were in his work time, in the place where he was employed and while he was carrying out his employed duty to care for the children.

Whether this 'close connection' between the employee's tort and his employment exists must be decided by the court on the facts of each case. Two further cases in which the test has been applied since the *Lister* case are:

Dubai Aluminium Co Ltd v Salaam and ors 2002
The facts: A, a solicitor, drafted bogus agreements.

Decision: the drafting of agreements of this nature (but for a proper purpose) would be within the ordinary course of business for a solicitor. Therefore, the dishonest acts were sufficiently closely connected to the course of his business for his employers to be vicariously liable for those acts.

Attorney General v Hartwell 2004
The facts: a police constable in the British Virgin Islands was on duty when he went to a restaurant where his partner worked as a waitress. He fired several shots at his partner and her male companion. One shot hit a British tourist, who sustained serious injuries.

Decision: the Privy Council found that the Attorney General (as the representative of the Government of the British Virgin Isles) was not vicariously liable for the personal injury sustained by the British tourist. The acts of the policeman were not closely connected to his employment, and in fact had nothing to do with his police duties. He was pursuing a personal vendetta.

3.4 Vicarious liability and agency

A principal is vicariously liable for a tort committed by an agent acting within the limits of his authority and carrying out the acts for which he was appointed as agent.

Ormrod v Crossville Motor Services 1953
The facts: a car owner asked a friend to drive his car to Monte Carlo where the owner was going to take part in a rally and then they were going to holiday together after the rally. The friend's negligent driving caused damage to the claimant's bus.

Decision: the owner was vicariously liable for his friend's negligence. It was irrelevant that the friend was driving to Monte Carlo partly for his own purposes.

Activity 3 (10 minutes)

A research chemist employed by a drug company works in a laboratory in which, for safety reasons, all experiments involving the application of heat are forbidden. The chemist tries a reaction in which heat is spontaneously generated, and an explosion results, injuring other employees. Discuss whether the chemist acted in the course of his employment.

3.5 Independent contractors

If someone works for someone else and is not an employee, they are likely to be described as an **independent contractor**. Normally the person who engages an independent contractor is not liable for the latter's tortious acts. Generally, independent contractors are liable for their own torts. For example a builder may engage casual workers, such as electricians and plumbers, to work on specific projects. Such individuals are likely to be liable for their own wrongful acts.

However, a person who has work done not by his employee but by an independent contractor, such as a freelance plumber used by a builder, is vicariously liable for torts of the contractor in the following circumstances.

(a) The operation creates a hazard for users of the highway, as in repair of a structure adjoining or overhanging a pavement or road.

(b) The operation is exceptionally risky.

> *Honeywill & Stein v Larkin Bros 1934*
> *The facts*: decorators who had redecorated the interior of a cinema brought in a photographer to take pictures of their work. The photographer's magnesium flare set fire to the cinema.
>
> *Decision*: in commissioning an inherently risky operation through a contractor the decorators were liable for his negligence in causing the fire.

(c) The duty is personal. For example, an employer has a common law duty to his employees to take reasonable care in providing safe plant and a safe working system. If he employs a contractor he remains liable for any negligence of the latter in his work.

(d) There is negligence in selecting a contractor who is not competent to do the work entrusted to him.

(e) The operation is one for which there is strict liability (see below).

4 STRICT LIABILITY

In many torts the defendant is liable because he acted intentionally or at least negligently. He may escape liability if he shows that he acted with reasonable care. That is essentially the position in the tort of negligence itself. But there are also torts which result from **breach of an absolute duty: the defendant is liable even though he took reasonable care.**

4.1 The rule in *Rylands v Fletcher*

The outstanding example of a tort of strict liability is the rule in *Rylands v Fletcher*.

'Where a person who, for his own purposes, brings and keeps on land in his occupation anything likely to do mischief if it escapes, he must keep it in at his peril, and if he fails to do so he is liable for all damage naturally accruing from the escape.'

> *Rylands v Fletcher 1868*
> *The facts*: F employed competent contractors to construct a reservoir to store water for his mill. In their work the contractors uncovered old mine workings which appeared to be blocked with earth. They did no more to seal them off and it was accepted at the trial that there was no want of reasonable care on their part. When the reservoir was filled, the water burst through the workings and flooded the mine of R on adjoining land.
>
> *Decision*: F was liable for the damage suffered by R, and the principle quoted above was laid down.

Activity 4   **(5 minutes)**

A is the owner of a piece of land, and he knows that natural gas tends to accumulate in caverns under the land. Building works by A cause one of the caverns holding this gas to fracture, and the resulting escape of gas causes a fire on B's adjoining land. Why could B not sue A under the rule in Rylands v Fletcher?

Many industrial processes entail the artificial ('non-natural') accumulation of water, gas or other materials which may cause damage if they escape. In such cases the occupier of the land is liable even if the escape occurs without negligence or want of care on his part. It has, however, been held in a more modern case (*British Celanese v Hunt 1969*) that not every escape of industrial materials gives rise to this strict liability. Industrial activities, as distinct from the accumulation of materials, can be a natural use of the land and so be outside the rule.

Polluters may be strictly liable for the tort of nuisance. However forseeability of damage is required for there to be liability for nuisance.

> *Cambridge Water Co v Eastern Counties Leather plc 1994*
> *The facts*: the defendant, a firm involved in the tanning industry, stored organochlorines on its premises. The only foreseeable damage at the time was that someone working there might become overcome by fumes. The chemical seeped into the ground and a nearby public water supply borehole, over a mile away, became polluted. The claimant, who had to spend nearly £1 million developing a new source of supply to meet an EC directive on the quality of water, made claims in nuisance and based on the rule in *Rylands v Fletcher*.
>
> *Held*: the defendants were not liable. The claimants had a right to extract water from beneath their land and liability for interference with this right was strict. However, the House of Lords decided unanimously that there could be no liability for unforeseeable damage.

It was argued in this case that the liability in *Rylands v Fletcher* is not intended to be any more strict than liability in nuisance. In *The Wagon Mound*, it was held that foreseeability of damage was essential for liability in nuisance. In addition, the language used in *Rylands v Fletcher* itself implies that damage must be foreseeable: 'anything likely to do mischief'. In giving judgement in the *Cambridge Water Co* case, the House of Lords made it clear that *Rylands v Fletcher* was broadly an extension of the principles of nuisance to cases of isolated escape from land. Thus the decision in *The Wagon Mound* should extend to determining whether there is liability in cases such as the *Cambridge Water Co* case.

The decision in the *Cambridge Water Co* case reduces the significance of *Rylands v Fletcher* and suggests that liability will in future be very close to 'ordinary' negligence liability, with foreseeability being a requirement

5 TRESPASS

5.1 Trespass

Trespass is one of oldest torts and takes three forms.

(a) Trespass to the **person**: battery, assault, false imprisonment

(b) Trespass to **land**: unlawful interference with the possession of someone's land

(c) Trespass to **goods**: wrongful interference with a person's possession of goods, eg destroying or stealing

We will look at trespass to land in more detail.

Trespass to land is one of the oldest actions known to the common law, and involves **direct** interference. No damage need be proved, as the **interference itself** is enough to establish liability. Being a wrong to **possession** rather than **ownership**, the claimant need not be the owner of the land. Thus a landlord cannot sue for trespass while a lease subsists. **Deliberate entry** to the land is sufficient, and it does not matter that the defendant did not know he was on the claimant's land, or believed the entry was authorised.

Actions in trespass and nuisance differ because nuisance normally requires proof of damage, and is concerned with consequential harm. To take an example, it is **trespass** to throw stones onto somebody's land, but **nuisance** to allow a fence to become so dilapidated that it collapses on to land (*Mann v Saulnier 1959*). In *Southport Corporation v Esso Petroleum Co Ltd 1954* there was a question as to whether discharging oil into the sea, which was then carried to shore, amounted to trespass.

Trespass to land may take the following forms.

- Entering onto land

- Remaining on the land for longer than entitled

- Placing objects or rubbish on the land: *Westripp v Baldock 1938* (ladder against a wall)

- Abusing permission to be on the land: *Hickman v Maisey 1900* (racing tout watching racehorses in training)

- Driving animals on to land

Rights to possession of land extend to the *subsoil* beneath and the *airspace* above. Trespass in airspace is limited to the height at which intrusion limits full use of the land (*Kelsen v Imperial Tobacco Co Ltd 1957*). So it is not trespass to fly an aircraft over land at a reasonable height (Civil Aviation Act 1982).

Justification of trespass

Trespass to land may be justified in the following circumstances.

- After the granting of a *licence* to enter the land (eg to view a sporting event)
- **Right of entry** conferred by the owner
- Public **right of way**
- **Statutory powers** of entry (eg police powers)
- Necessity

Trespass ab initio

This is a special rule that applies where the defendant entered land under the authority of the law, but subsequently abuses that authority (eg police entering and seizing documents unlawfully: *Elias v Pasmore 1934*.

The rule is that the authority to enter, having been abused by the subsequent wrongful act, is cancelled retrospectively so that the exercise of the authority becomes actionable as a trespass. The claimant may recover damages for the entire trespass, and not merely the wrongful portion of it.

There are limits to the rule.

(a)   It only applies to acts done in pursuance of an entry done under **authority of the law**.

(b)   It only applies when the abuse amounts to a **positive wrongful act**, not an omission. In the *Six Carpenters' Case 1610*, where the carpenters refused to pay for bread and wine they had consumed at an inn, it was held that they were not trespassers *ab initio*.

(c)   A lawful entry does not become a trespass *ab initio* unless the abuse takes away the entire grounds for the entry. Any independent grounds for entry which is unaffected by the abuse will protect it from the rule: *Chic Fashions (West Wales) Ltd v Jones 1968*.

5.2   Remedies to an action for trespass

The claimant may seek **damages** or an **injunction** or both. In the case of trivial trespass, damages are likely to be nominal, but where the trespass has caused physical damage, then damages are measured by **diminution in value** of the land.

A person who has been dispossessed may bring an action for **ejection**, or take it upon himself to effect **re-entry**. He is entitled to use reasonable force to expel a trespasser if he has first asked him to leave.

We shall look at remedies in more detail in Chapter 14.

6   OCCUPIERS' LIABILITY

6.1   Businesses as occupiers

One area of the law of tort which can potentially have a significant impact on businesses is occupiers' liability for damage or injury caused to people coming on to their premises.

An occupier of premises is any person (not necessarily the owner) who has control or possession of them. Occupation may be shared by two or more persons.

6.2   The liability to visitors

By statute (Occupiers' Liability Acts 1957 and 1984) an **occupier** owes a duty ('a common **duty of care**') to all **visitors** to the **premises** and must take such precautions as are necessary to make the premises reasonably safe for the purpose for which the visitor is permitted to enter them.

An occupier of premises is the person who has control of the premises. Ownership alone is not sufficient to constitute occupancy. In *Wheat v Lacon & Co Ltd 1966* it was held that the owners of a public house, which was managed by a manager, were nevertheless occupiers of it because of the degree of control they exercised over it.

Definition

A **visitor**:

(a) A person who enters the premises with the actual or implied permission (or invitation) of the occupier

(b) A person such as a health inspector who has a legal right of entry

A person who enters to do business with the occupier is deemed to have implied permission although he may in fact not wish to see the visitor – as an example, a casual call by a sales representative hoping to sell his products to the occupier would make him a visitor. But there is no duty of care to a visitor who, after entering the premises, **exceeds the limits of the permitted purpose**, say by straying into parts of the building unconnected with his visit; he then becomes a trespasser.

Premises include not only land and buildings, but also fixed and moveable structures. Case law suggests that this definition is wide enough to include a mechanical digger, scaffolding and a lift.

The duty of care may vary with the visitor. An occupier is entitled to assume that lawful visitors will display ordinary prudence while on his premises.

(a) If the visitor is a specialist, for example a technician called in to do repairs, he is deemed to be aware of special risks incidental to his calling (eg no liability for the death by carbon monoxide poisoning of two sweeps called in to close a hole in a boiler chimney: *Roles v Nathan 1963*).

(b) If he is a child, a higher standard of care is imposed on the occupier.

The occupier may discharge his duty to visitors as follows.

(a) **By taking reasonable measures**, such as repair work, to eliminate a hazard. He is not responsible for faulty work of an independent contractor, brought in to do specialist work. But he should inspect it. Thus an occupier will not be liable for the unsafe state of a lift due to negligence of the specialist firm employed to repair it but he remains liable when a school cleaner leaves slippery ice on a step (not a specialist task).

(b) **By giving warnings** where a warning is enough to enable the visitor to be reasonably safe. A visitor who ignores a warning may be consenting to the risk or may be guilty of contributory negligence. But a warning is not a sufficient precaution in some cases. It depends on the facts.

The occupier may in theory limit his liability to visitors on his premises by contract. But any such exclusion or limitation is restricted by the Unfair Contract Terms Act 1977 which among other provisions renders void a 'notice given to persons general' purporting to exclude or restrict liability for death or personal injury resulting from negligence. The position of employees is protected by the Health and Safety at Work Act 1974 and related statutes and regulations.

6.3 Occupier's liability to trespassers

The Occupiers' Liability Act 1984 has replaced the common law rules governing the duty of occupiers of premises to persons other than visitors. Prior to 1984, the occupier's duty to trespassers was to act with common sense and humanity. This required all the surrounding circumstances to be considered, for example the seriousness of the danger, the type of trespasser likely to enter, and in some cases the resources of the occupier.

There is no satisfactory definition of 'trespasser'. It may include the innocent as well as the malicious. Broadly speaking it is a person who knows he does not intend communication with the occupier or anyone else on the premises.

> *British Railways v Herrington 1972*
>
> *The facts*: the local management of British Rail were aware that children gained entry to an electrified railway line through a broken-down fence which divided the line from land open to the public. British Rail merely reported the matter to the police but did not repair the fence. A child of six was injured on the line.
>
> *Decision*: the occupier's duty must be set by reference to the particular circumstances of the trespassers. A warning may be sufficient for an adult but it falls short of the duty of common humanity owed to a child to safeguard it from accessible and tempting perils on the occupier's land.

The main provisions of the 1984 Act are set out below.

Duty owed

The occupier owes a duty in the following circumstances.

(a) He is aware of the danger or has reasonable grounds to believe that it exists

(b) He knows or should know that someone is in (or may come into) the vicinity of the danger

(c) The risk is one against which he may reasonably be expected to offer that person some protection

Duty broken

The duty is to take such care as is reasonable in all the circumstances to see that the person to whom a duty is owed does not suffer injury on the premises by reason of the danger.

Damage

The occupier can only be liable for injury to the person. The Act expressly provides that there can be no liability for loss or damage to property.

Warnings

The duty may be discharged (in appropriate cases) by taking reasonable steps to give warning of the danger.

A person using a right of way across land is neither a licensee nor an invitee and is therefore not a visitor. The occupier of the land is under no liability to users of the right of way for failure to keep it in good repair: *McGeown v Northern Ireland Housing Executive 1994.* Thus the 1984 Act applies to entrants other than trespassers.

6.4 Defective Premises Act 1972

This Act imposes on landlords a general liability, say to tenants' visitors, arising from a landlord's failure to repair the premises. It also imposes a statutory obligation on those who provide dwellings (landlords, builders, developers, local authorities etc) to ensure that each dwelling is fit for habitation. Furthermore, any work done (where a dwelling house is not built under an NHBC guarantee) must be carried out in a workmanlike or professional manner using proper materials A vendor of a house has similar duties towards a buyer and other persons reasonably expected to be affected.

Actions arising under the 1972 Act lie in tort. Section 1 of the Act imposes 'strict liability' regarding fitness for habitation while the duty imposed on landlords under s 3 requires proof of negligence on the part of the defendant.

7 NUISANCE

7.1 Private nuisance

Nuisance may be of two types – public and private. In private nuisance the central idea is that of interference with the claimant's enjoyment of his property. Public nuisance does not require any 'invasion' of private land, rather the annoyance of the general public.

Private nuisance is unlawful interference with the claimant's use of his property or with his health and comfort or convenience. It often takes the form of emitting noise, smell or vibration – it is essentially an indirect form of interference. If A throws garden rubbish over the fence into B's garden that is trespass; if A burns his rubbish by a series of smoky bonfires which causes real discomfort to B that may be private nuisance.

What constitutes private nuisance ?

It is important to note that private nuisance is unlawful interference. Many of the actions which constitute private nuisance are themselves lawful. It is only when they cause interference to such a degree as to be unreasonable that they become unlawful. Examples of interference which has been held to be unlawful are set out below.

(a) Physical damage to the claimant's land by flooding: *Sedleigh-Denfield v O'Callaghan 1940.*

(b) Encroachment onto the claimant's land by tree roots: *Davey v Harrow Corporation 1958.*

(c) Interference with the comfort of the claimant through smell: *Bone v Seal 1975.*

In private nuisance cases it is often necessary to strike a balance between the convenience and interests of two parties which conflict. The following factors may enter into the decision.

(a)   If the activity causes significant physical damage to property it will generally be restrained as private nuisance. If it merely causes personal discomfort the advantages and disadvantages may be balanced to determine whether the activity complained of is so unreasonable as to amount to nuisance.

(b)   Causing intentional discomfort to a neighbour is very likely to be restrained as unreasonable.

> *Christie v Davey 1893*
> *The facts*: C and D occupied adjoining semi-detached houses with a common party wall. D objected to the sounds of C's activities as a music teacher, so he made very loud noises, shouting and banging metal trays.
>
> *Held*: C's music lessons were a reasonable use of her house. D's deliberate racket, made purely to annoy, was unreasonable. D was restrained from this conduct by means of an injunction.

Physical damage

Where the claimant can establish actual damage to land or property, he is not normally required to show an additional element of interference.

> *St Helens Smelting Co v Tipping 1865*
> *The facts*: fumes from a copper smelting works damaged shrubs belonging to the claimant, who lived on an estate in a manufacturing area.
>
> *Held*: although locality was an important consideration where nuisance takes the form of interference with the occupier's comfort and enjoyment (one should not expect to breathe the clean air of the Lake District in an industrial town such as St Helens), the nature of the locality is irrelevant where the nuisance causes physical damage to property. An occupier is entitled to protection from physical damage wherever he lives.

Interference with comfort

Where there is no element of physical damage, and the alleged nuisance consists of interference with the occupier's comfort and convenience, it is for the courts to balance the conflicting interests of claimant and defendant. The test has been stated to be whether the interference is an 'inconvenience materially interfering with the ordinary comfort physically of human existence, not merely according to elegant or dainty modes and habits of living, but according to plain and sober and simple notions among the English people': *Walter v Selfe 1851*.

> *Halsey v Esso Petroleum Co Ltd 1961*
> *The facts*: the defendant operated an oil depot. The claimant lived nearby. Acid damaged clothing hanging out to dry in his garden and the paintwork of his car parked on the highway. Noise from the depot's boilers and from oil tankers arriving and departing during the night interfered with his sleep.

Held: the defendants were liable for private nuisance for the damage to clothes and the noise from the depot. (They were also liable for *public* nuisance for the damage to the motor vehicle and the noise of the oil tankers.)

By contrast in *Hunter and Others v Canary Wharf Ltd 1997* it was held that a landlord was generally entitled to build on his land as he wished and, accordingly, would not be liable in nuisance because a large building he had erected had interfered with television reception.

Abnormal sensitivity

If the claimant or the claimant's property has some abnormal sensitivity, he will be unable to restrain an interference from which a person of normal sensitivity would not require protection.

> *Robinson v Kilvert 1889*
> *The facts*: the claimant manufactured brown paper on his premises, which were situated directly above the defendant's premises. Heat from the defendant's manufacturing process damaged the brown paper, which was sensitive to heat. Ordinary paper would not have been affected.
>
> *Held*: the defendant was not liable, because his action was lawful and the claimant was carrying on an exceptionally delicate operation.

Malice

As noted above (*Christie v Davey 1893*) actions motivated by malice may constitute nuisance. Even in the case of the claimant's abnormal sensitivity, malice may tip the balance towards the defendant's conduct being unreasonable.

> *Hollywood Silver Fox Farm Ltd v Emmett 1936*
> *The facts*: the claimants bred silver foxes, which become very nervous during their breeding season and may, if disturbed, devour their own young. The defendant discharged guns on his own land in order to interfere with the foxes' breeding.
>
> *Held*: the defendant was liable – he had been motivated by the malicious intention of causing damage. His argument that the noise was no more than a reasonable landowner might create during the course of shooting failed.

7.2 Public nuisance

Public nuisance may be defined as follows.

> '*Any nuisance which materially affects the reasonable comfort and convenience of life of a class of Her Majesty's subjects. The sphere of the nuisance may be described generally as the neighbourhood; but the question whether the local community within that sphere comprises a sufficient number of persons to constitute a class of the public is a question of fact in each case*': *Attorney-General v PYA Quarries 1957.*

An action for public nuisance is conceptually different from an action for private nuisance, even though the two may arise from the same conduct: *Halsey v Esso Petroleum Co Ltd 1961.*

Public nuisance is essentially a criminal act for which the person at fault may be prosecuted. A criminal action ensues, involving either prosecution or an action by the

Attorney-General on behalf of the public. A claimant who wishes to commence an action in **tort** for public nuisance must show that he has suffered 'particular damage' beyond the damage sustained by the general public.

Various types of public nuisance are now governed by statute and have lost their significance in the law of tort. Legislation includes the Public Health Acts 1936 and 1961, the Clean Air Acts 1956 and 1968 and the Environmental Protection Act 1990.

Most cases of public nuisance in modern times concern obstruction of the highway or danger to the highway.

Obstruction of the highway

The public has a right of passage along the highway. Interference with this right by means of obstruction constitutes public nuisance. The test is one of whether the defendant's action is unreasonable.

> *Dymond v Pearce 1972*
> *The facts*: the defendant parked his lorry overnight on a dual-carriageway. The vehicle was parked under a street lamp and its lights were left on. The claimant, a pillion passenger on a motor cycle, was involved in a collision with the lorry.
>
> *Held*: this was an unreasonable action as it had been done solely for the defendant's convenience. (The claimant's action failed because the *cause* of the accident was the motor cyclist's failure to look where he was going, not the parking of the lorry.)

The courts will consider whether the obstruction could have been avoided.

> *Silservice v Supreme Bread 1949*
> *The facts*: the defendant sold fresh bread. Queues formed each day to buy the bread and spilled onto the road.
>
> *Held*: there was no other way in which the defendant could conduct his business. There was no public nuisance.

> *Lyons v Gulliver 1914*
> *The facts*: the defendant owned a theatre. Queues formed which obstructed access to the claimant's premises.
>
> *Held*: the accumulation of people could have been avoided if the defendant had opened his doors earlier. He was liable. Even though he had not intended the crowd to gather, this was the probable consequence of his actions.

Danger to the highway

This may take the form of an obstruction which is dangerous, for example an unlit spiked barrier: *Clark v Chambers 1878*. It may also take the form of danger from buildings or premises adjoining the highway. 'If owing to want of repair, premises on a highway become dangerous and therefore a nuisance, and a passer by or neighbouring owner suffers damage by their collapse, the occupier, or the owner if he has undertaken the duty of repair, is answerable whether he knew or ought to have known of the danger or not': *Wringe v Cohen 1940*.

Tarry v Ashton 1876

The facts: a lamp projecting over the highway fell on a passer-by.

Held: this was public nuisance.

8 DEFAMATION

As with other rights of individuals, limits are placed on freedom of speech, both to avoid disorder and to protect the reputations of others. The most important of these restrictions is the **law of defamation**. The essence of a defamatory statement is that it **damages the reputation** of the person defamed.

- Lowers his standing in society
- Causes him to be shunned or avoided
- Makes imputations which are damaging to him in his profession, business or occupation

Mere insults or 'abuse', spoken in the heat of a quarrel, are not necessarily defamatory, though the distinction is not always easy to make. To say to a man 'You devil!' might not be defamatory, but to say of him that 'He is a born criminal' probably would be. The law against defamation serves to protect 'interests in reputation', reputation being the estimation other people have of you. Injury to one's own self-respect, pride or dignity without further publication is not defamation.

Defamation involves the publishing of a statement which has the effect of causing 'right–minded persons' to think less of the person or to avoid him. If a person makes a statement – written or spoken – which is 'defamatory', he may be liable to the person he has defamed, unless one of a number of recognised defences is available. If a High Court judge allows, it is possible to bring a criminal prosecution for a particularly offensive statement. In general, however, the remedy for defamation is a *civil action* to recover damages. Less often an injunction, which is a prohibition against the repetition of a defamatory statement, may be obtained.

8.1 Libel and slander

There are two distinct forms of defamatory statement.

(a) A **libel** is typically made in writing, but it includes other statements made in a form which is likely to be disseminated widely or continuously, such as a film made for public exhibition (both sound and visual effects may be libellous), a programme broadcast by radio or television, a play (s 4 Theatres Act 1968) and effigies (*Monson v Tussauds Ltd 1894*).

Yousoupoff v MGM Pictures Ltd 1934
The facts: a film was produced in England depicting the rape of a lady by Rasputin, and his subsequent murder. The lady had been romantically linked with one of his murderers. The claimant, who was married to one of Rasputin's murderers, alleged that people thought she was the lady who had been raped.

Held: a talking film, even where the defamation is only in pictures, is libellous. Hence the claimant did not have to show special damage to obtain her damages.

(b)   A **slander** is typically spoken, or in some other transitory form, such as a gesture.

The distinction between these forms is important, since slander cannot be a criminal offence, whereas libel may be. In addition, many actions for slander will only produce a remedy if '**special loss**' is proved by the claimant, whereas libel is actionable *per se*.

A person may sue for slander without proof of damage in the following situations.

(a)   Aspersions are cast on his integrity or competence in his profession

(b)   Allegations are made that he has committed a criminal offence punishable by imprisonment (*Gray v Jones 1939*)

(c)   Unchastity to a woman is imputed (Slander of Women Act 1891)

(d)   Implications are made that he suffers from venereal disease or some other contagious disease

'Special loss' must be proved in any other case of alleged slander to gain a remedy. This may be easier for a business client to prove. Telling a supplier that his customer is a crook may lead to the latter losing a contract and so incur special expense in loss of profit or in finding another supplier. But mental suffering and social ostracism leading to loss of habitual hospitality have been seen as special losses for individuals.

You should note that **each occasion on which a statement is made can be a separate case of defamation** – there may be liability for a defamatory statement each time it is made, by whomever it is made. The defence of 'privilege' (as described later) is sometimes available to a person who repeats what was said by someone else (eg a newspaper reporter), but in principle it is no defence to assert that the statement is only a repetition and not an original statement.

A defamatory statement is assumed to be untrue, unless the person who made it can show that it is true – the defamed person is given the benefit of the doubt. With one minor exception a **true statement is not defamatory** since a person is not entitled to protect his reputation against the truth, even if the statement is made with malice. (The exception arises where a statement is made about a criminal conviction where the person has been 'rehabilitated' under the Rehabilitation of Offenders Act 1974. The defence of justification will not succeed if such a statement is prompted by malice.)

Normally an action for defamation is brought by an **individual** to protect his reputation. Previously it was held that a local authority, being a corporate body, had a **corporate reputation** – for conduct or performance – and might sue if it is defamed in that respect: *Bognor Regis UDC v Campion 1972.* However, in *Derbyshire County Council v Times Newspapers plc 1993* the House of Lords held that the public interest in free speech gives priority to the critic of the elected local authority. It is not clear whether a **company** can sue for defamation of its corporate reputation.

You should note, however, that an unincorporated body, such as a trade union, is merely an association of its individual members and officers – it has no corporate reputation to protect. A trade union may only sue for defamation if it is a 'special register' body within the meaning of s 10 Trade Union and Labour Relations (Consolidation) Act 1992: *Electrical Electronic Telecommunications and Plumbing Union (EETPU) v Times Newspapers Ltd 1980.*

To succeed in an action for defamation, the claimant must show three elements.

- The statement complained of was **defamatory**
- That it was **understood** to refer to him (the claimant)
- It was **published** so that third parties became aware of its contents

8.2 What is defamatory?

It is the **sense of the statement, as reasonably understood by those to whom it was communicated,** which determines whether it is defamatory. In other words, it does *not* have to be shown that the defendant intended to damage the claimant's reputation or even that he was aware of its defamatory nature.

This means that a statement may be defamatory by reason of facts which are unknown to the person who makes the statement. This is a risk to which newspapers are often exposed in reporting statements by others. The Press are given certain other defences, but mere innocence of intent to defame (or ignorance that a statement is defamatory) is not of itself a defence.

The statement must be both **false** and **capable of being construed in a defamatory way**. It is up to the judge to decide whether a statement *can* be defamatory (question of law). The jury decides whether it was (question of fact). This presents a number of problems.

Natural and ordinary meaning of words

This is deemed to be what an ordinary person would infer presuming he or she had no special information. But while some words – such as 'dishonest' or 'promiscuous' – can imply only one thing, many others – such as a popular euphemism, 'fun-loving' – may have different inferences for different persons depending on their dispositions. The judge therefore attempts to draw the most 'ordinary' inference, which is the one that most right-minded people would draw. It is not necessarily the literal meaning, nor will the judge set out to read something into a statement which is not reasonably there: *Sim v Stretch 1936.*

Fact and opinion

A statement of fact which proves to be false and which may be construed in a defamatory way – such as 'X is a thief' – can clearly lead to a claim for defamation. However, a statement of opinion – 'I believe that X will be struck off as a dentist for adultery with a patient' – is also defamatory.

Innuendo

A statement which on the face of it cannot have a defamatory meaning inferred may still qualify if the claimant can prove all of the following.

(a) That the statement contains a wider meaning.

(b) That reasonable people with special knowledge could and would infer such a meaning from the words or from facts which are represented in the words.

(c) That certain particular people with special knowledge did so infer.

(d) That those persons knew of the special facts before or at the time of publication.

Tolley v Fry 1931

The facts: Fry, a chocolate manufacturer, published an advertisement which was a drawing of Tolley, a famous amateur golfer, making a shot with a verse which said in effect that both Fry's chocolate and Tolley's golf were excellent. Tolley objected to the advertisement, which had been published without reference to him, on the grounds that those who saw it would conclude that Tolley had accepted a fee from Fry for his permission, thus compromising his amateur status.

Held: the advertisement did indeed convey the innuendo of which Tolley complained. It was therefore defamatory, since it tended to lower his reputation.

8.3 Did the statement refer to the claimant?

On this issue also, the deciding factor is not what was *intended* by the person who makes the statement, but what was *understood* by the persons to whom the statement was made: *Bourke v Warren 1826*.

Hulton v Jones 1910

The facts: a newspaper published a humorous article describing the peccadilloes, while on holiday in France, of a churchwarden from Peckham, giving the fictitious name (it was thought) of Artemus Jones. However there was a *real* Artemus Jones (a barrister who did *not* live in Peckham and who was *not* a churchwarden). He sued the newspaper, producing evidence from some of his acquaintances that they had understood the rather distinctive name to refer to him. The newspaper's defence was that it did not even know of the claimant's existence.

Held: the article must be taken to refer to the claimant since it had been understood in that sense. It was defamatory because it alleged sexual misconduct.

In a similar later case (*Newstead v London Express Newspaper 1931*) the paper made an unsuccessful defence that its report (on bigamy) was a true story about another man called Newstead. However, evidence was produced that some readers who knew the claimant took the article to refer to him.

An individual may sometimes sue for a defamatory statement which was *made with reference to a class of which he is a member*. There must be evidence that the statement was reasonably understood to *refer to the claimant as an individual*. Remember that an unincorporated body, such as a trade union, cannot sue for defamation on its own behalf, having no corporate reputation, nor as representative of its individual members, unless they were referred to as individuals.

Orme v Associated Newspaper Group Ltd 1981

The facts: the claimant was the leader in England of a religious sect ('the Moonies') and sued for damage to his own reputation arising from statements published in the newspaper about the sect in general.

Held: on the facts, the statements could be reasonably understood to refer to the claimant himself (among others). However, the court went on to find that the statements were true, and therefore not defamatory.

If reference to the individual cannot be shown, the court need not decide whether or not the statement is defamatory in nature, because the action has already failed.

Knupffer v London Express Newspaper Ltd 1944

The facts: the claimant was the head in the UK of a Russian refugee organisation, which had only 24 members in England, though it was also active in France and in the USA. The newspaper described as 'fascist' this 'minute body established in France and in the USA'. There was no mention of the English branch.

Held: the action must be dismissed, since there was no reference to the claimant. It was therefore unnecessary to decide whether the term 'fascist' was defamatory.

Certain other defamatory statements may not be actionable because of their object.

(a)   A dead person cannot be defamed.

(b)   Inanimate objects, such as goods or chattels, may not be defamed – though if the statement extends from a businessman's products to his person then it may be defamatory.

8.4   Was the statement published?

For a statement to be defamatory, it must have been *published*. This means that some person other than the claimant, the defendant and the defendant's spouse must have knowledge of its contents. There is no case for defamation if the only way in which the statement is published is the action of the claimant himself, in showing a third party a defamatory letter which was addressed to him alone.

A person will be liable for any publication which was intended or which he could reasonably have anticipated. Case law sheds some interesting light on aspects of publication, including the following.

Letters

A letter addressed to a particular person is presumed to be published to the addressee, but the sender should anticipate in some cases that it may be read by someone else.

(a)   If a sealed letter is addressed to someone at his *home address*, it will usually be accepted that the defendant expected it to be opened by the addressee and no-one else. If someone else opens it without authorisation – such as a butler in *Huth v Huth 1915* – that is not publication. However, this depends on the facts of the case.

Theaker v Richardson 1962
The facts: a defamatory letter was addressed to a married woman who was a member of the local council, along with the letter's author. It was sent in a style to suggest it was an election address. The woman's husband opened it believing this to be so.

Held: it was a natural and probable consequence that the husband would open it and hence the statement had been published.

(b)   A letter sent to someone at *work* may well be opened by a secretary: the sender/defendant will be assumed to have intended publication to a third party, unless it was marked 'private and confidential' or 'personal'.

Postcards

If a defamatory postcard has been sent through the post to the claimant, the law will assume that a post office employee, or some other third party, has read it.

'Mechanical distributors'

There is a distinction between the originators of defamatory material and those who merely disseminate it. Booksellers, libraries, newsagents etc are not generally liable for innocently spreading abroad a publication which they do not know to be defamatory. To escape liability, these 'mechanical distributors' must prove that they did not know of the libel and that there was no reason why they ought to have known of it. If the publisher asks the distributors to return all copies of a book which has been discovered to be defamatory, any distributor who ignores the request and continues to sell copies (by oversight) may be sued: *Vizetelly v Mudie's Select Library 1900*.

E-mail

The increasing popularity of e-mail has created an entirely new method of communication. There have already been defamation cases where publication on the Internet of a statement that would lower someone in the minds of 'right thinking people' has been held to be libellous in Australia and the US.

This can also be applied to internal company e-mail systems. In *Eggleton v Asda 1995*, a police officer brought an action for defamation against the supermarket, alleging that a defamatory message about him was on their e-mail system.

Activity 5	**(5 minutes)**
Distinguish between libel and slander.	

9 HEALTH AND SAFETY ISSUES

The workplace liability of employees often extends to health and safety issues. Much of health and safety is now covered by detailed legislation, and this applies to 'persons at work', so it protects both employees and independent contractors.

There is a wealth of legislation and codes of practice on health and safety at work, which is often industry specific. We are going to look at some of the more general legislation in detail.

Much of the law relating to health and safety in the UK is derived from the EU, and many of the regulations we shall mention implement EC Directives on these issues.

Statutory references in this section are to the Health and Safety at Work Act 1974 unless otherwise noted

9.1 Health and Safety At Work Act 1974

In this section, we are going to look at the duties employers have to 'persons at work' and 'persons other than persons at work' under the Health and Safety at Work Act 1974.

Section 1 of Part I of the Act states:

'The provisions of this Part shall have effect with a view to:

(a)   Securing the health, safety and welfare of **persons at work**

(b)   Protecting **persons other than persons at work** against risks to health and safety arising out of or in connection with the activities of persons at work

(c)   Controlling the keeping and use of explosive or highly flammable or otherwise dangerous substances, and generally preventing the unlawful acquisition, possession and use of such substances'

'Persons at work' and 'Persons other than persons at work'

As you will see in the following sections, the Act sometimes refers to employees and sometimes refers to others. The Act encompasses a wide variety of people to whom the employer may have responsibility as regards health and safety.

Definition

'Persons at work'. The Act does not define this term, but does define 'work' as 'work as an employee or a self-employed person'. This means that 'persons at work' appears to cover both categories. It is not restricted to persons at work for the employer, so appears to mean anyone who comes within the scope of the employer while undertaking their own work. This therefore would include employees, independent contractors, visitors who are visiting for business purposes (for example, suppliers or professional advisers).

'Persons other than persons at work' appears to mean any persons, extending to the general public.

'Reasonably practicable'

As you will also see in the following sections, the Act frequently uses the terms 'as far as is reasonably practicable'. It does not define what is meant by 'reasonably practicable' so this is a matter for the courts to consider as and when cases are brought under the Act.

Judges have determined that an employer must do what 'any reasonable employer' would have done. As a minimum, this means complying with the law, relevant Codes of Practice and guidance notes.

As we shall see later, such Codes of Practice and guidance notes are issued by the Health and Safety Commissions and Health and Safety Executive. There are a substantial number of such codes, and they can be extremely industry specific, so there is a significant burden on an employer to be up to date with the relevant guidance.

9.2 General duties

The Act contains a number of duties that we will look at in this section. We shall look at some of the more specific duties, such as the duties of landlords who are not the employer in considerably less detail than the specific duties of employees and employers to each other. However, ensure you are at least **aware** of all the general duties in this section.

The Act provides that it is a **criminal offence** for persons to fail to discharge a duty imposed by sections 2 to 7 or to contravene sections 8 or 9.

General duties of employers to their employees: s 2

There is a key, overriding duty owed by employers to their employees, which is: 'It shall be the duty of every employer to ensure, so far as is reasonably practicable, the health, safety and welfare at work of all his employees': s 2(1).

As discussed above, employers must, as a minimum, follow law and relevant Codes of Practice and guidance notes.

Section 2 also identifies a number of matters which that duty extends to in practice, although these do not preclude other matters covered by the general duty in s 2(1). These matters are that the employer ensures that:

- Plant and systems of work are provided and maintained so as to be safe and without risks to health.

- Arrangements are made so as to ensure safety and absence of risks to health in the use, handling, storage and transport of articles and substances.

- He provides such information, instruction, training and supervision necessary to ensure health and safety of employees at work.

- He maintains places of work, and access to and from such places, in such a condition as to ensure that they are safe and without risks to health.

- The working environment provided and maintained is safe, without risks to health and has adequate facilities and arrangements for employee welfare at work.

An employee has a duty to prepare a written policy on health and safety at the workplace: s2(3). He is also required to consult with employee representatives in making arrangements that assist him and his employees co-operating to ensure that the workplace is safe.

General duty of employers and self-employed to persons other than their employees: s 3

Employers and those who are self-employed have a duty to ensure that the business is conducted in such a way as ensures that people not in his employment are not exposed to risks to their health and safety.

General duty of persons concerned with premises to persons other than their employees: s 4

This section states that persons who are responsible for non-domestic premises where others (who are not their employees) work should take measures to ensure that the premises and all means of access and exit from the premises are safe and without risks to health.

General duty of manufacturers etc as regards articles and substances for use at work: s 6

This section imposes duties on people who manufacture articles for use at work to ensure that they are safe to so use.

General duty of employees at work: s 7

This important section looks at the corresponding duty that employees have to their employers in relation to health and safety at work.

Section 7 states that:

'It shall be the duty of every employee while at work

(a) *To take reasonable care for the health and safety of himself and of other persons who might be affected by his acts or omissions at work, and*

(b) *As regards any duty or requirement imposed on his employer or any other person by or under any relevant statutory provisions, to co-operate with him so far as is necessary to enable that duty or requirement to be performed or complied with'.*

It is important that you note that the employee has a duty here to three groups of people.

- **Himself** (an employee must take care of his own health and safety at work)

- **Other persons** affected by his acts/omissions at work (that is, both fellow employees and any other persons affected by his work, perhaps visitors, or the public)

- **His employer** (whose requirements in relation to health and safety he must obey)

Duty not to interfere with or misuse things provided pursuant to certain provisions: s 8

People must not intentionally or recklessly interfere with items provided for health and safety reasons. Examples might include letting off fire extinguishers or items in a first aid box.

Duty not to charge employees for things done or provided pursuant to certain specific requirements: s 9

Employers must not charge employees if they are obliged to provide additional equipment (for example, goggles or anti-glare screens for computer screens) to comply with Health and Safety Regulations.

9.3 Health and safety bodies

The 1974 Act provided that the Health and Safety Commission and the Health and Safety Executive should be set up. The Commission is a policy-making body and the Executive is the enforcement body. Both are non-governmental bodies that nonetheless have significant connections with the government.

The Health and Safety Commission (HSC)

The Commission is a body with a Chairman appointed by the Secretary of State and between six and nine appointed members. When appointing the members, the Secretary of State must consult employers' organisations, employees' organisations and local authority associations.

The HSC exists to:

- Assist and encourage others to further the purposes of the Act

- Carry out research related to health and safety at work and publish the results and encourage others to carry out research

- Provide information and training and advisory services in connection with health and safety at work

- Submit proposals to the Secretary of State for future regulations in connection with health and safety

- In general terms, the HSC furthers the work of the Secretary of State in relation to health and safety

The HSC is also empowered to set up enquiries into accidents at work.

The Health and Safety Executive (HSE)

The Executive is a body with three members, a Director General (appointed by the HSC with the approval of the Secretary of State) and two other members (appointed by the HSC in consultation with the Director General and the Secretary of State).

The HSE exists to:

- Carry out investigations as required by the HSC
- Act as a delegate for the HSC when required
- To give effect to HSC directions

The general operations division of the HSE is divided into 'directorates' in which most of the inspectors work, such as:

- Field operations directorate (split into seven sectors and the railway industry, it also has an occupational health and environment unit and a safety unit)

- Nuclear safety directorate (responsible for regulating nuclear safety)

- Hazardous installations directorate (concerned with petroleum industries, diving, sites where chemicals are used/stored or explosives are manufactured, pipelines and mining)

9.4 Health and Safety Regulations

Section 15 of the Health and Safety at Work Act 1974 confers the right on the Secretary of State to issue guidance, make regulations and issue Approved Codes of Practice in relation to health and safety. A substantial number of Regulations have been passed under this section. We are going to look in detail at the Health and Safety at Work Regulations 1999, but so that you are aware of some of the legislation that has been passed, we shall list some here.

The following are examples of Regulations that have been passed under the authority of s 15 of the Health and Safety at Work Act 1974. Many implement EC Directives.

- The Classification of Hazards, Information and Packaging Regulations 1999
- The Confined Spaces Regulations 1997
- The Control of Substances Hazardous to Health Regulations 1999
- The Electricity at Work Regulations 1989
- The Health and Safety (Display Screen Equipment) Regulations 1992
- The Lifting Operation and Lifting Equipment Regulations 1998
- The Management of Health and Safety at Work Regulations 1999
- The Manual Handling Operations Regulations 1992
- The Noise at Work Regulations 1989
- The Personal Protective Equipment at work Regulations 1992
- The Provision and Use of Workplace Equipment Regulations 1998
- The Working Time Regulations 1998 (as amended)
- The Workplace (Health Safety and Welfare) Regulations 1992
- The Health and Safety (First Aid) Regulations 1981

Activity 6	**(30 minutes)**

Go to www.hse.gov.uk and download the booklet entitled *Health and Safety Regulations. A Short Guide.* This will help you identify the full range of regulations, and the way they fit into the overall scheme.

Activity 7	**(30 minutes)**

Using the same website address given in Activity 1, look specifically this time at the Workplace (Health, Safety and Welfare) Regulations 1992 (SI No 3004 in 1992). These Regulations include some specific requirements which employers should comply with, such as temperature and lighting. Including these two issues, what requirements do the Regulations impose on employers?

Activity 8	**(30 minutes)**

Using the same website address given in Activity 1, look specifically at the Working Time Regulations 1998 (SI No 1833 in 1998). These Regulations deal with the amount of time for which it is safe for workers to work. What general duties do the Regulations impose upon employers and what rights do the Regulations give to employees?

9.5 Health and Safety at Work Regulations 1999

In the rest of this chapter we shall look at the requirements of the Health and Safety at Work Regulations 1999.

Statutory references in this section are to Health and Safety at Work Regulations 1999.

Risk assessments

One of the most significant requirements of the Health and Safety at Work Regulations 1999 is the requirement on employers and self-employed people to make assessments of the health and safety risks which employees and others are exposed to as a result of the undertaking. The risk assessment is designed to show the employer what requirements and prohibitions he must comply with.

The risk assessment itself must be reassessed if there is reason to believe that it is no longer valid or there has been a significant change.

If the employer employs five or more persons, the significant findings of the assessment must be recorded, as must any group of people who are particularly at risk.

Young people

The regulations identify young people as being people who are particularly at risk and imposes specific requirements on the employer in relation to them. A young person is classed as someone between the ages of 16 and 18. The employer must take particular note of:

- The inexperience, lack of awareness and immaturity of young persons

- The fitting out and layout of the workplace and the workstation

- The nature, degree and duration of exposure to physical, biological and chemical agents

- The form, range and use of work equipment and the way in which it is handled

- The organisation of processes and activities

- The extent of health and safety training provided or to be provided to young persons, and

- Risks from agents, processes and work listed in Directive 94/33/EC

Principles of prevention

Having conducted a risk assessment, the employer must implement procedures, as will be discussed later. The Regulations require the employer to implement those procedures on the basis of the EC's principles of prevention, as set out in Directive 89/391.

> **GENERAL PRINCIPLES OF PREVENTION**
> (a) Avoiding risks
> (b) Evaluating risks that cannot be avoided
> (c) Combating the risks at source
> (d) Adapting the work to the individual, especially as regards the design of workplaces, the choice of work equipment and the choice of working and production methods, with a view, in particular, to alleviating monotonous work and work at a pre-determined work-rate and to reducing their effect on health
> (e) Adapting to technical progress

(f) Replacing the dangerous by the non-dangerous or the less dangerous

(g) Developing a coherent overall prevention policy which covers technology, organisation of work, working conditions, social relationships and the influence of factors relating to the working environment

(h) Giving collective protective measures priority over individual protective measures, and

(i) Giving appropriate instructions to employees

Health and safety arrangements

The general requirement to make health and safety arrangements is found in Section 5:

'Every employer shall make and give effect to such arrangements as are appropriate, having regard to the nature of his activities and the size of his undertaking, for the effective planning, organisation, control, monitoring and review of the preventative and protective measures': s 5(1) HSWR 1999.

Where there are five or more employees, the arrangements made must be recorded.

Procedures

There are various procedures that an employer must consider:

- Health surveillance, where appropriate
- Appointment of competent persons to assist (this is mandatory)
- Implement procedures for areas of serious and imminent danger areas

Information

Employers are required to give information to their employees on:

- The risks identified by the assessment
- The preventative and productive measures taken
- Procedures for serious and imminent danger areas

Considering capabilities

When appointing competent persons from amongst his employees to assist in heath and safety issues, the employer must give consideration to the capability of the employees chosen.

Special cases

The regulations go on to consider the employer's duties to persons who may be at particular risk for specific reasons. Young persons have already been mentioned above. The regulations also refer to the requirement to consider health and safety issues specifically in relation to new or expectant mothers, and also the requirement on employers to advise temporary workers of health and safety policies in force at the undertaking.

Employees' duties

Lastly, we shall consider the duties that the Health and Safety at Work Regulations 1999 put on employees, which are contained in Section 14.

Employees are required to use machinery or dangerous substances **in accordance with training** they have received **and** in accordance with **the instructions they have been given** by the employer.

An employer is also required to inform

- the employer
- anyone else charged with health and safety duties in the organisation

of any serious and imminent dangers to health and safety.

FOR DISCUSSION

What policies and procedures does your employer have in place in respect of health and safety? Are there any significant health and safety risks in the place where you work, to your knowledge? Have you been given a summary of the health and safety risk assessment carried out at your place of work? What did you think of it?

Chapter roundup

- A tort is a civil wrong arising from a general duty rather than from a contractual relationship.

- If a claimant has suffered damage but no legal wrong has been done, he will not succeed in his action. If a legal wrong has been done but no damage has been suffered, damages may be awarded in some cases, but they may be only nominal.

- In most torts, the claimant need not show that the defendant acted maliciously, only that he acted voluntarily.

- Damages will only be awarded for loss which is not too remote from the actions of the defendant. Chains of causation may be broken by the actions of others, or may become too tenuous when the consequences go beyond what could reasonably have been foreseen. However, the thin skull principle may allow damages to be awarded for unexpected damage.

- An employer is liable for torts committed by his employees in the course of their employment. Vicarious liability can also arise for the torts of independent contractors.

- The rule in *Rylands v Fletcher* defines a tort of strict liability, in which reasonable care is no defence. It covers the escape of anything brought onto the defendant's land and likely to do mischief if it escapes, but it does not cover things naturally on the land.

Chapter roundup (cont'd)

- Trespass to land is the most common form of trespass. Claimants may seek damages, an injunction, or both.

- The occupier of premises has a duty of care to trespassers, where he is aware of the danger, he knows that someone may come into the vicinity of the danger, and the risk is one against which the occupier may reasonably be expected to offer that person some protection.

- Nuisance may be of two types – public and private. In private nuisance the central idea is that of interference with the claimant's enjoyment of his property. Public nuisance does not require any 'invasion' of private land, rather the annoyance of the general public.

- As with other rights of individuals, limits are placed on freedom of speech, both to avoid disorder and to protect the reputations of others. The most important of these restrictions is the law of defamation. The essence of a defamatory statement is that it damages the reputation of the person defamed.

- An occupier owes a duty of care to all visitors to his premises, and to a certain extent to trespassers.

- The Health and Safety at Work Act 1974 puts a requirement on employers and self-employed to consider and protect the health and safety of persons at work and persons other than persons at work.

- The Act imposes several general duties.

  – s 2: General duties of employers to employees

  – s 3: General duties of employers (self employed to persons other than employees

  – s 4: General duty of persons concerned with premises to persons other than their employees

  – s 6: General duty of manufacturers as regards articles/substances for use at work

  – s 7: General duty of employees at work

  – s 8: Duty not to interfere with/misuse things provided under regulations

  – s 9 Duty not to charge employees for things done pursuant to Regulations

- Employers general duty (s 2) is to ensure the health and safety of employees (as far as is reasonably practicable).

- Employees must take care for their health and safety of themselves and other persons and they must obey employers' health and safety requirements.

- The Health and Safety commission and Executive were set up to oversee health and safety in the UK.

Chapter roundup (cont'd)

- Many regulations have been issued under the authority of s 15 of the Act.

- The most key recent Regulations are the Health and Safety at Work Regulations 1999.

- The Regulations require employers to conduct health and safety assessments and then to implement procedures in response to the assessments.

- The employer must pay particular regard to persons who may be at high risk, for example, young persons and expectant mothers.

- Employees must use any equipment used at work in accordance with training and instructions given by the employer.

Quick quiz

1   What is a tort?

2   Distinguish wrong from damage, and identify the factors which must be present for there to be liability in tort.

3   How may remoteness of damage affect a claim in tort?

4   What two factors must be present for an employer's vicarious liability to be established?

5   When is a person liable for the torts of his independent contractor?

6   What is the rule in *Rylands v Fletcher*?

7   What forms may trespass to land take?

8   What is a visitor in the context of the Occupiers' Liability Acts?

9   What is meant by private nuisance?

10 What is public nuisance?

11 Who does an employer have responsibility to in relation to health and safety?

12 What are the general duties given in the 1974 Health and Safety at Work Act?

13 What is the Health and Safety Commission?

14 Name five sets of Regulations made under the authority of s 15 of HASAWA.

15 What matters must an employer consider when conducting a risk assessment in relation to young persons?

16 What are the employees' duties under the Health and Safety at Work Regulations 1999?

Answers to quick quiz

1 A tort is the infringement of someone else's rights. (see Introduction)

2 Wrong is breach of a legal duty. Damage is a loss suffered by the claimant. Usually both are required. (para 1.1)

3 If the damage is too remote, the claimant will not be able to claim a remedy. (para 2.1)

4 Employer-employee relationship
Tort is committed in the course of employment. (Section 3)

5 Where the operation is hazardous, risky, personal. (para 3.5)

6 The rule of strict liability. (para 4.1)

7 Entering onto or driving animals on to land, remaining on the land for longer than entitled, placing objects on the land and abusing permission to be there. (para 5.1)

8 A person who enters the premises with the actual or implied permission of the occupier, and a person with a legal right of entry. (para 6.2)

9 Unlawful interference with the claimant's use of his property or with his health and comfort or convenience. (para 7.1)

10 Any nuisance that materially affects the reasonable comfort and convenience of life of a class of Her Majesty's subjects. (para 7.2)

11 'Persons at work' and 'persons other than persons at work'. (para 9.2)

12 s 2: Employers to their employees
s 3: Employers/self-employed to others
s 4: Persons concerned with premises to users
s 6: Manufacturers of articles for use of work
s 7: Employees
s 8: Not to interfere with articles provided for health and safety
s 9: Employer not to charge employee for health and safety items.
(para 9.3)

13 A body formed to encourage persons to further the provisions of the 1974 Act. (para 9.4)

14 See the list given under Paragraph 9.5.

15 Their inexperience/immaturity/lack of awareness
The fitting out of the workplace/station
The nature, degree and duration of exposure to physical, biological, chemical agents
The form, range, use of work equipment/way in which it is handled
The organisation of processes/activities
The extent of health and safety training provided
Risk from agents, processes, work listing in Directive 94/33
(para 9.6)

16 To use machinery etc in accordance with training/instructions given by the employer. (para 9.6)

Answers to activities

1   There is *damnum* but no *injuria*. There is not therefore an actionable tort.

2   It was reasonably foreseeable that the part of the machine would break loose. The harm caused by large parts is of the same type as that caused by smaller parts.

3   It can be argued that the employee was doing the work for which he was employed, ie chemical experiments. Therefore the employer would be liable for the injuries. This follows cases such as *Limpus v London General Ombibus Co* and *Rose v Plenty*.

4   A did not bring the gas onto his land.

5   Libel is the making of a defamatory statement in a permanent form, typically in writing. This includes visual (eg film) or aural (eg a radio broadcast), media. Slander is a statement which is not recorded, and which is usually spoken.

6   This will depend on which Regulations you have looked at.

7   The employer is required to ensure that every workplace complies with the regulations in respect of maintenance, ventilation, temperature, lighting, cleanliness, waste, dimensions/space, seating, floors and traffic routes, falls, falling objects, windows etc, doors, escalators, sanitary conveniences, washing facilities, drinking waters, accommodation for clothing/changes, facilities to rest/eat meals

8   Employers are required to take 'all reasonable steps' to ensure that employees don't work more hours than the time limits specified.

Employees are entitled to rest periods:
- 11 hours in every 24 hours
- 24 hours in every 7 days
- A break for every 6 hours worked consecutively

They are also entitled to four weeks' paid annual leave.

Chapter 13:
BUSINESS AND ECONOMIC TORTS

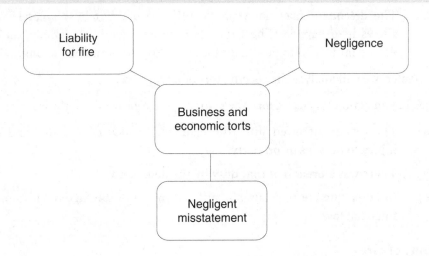

Introduction

Many torts may be committed by mere carelessness rather than intentionally. But in modern times the law has developed a *tort of negligence in itself* which is liability for a failure to take proper care to avoid inflicting foreseeable injury. It has become the most important and far-reaching of modern torts.

Most torts are wrongful *acts*. There can however be liability for an *omission*, or a failure to act in circumstances where there is a duty to do so. For example, as we saw in the previous chapter, the occupier of premises who knows that they are in a dangerous condition may be liable in tort if he fails to make the premises safe and a visitor is injured in consequence.

Your objectives

In this chapter you will learn about the following.

(a)   The tort of negligence and the three elements that a successful claimant must demonstrate

(b)   The tort of negligent misstatement

(c)   The law concerning liability for fire

BPP
LEARNING MEDIA

1 NEGLIGENCE

In the law of tort the concept of negligence appears in two different senses.

(a)   There is a distinct tort of negligence which is (briefly) causing loss by a failure to take reasonable care when there is a duty to do so.

(b)   The defendant may not wish to inflict injury but by his carelessness he allows it to happen. The wrong is unintentional but negligent and so the defendant is held to be at fault for the negligent doing of a wrong.

In this chapter, we will analyse the specific tort of negligence.

To succeed in an action for negligence the claimant must prove three things.

(a)   The defendant owed him (the claimant) *a duty of care* to avoid causing injury to persons or property.

(b)   There was a **breach of that duty** by the defendant.

(c)   **In consequence** the claimant suffered **injury or damage** or (in some cases) financial loss.

1.1 Duty of care

Whether or not a duty of care exists in any situation is generally decided by the courts.

In the famed case of *Donoghue v Stevenson* the House of Lords ruled that a person might owe a general duty of care to another with whom he had no contractual relationship at all.

> *Donoghue v Stevenson 1932*
>
> *The facts*: A purchased from a retailer a bottle of ginger beer for consumption by A's companion B. The bottle was opaque so that its contents were not visible. B drank part of the contents from the bottle and topped up her glass with the rest. As she poured it out the remains of a decomposed snail emerged from the bottle. She became seriously ill, and sued C, the manufacturer, who argued that as there was no contract between himself and B he owed her no duty of care and so was not liable to her.
>
> *Held*: C was liable to B. Every person owes a general duty of care to his 'neighbour', to 'persons so closely and directly affected by my act that I ought reasonably to have them in contemplation as being so affected'. In supplying polluted ginger beer in an opaque bottle the manufacturer must be held to contemplate that the person who drank the contents of the bottle would be affected by the consequences of the manufacturer's failure to take care to supply his product in a clean bottle.

Development of the doctrine of duty of care

The narrow doctrine of the neighbourhood principle has been much refined in the seventy-odd years since the snail made its celebrated appearance.

At the present time, it is perhaps fair to say that whether or not a duty of care exists will be assessed on the basis of some or all of the following four tests. These were formulated by the House of Lords in *The Nicholas H (Marc Rich & Co v Bishops Rock Marine) 1995* case.

Test	Meaning
1 Reasonably foreseeable	Was the damage reasonably foreseeable by the defendant as damage to the claimant at the time of the negligent act or omission?
2 Proximity	Is there sufficient proximity, or neighbourhood, between the parties?
3 Fair, just and reasonable	Is it fair, just and reasonable that the law should impose a duty on the defendant on the facts of the case?
4 Public policy	Is there a matter of public policy that requires that no duty of care should exist?

In applying these tests, the court is essentially looking at the relationship between the claimant and the defendant in the context of the damage suffered. *The Nicholas H* case was concerned with economic loss, but the court held that the requirements would be equally applicable in cases of physical damage to property.

Activity 1   **(5 minutes)**

Which of the following elements must be present for a duty of care to exist?

1   There must be a sufficient relationship of proximity between defendant and claimant

2   It must be reasonable that the defendant should foresee that damage might arise from his carelessness

3   The claimant must have acted in good faith and without carelessness

4   It must be just and reasonable for the law to impose liability

A   1 and 2 only
B   3 and 4 only
C   1, 2 and 3 only
D   1, 2 and 4 only

1.2 Restricting the duty of care

In any given case, if a reasonable man could have foreseen the consequences then a duty of care may be owed; whether it has actually arisen or not depends on the facts. The duty may be restricted or ignored completely in the following circumstances.

    (a)   A person is not normally liable for the acts of third parties unless they were under his control. In an employment relationship, where there is control by the employer, the latter normally has vicarious liability for the acts of his servants done in the course of their employment.

    (b)   Certain persons involved in judicial process are immune from all civil action, particularly judges, lawyers and jurors during a trial. Arbitrators are immune when they act in that capacity, as are valuers acting as arbitrators or quasi-arbitrators.

(c)   A person may be liable for omission, such as where an accountant carelessly leaves out part of his report, but a duty of care rarely arises from an obligation to take positive action which has not been taken.

> **Activity 2**   (5 minutes)
>
> Consider the reasons why a barrister acting as an advocate in legal proceedings should be immune from being sued in negligence.

There is generally no duty to take care to prevent third parties from doing damage: mere foreseeability of damage is not enough.

Perl v Camden LBC 1983
The facts: thieves entered an empty house owned by the defendant and broke through from there into the adjacent property, stealing a number of high-value items.

Held: although it was foreseeable that such an event may occur, because there was no special relationship by which the house-owner could control the acts of the thieves, no duty of care to the claimants arose.

Lamb v London Borough of Camden 1981
The facts: by their negligence, the defendants had caused damages to the foundations of the claimant's house so that his tenant had to vacate it. Two sets of squatters then moved in, causing much damage, until strong barricades prevented further intrusion.

Held: the damage was reasonably foreseeable but was only 'possible' rather than 'likely to occur' and the workmen who damaged the water main which damaged the foundations could not, at the time, have foreseen the damage which would be wreaked by squatters. The defendants were therefore not liable.

But if the defendant is in control of third parties he has a duty of care in the exercise of that control.

Home Office v Dorset Yacht Club 1970
The facts: DY's property was damaged by a number of boys who escaped at night from a Borstal institution. The escape was due to lack of care by the guards for whom the Home Office was responsible.

Held: the Home Office was vicariously liable for the negligence of its staff as it owed a duty of care to persons whose property it could be foreseen might be damaged if the boys escaped.

1.3   Liability for economic loss

One of the most uncertain areas in the law on negligence is how far and in what circumstances there is liability for financial (usually called 'economic') loss, if it is not the direct consequence of physical damage caused by negligence. The most common example of economic loss is where a person who has suffered physical damage makes a claim for loss of business profits while the damage is put right.

But in more recently, successful claims have been made for loss of profits both in cases where the root cause was physical damage and in cases where no actual physical damage occurred at all.

Ross v Caunters 1980
The facts: a solicitor gave negligent advice to a testator and drew up a will carelessly. A gift to the claimant (an intended beneficiary) failed as a result.

Held: the solicitor owed a duty of care to beneficiaries since it was reasonably foreseeable that they would be damaged by negligent advice. The beneficiary could therefore sue for loss since he was actually in mind when the solicitor drew up the will.

Liability to pay damages for economic loss is limited to situations where the parties are linked by some special relationship, such as solicitor and beneficiary or takeover bidder and accountant. In the *Caparo* case the situation was analysed as being one where the defendant knew the following.

(a) The nature of the transactions which the claimant had in mind

(b) That the advice or information would be communicated to the claimant

(c) It was likely that the claimant would rely on that advice or information when deciding whether to go ahead with the transaction in mind

Damages for economic loss are generally awarded only where that loss is attached to physical loss.

Muirhead v Industrial Tank Specialities Ltd 1986
The facts: the claimants, wholesale fish merchants, purchased lobsters in the summer with the intention of selling them at Christmas when prices were higher. The pumps which they purchased to oxygenate the water were inadequate. The lobsters died.

Held: the death of the lobsters was reasonably foreseeable and this loss was recoverable. The additional losses were purely economic and were not recoverable.

Activity 3 **(5 minutes)**

As a security measure, A installs lights outside his house. The house of B, his neighbour, is thereby illuminated, and B expresses his gratitude to A for choosing a security measure which benefits both of them. A later removes the lights without warning B, and the night after he does so B's house is burgled. Could B sue A?

1.4 Liability for 'nervous shock'

The claimant may claim compensation for nervous shock caused by the defendant's negligent act. Typically the claimant has suffered a reaction when they have witnessed an accident in which a close relative is injured. Compensation will not be awarded for mere grief or distress: the claimant must prove a definite and identifiable psychiatric illness.

Nervous shock is dealt with separately from ordinary physical damage because it has been perceived as a potential area for a vast litigation and therefore particular rules have developed. A duty of care is not owed to everyone who may in fact be affected by the defendant's act.

There is a duty of care not to cause nervous shock by putting a person in fear of his own safety *Dulieu v White & Sons 1901*, or in fear for the safety of his children *Hanbrook v Stoke Bros 1925*, or by making him an actual witness to an act of negligence by which he suffers nervous shock such as seeing his house on fire: *Attia v British Gas plc 1987*.

A person suffering nervous shock may have a claim if they can show that there was a sufficiently close relationship between themselves and the primary victim and that they either saw the accident with their unaided senses or came upon the 'immediate aftermath'.

> *McLoughlin v O'Brien 1982*
> *The facts*: the claimant was called to the hospital where her husband and children were receiving emergency treatment shortly after an accident caused by the defendant. She was informed that her daughter had died. She suffered nervous shock.
>
> *Decision*: it was reasonably foreseeable that the claimant would be affected. She had a close relationship with the primary victims and came upon the immediate aftermath. Therefore, she could recover damages.

It appears then that a distinction can be drawn between those who have a close family tie to the victim and a mere bystander. There is also a distinction between those who witness an event and are proximate to the accident in terms of time and space and those who are told of the accident or witness it via simultaneous television broadcast.

> *Alcock & Others v Chief Constable of South Yorkshire Police 1991*
> *The facts*: this case involves the Hillsborough disaster when 95 people were killed and another 400 injured due to being crushed in crowded stands. Various relatives of the victims, who had proved various psychiatric illnesses as a result of learning of the tragedy, being at the ground or witnessing it on television, brought an action against the defendants in negligence.
>
> *Decision*: the claimants' claim must fail either because they could not establish a sufficient degree of kinship to make it reasonably foreseeable that psychiatric illness would result, or because they witnessed the accident via simultaneous (or recorded) broadcasts and therefore were not sufficiently proximate in time and space.

> *Vernon v Bosley 1997*
> *The facts*: two young children were passengers in a car driven by the defendant, their nanny, when it went off the road and crashed into the river. The claimant, their father, did not see the accident but was called to the scene and witnessed the unsuccessful attempt to rescue the children. The claimant suffered nervous shock.
>
> *Decision*: the claimant could recover damages from the defendant.

The Piper Alpha disaster in the North Sea produced further developments in this area. The issue was whether a duty of care was owed to a mere bystander who witnessed a horrific accident with his own unaided senses and subsequently suffered nervous shock.

McFarlane v E E Caledonia Ltd 1994

The facts: the claimant, an employee of the defendants, stood and witnessed the massive explosions on the oil rig in which 164 men were killed, before being evacuated by helicopter. As a result he suffered psychiatric illness and sued the defendants in negligence.

Decision: no duty of care was owed in these circumstances. The claimant had not been in fear for his own safety nor had he been in actual danger. He had no close relationship with the primary victims and had taken no active part in rescue operations. As a mere bystander he had no claim.

It is established then that a person who suffers nervous shock as a result of participating in the rescue of injured victims in an accident would be owed a duty of care.

Chadwick v British Railways Board 1967

The facts: a serious train crash occurred as a result of the negligence of the train driver. The claimant attended the scene and over a prolonged period of time helped in the rescue work. As a result he suffered nervous shock.

Decision: a duty of care was held to rescuers and as nervous shock was foreseeable in the circumstances. The defendants were liable.

Activity 4   **(5 minutes)**

S and her daughter, A, visit the local fair owned by C. A has a ride on the big wheel. S watches in horror as the carriage in which A is riding becomes disconnected due to rust and decay and plummets to the ground. S suffers nervous shock. Consider whether S could sue C in negligence.

1.5 Breach of duty of care: the reasonable man

The second element that must be proven by a claimant in an action for negligence is that there was a breach of the duty of care by the defendant.

The standard of care

The standard of reasonable care requires that the person concerned should do what a reasonable man 'guided upon those considerations which ordinarily regulate the conduct of human affairs' would do and abstain from doing what a reasonable man would not do: *Blyth v Birmingham Water Works 1856*. The standard of 'a reasonable man' is not that of an average man – for instance, the standard of a 'reasonable' car driver is a very high standard indeed.

Nettleship v Weston 1971

The facts: the defendant was a learner driver who crashed and injured the passenger, despite doing her best to control the car.

Held: the standard required of a learner driver is the same as that of any other driver. 'Incompetent best is not good enough'. A variable standard for different levels of experience would create too much uncertainty.

Principle	Explanation
Particular skill	If the defendant professes a **particular skill,** the standard is that of a reasonable person with that skill, ie a reasonable accountant or reasonable electrician.
Lack of skill	**Peculiarities or disabilities** of the defendant are not relevant, so the standard for a learner driver is that of a reasonable driver and for a trainee accountant, that of a reasonable accountant.
No hindsight	The test is one of **knowledge and general practice existing at the time,** not hindsight or subsequent change of practice. *Roe v Minister of Health* 1954 A doctor gave a patient an injection taking normal precautions at that time. The drug became contaminated in a way that was not understood at the time and the patient was paralysed. *Held*: The proper test was normal practice based on the state of medical knowledge at the time. The doctor was not at fault in failing to anticipate later developments.
Body of opinion	In broad terms, a claim against a professional person will fail if he or she can point to a **body of professional opinion that supports the approach taken** and which the court concedes to be reasonable.
Advantage and risk	In deciding what is reasonable care, the balance must be struck between **advantage and risk**. (For example, a driver of a fire engine may exceed the normal speed on his way to the fire but not on the way back.)
Emergency	If a defendant acts negligently in an **emergency situation**, this will be taken into account – the test is that of a reasonable man in the defendant's situation.
Vulnerability	If A owes a duty of care to B and A knows that B is **unusually vulnerable,** a higher standard of care is expected. *Paris v Stepney Borough Council* 1951 *The facts*: C was blind in one eye and was employed by D on vehicle maintenance. It was not the normal practice to issue protective goggles since the risk of eye injury was small. A chip of metal flew into C's eye and blinded him. *Decision*: there was a higher standard of care owed to C because an injury to his remaining good eye would blind him.

Activity 5 **(10 minutes)**

An accountant advises a client to use a well known tax avoidance scheme. At the time when he does so, HM Revenue and Customs (HMRC) is challenging the scheme in the courts. In a test case, the High Court has found in favour of the HMRC but the Court of Appeal has found in favour of the taxpayer, and a HMRC appeal to the House of Lords is pending. If the HMRC succeed, any taxpayer who has used the scheme will be substantially worse off than if he had not used the scheme. If the HMRC were to succeed in the House of Lords and the client were to sue the accountant, would the accountant be able to rely on *Roe v Minister of Health 1954* in his defence?

Res ipsa loquitur

Whether or not there has been a breach of a duty of care is a question of fact.

It rests on the claimant to show both that the defendant owed him a duty of reasonable care and that the defendant failed in that duty. In some circumstances the claimant may argue that the facts speak for themselves (*res ipsa loquitur*) – that want of care is the only possible explanation for what happened and negligence on the part of the defendant must be presumed.

To rely on this principle the claimant must first show the following.

(a) The thing which caused the injury was under the management and control of the defendant

(b) The accident was such as would not occur if those in control used proper care

Scott v London & St Katharine Docks Co 1865
The facts: S was passing in front of the defendant's warehouse. Six bags of sugar fell on him.

Held: in the absence of explanation it must be presumed that the fall of the bags of sugar was due to want of care on the part of the defendants. Principles (a) and (b) above were formulated in this case.

Easson v LNE Railway Co 1944
The facts: a four year old boy fell through the open door of a train seven miles from its last stopping place.

Held: the principle of *res ipsa loquitur* did not apply since the railway company was not sufficiently in control of the doors of the train. After it left the last station a passenger might have opened the door.

1.6 Loss carried by the breach: Consequential harm

A claim for compensation for negligence will not succeed unless the third element (damage or loss) is proved. In deciding whether a claim should be allowed, the court considers whether:

- The breach of duty gave rise to the harm (fact)
- The harm was not too remote from the breach (law)

A person will only be compensated if he has suffered actual loss, injury, damage or harm as a consequence of another's actions. The claim will not be proved in the following circumstances.

(a) The claimant followed a course of action regardless of the acts of the defendant.

(b) A third party is the actual cause of harm.

(c) A complicated series of events takes place such that no one act was the cause of all the harm.

(d) An intervening act by the claimant or a third party breaks the 'chain of causation' (*novus actus interveniens*).

The 'but for' test

If harm to the claimant would not have occurred 'but for' the defendant's negligence, then that negligence is a cause of harm. If the loss would have occurred anyway, then it is not.

> *Barnett v Chelsea & Kensington Hospital Management Committee 1969*
> *The facts*: a doctor sent a patient away from a casualty department and told him to see his own doctor. The patient died from arsenic poisoning.
>
> *Held*: because the patient was beyond help anyway, the negligence of the doctor did not cause the death.

Loss of a chance

Another assessment of liability for damages refers to the **loss of chance**. This can come down to a consideration of statistics.

> *Hotson v East Berkshire Health Authority 1987*
> *The facts*: the patient suffered an injury to his hip in a fall, which carried a 75% risk of permanent disability. Due to negligent (ie delayed) medical attention the likelihood of disability became 100%. The claimant contended that the delay had cost him that 25% chance of recovery. The defendant argued that negligence had not caused the disability.
>
> *Held*: the case went to the House of Lords who decided that, on the balance of probabilities, it was the fall which caused the disability, and that the 'lost chance' test became irrelevant.

1.7 Multiple causes

The courts often have difficulty in determining **causation** where there are a number of possible causes of injury including the negligent act. The courts must decide on the **facts** if the negligent act was the one that most likely caused the injury.

> *Wilsher v Essex AHA (1988)*
> *The facts*: a premature baby suffered blindness after birth. It was claimed that a doctor failed to notice that the baby received high doses of oxygen and this caused the blindness.

Decision: evidence was provided that there was six possible causes of the blindness including the one claimed. However, the court could not ascertain which of the six actually occurred and therefore could not create a direct causal link.

The case below indicates the court's flexibility when applying legal principles in **exceptional** cases.

Fairchild v Glenhaven Funeral Services Ltd & Ors (2002)
The facts: the claimants all contracted a disease caused by contact with asbestos over extended periods of time with several different employers. In defence it was claimed that the disease could be contracted with exposure to one asbestos fibre and as the claimants were employed by a number of employers it could not be established at which employer they contracted the disease.

Decision: the House of Lords held that all the employers (who had failed to take reasonable care), contributed to the cause and where all liable.

Having decided whether harm arose from a breach of duty, the court will finally look at whether the harm which occurred was reasonably foreseeable. This is the question of **remoteness of damage**, which we saw in Chapter 12

2   NEGLIGENT MISSTATEMENT

2.1   Special relationship

There is a duty of care not to cause economic loss by negligent misstatement, but the duty exists only where the person who makes the statement foresees that it may be relied on. There must therefore be a **special relationship**. To establish such a special relationship the person who makes the statement:

(a)   **Must do so in some professional or expert capacity which makes it likely that others will rely on what he says.** This is the position of an accountant providing information or advice in a professional capacity (or indeed any other person 'professing' special knowledge, skill and care), but the principle has also been extended to a friendly relationship with business overtones.

Chaudry v Prabhakar 1989
The facts: a friend of the claimant undertook (as a favour) to find a suitable car for her to buy; the claimant stipulated that any such car should not have been involved in an accident. The friend (who knew more about cars than the claimant did) failed to enquire of the owner of a car (which had, to the friend's knowledge, a straightened or replaced bonnet) whether it had been in an accident. In fact, the car had been in a serious accident and it was unroadworthy and worthless. The claimant sued the friend for £5,500.

Held: the friend owed a duty to take such care as was reasonable in the circumstances and had broken that duty; there had been a voluntary assumption of responsibility against the background of a business transaction; hence the friend was liable for the claimant's loss.

Coulthard v Neville Russell 1997
The facts: the Court of Appeal held that, as a matter of principle, auditors could owe a duty of care to client company directors to advise them that

intended payments might breach the financial assistance provisions of the Companies Act even if advice on the matter was not specifically sought. Whether a duty was owed in a particular case would depend on the facts.

(b)   *Must foresee that it is likely to be relied on by another person.*

Hedley Byrne v Heller and Partners 1963
The facts: HB were advertising agents acting for a new client E. If E failed to pay bills for advertising arranged by HB then HB would have to pay the advertising charges. HB through its bank requested information from E's bank (HP) on the financial position of E. HP returned non-committal replies which were held to be negligent misstatement of E's financial resources. In replying HP expressly disclaimed legal responsibility.

Decision: while HP were able to avoid liability by virtue of their disclaimer, the House of Lords went on to consider whether there ever could be a duty of care to avoid causing financial loss by negligent misstatement where there was no contractual or fiduciary relationship. It decided (as *obiter dicta*) that HP were guilty of negligence having breached the duty of care, because a special relationship did exist. Had it not been for the disclaimer, a claim for negligence would have succeeded.

In reaching the decision in *Hedley Byrne*, Lord Morris said the following.

> 'If someone possessed of a special skill undertakes....to apply that skill for the assistance of another person who **relies** on that skill, a duty of care will arise....If, in a sphere in which a person is so placed that others could reasonably rely on his skill....a person takes it on himself to give information or advice to....another person who, as he **knows or should know**, will place reliance on it, then a duty of care will arise.'

As you already know from your reading of Chapter 3, Section 2.2, obiter dicta *such as those made in 1963 do not form part of the ratio decidendi, and are not binding on future cases. They will, however, be persuasive.*

Note that at the time liability did not extend to those who the advisor might merely **foresee as a possible user** of the statement.

The principle of liability for negligent misstatement was refined in the area of professional negligence to take account of the test of **reasonable foresight** being present to create a duty of care.

JEB Fasteners Ltd v Marks, Bloom & Co 1982
The facts: the defendants, a firm of accountants, prepared an audited set of accounts showing stock valued at £23,080. It had been purchased for £11,000, but was nevertheless described as being valued 'at the lower of cost and net realisable value'. Hence profit was inflated. The auditors knew there were liquidity problems and that the company was seeking outside finance. The claimants were shown the accounts; they doubted the stock figure but took over the company for a nominal amount nevertheless, since by that means they could obtain the services of the company's two directors. At no time did MB tell JEB that stock was inflated. With the investment's failure, JEB sued MB claiming:

(a)   The accounts had been prepared negligently

(b)   They had relied on those accounts

(c)   They would not have invested had they been aware of the company's true position

(d)   MB owed a duty of care to all persons whom they could reasonably foresee would rely on the accounts

Held: MB owed a duty of care (d) and had been negligent in preparing the accounts (a). But even though JEB had relied on the accounts (b), they would not have acted differently if the true position had been known (c), since they had really wanted the directors, not the company. Hence the accountants were not the cause of the consequential harm and were not liable.

This case implied that an auditor should 'reasonably foresee' that he has a legal duty of care to a stranger. The decision was confirmed in *Twomax Ltd and Goode v Dickson, McFarlane & Robinson 1983*, where the auditors had to pay damages to three investors who purchased shares on the strength of accounts which had been negligently audited.

The **JEB Fasteners** *case also reinforces the important point that the person suing for negligent misstatement must actually have relied on the advice. There is no case if he would have proceeded come what may.*

Decisions since *JEB Fasteners* have, however, shied away from the reasonable foresight principle and gone back to looking at that the adviser has knowledge of the user, and the use to which the statement will be put.

2.2   The Caparo decision

The Caparo case is fundamental to an understanding of this area.

The case below made considerable changes to the tort of negligence as a whole, and the negligence of professionals in particular, and set a precedent which now forms the basis for courts when considering the liability of professional advisers.

> *Caparo Industries plc v Dickman and Others 1990*
> *The facts*: in March 1984 Caparo Industries purchased 100,000 Fidelity shares in the open market. On 12 June 1984, the date on which the accounts were published, they purchased a further 50,000 shares. Relying on information in the accounts, which showed a profit of £1.3 million, further shares were acquired. On 25 October the claimants announced that they owned or had received acceptances amounting to 91.8% of the issued shares and subsequently acquired the balance. Caparo claimed against the directors (the brothers Dickman) and the auditors for the fact that the accounts should have shown a loss of £400,000. The claimants argued that the auditors owed a duty of care to investors and potential investors in respect of the audit. They should have been aware that in March 1984 a press release stating that profits would fall significantly had made Fidelity vulnerable to a takeover bid and that bidders might well rely upon the accounts.

> *Held*: the auditor's duty did not extend to potential investors nor to existing shareholders increasing their stakes. It was a duty owed to the body of shareholders as a whole.

In the *Caparo* case the House of Lords decided that there were two very different situations facing a person giving professional advice.

(a) Preparing advice or information in the knowledge that a particular person was contemplating a transaction and was expecting to receive the advice or information in order to rely on it to decide whether or not to proceed with the transaction (a special relationship).

(b) Preparing a statement (such as an audit report) for more or less general circulation which could foreseeably be relied upon by persons unknown to the professional for a variety of different purposes.

It was held therefore that a public company's auditors owed no duty of care to the public at large who relied on the audit report in deciding to invest – and, in purchasing additional shares, an existing shareholder was in no different position to the public at large.

In *MacNaughton (James) Papers Group Ltd v Hicks Anderson & Co 1991*, it was stated that, in the absence of some general principle establishing a duty of care, it was necessary to examine each case in the light of three concepts.

- Foreseeability
- Proximity
- Fairness

This is because there is no single overriding principle establishing a duty of care that could be applied to the individual complexities of every case. So the court had to consider whether it was fair, just and reasonable for a legal duty of care to arise in the particular circumstances of each case. Lord Justice Neill set out the matters to be taken into account in considering this.

- The purpose for which the statement was made
- The purpose for which the statement was communicated
- The relationship between the maker of the statement, the recipient and any relevant third party
- The size of any class to which the recipient belonged
- The state of knowledge of the maker
- Any reliance by the recipient

In spite of this decision, it is still possible for professional advisers to owe a duty of care to an individual. The directors and financial advisors of the target company in a contested takeover bid were held to owe a duty of care to a known take-over bidder in respect of financial statements and other documents prepared for the purpose of contesting the bid: *Morgan Crucible Co plc v Hill Samuel Bank Ltd and others 1990*. It was found that the directors and financial advisers of the target company had made express representations to a known bidder, intending that the bidder should rely on those representations. In this case they owed the bidder a duty of care not to be negligent in making representations which might mislead him.

A more recent case highlights the need for a cautious approach and careful evaluation of the circumstances when giving financial advice.

ADT Ltd v BDO Binder Hamlyn 1995

The facts: Binder Hamlyn was the joint auditor (along with McCabe & Ford) of BSG. In October 1989, BSG's audited accounts for the year to 30 June 1989 were published. Binder Hamlyn signed off the audit as showing a true and fair view of BSG's position. ADT was thinking of buying BSG and, as a potential buyer, sought Binder Hamlyn's confirmation of the audited results. On 5 January 1990, the Binder Hamlyn audit partner, Martyn Bishop, attended a meeting with John Jermine, a director of ADT. This meeting was described by the judge as the 'final hurdle' before ADT finalised its bid for BSG. At the meeting, Mr Bishop specifically confirmed that he 'stood by' the audit of October 1989, thereby reconfirming the true and fair view given in that audit. ADT proceeded to purchase BSG for £105m on the strength of Binder Hamlyn's advice. It was subsequently alleged that BSG's true value was only £40m. ADT therefore sued Binder Hamlyn for the difference, £65m plus interest.

Held: Binder Hamlyn assumed a responsibility for the statement that the audited accounts showed a true and fair view of BSG. Furthermore, ADT relied to its subsequent detriment on the information provided by Mr Bishop. Since the underlying audit work had been carried out negligently, Binder Hamlyn was held liable for the difference in the amount paid by ADT and true value of BSG, amounting to £65m.

This situation was different from *Caparo* since the court was concerned with the purpose of the **statement made at the meeting** and not with the purpose for which the audit had been performed. Binder Hamlyn appealed against the decision but in 1997 reached an out of court settlement with ADT.

The following case on duty of care had parallels with the *ADT* decision, but the Court of Appeal found for the accountants.

Peach Publishing Lt v Slater & Co 1997

The facts: the defendant represented at a meeting that a set of management accounts of a company that the claimant was seeking to acquire were 'right'. It later turned out that the accounts were inaccurate.

Held: the Court of Appeal decided that on the facts of the case that the defendant had not assumed responsibility to the claimant for the accuracy of the information. There was evidence that at the meeting the claimant was not seeking assurance on the accounts as an end in itself, but in order to obtain a warranty from the vendor. Thus there is no automatic link between the giving of an assurance and the finding of liability.

There have been other important clarifications of the law affecting accountants' liability in the area of responsibility towards non-clients. The following two cases both concerned authors' liability to part of a group for losses incurred elsewhere in the group.

Barings plc v Coopers & Lybrand 1997

The facts: Barings collapsed in 1995 after heavily loss-making trading by the general manager of its Singapore subsidiary, BFS. BFS was audited by the defendant's Singapore firm, which provided Barings directors with consolidation schedules and a copy of the BFS audit report. The defendant tried to argue that there was no duty of care owed to Barings, only to BFS.

Held: duty of care was owed to Barings, as the defendants must have known that their audit report and consolidation schedules would be relied upon at group level by the parent company.

NOTES

BCCI (Overseas) Ltd v Ernst & Whinney 1997

The facts: in this case, the defendants audited the group holding company's accounts, but not those of the claimant subsidiary. The claimant tried to claim that the defendants had a duty of care to them.

Held: no duty of care was owed to the subsidiary because no specific information is normally channelled down by a holding company's auditor to its subsidiaries.

UK accountancy firms have been investigating ways of limiting liability in the face of increasing litigation. KPMG, for example, incorporated its audit practice in 1995.

In 2000, the Limited Liability Partnerships Act 2000 was passed, and limited liability partnerships have been permitted under law since 2001.

This protects the partners of accountancy firms from the financial consequences of negligent actions as their liability to third parties (previously unlimited) can now be limited.

Activity 6   **(10 minutes)**

At a party, A asks B, a friend of his and a solicitor, about a dispute which he is having with his neighbour. B suggests that A comes to her office for a chat about it the next day. He does so, and B gives him some advice without charge. He acts upon that advice, and in consequence loses his right to sue his neighbour. Discuss whether A could sue B.

Activity 7   **(10 minutes)**

An electrical engineer writes a book for general publication on the safe use of electricity. The advice given is generally sound, but there are certain circumstances in which precautions not mentioned in the book should be taken. Consider whether someone who suffers injury through not taking these precautions could sue the author in negligence.

2.3 Statutory liability for auditor's report and audited accounts

In addition to any liability in tort, an auditor also commits an offence under the Companies Act 2006 if he recklessly causes an auditor's report to contain any matter that is misleading or false to a material extent (s 507). Such an offence is punishable by fine.

Also relevant to this question of professional liability are the following provisions of that Act.

- Any provision which exempts an auditor of a company (to any extent) from, or indemnifies him against, liability for negligence (among other things) in relation to providing audited accounts is **void** (save for an indemnity for costs against successfully defending proceedings or where a liability limitation agreement applies), s 532

- A company may enter into a liability limitation agreement with an auditor, limiting his liability for negligence (among other things) in the course of auditing accounts, s 534

Activity 8 **(10 minutes)**

Claudia is a trainee accountant employed in an accountancy firm. She meets Daniel at a party and they date for three months. During that time, Daniel asks for some tax advice. Claudia looks up some information at work and then goes home and gives him advice, based on the information she has obtained from the office. She has misinterpreted the tax law and gives incorrect advice to Daniel. A reasonably competent accountant would not have given the same advice to Daniel.

If Daniel decides to sue Claudia, indicate whether or not she could rely on any of the following factors as a complete or partial defence.

		Yes	No
A	She is merely a trainee and therefore the objective standard of care required is lower.	☐	☐
B	She was in a relationship with Daniel, therefore there is a reputable presumption that she is not intending him to use here advice professionally	☐	☐
C	Daniel had intended to do as she advised anyway, so was not affected by her advice.	☐	☐

Daniel might succeed in a claim for negligence against		Yes	No
D	Claudia	☐	☐
E	Claudia's firm	☐	☐
F	Claudia' firm and Claudia	☐	☐

---

3 LIABILITY FOR FIRE

Common law

A person may be liable under common law for damage caused by fire in two different ways. The injured party may seek to demonstrate that the damage was caused:

(a) By negligence; or

(b) By the escape, without negligence, of a fire which was brought into existence by some 'non-natural' use of the land. This principle is similar to, but can be distinguished from, the rule in *Rylands v Fletcher*, which we discussed in Chapter 12.

The principles for this were set out in *Mason v Levy Auto Parts 1967*. The defendant will be liable if:

(a) He brought on to his land things likely to catch fire, and kept them there in such conditions that, if they did ignite, the fire would be likely to spread to the plaintiff's land;

(b)   He did so in the course of some non-natural use; and

(c)   The thing ignited and the fire spread.

Statute

Under statute, s 86 of the Fires Prevention (Metropolis) Act 1774 may apply. It provides that 'no action, suit or process whatever shall be had, maintained or prosecuted against any person in whose house, chamber, stable, barn or other building, or on whose estate any fire shall ... accidentally begin'.

Chapter roundup

- Negligence is the most important modern tort. To succeed in an action for negligence the claimant must prove three things. He must show that the defendant owed him (the claimant) a duty of care to avoid causing injury to persons or property. He must show that there was a breach of that duty by the defendant. He must show that in consequence the claimant suffered injury or damage or (in some cases) financial loss.

- Professional individuals and organisations have a special relationship with their clients and those who rely on their work. This is because they act in an **expert capacity**.

- To establish a **special relationship** the person who made the statement must have done so in some professional or expert capacity which made it likely that others would rely on what he said. This is the position of an adviser such as an accountant, banker, solicitor or surveyor.

- The Caparo case is fundamental to understanding professional negligence. It was decided that auditors do not owe a duty of care to the public at large or to shareholders increasing their stakes

- A person may be liable at common law for damage caused by fire through negligence or non-natural use of the land.

Quick quiz

1   How is a special relationship established in a case of negligent professional advice?

2   Outline the facts of *Caparo v Dickman and Others 1990*.

Chapter 13: Business and economic torts

NOTES

Answers to quick quiz

1   Person acts in a professional or expert capacity.
    Likely that others will rely on what he says.
    Must foresee that it is likely to be relied upon. (see para 1.4)

2   Refer to Section 2.

Answers to activities

1   D. The elements in options 1, 2 and 4 are the formulation of the tort of negligence as in *Anns* and *Caparo*. If these are present then there is a right of action for the tort of negligence.

2   It is for public policy reasons that barristers may not be sued in negligence. If every unsuccessful litigant sued his barrister this would effectively lead to a retrial and excessive litigation which would be detrimental to the legal system and justice.

3   No, A is not responsible for the actions of third parties and he has no duty of care or responsibility to B.

4   S could claim damages for nervous shock because she witnessed the accident with her own unaided senses and has a sufficiently close relationship (mother and child) with the primary victim, A.

5   No, the accountant knew (or at least should have known) of the risk.

6   A could sue B for negligent misstatement because B is giving advice in the capacity of solicitor (rather than friend) in a formal business context.

7   An action for negligent misstatement in these circumstances would fail due to the absence of a special relationship between the author and injured party.

8   A   No – the objective standard of care is the same for a trainee as a qualified accountant.

    B   No – there is no such rebuttable presumption (as there is in contract law). However, the position would be different had Claudia given the advice at the party over a drink or two.

    C   Yes – if Daniel's acts and therefore loss were unconnected with her advice then Claudia will not be liable. Daniel will have to prove that the reverse was true.

    D   Yes – if he can prove that the loss was due to her advice (ie the defence in (C) is removed).

    E   No – Claudia's firm will not be vicariously liable, as although she researched the matter at work, she gave the advice in her own time and away from work premises and therefore not in the course of her employment.

    F   No – because of answer to (E).

BPP
LEARNING MEDIA

Chapter 14:

DEFENCES AGAINST ACTIONS IN TORT

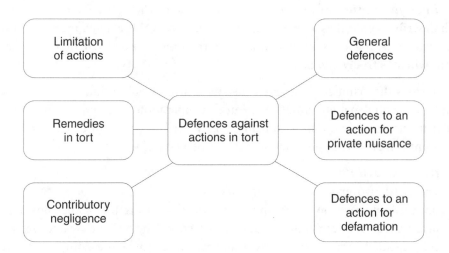

Introduction

In this chapter we describe the defences to an action in tort and the remedies available. We introduce the concept of vicarious liability.

Your objectives

In this chapter you will learn about the following.

(a) The general defences to an action in tort

(b) Specific defences available in repeat of nuisance and defamation.

(c) The remedies that may be awarded, both compensatory and non-compensatory

(d) The calculation of damages and different forms of loss

1 GENERAL DEFENCES

In an action for a particular tort the defendant may be able to rely on a defence applicable to that tort, such as justification in an action for defamation or that he took reasonable care if he is sued for negligence. But those particular defences are not available in every tort action. For example, reasonable care is no defence in a tort of strict liability. There are, however, general defences which may be pleaded in any action in tort. Of these general defences the most important is consent.

1.1 Consent

Volenti non fit injuria (no wrong is done to a person who consents to it) is the maxim which describes consent as a defence in tort (sometimes abbreviated merely to *volenti*). It must however be *true* consent, which is more than mere knowledge of a risk, and also a consent which is **freely given**.

In some cases the claimant expressly consents to what would otherwise be a wrong. For example a hospital patient awaiting a surgical operation is asked to give his written consent to the operation, that is to being cut by the surgeon's knife etc. But more often the consent is merely the voluntary acceptance of a risk of injury.

> *ICI v Shatwell 1965*
> *The facts*: two experienced shotfirers were working in a quarry. Statutory rules imposed on them (not their employer) a duty to ensure that all persons nearby had taken cover before making a dangerous test. As their electric cable was too short they decided to make the test without taking cover before doing so. There was a premature explosion and both were injured. They sued the employer.
>
> *Held*: (in the House of Lords) they had consented to the risk. The employer was not liable since it had not been negligent nor had it committed or permitted a breach of statutory duty over safety procedures. The injured men were trained for their work and properly left to carry out safety procedures of which they were well aware. (Lower courts, however, had taken the view that there had been negligence of the employer modified as to 50 per cent by contributory negligence of the employees – very much a borderline case.)

Consent in taking a normal risk may be implied. A competitor in a boxing contest or a rugby match gives an implied consent to the risks incidental to the sports played fairly in accordance with its rules – even if the actual injury is exceptional.

> *Simms v Leigh Rugby Football Club 1969*
> *The facts*: Northern rugby league rules required that any wall or other obstacle should be at least seven feet from the touchline. S was tackled fairly but broke his leg against a concrete wall 7ft 3ins from the touchline. He sued the home club.
>
> *Held*: the defendants were not at fault since their pitch complied with the rules. S, by playing on such a pitch, consented to the risk of injury in these circumstances.

However, in *Smaldon v Whitworth and Another 1996* it was held that a *referee* in a rugby match owed a duty of care in negligence to ensure that scrummages did not collapse dangerously.

In the same way a spectator at a motor race, or an employee engaged on inherently dangerous work, such as a test pilot of experimental aircraft or a steeplejack, is deemed to accept the inherent risks. But an employee, by accepting a job or continuing in it, does not consent to abnormal or unnecessary risks created by his employer merely because the employee is aware of them.

Smith v Baker & Sons 1891

The facts: S was put to work by B (his employer) in a position where heavy stones were swung over his head on a crane. Both S and B were aware of the risk. S was injured by a falling stone.

Held: S could recover damages. In working in circumstances of known risk he was not deemed to consent to the risk of the employer's negligence. This principle has been developed in later cases to impose on the employer a common law duty to provide a safe working system.

In other circumstances it has to be decided on the facts how far knowledge implies consent.

Dann v Hamilton 1939

The facts: D and H drove with others to a party at which H became very drunk. On their return to their original starting point in H's car, the party dispersed but H offered to drive D to her home nearby and she accepted. In this last part of the journey there was a serious accident due to the negligent driving of H.

Held: D was aware of the potential danger of an accident but she had not, by virtue merely of her knowledge, assented to it. However, damages were reduced because of her contributory negligence.

Morris v Murray 1990

The facts: the claimant and defendant spent all afternoon drinking together with another man. Despite the fact that the weather was poor, the two decided to go flying in a plane owned by the defendant, who piloted it. The plane crashed, killing the defendant and severely injuring the claimant, who sued the former's estate. On his behalf his administrators claimed *volenti non fit injuria* and/or contributory negligence on the part of the claimant.

Held: right from the beginning the drunken escapade was fraught with danger and, although drunk, the claimant knew what he was doing. It was very foreseeable that such an escapade would end tragically and so, by embarking on the flight, the claimant had implicitly waived his rights in the event of injury consequent on the deceased's failure to fly with reasonable care. In contrast to *Dann v Hamilton* the claimant had no reason to be involved in the escapade and every opportunity for avoiding it.

Kirkham v Chief Constable of Greater Manchester 1990

The facts: the deceased had hanged himself while in custody and his estate sued the police for negligence for failing to inform the prison authorities of the deceased's suicidal tendencies, contrary to official procedure.

Decision: the defendants could not plead the defence of *volenti non fit injuria* because the claimant was suffering from a mental illness at the time of the suicide and therefore was not capable of consenting.

1.2 Rescue cases

A person who accepts a risk in order to effect a 'rescue' does not lose his rights against the defendant if he is injured since his consent to the risk was constrained and not freely given. But the principle only applies when the risk is taken in order to safeguard others from the probability of injury for which the defendant is responsible.

> *Haynes v Harwood & Son 1935*
> *The facts*: the defendant's driver left his horse-drawn van unattended in a street. The horses bolted and a policeman (the claimant) ran out of the nearby police station to stop the horses since there was risk of injury to persons, including children, in the crowded street. He suffered injury in taking this action. The defendant pleaded *volenti*.
>
> *Held*: the policeman had not forfeited his claim by exposing himself to the risk, since consent to the risk was not freely given, and the risk was taken to safeguard others from injury that would have been the defendant's fault.

> *Cutler v United Dairies 1933*
> *The facts*: an unattended horse-drawn van bolted into an empty field. The driver called for help and a spectator who responded was injured.
>
> *Held*: the spectator had consented to the risk. He was not impelled by the need to save others from danger. His claim was barred by his consent.

If a person creates a hazard through his own negligence and a rescuer is injured, there need not be an exceptional risk over and above the inherent risks of rescue for that person to be liable for damages.

> *Ogwo v Taylor 1987*
> *The facts*: the defendant negligently set fire to his roof. Despite being well-protected, a fireman was badly scalded by steam produced by the water from his hose hitting the flames.
>
> *Held*: the defendant's action created a real risk of injury to others, of which scalding was only one. He was therefore liable for damages.

A person who creates a risk of personal injury to others cannot contract out of his liability for personal injury or death, for instance by giving notice (in circumstances of 'business liability'): Unfair Contract Terms Act 1977.

Activity 1   **(10 minutes)**

A petrol tanker is supplying petrol to a filling station next to a busy road. A small fire starts on the forecourt, and a bystander picks up a fire extinguisher and goes to put it out. Because some petrol has been spilled, there is an explosion and the bystander is injured. If the bystander were to sue the petrol company, could the company plead *volenti non fit injuria*?

1.3 Unavoidable accident

Accident is a defence only if it could not have been foreseen nor avoided by any reasonable care of the defendant.

Stanley v Powell 1891

The facts: P, a member of a shooting party, fired at a pheasant. A pellet glanced off a tree and injured a beater (the claimant).

Held: the defendant was not liable as the ricochet and subsequent injury could not reasonably be foreseen.

1.4 Act of God

Act of God, which is an unforeseeable catastrophe, is a special type of unavoidable accident. This defence is rarely available.

1.5 Statutory authority

If a statute requires that something be done, there is no liability in doing it unless it is done negligently. If a statute merely permits an action it must be done in the manner least likely to cause harm and there is liability in tort, for nuisance, if it is done in some other way.

1.6 Act of State

If a person causes damage or loss in the course of his duties for the State, he may claim Act of State. But it is not a defence in any case where the claimant is a British subject or the subject of a friendly foreign power (eg the US).

Buron v Denman 1848

The facts: D was captain of a British warship who had a general duty to suppress the slave trade. He set fire to a Spanish ship carrying slaves and released them. The Crown later ratified his act.

Held: neither D nor the Crown were liable.

1.7 Necessity

An act which causes damage may be intentional. If this is so, the defence of necessity may be raised in the following circumstances.

(a) The act is reasonable – such as shooting a dog to prevent it worrying sheep
(b) The act was done to prevent a greater evil
(c) It was done to defend the realm

1.8 Mistake

An intentional act done out of mistake may occasionally be defendable if it was reasonable. Such a case may be where a person makes a citizen's arrest in the reasonable and sincere belief that the claimant committed a crime.

1.9 Self-defence

Similarly, self-defence is a valid defence if the defendant acted to preserve himself, his family or his property, so long as the act was reasonable and in keeping with the nature of the threat. But if a blow is struck in response only to verbal attack, there is no defence.

Lastly, no claim for damages will succeed if both claimant and defendant were engaged in illegal activity at the time of the damage, and it arose naturally out of that activity. Hence a burglar could not sue his getaway driver for damages when the latter crashed the car: *Ashton v Turner 1980.*

Activity 2   (5 minutes)

A lorry is carrying mirrors which are standing upright. The whole cargo is covered by a tarpaulin. The tarpaulin breaks free, exposing one of the mirrors. The sun is reflected off this mirror into the eyes of the driver of another vehicle, which then crashes injuring a pedestrian. If the lorry owner is sued by the pedestrian, which defence should he put forward?

---

2   DEFENCES TO AN ACTION FOR PRIVATE NUISANCE

Prescription

The right to commit private nuisance may be acquired by prescription. The defendant must show that the actions causing the nuisance have been carried on for 20 years. The actions must have been carried on as of right: *nec vi, nec clam, nec precario* (neither forcibly, nor secretly, nor with permission).

The actions must have amounted to an actionable nuisance for the full 20 year period.

> *Sturges v Bridgman 1879*
> *The facts*: the claimant built a consulting room in his garden for use in his medical practice. The defendant operated machinery in his business as a confectioner. This created noise which caused interference to the claimant. The defendant pleaded prescription as a defence.
>
> *Held*: although the defendant's business had continued for over 20 years, it only constituted a nuisance from the time that the consulting room was built. The defence was not available.

Statutory authority

The defendant may plead that an activity which causes interference is authorised by statute. He must demonstrate that the interference is inevitable and that he has not been negligent. Negligence here means behaviour without reasonable regard and care for the interests of other persons.

> *Allen v Gulf Oil Refining Ltd 1981*
> *The facts*: the claimants alleged that noise, smell and vibrations from an oil refinery caused a nuisance. The Gulf Oil Refining Act 1965 (a private Act of Parliament) authorised the defendants to make compulsory purchases of land for the construction of a refinery, but did not authorise the construction or use of the refinery.
>
> *Held*: construction and operation of the refinery were impliedly authorised by statute.

Consent

Consent may be a defence to an action.

> *Kiddle v City Business Properties Ltd 1942*
> *The facts*: the claimant was a tenant of part of premises of which the defendant landlord also retained part. The landlord's guttering overflowed and water damaged the claimant's stock.
>
> *Held*: the tenant had, by becoming tenant of part of the premises, consented to run the risk of nuisance arising from the condition of that part of the premises retained by the landlord, in the absence of negligence on the part of the landlord.

Act of God and act of a third party

Act of God or act of a third party may constitute a defence.

Coming to the nuisance

'Coming to the nuisance', a claim that the claimant acquired land with knowledge of an existing nuisance, is no defence: *Sturges v Bridgman 1879*. It would be unreasonable to expect someone not to purchase a property because a neighbour is committing an actionable nuisance.

Remedies

There are three remedies available to a victim of private nuisance.

(a) An award of **damages** may be made. This will be calculated on the same basis as an award of damages for other torts.

(b) The award of an **injunction** is, as an equitable remedy, discretionary: *Miller v Jackson 1977*. In spite of this the courts will usually grant an injunction where the nuisance is continuing. Principles have been laid down to determine when damages should be awarded instead of an injunction: *Shelfer v City of London Electric Lighting Co 1895*. 'If the injury to the claimant's legal rights is small, and is one which is capable of being estimated in money, and is one which can be adequately compensated by a small money payment, and the case is one in which it would be oppressive to the defendant to grant an injunction,' then damages will be substituted.

(c) The third remedy is **abatement**. Abatement can be defined as removal of the nuisance by the victim. This is, as might be expected, not a remedy encouraged by the law. Notice must usually be given to the wrongdoer, except where there is an emergency or where the nuisance can be removed without entering the wrongdoer's land, for example to remove tree roots and branches: *Lemmon v Webb 1895*. The abater cannot use force and should use the remedy only if this can be done peaceably.

> *Perry v Fitzhowe 1846*
> *The facts*: the defendant demolished the claimant's inhabited house because the building interfered with the defendant's easement of pasture over the claimant's land.
>
> *Held*: abatement was no defence.

NOTES

3 DEFENCES TO AN ACTION FOR DEFAMATION

There are a variety of specific defences available regarding the tort of defamation, which we saw in Chapter 12.

- Consent
- Justification
- Fair comment
- Privilege
- Innocence
- Apology

Consent

It is a defence that the claimant gave his consent, possibly only by implication, to the publication of a defamatory statement about himself *Cookson v Harewood 1932*. This sounds unlikely, but, for example, the subject of a defamatory statement made at a company meeting may fail to object to it – thereby 'consenting' to its inevitable publication in the minutes of that meeting.

Justification

Justification is a defence; the defendant must show that the statement was true in all material particulars. Defamation cannot be committed by telling the truth. The defendant need only prove the facts which constitute the 'sting of the charge'.

> *Alexander v North Eastern Railway Co 1865*
> *The facts*: a statement had been made to the effect that the claimant had been convicted of dishonesty and sentenced to three weeks imprisonment for failing to pay his rail fare. In fact he had been sentenced to two weeks imprisonment for non payment.
> *Held*: the statement could be justified.

Fair comment

For the defence of fair comment to succeed, it must be shown that the statement was:

- A fair comment
- On a matter of public interest
- Insofar as it gave facts they were accurate
- The defendant was not actuated by malice

This allows room for an individual – eg a writer or preacher – to speak out with an opinion on a matter of genuine concern. It is an important element of the principle of freedom of speech.

- The opinion expressed on the facts must be honestly held
- The defendant must have believed the facts to be true

Fair comment, then, must be an opinion rather than a statement of fact – it is a particular reaction to facts, however extreme or prejudiced that reaction may be.

London Artists Ltd v Littler 1969

The facts: the defendant, an impresario, had received four letters simultaneously from the four top performers in his West End play, each of them cancelling his contract. Littler was convinced that this was a plot and sent a letter alleging this to each claimant, and to the press. He was sued for libel.

Held: the matter was one of public interest and he could have made fair comment on it, but in leaping to a conclusion of a plot (which was never proved) he had made a statement of fact for which fair comment was not a defence.

Privilege

It is a defence that the statement was protected by *privilege*, which may be 'absolute' or 'qualified'. This is the most important defence in practice. The difference between absolute and qualified privilege is that absolute privilege remains available as a defence despite any evidence of malice on the part of the person who makes the statement. It enables Members of Parliament, for example, to make statements with the deliberate intention of causing prejudice to the person about whom the statement is made.

Absolute privilege

Absolute privilege is given to enable a person to make statements in the public interest, without fear of personal liability. It extends to:

(a) Statements made in Parliament, and papers laid before Parliament

(b) Statements made by judge, jury, witnesses, counsel or parties in judicial proceedings and contemporary newspaper reports of those proceedings and other (fair and accurate) reports of those proceedings, such as the Law Reports

(c) Communications between high officers of state, in the course of their official duties

(d) Statements between solicitor and client, in some cases

Qualified privilege

The defence of qualified privilege evolved through case law. It was extended to newspapers (subject to certain conditions) by the Defamation Act 1952.

Qualified privilege is applicable to statements made *without* malice or improper intent.

- By a person who has an interest or a (social, moral or legal) duty to make it
- To a person who has a corresponding interest or duty to receive it.

This reciprocity is essential: *Adam v Ward 1917*.

Qualified privilege has been held to arise in the following cases.

(a) Common interest, eg references to prospective employers or credit agencies: *London Association for the Protection of Trade v Greenlands 1916*

(b) Statements in protection of one's private interests: *Osborn v Thos Boulter 1930*

(c)   Statements made by way of complaint to a proper authority, eg to the Panel on Take-overs and Mergers

(d)   Professional communications between solicitor and client

(e)   Fair and accurate reports of Parliamentary or public judicial proceedings

If a statement to which qualified privilege might otherwise apply is made in circumstances which give it wider circulation than is necessary to protect the common interest, malice may be inferred, and the privilege will be lost.

> *Parsons v Surgey 1864*
>
> *The facts*: a shareholder of a railway company called a general meeting to which he invited non-members, including representatives of the press. At the meeting he made defamatory statements about one of the directors, who sued him. He pleaded qualified privilege.
>
> *Held*: qualified privilege would extend to communications made to other shareholders since they had a common interest in the affairs of the company. But the privilege was lost owing to the invitation to the press and other publicity about the meeting.

Comments made in protection of one's own interests and fair and accurate reports of parliamentary and judicial proceedings are protected by qualified privilege. But a statement published by, or on behalf of, a candidate for election to Parliament or to a local authority is *not* privileged, because of the candidate's vested interest in prejudicing the public's opinion. A statement might, however, be defended as a 'fair comment' on a matter of public interest.

Qualified privilege and the press

The difficulty which confronts a newspaper in pleading common law 'qualified privilege' is that usually it has no duty (in the legal sense) to its readers to disclose the information which it prints. It is not a sufficient defence to show that the material is 'of interest' to readers. But s 7 Defamation Act 1952 offers newspapers and broadcasters statutory qualified privilege in respect of various types of report.

For the purpose of this defence, a 'newspaper' is defined as follows.

- It contains public news and comment thereon
- It is published in the UK at intervals of not more than 36 days

The list of newspaper reports to which qualified privilege is given under the Act is divided into two parts. Part 1 comprises reports of:

(a)   Public proceedings of foreign legislatures and courts

(b)   The contents of UK public registers and notices published by order of the courts

(c)   British courts martial

It is unnecessary to give this protection to newspaper reports of the proceedings of the UK Parliament and courts since these already have absolute privilege. Where a report is covered by Part 1, the claimant need not be given the opportunity of rebuttal in the newspaper itself.

Part 2 lists mainly the reports of various kinds of meetings, whose appearance in the newspapers may be protected.

(a)   Public meetings – meetings *bona fide* and lawfully held in the UK to discuss a matter of common concern, whether or not admission to the meeting is restricted.

(b)   Meetings of almost very kind of common interest association – artistic, scientific, religious, learned, commercial, professional, athletic or recreational – insofar as the report related to the conduct of members, officers or employees of the association. If a meeting of an association defames someone not directly associated with it, a newspaper does not have qualified privilege to report that statement.

(c)   Meetings of local authorities and of their committees.

(d)   Meetings of public (but not of private) companies, including corporate bodies formed under royal charter or special statute (although most companies are formed under the Companies Act).

Additional conditions apply to the reports covered by Part 2. Unlike those of Part 1, they enjoy qualified privilege only if the newspaper has responded to a request by the claimant that it publish a reasonable letter of statement explaining or contradicting the original report. Note that this point only arises if the **claimant makes a request** for an opportunity to publish a rebuttal, and the newspaper must make an **adequate and reasonable response**. If it distorts or suppresses the claimants rebuttal, with selective quotation, long delay or illegible print, it might lose the protection of privilege.

Innocence

As noted above, mechanical distributors of a libel may plead **innocent defamation**. The Defamation Act 1996 introduced an 'offer to make amends.' Under this procedure the offer is one to pay *compensation*, as distinct from merely costs and expenses, and to publish a correction and apology. The disseminator of defamatory material must show the following.

(a)   He was not the author, editor or publisher of the statement.

(b)   He took reasonable care in relation to its publication.

(c)   He did not know, and had no reason to believe, that what he did caused or contributed to the publication of a defamatory statement.

These principles may soon be tested in cases involving 'e-mail libel': In the first case of its kind, the High Court ruled that an Internet provider could face defamation proceedings if it fails to remove a statement which has been **brought to its attention** as being libellous. It cannot necessarily rely on the defence of **innocent defamation** if it has failed to take reasonable care by failing to remove the statement when told about it. (*Godfrey v Demon Internet Ltd 1999*).

Apology

If the statement was published in a newspaper or other periodical, the paper may plead *apology* if it can show the following.

- It published the statement without malice or gross negligence
- It has since published a full apology
- It has paid a sum of money into court as an offer of compensation

In other words, it has 'made amends' for its error.

4   CONTRIBUTORY NEGLIGENCE

If the damage suffered as a result of negligence was partly caused by contributory negligence of the claimant his claim is proportionately reduced: Law Reform (Contributory Negligence) Act 1945.

4.1   Degree of proof

The defendant need not prove that the claimant owed him a duty of care. It is sufficient if part of the damage was due to the claimant's failure to take reasonable precautions to avoid a risk which he could foresee. If a motor cyclist, injured in a crash caused by the negligence of another driver, suffers avoidable hurt by failure to wear a crash helmet (which is compulsory by law) that is contributory negligence (*O'Connell v Jackson 1971*), which will reduce damages by 15% if injury would have been less and 25% if it would not have happened at all had the helmet been worn: *Froom v Butcher 1976*. So too is failure of a front seat passenger in a car to use a seat belt (even before it became compulsory).

The test of contributory negligence is what caused the damage, not what caused the accident.

4.2   Standard of reasonableness

There is however a standard of reasonableness. Mere failure to take a possible precaution or even thoughtlessness or inattention are not contributory negligence, unless there is a failure to do what a prudent person should do to avoid or reduce a foreseeable risk, If the claimant is a workman working at a monotonous task or in factory noise which may dull his concentration, due allowance is made in determining whether he is guilty of contributory negligence. A child of any age may be guilty of contributory negligence but in deciding whether he has been negligent the standard of reasonable behaviour is adjusted to take account of his inexperience.

Yachuk v Oliver Blais 1949
The facts: a boy of nine bought petrol from a garage stating falsely that his mother's car had run out of petrol down the road. It was supplied in an open margarine tub. He set fire to the petrol and was badly burned. The garage pleaded contributory negligence.

Held: the garage was negligent in selling the petrol in this way. There was no evidence that the boy realised the danger of what he did and so it was not a case of contributory negligence.

The contributory negligence of an adult who accompanies a child is not a defence to an action by the child.

> **Activity 3** **(10 minutes)**
>
> A factory has its own electrical generator. The building containing the generator is left unlocked so as to allow rapid access in the event of fire, but there is a notice on the door which reads (in full): 'High voltage. Trained electricians only'. A child of ten is negligently allowed by his parents to play near the building. The child enters the building, suffers an electric shock and is injured. To what extent could the building's owner plead contributory negligence to reduce damages payable to the child?

Employer/employee relationship

In the special circumstances of the employer/employee relationship, certain principles relating to contributory negligence have been developed by the courts. Due allowance is made for ordinary human failings.

(a) An employee is not deemed to consent to the risk of injury because he is aware of the risk. It is the employer's duty to provide a safe working system.

(b) Employees can become inattentive or careless in doing work which is monotonous or imposes stress. This factor too must be allowed for in the employer's safety precautions.

(c) It is not always a sufficient defence that the employer provided safety equipment etc. The employer has some duty to encourage if not to insist on its proper use. Much depends on the nature of the risk and the experience and responsibility (or want of it) of the employee.

(d) Many dangers can be caused by carelessness or other fault of an otherwise competent employee. It is the employer's duty to be watchful and to keep such tendencies in check.

(e) Employees do not work continuously. The employer's duty is to take reasonable care for their safety in all acts which are normally and reasonably incidental to the day's work.

Davidson v Handley Page 1945
The facts: a woman employee went to wash her tea-cup after use. She slipped on a wet surface and was injured.

Held: the employer had failed in his duty to take reasonable care to provide safe premises. The employee's injury had occurred in the course of her employment and the employer was liable.

5   REMEDIES IN TORT

5.1   Damages in tort

The rules on remoteness of damage in tort have already been considered. The amount of damages is based on the principle of compensating the claimant for his financial loss and not of punishing the defendant for his wrong. But there are several categories of damages related to the circumstances.

Ordinary damages

Ordinary damages are assessed by the court as compensation for losses which cannot be positively proved or ascertained, and depend on the court's view of the nature of the claimant's injury.

Special damages

Special damages are those which can be positively proved, such as damage to clothing, cars and so on.

Exemplary damages

Exemplary or aggravated damages are intended to punish the defendant for his act, and to deter him and others from a similar course of action in the future. These damages are only rarely awarded, eg where in a defamation case the defendant raises the defence of justification but loses. In *Rookes v Barnard 1964* the House of Lords set down that exemplary damages could only be awarded for torts where the defendant calculated to make more money from the tort than he would have to pay in damages (as is sometimes the situation in newspaper libel cases), where a government official acts oppressively, arbitrarily or unconstitutionally, or where statute permits.

Nominal damages

Nominal damages are given where the claimant has suffered injury, but has suffered no real damage (eg trespass to land without damage to that land).

5.2   Non-monetary remedies in tort

Injunction

This is an order by the court which requires an individual to refrain from doing a certain act, or orders him to do a certain act. There are two types of injunction.

(a)   **Interlocutory injunctions**: these are awarded before the hearing of an action so as to preserve the *status quo*. Here, the claimant enters into an undertaking to pay the defendant for any loss arising out of the granting of the injunction.

(b)   **Perpetual injunctions**: these are granted after the full hearing and continue until revoked by the court.

Failure to comply with an injunction is a contempt of court, which then empowers the court to fine the person in default or imprison him until his contempt is purged, when he apologises and promises not to breach the court order again in the future.

6 LIMITATION OF ACTIONS

The right of action in tort is generally barred by lapse of time six years after the right of action accrues: Limitation Act 1980. But where the claim is for personal injury resulting from negligence, a limitation period of three years runs from the time when the right of action accrued or (if later), from the date when the claimant first knew of it. The purpose of this rule is to allow a claimant to sue when the consequences of a tort only become apparent long after the tort is committed.

The Latent Damage Act 1986 provides that in non-personal injury claims where damage is latent (undiscoverable), the limitation period will be either the usual six year period or (if longer) three years from the date that the claimant discovered or should have discovered the damage. The Act also provides for a 'long-stop' – a bar on all claims (except personal injury claims) brought more than fifteen years from the act or omission alleged to constitute the negligence.

Chapter roundup

- There are a number of general defences which may be pleaded in any action for tort. The most important of these is consent.

- If the damage suffered as a result of negligence was partly caused by contributory negligence of the claimant the claim is proportionately reduced: Law Reform (Contributory Negligence) Act 1945.

- The amount of damages is based on the principle of compensating the claimant for his financial loss and not of punishing the defendant for his wrong. There are several categories of damages related to the circumstances.

- The right of action in tort is generally barred by lapse of time six years after the right of action accrues: Limitation Act 1980. But where the claim is for personal injury resulting from negligence, a limitation period of three years runs from the time when the right of action accrued or (if later), from the date when the claimant first knew of it.

Quick quiz

1   What is a 'general defence'?

2   List five general defences besides consent.

3   What are the categories of damages in tort?

4   What is an injunction?

Answers to quick quiz

1   Consent is the most important, which may be pleaded in any action in tort. (see para 1)

2   Rescue cases, accident, Act of God, statutory authority, Act of State. (para 1)

3   Ordinary, special, exemplary, nominal. (para 4.1)

4   An order by the court which requires an individual to refrain from or perform a certain act. (para 4.2)

Answers to activities

1   No, the bystander acted to prevent injury to other persons.

2   Unavoidable accident.

3   Not at all: the parents' negligence is irrelevant, and the child was too young to understand the risk.

PART E

EUROPEAN LAW

Chapter 15:
THE EU INSTITUTIONS

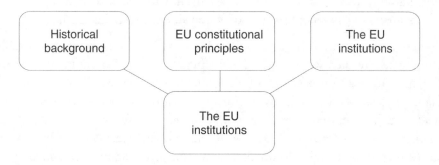

Introduction

This part of Unit 28 deals with the **law of the European Union** ('EU'). Originally set up as the European Economic Community under the Treaty of Rome 1957, the Community has evolved, both through Treaty revisions and by the way the Treaty has been interpreted by the European Court of Justice, into an organisation uniting 27 European states. Other pan-European organisations exist, as do other treaties, but these have nothing to do with the EU.

The EU has its own legal principles and its own institutions which are quite separate from those of the constituent parts of the UK. It is important to learn what these principles and institutions are and how they operate. Only then will you be able to understand how the EU makes law on practical subjects such as workers' rights.

Your objectives

In this chapter you will learn about the following.

(a) The EU constitutional principles of European citizenship, federalism and subsidiarity

(b) The structure of the EU institutions and their roles

1 HISTORICAL BACKGROUND

1.1 Development of the EU

The history of Europe is one of almost constant warfare. It was not until 1919 that going to war was outlawed as a method of resolving disputes over international treaties. Various factors came together after the end of the Second World War that made an attempt to find a method of ensuring peace in Europe more likely; not least the economic and physical destruction of the war itself, which had turned relatively wealthy European states into paupers regardless of which side they had been on.

The French civil servant, Monnet, convinced that nation states would not be able to act alone to re-generate themselves, formulated a plan to build a community of nations that would ensure peace and prosperity. Monnet's plan was adopted by the French minister Schuman. They started by inviting all European nations to pool their resources in coal and steel, the two commodities essential to wage war. Only six countries accepted, signing the **Treaty of Paris** in 1951 – Belgium, France, Germany, Italy, Luxembourg and the Netherlands. Britain declined to join, concerned about its empire and its ties with the USA and also with the movement towards a federal Europe envisaged by Monnet and Schuman.

Subsequent attempts at extending the Community sector by sector to cover all industry failed. Monnet and Schuman then decided to set up a **European Economic Community** and, at the same time, put atomic energy production in the hands of a supranational body. Once again all European states were invited to join and, once again, only six accepted, with the UK declining for the same reasons as before. The two **Treaties of Rome** were signed in 1957 setting up the EEC and Euratom.

The USA had been very influential, as they were providing the money to help Europe re-generate itself. They wanted to withdraw their own forces from Europe in order to fight the Korean War and then the Vietnam War. They needed to reconcile France and Germany to achieve this.

Initially the three Communities, ECSC, EEC & Euratom were set up with different institutional actors. In the nineteen sixties the decision was taken to merge the ECSC's High Authority with the Commissions of the EEC & Euratom. The first major revision of the founding treaties was that which led to the **Merger Treaty** in 1965. Revisions also occurred every time the communities grew, starting in 1973 with the accession of Denmark, Ireland and the UK. Greece joined in 1981 with Spain & Portugal following in 1986. Austria, Finland and Sweden joined in 1995 after the cessation of the cold war removed the need for political neutrality for those countries that had bordered Communist Eastern Europe. The largest increase was in 2004 when ten countries (Cyprus, Czech Republic, Estonia, Hungary, Latvia, Lithuania, Malta, Poland, Slovakia and Slovenia) joined, most of which had been under soviet domination since the end of the Second World War. Finally, in January 2007, Bulgaria and Romania became part of the EU.

During the seventies and the early eighties the EEC stagnated, due to a number of factors, including an oil crisis. Eventually the **Single European Act** was passed in 1986 to remove the final obstructions to the free movement of goods. The other major revisions of the Treaties were intended to prepare for enlargement, but never quite succeeded. They are the Treaties of Maastricht in 1992, Amsterdam in 1997, and Nice in 2001. A further Treaty, known as the Constitutional Treaty was signed in 2004. However it did not come into effect after it was rejected by referenda held in France and the Netherlands in 2005. However late in 2007 many of the changes agreed for the Constitutional Treaty were adopted in the new **Treaty of Lisbon**, also known as the **reform treaty**. Whether or not this new Treaty comes into force remains to be seen.

The **Maastricht Treaty**, also known as the **Treaty on European Union** was significant because it set up the three pillar system that will remain in place until the Reform Treaty comes into force. Under this system the old EEC became the EC, remaining a supranational pillar. The other two pillars, Common Foreign and Security Policy and Justice and Home Affairs (JHA) were introduced on an intergovernmental basis – the usual format for international treaties. This allowed those members of the EEC that wanted to move towards closer integration a forum for discussions whilst at the same time keeping on board those countries that were uncomfortable with the concept of a federal Europe.

The Amsterdam Treaty shifted some of the topics that Maastricht had placed in the JHA pillar into the EC pillar. JHA was then renamed Police and Judicial Co-operation in Criminal Matters. The Treaty of Amsterdam also re-numbered all the Treaty articles. The Treaty of Nice dealt mainly with voting rights and the number of Commissioners, MEPs and Judges in an enlarged union. The Treaty of Nice also dealt with what was to happen regarding coal and steel when the ECSC reached the end of its planned 50 year life in July 2002. Lisbon will, if ratified, strengthen the role of the European Parliament regarding legislation, increase the number of areas covered by qualified majority voting (QMV) and appoint a President of the Council for a term of two and a half years instead of the current six months, allowing for better long term planning. It will also enable the appointment of a 'High Representative' to give the appearance of a more coherent foreign policy for the EU as a whole.

1.2 The provisions and treaties relevant to this part of the Unit

Article 12 of the Treaty of Amsterdam amends the old article numbers of the EC Treaty.

The European Communities (Amendment) Act 1998 implements the TOA, which came into force in May 1999. The Act makes the TOA an integral part of UK Law.

The following is a list of key Treaty provisions, the subjects they cover and the new and old article numbers that relate to them. (Note, the new numbers will be used in this book – even when the old number was in place at the time of, for example, the ECJ judgment – but the old ones are also given here for cross-referencing to other texts.)

Activities of the Community	Article 3 (formerly Article 3) as amended by Article G (3) TEU.
Free movement of goods – financial restrictions	Articles of Goods 23 – 27 (formerly Articles 9 – 29) which prohibit financial trade restrictions.
Free movement of goods – non-financial restrictions	Articles 28 – 31 (formerly Articles 30 – 37) which prohibit non-financial trade restrictions.
Free movement of workers	Articles 39 – 40 (formerly Articles 48 and 49) which prohibit restrictions on the free movement of employed persons.

Free movement of services	Articles 49 – 55 (formerly Articles 59 – 66) which prohibit restrictions on the movement of self-employed persons.
Rights of establishment	Articles 43 – 48 (formerly Articles 52 – 58) which prohibit restrictions on self-employed workers to setting up business in other member states.
Free movement of capital and the EMU	Articles 56 – 60 (formerly Articles 73b – 73g) and Articles 105 – 111 (formerly Articles 105 – 109), which provide for free movement of capital and the European Monetary Union.
Competition	Article 81 (formerly Article 85) and Article 82 (formerly article 86). See also Regulation 17/62.
The Institutions of the Community	Articles 7 – 9 (formerly Articles 4 – 10) and Articles 189 onwards (formerly Article 137 onwards).
Enforcement actions against member states	Articles 226 – 227 (formerly Articles 169 – 170).
References to the ECJ	Article 234 (formerly Article 177).
Actions against the Community	Articles 230 – 233 (formerly Articles 173 – 176) and Article 241 (formerly Article 184).
The Lomé Conventions	These conventions are examples of preferential trade agreements between the Community and contain ACP.

Note. A reference to an Article of the EC Treaty in this unit will be identified as, for example, 'Article 189 EC'. Other references to Articles will be Articles of Directives and so no.

1.3 Important substantive provisions of the EC Treaty relating to general interpretation of EU Law

Article 7 EC – *Ultra Vires* and the EU institutions:

> '*Each institution shall act within the limits of the powers conferred upon it by this Treaty.*'

Article 10 EC – Member State obligation to follow the laws of the EU

Member states are required to:

> '*take all appropriate measures whether general or particular, to ensure fulfilment of the obligations arising out of this Treaty or resulting from action taken by the institution.....*'

Article 10 EC places obligations on the member states to follow the laws of the EU. In essence these are the following.

- To give effect to such laws within the member states
- To obey the laws of the EU
- To facilitate achievement of EU objectives
- To abstain from jeopardising such objectives

Article 12 EC – Prohibition against discrimination:

> '*... any discrimination on grounds of nationality shall be prohibited.*'

2   EU CONSTITUTIONAL PRINCIPLES

2.1   European Citizenship

Article 17 of the TEU stated:

> '*(1) Citizenship of the Union is hereby established. Every person holding the nationality of a Member State shall be a citizen of the Union. Citizenship of the Union shall complement and not replace national citizenship.*
>
> *(2) Citizens of the Union shall enjoy the rights conferred by this Treaty and shall be subject to the duties imposed thereby.* '

EU citizenship is obligatory for all the member states' nationals – neither you nor your member state can opt out of this provision.

Article 18 of the TEU granted every citizen the right to '*move and reside freely*' with all the member states' territory. This right is, however, capable of being restricted by both the provisions of the EC Treaty itself and any measures adopted to put it into effect. The actual scope of this free movement will be dealt with in Chapters 17 and 18.

In addition, EU citizens have a number of other rights. For example, you are entitled to vote or stand as a candidate in any local authority elections (formally referred to as 'municipal' elections) or the elections to the European Parliament ('EP' – see below) in another member state. You are not, however, entitled to stand for election to another member state's national parliament by virtue of your EU citizenship.

An EU citizen is also entitled to be represented (and be protected) by the diplomatic authorities of another member state if he is in a third (non-EU) country in which his own member state has no diplomatic presence (eg the UK had no diplomatic represent-ation in Iraq for many years).

Article 21 of the TEU states that EU citizens may petition the EP and complain to the EU Ombudsman about the activities of EU institutions. Further, if you do write to the EU institutions you may do so in any of its official languages and expect to be answered in that same language.

2.2   Federalism

Many of the early supporters of the ECSC, Euratom and the EEC (as it then was) in the 1950s described themselves as 'federalists'. They believed in the creation of a Europe-wide political body that would assume many of the functions and powers of the individual European nation states. They hoped that, eventually, these various nation states, such as France and the UK, would be replaced by a country called 'Europe' with its own government, currency, army, flag etc. These ambitions have not, however, been universally welcomed – even by other supporters of, first, the EEC and then the EC and EU.

For example, a draft statute for a 'European Political Community' was drawn up in 1953 which envisaged a European federation. This fell victim, however, to France's fear of Germany. Other projects advanced by federalists, such as monetary union, have also taken much longer to put into practice than their champions had envisaged. Often, as with monetary union itself, these projects have also been implemented on 'functionalist' basis. The functionalist preference has been for a step-by-step or subject area-by-subject area approach to European integration with supranational institutions for specific disciplines or tasks rather than pan-European political bodies.

This tension between federalists and functionalists explains, in part, the development of the EU's institutions over the years since 1957 including the UK's opt-out from the Social Chapter under the TEU, the principle of subsidiarity and the emergence of practices such as '**enhanced co-operation**'.

2.3 Subsidiarity

The preamble to the TEU states:

'...*the process of creating an ever closer Union among the peoples of Europe in which decisions are taken as closely as possible to the citizens in accordance with the principle of subsidiarity*'.

Article 5 of the TEU goes on:

'*In areas which do not fall within its exclusive competence, the Community shall take action, in accordance with the principle of subsidiarity, only if and in so far as the objectives of the proposed action cannot be sufficiently achieved by the Member States and can therefore by reason of the scale or effects of the proposed action, be better achieved by the Community. Any action by the Community shall not go beyond what is necessary to achieve the objectives of this Treaty*'.

There are, therefore, three parts to this principle.

- The EU only takes action if the objectives for that action cannot be sufficiently achieved by the individual member states,

- The EU can achieve the objectives because of its scale or effects, and

- If the EU does take any action it should not go beyond what is needed to achieve the Treaty objectives.

Hence, it is for the Commission to justify its proposals under the above principle. This was specifically required by the TOA, which contains a Protocol on the subsidiarity principle. This Protocol contains the following conditions for deciding whether the principle has been complied with.

- Does the action have Europe-wide aspects that could not be dealt with by individual member states?

- Would action by individual member states undermine the objectives of the EC Treaty?

- Would action at a EU level produce clear benefits?

Activity 1   **(5 minutes)**

Does the principle of subsidiarity reflect a federalist or functionalist view of the EU?

3 THE EU INSTITUTIONS

The primary institutions of the EU are the:

1. Commission
2. Council of the European Union (Council of Ministers prior to 1993)
3. European Council
4. European Parliament ('EP')
5. European Court of Justice ('ECJ') – including the Court of First Instance

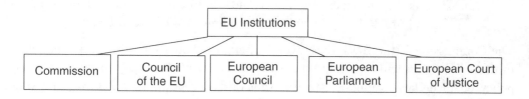

We shall cover each of these institutions in turn.

3.1 The Commission (Articles 211 – 219 EC)

Structure

The Commission is based in Brussels (with a subsidiary base in Luxembourg). There are currently twenty-seven Commissioners (one per member state). They are '**chosen on the grounds of their general competence and whose independence is beyond doubt**' and serve for five years (renewable). The whole Commission retires at the same time.

Commission appointments require the EP's approval. The EP can also force the entire Commission to resign through a vote of censure or no confidence. Further, the Commission attends EP sessions to explain and justify its policies. The Commission itself meets weekly, normally on Wednesdays. Although decisions can be by simple majority, in practice they are by consensus.

The Commission's President is nominated by the common accord of the member states and approved by the EP. He is the figurehead of the EU, participating in the twice-yearly meetings of the European Council and representing the EU at various international summits.

Beneath the President, each Commissioner is responsible for a particular subject area (allocated by the President) and is assisted by a personal 'Cabinet' of six civil servants who link him with the Directors General and keep him informed of developments. Any Commissioner who is guilty of serious misconduct may be compulsorily retired by the ECJ on application by the Council or Commission, or can be required to resign by the President of the Commission, making such a request with the agreement of all the other Commissioners.

The Commission operates through 36 Directorates General, each headed by a Director General reporting to individual Commissioners. Fifteen thousand civil servants ('fonctionnaires') work for the Commission.

The role of the Commission

The powers of the Commission are set out in Article 211. It may:

(a) Make references to ECJ

(b) Make recommendations or opinions on matters covered by the Treaty

(c) Exercise its own power of decision (autonomous role in competition policy)

(d) Exercise its right of initiative in the legislative process

(e) Exercise its management role in the day-to-day operation of the Common Agricultural Policy ('CAP') and the Common Commercial Policy.

The Commission is the EU's 'Executive', although it holds some legislative powers. It initiates EU policy and represents the general interest of the EU. This right to initiate policy enabled the Commission to drive forward European integration eg the single European market in early 1993.

The EP can request a proposal from the Commission to the Council or the Council itself can request the Commission to undertake studies for possible legislation. Before issuing draft legislation the Commission seeks any affected parties' views to achieve a balance of interests. Any Commission proposals must be agreed before being sent to the Council. Due to the principle of subsidiarity the Commission only initiates legislation where individual member states are not in as effective a position as the EU to take action.

The Commission also ensures that Treaty provisions are applied, giving recommendations and opinions where necessary and exercising powers conferred upon it to implement the rules. These powers enable the Commission to take the lead in developing the EU by submitting policies to the Council for decisions. It may also take policy decisions itself, eg social policy.

The Commission is the guardian of the Treaties, ensuring the member states' compliance by delivering reasoned opinions and, if necessary, by reference to the ECJ. The Commission may apply to the ECJ for a fine if a member state continuously fails to comply with the judgment. The Commission may also refer any Act contrary to EU law for annulment by the ECJ.

The Commission drafts the Community's annual budget. This role is scrutinised by the Court of Auditors to ensure sound financial management, legality and the elimination of fraud and waste. The Auditor reports to the EP, which judges the Commission's execution of the budget.

The Commission also ensures member states comply with established policies under powers delegated by the Council. It achieves this through supervising committees comprising member state representatives under the chairmanship of a Commission representative (Comitology).

Other tasks of the Commission include:

(a) Enforcement of competition policy
(b) Elimination of customs duties
(c) Abolition of obstacles to free movement of goods, services, persons and capital
(d) Administration of the European social fund and Regional Development
(e) Negotiation of trade agreements with external countries.

The Commission has a more circumscribed role with regard to the two pillars of 'Common Foreign and Social Policy' and 'Justice and Home Affairs' under the TEU.

Activity 2 **(10 minutes)**

How does the Commission act as 'Guardian of the Treaties'? Why does it have this role?

3.2 Council of the European Union (formerly the 'Council of Ministers') (Articles 202 – 210 EC)

Structure

The Council is based in Brussels with a subsidiary location in Luxembourg.

The Council is the EU's main decision-making body, with both executive and legislative powers although many executive powers are devolved to the Commission and some legislative powers are shared with the EP.

The membership comprises **'a representative of each member state at Ministerial level, authorised to commit the Government of that member state'**. Generally these are the foreign ministers of the member states. This is the basic, senior, council called 'The General Affairs Council' but the membership can comprise any ministers relevant to the topics under discussion eg agriculture. Council members are politically accountable to their member states and not to each other.

Most Council decisions are taken using a complicated system of weighted voting intended to ensure a compromise between equality (one vote per country) and the different populations of the Member States. Even here the Council endeavours to reach a consensus decision on matters that a Member State regards as vital to its interests. Some decisions have to be agreed by all Member States (accession of new members for instance) and a few by simple majority.

Note. Council meetings do have agendas. They are prepared by the Committee of Personal Representatives (Coreper) in two parts. Part A covers those matters that are agreed. Part B covers those requiring discussion in Council.

Council decisions are either unanimous eg on EU membership; by simple majority (13 out of 27 votes); or qualified majority (the large states' votes being restricted to ensure no single state veto is possible). Although Article 205 EC states that **'the Council shall act by a majority of its members'** most decisions are made by a qualified majority. No official agenda is drawn up for its meetings, no Council documents prepared or formal conclusions arrived at.

The Council also ensures Treaty objectives are achieved and should **'ensure co-ordination of the general economic policies of the Member States'**. It concludes international agreements between the EU and other states/organisations and – with the EP – adopts the EU budget. It takes the decisions needed to implement the common foreign and security policy following guidance from the European Council.

Law-making power

By Article 308 EC, the Council, acting unanimously on a proposal from the Commission and following consultation with the EP may pass legislation. This power is restricted.

(a) It must be used to attain one of the objectives of the EU.

(b) It must be necessary for that purpose (a question of fact determined by ECJ).

(c) Such attainment must take place within the operations of the single market.

(d) There must be no alternative article or legislative provision, which can be used to fulfil the same objectives.

(e) The use of the power must be appropriate (ie 'proportional').

Proportionality is covered in greater depth in the next chapter.

The Presidency

The Presidency of the Council is held by each member state for six months. The President organises the meetings and signs any resulting acts and issues a programme of action at the start of its term of office. The President acts as mediator between member states and ensures a smooth organisation of Council meetings.

The Council presidential rota for 2007-2008 is:

2007   Germany and Portugal
2008   Slovenia and France

The Treaty of Nice 2000 recognised the difficulty of getting unanimous agreement in a future EU of 20 to 30 states, and provided for a change in the weighting of votes from 1 January 2005. Thereafter qualified majority voting will be used whenever a decision receives a specified number of votes (only to be specified after each accession) or where a decision is approved by a majority of member states. Additionally such a majority must represent at least 62% of the EU's population.

'Enhanced Co-operation'

The Treaty of Amsterdam introduced 'Closer co-operation'. Member states that wanted to work together more closely were free to do so. The Treaty of Nice removed the member states' veto over such enhanced co-operation, allowed it go ahead amongst those states wishing and left it open to other states to join in later if they wish to do so. There is a minimum of eight states needed for enhanced co-operation. It is allowed in the area of foreign and security policy.

The Committee of Permanent Representatives (COREPER)

This group of diplomats carries on the work of each ministerial council meeting during the intervening periods and also oversees the work of around 250 committees and working parties. It is based in Brussels and meets every week. The chair is taken by the delegate of the state which is President of the Council.

Due to its volume of work COREPER is split into two equal committees: COREPER 1 comprises the deputy ambassadors to the EU and deals with internal matters. COREPER 2 comprises the ambassadors themselves and handles the more important political issues. The two committees are, however, equal in status.

Activity 3   **(10 minutes)**

Why do you think the EU introduced 'enhanced co-operation'?

3.3 The European Council

The European Council is a meeting of the heads of government of the member states and the President of the Commission. It is **not** the same as the Council for the European Union (the Council of Ministers) **nor** is it the Council of Europe (which is responsible for the ECHR). It meets at least twice a year (June and December). It takes long-term strategic decisions about EU development. Decisions are made by common accord.

It is not legally an institution of the EU as it possesses no formal powers. It was not mentioned in any of the EU treaties until the SEA 1986. Today it is formally recognised in Article 4 of the TEU, its role being to:

> *'provide the Union with the necessary impetus for its development and ... define the general political guidelines thereof '.*

Its role under the TEU is predominantly in the area of Common Foreign and Security Policy particularly involving the Western European Union. The Council must also determine any serious persistent breaches by any member state.

3.4 The European Parliament ('EP') (Articles 189 – 201 EC)

Structure

Officially based in Strasbourg, its committees sit in Brussels and its secretariat is divided between Brussels and Luxembourg.

It comprises 736 MEPs directly elected under proportional representation for five years. A citizen residing in another member state may both vote and stand for election in the state of residence. MEPs form political parties of a pan-European nature based on ideology rather than nationality. The number of MEPs for each member state is based on their populations (eg UK has 72 MEPs).

The EP is governed by the Conference of Presidents, chaired by the President himself, comprising the leaders of the political groupings. The President is assisted by fourteen vice presidents and five Quaestors (handling financial and administrative matters) who are collectively referred to as the Bureau (elected for two-and-a-half years).

A Secretariat headed by a Secretary General forms the EP's civil service (around 4,900 members).

Role

The EP's role is legislative, supervisory and budgetary. It includes:

(a) Making informal representations,

(b) Requesting the Commission to make legislation proposals, and

(c) Giving a formal opinion on legislation to the Council.

The EP's role in the legislation procedure varies according to which of the three procedures is being followed. In some areas it may not even be consulted eg common commercial policy.

The EP must approve the EU budget and may amend this with the authority of the Council. Should the EP and Council fail to agree after two readings of the budget (between May and December) the EP may reject it in its entirety and the whole process start again. The Council has the final say over compulsory expenditure (CAP) and the Parliament has the final say over non-compulsory expenditure (social and regional policy). A further power includes granting a discharge to the Commission on its spending for previous years.

Other powers include:

(a) Democratic supervision of all the Institutions, which includes setting up committees of enquiry, receiving petitions from EU citizens and appointing an ombudsman to investigate disputes between citizens and EU administrative authorities

(b) The Commission is obliged to reply to questions put by Parliament

(c) Motions of censure of the Commission (to be carried by a two-thirds majority) upon which the Commission should resign as a body

(d) Approval of a new Commission

(e) A veto over new member states

The EP may challenge the acts of the other institutions where these affect the institutional balance. It can also bring proceedings in the ECJ where the Council has failed to act.

Consultation procedure (Articles 19 – 20 EC)

No single Article sets out when the Consultation procedure is to be used, so it is used when no other procedure is mentioned. It has been used to achieve harmonisation of:

- Environment policy
- Indirect taxation
- Voting and elections
- Visas

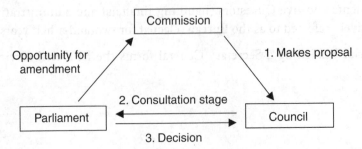

Figure 15.1: Constitution procedures

Stage 1. **Proposal** (normally a complete and detailed text).

Stage 2. If there is no treaty requirement to consult, the **Council decides**. Normally the Council does consult on all political matters to enable the EP to fulfil role of representing the people.

Stage 3. Parliament is not obliged to follow the Decision but failure to consult is breach of '**essential procedural requirement**' and legislation will be annulled. Reconsultation will happen if change differs in substance. **Voting** is done by unanimous or qualified majority.

Co-decision procedure (Article 251 EC)

This is more complex than the consultation procedure (shown above) but the co-decision procedure gives Parliament the most power (veto). Again, there is no information on when this procedure is to be used – it is stated in individual articles eg internal market.

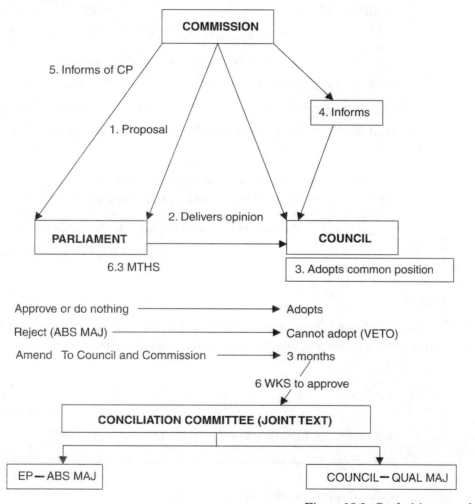

Figure 15.2: Co-decision procedure

If both accept, the measure becomes law; if only one accepts it fails (EP VETO).

Co-operation procedure (Article 252 EC)

Individual Articles state when Co-operation is to be used eg **'where reference is made in this treaty to this Article for the adoption of an act'**.

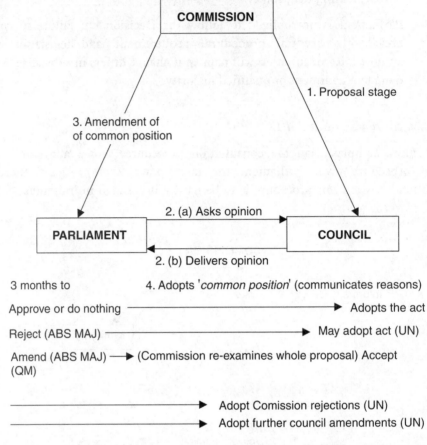

Figure 15.3: Co-operation procedure

Assent procedure

There is also the **Assent Procedure**, by which Parliaments assent to a number of matters, including admission of new members and association agreements.

Activity 4 **(10 minutes)**

Why is it important for the EP to have a role in the creation of EU law?

3.5 The European Court of Justice (Article 220 EC)

It is important you can distinguish the ECJ from the European Court of Human Rights (Strasbourg) and the International Court of Justice (The Hague).

Structure

The ECJ is based in Luxembourg and comprises 27 judges (one from each member state). They are assisted by eight Advocates General ('AGs') whose role is to deliver *'reasoned submissions'* which are impartial and independent opinions on the cases before the court. The AGs do not prosecute cases nor do they take part in the court's deliberations The AGs' opinions have no legal force and need not be followed by the ECJ.

Both Judges and AGs hold office for six years (renewable) and are appointed by common accord of the member states. They must be *'persons whose independence is beyond doubt and who possess the qualifications required for appointment to the highest judicial offices in their respective countries or who are jurisconsults of recognised competence'*. The President of the ECJ is appointed for three years and is selected by the judges themselves. His role is to direct the court's work and act as its figurehead.

The ECJ normally sits in Chambers of three or five judges. It will sit in Grand Chamber (13 judges or more) at the request of a Member State or institution that is a party to the case and it sits in plenary session rarely, when required to do so by the Statute of the Court.

Jurisdiction and role

The ECJ ensures the application of EU law to the EU institutions. It has also 'created' EU law as an independent and separate body of law which is both superior to and separate from national law and yet uniform throughout the EU. The doctrines of 'direct applicability' (created by Treaty) and 'direct effect' (created by the ECJ) have enabled individuals to have access to this law.

The ECJ has furthered the objectives of the EU treaties by taking account of the ultimate purpose of any EU legislation. It looks to the intention behind the words of such treaties rather than interpreting them literally in the classic English procedure. Precedent is interpreted far more flexibly than in England.

The jurisdiction falls into three main bands.

(a) **Ensuring EU institutions act lawfully**

There are disputes between member states, individuals or EU institutions concerning the wrongful exercise of power by the institutions. The ECJ reviews the legality of the acts of the institutions (Parliament, Council, Commission or ECB) and can annul them. EU institutions may be held liable by the ECJ where they have caused damage based on non-contractual liability.

(b) **Ensuring the member states fulfil their obligations under EU law**

Once the ECJ has decided there is a breach the member state must comply (*'take the necessary measures'*) and should it fail to do so the Commission brings a new action to enable the ECJ to impose a penalty eg 'A lump sum or penalty payment'.

(c) **Preliminary references**

A preliminary reference to the ECJ by national courts can be made to clarify European Law. This specifically covers:

(i)   The interpretation of Treaties

(ii)   The validity and interpretation of Acts of the institutions

(iii)   The interpretation of statements of bodies established by Act of the Council.

Whilst national courts are empowered to apply EU law, preliminary rulings are often essential to prevent different national interpretations. If the issue is before a final Court of Appeal in a member state that court must seek a preliminary ruling. A preliminary ruling will be applied by the national court to decide the case before it and will also be applied throughout all other national courts in the EU on that issue.

Court of First Instance

The Court of First Instance (CFI) was created by the SEA 1986 to act as a 'filter' for the ECJ because of the pressure of work on the ECJ. It has been in operation since 1 November 1989; it decides particular actions with appeals only on points of law lying to the ECJ within a two-month deadline. Its jurisdiction now includes:

(a)   Annulment actions

(b)   Failure to act brought by individual parties against the community

(c)   Disputes between institutions and their staff

(d)   Actions by individuals regarding competition laws

(e)   Particular aspects of the treaty related to ECSC eg actions brought against the Commission

The ECJ hears appeals from the Court of First Instance on three grounds:

(a)   Lack of CFI competence
(b)   Infringement of EU law by CFI
(c)   Procedural breach by CFI so as to adversely affect an applicant's interest

The problem of delay

The creation of the CFI has not been enough to resolve the workload problems. On January 1 2000, 896 cases awaited a decision before the ECJ and 732 before the CFI, compared to 130 cases before the ECJ alone in 1975. The time taken for a preliminary reference has increased from six months in 1975 to just over 23 months in 1999. This delay must be added to the time taken for the issue to pass through the national courts.

Also cases brought directly to the ECJ rarely take less than two years. Added to this, both the TEU and TOA gave initial jurisdiction to the ECJ with regard to asylum and immigration and economic and monetary union. When the EU is enlarged the delays will become even worse.

The Treaty of Nice acknowledged that the ECJ had too many cases to decide and that with the accession of new states this could only get worse. In consequence the Treaty allows for a more effective sharing of the workload between the ECJ and CFI and that the ECJ may sit in a 'Grand Chamber' of thirteen judges rather than plenary sessions requiring all judges' attendance. Specialised chambers to deal with limited areas are also envisaged. It also changed the status of the CFI so that it will no longer be attached to the ECJ.

3.6 Other EU Institutions

The Court of Auditors carries out audits of all income and expenditure of the EU institutions. At the end of the financial year, it draws up a report which is presented to the other EU institutions and is printed in the Official Journal.

The Economic and Social Committee was established by the EC Treaty in 1957; it is an advisory committee comprising representatives of economic and social life – the 'Employers Group' made up of representatives of employers organisations (eg the UK's CBI); the 'Workers Group' consisting of trade unionists; and 'Other Interests' comprising small businesses, family-policy groups and environmentalist organisations.

The Committee of the Regions was set up by the TEU and comprises representatives of regional and local authorities.

Chapter roundup

- The EU has its own body of laws, principles and institutions that are quite separate from those of its member states.

- EU law is supreme over the law of individual member states.

- The principal institutions of the EU are the Commission; Council of the EU, European Council, European Parliament and European Court of Justice.

- The Commission is the 'Executive' of the EU.

- The Council of the EU is its main decision-making body.

- The European Parliament's role is legislative, supervisory and budgetary.

- The ECJ has developed EU case law over the years which has built upon and extended the provisions of individual Treaties and other EU legislation.

Quick quiz

1   Give two examples of the rights conferred by EU citizenship.

2   What do 'federalists' believe in?

3   What are the main powers of the Commission?

4   How are Council of the EU decisions reached?

5   How are MEPs elected and how long do they serve for?

6   What are the three bands of ECJ jurisdiction?

BPP
LEARNING MEDIA

Answers to quick quiz

1　Two from: Move and reside freely; vote and stand in other member states' municipal and EP elections; be represented by other member states' diplomats; petition the EP and complain to the EU Ombudsman; write to and be replied to by any EU institution in any of its official languages. (see para 2.1)

2　They believe in the creation of a Europe-wide political body that would assume many of the functions and powers of the individual European nation states. (para 2.2)

3　The powers of the Commission are set out in Article 211. It may make references to ECJ; make recommendations or opinions on matters covered by the Treaty; exercise its own power of decision (autonomous role in competition policy) or exercise its right of initiative in the legislative process; exercise its management role in the day to day operation of the Common Agricultural Policy ('CAP') and the common commercial policy. (para 3.1)

4　Council decisions are either unanimous eg on EU membership; by simple majority; or qualified majority (the large states' votes being restricted to ensure no single state veto is possible). (para 3.2)

5　They are directly elected under proportional representation and serve for five years. (para 3.4)

6　Ensuring EU institutions act lawfully; ensuring the member states fulfil their obligations under EU law; preliminary references. (para 3.5)

Answers to activities

1　It is a functionalist antidote to the federalist view. It is also designed to correct what was seen as a 'democratic deficit' in the EU institutions, whereby individuals would not become alienated by the fact that decisions affecting them were apparently made by unaccountable bureaucrats many miles away (and even in a different country).

2　The Commission ensures the member states' compliance by delivering reasoned opinions and, if necessary, by reference to the ECJ. The Commission may apply to the ECJ for a fine if a member state continuously fails to comply with the judgment. The Commission may also refer any Act contrary to EU law for annulment by the ECJ. It has this role as it is an independent and neutral body with allegiance only to the EU and the EC Treaty itself rather than any individual member state(s).

3　'Enhanced co-operation' was designed to reflect the growth in numbers of member states in, and the competencies of, the EU together with the legitimate differences in opinion between the member states on various matters. It recognised that some states would wish to develop policies and practices within the EU 'ambit' that others would not wish to be involved in. 'Enhanced co-operation' allows them to do so.

4　The populations of the member states directly elect the MEPs. Their involvement in the legislative process increases the democratic accountability of the EU to its people.

Chapter 16:

SOURCES OF EU LAW AND ISSUES OF SOVEREIGNTY

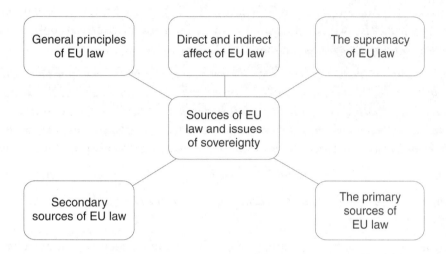

Introduction

We have already seen that the institutions of the EU are quite separate and distinct from those of the individual member states. In this chapter we will discover the different sources of EU law and their relationship with each other and the laws of the individual member states.

Your objectives

In this chapter you will learn about the following.

(a) The supremacy of EU law over domestic legislation

(b) The different sources of EU law and the relationship between them

(c) What is meant by 'General Principles' and give examples of the main General Principles.

1 THE SUPREMACY OF EU LAW

Although it is not specifically set out in any of the Treaties, the principle that EU law has supremacy over the national laws of the individual member states has been established in a number of ECJ decisions.

The basic principle was set down in *Case 26/62 Van Gend en Loos* (see below at Paragraph 5.3). It was reiterated in *Case 6/64 Costa v ENEL*, in which Mr Costa claimed that he was not obliged to pay a 1,950 lira bill to the nationalised Italian National Electricity Board as the nationalisation had been contrary to Italian and EU law. The Italian government argued that the Italian court's reference to the ECJ (see Chapter 1, Paragraph 2.5.2) under Article 234 EC was 'inadmissible' because the national court was obliged to apply Italian law. The ECJ stated (to the contrary):

> *'the Treaty has created its own legal system which...became an integral part of the legal systems of the Member States and which their courts are bound to apply...the member states have limited their sovereign rights, albeit within limited fields, and thus created a body of laws which binds both their nationals and themselves...It follows...that the law stemming from the Treaty...could not...be overridden by domestic legal provisions, however framed'*

Similarly in *Case 92/78 Simmenthal v Commission*, the ECJ stated that EU law was:

> *'an integral part of, and takes precedence in, the legal order applicable in the territory of each of the member states'*

The principle has also been accepted – not without some dispute – the member states' own courts. In *Case 221/89 R v Secretary of State for Transport ex p. Factortame*, Lord Bridge's judgment in the House of Lords contained the following passage:

> *'Under the terms of the Act of 1972 [by which the UK joined the EEC] it has always been clear that it was the duty of a United Kingdom court, when delivering final judgment, to override any rule of national law found to be in conflict with any directly enforceable rule of Community law. Similarly, when decisions of the European Court of Justice have exposed areas of United Kingdom statute law which failed to implement Council directives, Parliament has always loyally accepted the obligation to make appropriate and prompt amendments. Thus there is nothing in any way novel in according supremacy to rules of Community law in those areas to which they apply and to insist that, in the protection of rights under Community law, national courts must not be inhibited by rules of national law from granting interim relief in appropriate cases where it is no more than a logical recognition of that supremacy.'*

It follows on from this principle that, when it joins the EU, a new member state is obliged to reconcile its constitution and national laws with EU law. In the UK, this was done by the European Communities Act 1972.

The most important consequence of the principle of the supremacy of EU law is the doctrine of 'direct effect'.

2 THE PRIMARY SOURCES OF EU LAW

2.1 The Treaties

The various treaties referred to in the list in Chapter 19 are the first source of EU law. These are the European Coal & Steel Community (1952 – 2002), the European Economic Community (1957), the Euratom (1957) and the Merger Treaties, Budgetary Treaties, the Accession Treaties, the Single European Act (1986), the Treaty of European Union (1992), the Treaty of Amsterdam (1997), Treaty of Nice 2000 and the Annexes and Protocols of these Treaties.

2.2 Amendment to the Treaties

All amendments made to the Treaties listed above are primary sources of EU law. The EU Treaty can only be amended by the procedures specified within it. The procedures, which must be used, depend on the subject area concerned.

Each time a new country joins the EU, the EC Treaty is amended by an Accession Treaty. In order to become a member state of the EU a state must comply with the following 'Accession' procedure.

Stage 1. Apply to the Council of the EU.

Stage 2. Membership is open to any 'European' state, provided it respects the principles of liberty, democracy, human rights, fundamental freedoms and the rule of law.

Stage 3. The Council must unanimously approve an application for membership, having first taken the advice of the Commission and obtained approval of the Parliament.

Stage 4. The new member state enters into an Accession Treaty, which is also ratified by all member states, setting out the terms and conditions of their membership.

Stage 5. The new member must also accept existing EU law (known as the '*acquis communautaire*').

2.3 Third Country Treaties

Treaties or other Agreements between the EU and Third Parties are also primary sources of EU law; an example is the Lomé Conventions between the ACP (African Caribbean and Pacific Countries) group and the EU aimed at supporting the 'ACP States' efforts to achieve comprehensive, self-reliant and self-sustained development.

Activity 1   **(5 minutes)**

Why must a new member country accept existing EU law?

LEARNING MEDIA

3 SECONDARY SOURCES OF EU LAW

3.1 Generally: Regulations, Directives, Decisions, Recommendations and Opinions

Article 249 EC states:

'In order to carry out their task in accordance with the provisions of this Treaty, the European Parliament acting jointly with the Council, the Council and the Commission shall make regulations and issue Directives, take decisions, make recommendations or deliver opinions'

Definitions

> A **Regulation** has general application. It is binding in its entirety and directly applicable in all member states.
>
> A **Directive** is binding, as to the result to be achieved, upon each member state to which it is addressed, but leaves to the national authorities the choice of form and methods.
>
> A **Decision** is binding in its entirety upon those to whom it is addressed.
>
> **Recommendations** and **Opinions** have no binding force.

Key points to remember about Regulations

(a) Regulations **apply to everybody** and are binding, throughout the EU.

(b) Regulations are intended to take **immediate effect** without further steps. They are 'directly applicable' in that they are automatically law per se within member states (*H. P. Bulmer Ltd v J. Bollinger SA [1974] 2 CMLR 91*).

(c) Regulations set out general rules to create **uniformity** amongst the laws of the member states.

(d) Regulations are cited in the following manner – *'Regulation 17/62'*. '17' refers to the number of the Regulation and '62' refers to the year in which it is issued.

Key points to remember about Directives

(a) Directives are **not directly applicable**. They apply to the member state(s) to whom they are specifically addressed.

(b) They **do not automatically become law** within the member states to whom they are addressed. It is for each member state to decide how the Directive is to be implemented or achieved. In the UK, they are implemented by Statutory Instrument.

(c) While each member state has discretion as to the method of implementation, Directives are binding as to the result to be achieved and deadlines are specified for implementation.

(d)   Directives are cited in the following manner: '*64/221*'. '64' refers to the year of the Directive and '221' refers to the number of the Directive.

Key points to remember about Decisions

    (a)   Decisions are **binding on their addressees only**. They do not require further implementation.

    (b)   Decisions may be addressed to **member states**, collectively or singularly or to **individuals**.

Key points to remember about Recommendations and Opinions

    (a)   **Recommendations and opinions have no binding force**. Therefore, they are not legal acts.

    (b)   In order to determine whether a EU measure is a recommendation or opinion regard should be had to its **true nature**. This is determined by reference to its **content and object** and not its form. The label normally given to the measure is not decisive.

3.2   Miscellaneous

Article 253 EC states that reasons must be given for the making of EU measures. Failure to give reasons will render a measure invalid ie *Case 24/62 Germany v Commission (the Tariff Quotas on Wine case) [1963] ECR 63*.

Article 254 EC provides that most Regulations, Directions and Decisions must be signed by the Presidents of the Parliament and the Council and published in the *Official Journal* (OJ). Regulations come into force on the date specified in them or, if no date is specified, on the 20th day after publication in the Official Journal. All Directives and Decisions, which need not be published, must be notified to the member state or persons to which they are addressed. Failure to publish or notify does not affect the validity of an EC measure ie *Case 185/73 Hauptzollamt Bielefeld*.

Activity 2   **(10 minutes)**

Distinguish primary from secondary sources of European law.

---

4   GENERAL PRINCIPLES OF EU LAW

4.1   Introduction

The general principles have their foundation within the EC Treaty but were introduced into law by the ECJ. They are the principles by which the ECJ has been guided in its interpretation of EU law and which it has derived as common principles shared by the legal systems of the member states.

General principles may be used in the following ways.

(a) As an aid to interpretation
(b) By member states and individuals to challenge EU action
(c) More rarely, to challenge an action of a member state
(d) To support a claim for damages against the EU

Examples of what have become accepted as General Principles are set out below with a brief explanation of each one.

4.2 Equality

Article 12 EC provides that discrimination on grounds of nationality is not permitted. The TOA created a new Article 13 EC, which extends the EU's express competence to act against discrimination

> *'based on sex, racial or ethnic origin, religion or belief, disability, age or sexual orientation'.*

Article 13 EC and other anti-discrimination articles in the EC Treaty are supplemented by declarations and resolutions eg *Council Regulation 1035/97* created the European Monitoring Centre on Racism and Xenophobia under Article 213 EC.

General points to remember about the principle of equality are:

- Violation of the principle will render an EU provision invalid

- While the principle will invalidate an EU provision it will not give positive rights

4.3 Legal certainty and legitimate expectation

The principle of **legal certainty** prevents an EU measure from taking effect from a point in time before its publication. Retroactive measures will only be considered valid in exceptional cases eg if it is needed to achieve an EU objective or to meet certain legitimate expectations.

A **legitimate expectation** is one which may be held by a reasonable man with regard to events likely to occur in the normal cause of his affairs. In the absence of an overriding matter of public interest, EU law must not violate the legitimate expectation of those affected by it.

4.4 The right to a hearing – natural justice

An illustration of this general principle occurs in *Transocean Marine Paint Association v Commission [1974] 2 CMLR 459.* Advocate General Warner asserted a general rule that:

> *'a person whose interests are perceptibly affected by a decision taken by a public authority, must be given the opportunity to make his point of view known'.*

This amounted to the expression of the General Principle of a right to a fair hearing.

4.5 Legal professional privilege

An illustration of this concept can be seen in *AM & S Ltd v Commission [1982] 2 CMLR 264.* The Claimant Company brought an action for the annulment of a Commission

Decision, which had required it to produce various documents to assist a Commission investigation into suspected breaches of competition law. The company argued that it did not have to produce its communications with its lawyers, on the basis of legal professional privilege, a concept it claimed was recognised in most member states. The ECJ carried out a comparative survey and found that:

'provided that ...such communications are made for the purposes and in the interests of the client's rights of defence, and.. they emanate from independent lawyers, that is... lawyers who are not bound to the client by...employment then privilege will be recognised'.

4.6 Proportionality

The concept of **proportionality** means that any measure taken by the EU must be proportionate and suitable to the purposes to be achieved. No burden should be imposed on the citizen, which is disproportionate to the objective of the measures. It is in effect a three-fold test:

- Is the measure likely to bring about the objective?
- Is there no other measure that is less restrictive?
- Is the detriment disproportionate to the benefit?

4.7 Fundamental human rights

It is important to note that the development of the protection of human rights has undergone four main stages.

(a) No human rights protection was provided in the foundation Treaties.

(b) The ECJ was forced to confront this issue in its application of ECSC law. Could 'Community' acts violate the rights of member state citizens? At first the ECJ denied this but then accepted it and developed it by reference to the constitutional traditions of the member states and to Human Rights Treaties (such as the European Convention on Human Rights). The ECJ changed its approach over the years so as to acknowledge Human Rights as a 'General Principle' due to pressure from the constitutional courts of member states.

(c) The inclusion of Article 6(2) TEU gave Treaty recognition to the protection of Human Rights as a General Principle of law.

> *'The Union shall respect fundamental rights, as guaranteed by the European Convention for the Protection of Human Rights and Fundamental Freedoms ... and as they result from the constitutional traditions common to the Member States, as general principles of Community law'.*

(d) The draft Charter of Fundamental Rights attached to the ill-fated Constitutional Treaty was adapted and adopted by the Council, Commission and Parliament in December 2007 and comes into effect at the same time as the Treaty of Lisbon. It is a mixture of Human Rights and the social chapters adopted by the EU and the Council of Europe and will be interpreted with due regard to the judgments of the European Court of Human Rights.

Activity 3	(10 minutes)
Why did the founding Treaties lack any reference to human rights?	

5 DIRECT AND INDIRECT EFFECT OF EU LAW

5.1 Introduction

The ECJ is aware that, without enforcement, the provisions of the Treaties and subsequent legislation will have little effect. Hence, it has developed four 'routes' to allow individual claimants to enforce their EU legal rights. These are the concepts of:

- Direct applicability
- Direct effect
- Indirect effect
- State liability

5.2 Direct Applicability

This is capable of two meanings. Firstly, the ECJ has interpreted it as applying to any aspect of EU Law, which gives rise to rights, which individuals can enforce through national courts. In other words it has been held to have the same meaning as **direct effect**.

The second, and more common meaning given to '**Direct Applicability**' arises from Article 249 EC, which provides, amongst other things that Regulations:

'shall have general application. [They] shall be binding in [their] entirety and directly applicable in all Member States'.

This means that once Regulations are made they automatically become part of the national legal systems of member states, without the need for separate national measures to implement them.

5.3 Direct Effect

Direct Effect is the concept established by the ECJ in Case 26/62 *Van Gend en Loos*, that certain provisions of EU law give rise to rights, which can be enforced by individuals in their national courts.

The ECJ has established that in order for a provision of EU Law to be directly effective it must have certain characteristics. The provision must be:

- Clear and precise
- Unconditional and not dependant on any national implementing measure
- Capable of giving rights

5.4   EU Laws capable of Direct Effect

Treaty Articles

The following have all been held to have direct effect.

(a) Articles imposing a **negative duty** – that is, an obligation not to do something – on member states

(b) Articles imposing a **positive duty** on member states – held to be directly effective, despite the earlier belief that only 'standstill' articles like Article 25 EC would be directly effective. See *Case 57/65 Alfons Lütticke GmbH v Hauptzollamt Saarlouis*

(c) **Social Articles** – including Article 39 EC on Free Movement of Workers; Article 43 EC on Rights of Establishment; and Article 141 EC on Equal Pay for Workers

Regulations

The ECJ has held that Regulations can be directly effective. They are also directly applicable, ie, automatically part of national law. Indeed 'member states are under an obligation not to introduce any measure which seeks to implement a Regulation' (*Variola* 1973). But it is important to remember that Regulations must be 'significantly precise' in order to be directly effective.

Directives

Generally

A Directive cannot become part of the law of a member state unless that state takes national measures to implement it. This is due to Article 249 EC, whereby, a directive is only binding as to the result to be achieved; the form of implementation being left to the state.

Directives are usually subject to a time limit within which they must be implemented. If a member state fails to implement a Directive within the time provided, the ECJ has held that the provisions of the Directive may be held to be directly effective. This is a method of enforcement and a means of ensuring that Directives are implemented.

The ECJ's reasoning was as follows:

- That for a Directive *not* to be Directly Effective would be incompatible with the binding nature attributed under Article 249 EC.

- That their effect could be 'weakened if institutions were prevented from relying on it before their national courts'.

- The Preliminary Reference to the ECJ under Article 234 EC implies that individuals may invoke Directives in the national courts.

Directives which were closely related to a directly effective Treaty Article

Those Directives which are closely related to a Directly Effective Treaty Article are considered as being particularly capable of Direct Effect. *Case 41/74 Van Duyn v Home Office* concerned *Directive 64/1221* which was made under Article 39 EC, and is closely related to *Regulation 1612/68*. The Directive was held to be Directly Effective. Therefore, the provisions it contained could be enforced by an individual in national courts.

Various cases, including *Case 148/78 Pubblico v Ratti*, have established that to be Directly Effective, a Directive must be:

- Clear and precise
- Unconditional
- The time limit for implementation must have expired

Horizontal and vertical rights.

The ECJ has held that Articles of the EC Treaty and Regulations are capable of giving rise to horizontal and vertical rights.

Definitions

Horizontal rights: rights which are Directly Effective and horizontal, are those which can be enforced by an individual against other individuals in member states' national courts.

Vertical rights: rights which are Directly Effective and vertical, are rights which can only be enforced against states.

Directives are vertically effective only if the conditions referred to above are satisfied. They are **not** horizontally effective. This principle was affirmed by the ECJ in *Case 188/89 Foster v British Gas*, which concerned equal treatment of employees in respect of compulsory retirement ages (also see below with respect to 'emanations of the state'). There has, however, continued to be considerable debate as to whether the Direct Effect of Directives can be horizontal or vertical.

The Direct Effect of Directives and the concept of 'emanation of the State'

Directives require implementation by the member states to whom they are addressed. The member states have discretion on the type of implementing methods to be employed, but they must comply with the deadline set for implementation. This does not sit well with the conditions required to make a provision Directly Effective, in particular, the condition that the provision should not be dependent on any national implementing measure.

In *Case 152/84 Marshall v Southampton Area Health Authority* the ECJ held that the *Equal Treatment Directive 76/207* was Directly Effective and could be enforced vertically against:

- A member state, or
- An emanation of a member state.

The ECJ held that Southampton AHA was an emanation of the State. In addition the ECJ held that the State could not cite its own failure to implement the Directive as a defence. The ECJ also held that a directive cannot be horizontally Directly Effective:

'a directive may not be relied upon against an individual...according to [Article 249 (formerly Article 189)] the binding nature of a Directive, which constitutes the basis for the possibility of relying on the Directive before a national court, exists only in relation to 'each Member State to which it is addressed'. It follows that a Directive may not of itself impose obligations on an individual and that a provision of a Directive may not be relied upon... against such a person'.

The basic test for determining whether or not an organisation or body is an 'emanation of the State' is set out in *Case 188/89 Foster v British Gas*. The ECJ held that a Directive may be invoked against a body, whatever its legal form, which had been made responsible, pursuant to a measure adopted by the State, for providing a public service under the contract of the State and had for that purpose special powers beyond those which result from the normal rules applicable in relations between individuals.

Subsequent cases have created further tests, such as the bipartite test used in *NUS v St Mary's Church of England Aided Junior School [1997] 3 CMLR 630*, by which an 'emanation' needed to be:

- Under state control, and
- Providing a public service.

On this basis the governors of the school were capable of being seen as an emanation of the state. The ECJ developed an even wider test in *Cases C-253/96-C258/96 Kampelmann*, where it was argued that it was sufficient if there was responsibility for public service or if it was under public supervision. There was no need for a number of cumulative factors to be added together before a State emanation could be made out.

In addition to British Gas in its pre-privatisation days, the following organisations/ bodies have been held to be 'emanations of the State'.

- **Tax authorities** – *Case 8/81 Becker v Finanzamt Münster-Innenstadt*

- **Local or regional authorities** – *Case 103/88 Fratelli Costanzo Spa v Comune di Milano*

- The **RUC** and any other body, which is constitutionally independent and responsible for the maintenance public order and safety – *Case 222/84 Johnston v Chief Constable of the RUC*

- **Public health authorities** – *Case 152/84 Marshall (No.1)*

- Various types of **educational institution** – *Case 419/92 Scholz v Opera Universitaria di Cagliari*, where the ECJ held that the University of Cagliari was an emanation of the State.

Activity 4	(10 minutes)

Summarise the decision reached by the ECJ in *Van Gend*.

BPP
LEARNING MEDIA

5.5   Indirect Effect

Generally

In order to resolve some of the weaknesses of Direct Effect the ECJ argued that the courts of the member states had an obligation to ensure that EU Law has been effectively carried out.

The ECJ has required national courts to interpret and apply national laws which seek to implement Directives in a way that conforms to the provisions of those Directives. The principle was established in the cases of *Case 14/83 Von Colson & Kamann v Land Nordhein-Westfalen* and *Case 79/83 Harz v Deutsche Tradax*.

The ECJ has applied this principle of Indirect Effect in the following instances.

(a)   Where Directives have been inadequately implemented by national measures.

(b)   Where Directives have not been implemented by national measures. This was stated in *Von Colson* as meaning:

> *'National courts are required to interpret their national law in the light of the wording and purpose of the Directive in order to achieve the result referred to in the...article' 'In so far as it is given discretion to do so under national law'.*

(c)   Where the rights arising from the relevant Directive are to be enforced against an 'emanation of the State'.

(d)   Where the rights arising from the relevant Directive are to be enforced in horizontal actions.

(e)   Where the national measure which is being interpreted, pre-dates the relevant Directive so long as there is some national law relevant to the situation and thus is capable of being given a 'European' interpretation.

(f)   Wide departure from the wording of national law may be allowable (and indeed expected) but wording cannot be interpreted as *contra legum* (against the clear meaning of the legislation).

Development of the doctrine of Indirect Effect in the UK

As a result of a Commission action, the UK passed the Equal Pay Regulations to fill in the gap left by the British implementation of *Directive 75/117*. These added S1 (2)(c) to the Equal Pay Act and the House of Lords took a purposive interpretation of this, specifying that the 'manifest purpose of the Act' should be looked at rather than a strict reference to the words (*Pickstone v Freemans PLC [1989] AC 66*).

Defects of Indirect Effect

The ECJ has held that the principle cannot be applied where it would contradict General Principles of EU Law.

(a)   The national court cannot refer to a Directive when interpreting a national measure, with a view to determining or aggravating any criminal sanction that could be imposed against those who breach the Directive. In *Case 80/86 Officier van Justitie v Kolpinghuis Nijmegen BV*, a criminal case was bought against Kolpinghuis for breach of a Directive that had as yet not been implemented by Dutch authorities. The ECJ held that such a retrospective implementation of the measure went against that General Principle of Legal Certainty and should not be interpreted in such a way.

(b) Where it would infringe principles of Legal Certainty.

(c) There should be no 'distorting' of national law (Lord Keith in *Webb v EMO*).

As a result, Indirect Effect is not always possible.

5.6 State liability

Generally

As the principle of Indirect Effect had its own problems (just as with Direct Effect) the ECJ later held that an individual can recover damages from a member state where s/he had incurred loss as a result of the State's failure to implement a Directive. This action exists independently of Direct Effect and Indirect Effect.

The leading case is *Case 6/90 Francovich v Italy*, which concerned an action taken by employees of an insolvent company, who were owed outstanding wages. The Italian government failed to implement *Directive 80/987*, which would have provided the financial protection needed for employees of private companies.

Direct Effect was not available because the Directive did not fulfil the conditions for Direct Effect and, as there was no pre-existing national law, it could not be interpreted through Indirect Effect. The employees sued the Italian government to recover their outstanding wages.

The ECJ held that an action in damages for a state's failure to implement a Directive was possible. A member state may be liable 'to make good damage to individuals caused by a breach of EU law for which it is responsible'. This liability is wholly independent of the principle of Direct Effect. Three conditions had to be satisfied:

- The Directive must intend to grant rights to individuals
- It should be possible to identify those rights in the Directive
- There must be a causal link between the state's breach and the claimant's loss

The scope of the doctrine was vastly extended by *R v Secretary of State for Transport ex parte Factortame Ltd and Others (3)* [1996] *ECR 1-1029* and *Brasserie du Pecheur SA v Germany* [1996] *1 CMLR 889*. These cases decided that the breach need not be total, it was enough for it to be 'sufficiently serious' and there must be a causal link between the breach and the claimant's loss.

In *Brasserie*, the court held that liability should be available for **all** breaches, not merely a failure to implement a Directive.

What is 'sufficiently serious'?

Has the institution 'manifestly and gravely exceeded the limits of its discretion'? Factors to be taken into account include the following.

(a) The clarity and precision of the rule

(b) The measure of discretion left by that rule to the national authorities

(c) Whether the infringement was intentional or excusable

NOTES

(d) Was any contribution made by the EU to the state's breach? ie if the state is given wide discretion to implement the measure then the failure must be manifest and grave. If the state has no discretion and still does not implement, this alone is **sufficiently serious**.

An illustration of the application of these principles can be seen in *R v HM Treasury Exp BT [1996] 2 CMLR 217* in which one of the factors included:

'the interpretation, which was also shared by other member states, was not manifestly contrary to the wording of the Directive or to the objective pursued by it'.

Activity 5   **(5 minutes)**

How did the legal reasoning in *Factortame* differ from *Francovich*?

Chapter roundup

- EU law is supreme over the laws of individual member states.

- The primary sources of EU law are EU Treaties, amendments to EU Treaties and Treaties with third countries.

- The secondary sources of law are Regulations, Directives, Decisions, Recommendations and Opinions.

- The General Principles of EU law are the principles by which the ECJ has been guided in its interpretation of EU law.

- The ECJ has developed four routes to allow individuals to enforce their EU legal rights – Direct Applicability; Direct Effect; Indirect Effect and State Liability.

Quick quiz

1   What did the ECJ state in *Simmenthal v Commission*?

2   Name three of the treaties which are the first source of EU law.

3   What are the key points to remember about Decisions?

4   What is the three-fold test of 'proportionality'?

5   What did *Ratti* establish as the preconditions for a Directive to have Direct Effect?

Answers to quick quiz

1 The ECJ stated that EU law was 'an integral part of, and takes precedence in, the legal order applicable in the territory of each of the member states'. (see para 1)

2 Three from: European Coal & Steel Community (1951), the European Economic Community (1957), the Euratom (1957) and the Merger Treaties, Budgetary Treaties, the Accession Treaties, the Single European Act (1986), the Treaty of European Union (1992), the Treaty of Amsterdam (1997), Treaty of Nice 2000 and the Annexes and Protocols of these Treaties. (para 2.1)

3 (i) Decisions are binding on their addressees only. (ii) They do not require further implementation. (iii) Decisions may be addressed to member states, collectively or singularly or to individuals. (para 3.1)

4 Is the measure likely to bring about the objective? Is there no other measure that is less restrictive? Is the detriment disproportionate to the benefit? (para 4.6)

5 A Directive must be: clear and precise; unconditional; the time limit for implementation must have expired. (para 5.4)

Answers to activities

1 The principle that EU law has supremacy over the national laws of the individual member states has been established in a number of ECJ decisions. It follows on from this principle that, when it joins the EU, a new member state is obliged to reconcile its constitution and national laws with EU law.

2 The primary and most obvious source of EU law is that set out in the Treaties themselves. These are directly agreed to by the signatory states and as such form the backbone of all subsequent legal measures. Secondary legislation are those measures enacted by the Institutions authorised to do so by the Treaties. These include Regulations, Directives, Decisions, Recommendations and Opinions.

3 The failure of the projected European Political Union that would have contained references to Human Rights. In order to get an agreement the following EEC Treaty was restricted to economic issues. Also it was not immediately apparent that an economic Treaty would encroach on Human Rights.

4 The ECJ ruled that the statement in Article 12 EC concerning customs duties imposed a clear prohibition on such measures. Thus, this could be relied upon by the individual in a national court. However, the court did state that Direct Effect should be restricted to Treaty Articles which were clear, unconditional and not subject to intervening, particularly implementing, action by the member states.

5 In *Francovich* the infringement consists of a breach of EU law which has caused loss to the applicant. This was modified in *Factortame* to include any 'sufficiently serious' breach.

Chapter 17:

FREE MOVEMENT OF PERSONS

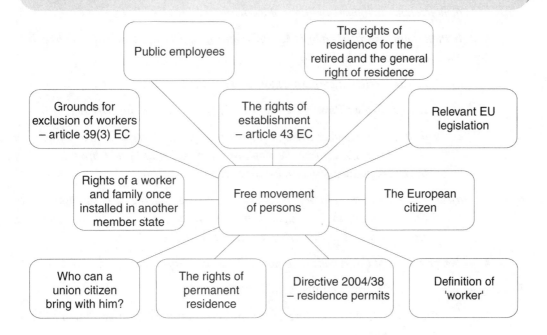

Introduction

Securing the free movement of persons within the EU is one of the central aims of the EC Treaty. It is also one of the more controversial areas of EU law. This is because, unlike the free movement of goods, Member States have traditionally viewed the control of aliens as one of their main functions. This is linked to concerns about national security, crime, welfare and employment issues. For this reason, the EC Treaty was drafted in fairly conservative terms so as to give Member States continuing control over migrants. However, the ECJ has caused alarm for Member States by its very broad reading of the EC Treaty and secondary legislation.

This chapter will focus upon workers because they form the most important category in economic and social terms. We will also consider the other types of persons who are entitled to free movement rights under EU law.

Your objectives

In this chapter you will learn about the following.

(a) The range of persons who have rights of movement under EU law

(b) That workers are a special category of persons

(c) The rights of movement and equality granted to workers

(d) The restrictions on deportation of workers

(e) The position of other persons

1 RELEVANT EU LEGISLATION

The key article in this area is Article 39 EC, which provides as follows.

'1. *Freedom of movement of workers shall be secured within the Community.*

2. *Such freedom of movement shall entail the abolition of any discrimination based on nationality between workers of the Member States as regards employment, remuneration and other conditions of work and employment.*

3. *It shall entail the right, subject to limitations justified on grounds of public policy, public security or public health:*

   a) *to accept offers of employment actually made;*

   b) *to move freely within the territory of Member States for this purpose;*

   c) *to stay in a Member State for the purpose of employment in accordance with the provisions governing the employment of nationals of that State laid down by law, regulation or administrative action;*

   d) *to remain in the territory of a Member State after having been employed in that State, subject to conditions which shall be embodied in implementing regulations to be drawn up by the Commission.*

4. *The provisions of this Article shall not apply to employment in the public service.'* '

The key legislation which supplements Article 39 EC is:

1. *Directive 68/360*, which covers **entry and residence formalities** such as visas and residence permits.

2. *Regulation 1612/68*, which confers **rights of equal treatment** and **residence for family members.**

3. *Directive 64/221*, which provides greater **security against deportation** for workers and families.

4. *Directive 68/360*, 64/221 and *Regulation 1612/68* have been partly amended and replaced by *Directive 2004/38*.

Directive 2004/38 confers rights on the citizens of the Union and their family members to move and reside feely within the territory of the Member States. This incorporates the more recent jurisprudence of the ECJ, going beyond the rights of workers, and giving rights to citizens of the Union, as citizens in their own right.

2 THE EUROPEAN CITIZEN

An important provision recently inserted into the Treaty is that regarding European citizenship. Articles 17 and 18 EC provide as follows;

'Every person holding the nationality of a member state shall be a citizen of the Union.'

'Every citizen of the Union shall have the right to move and reside freely within the territory of the member states, subject to the limitations and conditions laid down in this Treaty and by the measures adopted to give it effect.'

Much of the recent ECJ jurisprudence in the area of the free movement of persons concerns the idea of citizenship, and as a result, the importance of the EU citizen has begun to replace the importance of the worker.

3 DEFINITION OF 'WORKER'

The route to obtaining the full rights under EU law is to be a 'worker'. Self-employed people have similar rights to workers under the self-employed provisions of the Treaty (Article 43 EC).

3.1 EU definition

The ECJ has held that whether or not a person was a worker is a matter for the ECJ, and not for national law. This ensures that the definition is consistent across Member States.

3.2 The three point definition of a worker

A key feature of the meaning of 'worker' is that a person must only show that s/he

    (a) Performs services
    (b) For, and under, the direction of another
    (c) In return for remuneration.

Their particular designation is irrelevant. Thus a trainee teacher was deemed to be a worker in *Case 66/85 Lawrie-Blum v Land Baden-Württemberg*.

3.3 A 'genuine and effective activity'

A worker for the purposes of Article 39 EC is as a person who is pursuing an 'effective and genuine activity'. This does not include those who conduct what appear to be activities on such a small scale as to be regarded as marginal or ancillary. See *Case 53/81 Levin v Staatssecretaris van Justitie* concerning a claim made under Article 39 EC by a part-time chamber-maid, whose application for a residence permit had been refused by the Dutch authorities.

3.4 What is an 'economic activity'?

A person who claims to be a 'worker' must actually be performing an 'economic activity' (in the words of the *Lawrie Blum* test, 'providing services' of an economic value).

In *Case 36/74 Walrave & Koch* the ECJ held that a cycling race pace maker was a 'worker'. This and subsequent cases, including *Case C-415/93 Union Royal Belge des Sociétés de Football Assoc. v Bosman* concerning the transfer rights of a professional footballer, have been interpreted as meaning that 'workers' include those who participate in all professional sports.

3.5 Must a 'worker' be self-sufficient?

In *Case 139/85 Kempf v Staatssecretaris van Justitie* a German music teacher worked part-time in the Netherlands, during which time he received social security benefits on top of his modest earnings. He gave twelve music lessons per week in a school. His application for a Dutch residence permit was refused on the ground that his income was not sufficient to meet his needs. The ECJ held that a person pursuing a genuine and effective economic activity (as an employed person), even though the income produced was insufficient to meet his needs, could not be excluded from the scope of EU law.

3.6 Job seekers

Article 39 EC refers only to those who have already secured work in another member state having the right to move to take up that employment. The ECJ has however extended the scope of Article 39 to cover those seeking work (see *Case 48/75 Procureur du Roi v Royer*).

Job seekers have rights of entry and residence for a period of time in order to secure work. If they do not secure work within a reasonable period of time, they must provide evidence that they are continuing to seek employment and that they have genuine chances of being engaged (see Case C-292/89 *Antonissen* paragraph 21) or then they may lose the rights of residence. Pending their obtaining work, they are not entitled to the social benefits which accrue to those who have work.

Prior to 2002, it was held that 'Member State nationals who move in search of employment qualify for equal treatment only as regards *access* to employment in accordance with Article 48 of the Treaty and Articles 2 and 5 of Regulation No 1612/68.' This explicitly excluded social and tax advantages to those who took advantage of the right to free movement to search for employment (Case 316/85 *Lebon*, paragraph 26.)

However in the *Case 138/02 Collins v Secretary of State for Work and Pensions*, the ECJ held that following the inclusion of Articles 17 and 18 EC on citizenship of the European Union, 'citizens of the Union lawfully resident in the territory of a host Member State can rely on Article 6 of the Treaty in all situations which fall within the scope *ratione materiae* of Community law. Citizenship of the Union is destined to be the fundamental status of nationals of the Member States, enabling those who find themselves in the same situation to enjoy the same treatment in law irrespective of their nationality, subject to such exceptions as are expressly provided for.'(para. 61.)

This now means that a European citizen, lawfully resident in a member state has the right to equal treatment in the field of social benefits, as if he or she were a national of the host State. The State may impose certain requirements in order to meet the criteria for the benefit, but the requirements must pursue a legitimate objective and not be a form of disguised discrimination against non-nationals. In the case of *Collins* the right was to include access to job seekers allowance

Activity 1	**(10 minutes)**
What are the key tests on who is a 'worker'?	

4 DIRECTIVE 2004/38 – RESIDENCE PERMITS

This Directive sets out the formalities which regulate exercise of the rights conferred under Article 39 EC and *Regulation 1612/68*. In particular, it lays down rules on residence permits for, and entry into, other member states.

Article 6 gives a general right of entry and residence to European citizens and their families for a period of up to three months. Under Article 6(2) all they are required to show is a valid passport or identity card upon entry.

Article 2(2) requires host Member States to facilitate the entry and residence of the Union citizen's immediate family and dependants.

Under Directive 2004/38 the rules on registration of an EU citizen or a member of his/her family have been relaxed. For Union citizens, if they are to remain longer than three months, they are to register the relevant authorities within three months of their arrival by producing;

  (a) valid identity card or passport; together with

  (b) proof of either employment, enrolment at an educational establishment, or

  (c) evidence that they are self-sufficient (and hence will not become a burden on the host Member State (Article 8.)

They shall then be issued with a residence certificate.

A family member accompanying a Union citizen, who is a non-national of a Member State, must provide;

  (a) valid passport;

  (b) a document attesting to the existence of a family relationship or of a registered partnership; and

  (c) proof of residence in the host Member State of the Union citizen whom they are accompanying or joining.

They shall then be issued with a residence card.

The residence permit issued, under Article 11(1) entitles workers and their families to a five-year renewable residence permit. This 'permit' is in fact declaratory of rights conferred by Article 39 EC and the worker's rights do not depend upon possession of one.

Article 4(1) provides that the validity of the residence card shall not be affected by temporary absences not exceeding six months a year, or by absences of a longer duration for compulsory military service or by one absence of a maximum of 12 consecutive months for important reasons such as pregnancy and childbirth, serious illness, study or vocational training, or a posting in another Member State or a third country.

5 THE RIGHT OF PERMANENT RESIDENCE

Having been in the EU for at least five years, application can be made for a right of permanent residence for both the EU citizen and his/her family members in the host State.

Article 16 provides that Union citizens and their family members who have resided legally for a continuous period of five years in the host Member State shall have the right of permanent residence there. Article 16(3) provides that the continuous period shall not be affected by temporary absences in accordance with the same criteria given in Article 4(1) (shown above.) A EU citizen will be issued with a registration certificate. A family member who is not a national of a Member State shall be issued with a registration card.

Article 16(4) states that once acquired, the right of permanent residence can only be lost through absence from the Member State for a period exceeding two years.

Under Article 20(1) family members who are not nationals of a Member State, but entitled to permanent residence shall have their permanent residence card automatically renewed every 10 years.

Articles 13 – 14 provide rights to those having entered the EU, in particular they cover situations where the accompanying family separates from the EU citizen whilst still residing in the host Member State. Reasons for this separation could be due to illness, the EU citizen working outside the EU or on death or divorce from the EU citizen. The clear undertone of Directive 2004/38 is that, except in certain circumstances, the host Member State cannot expel the Union citizen or his/her family members who are not nationals of a Member State, where they have sufficient financial provision so as not to become a burden on the social security system of the Member State.

6 WHO CAN A UNION CITIZEN BRING WITH HIM?

Both *Regulation 1612/68 and Directive 2004/38* deal with the equality rights of Union citizens, of workers and also details the family members who may be brought with the worker (or later join the worker).

Article 1 of the Directive 2004/38 provides for a general right of free movement and residence for a Union citizen and his family members.

Family members are defined in Article 2 as:

(a) The worker's **spouse** and their **descendants** who are under the age of 21 or dependants.

(b) The worker's **dependant relatives** in the ascending line of the worker and his spouse.

(c) The partner with whom the Union citizen has contracted a registered partnership (though this is restricted to circumstances in which the host Member State treats registered partnerships as equivalent to marriage.)

Article 3 also promotes host States to facilitate entry to any other family member, irrespective of nationality, who is a partner with whom the Union citizen has a durable relationship, and those who are dependant or members of the household of the Union citizen or where health grounds *strictly* require the personal care of the family member by the Union citizen. (See *Case C-459/99 MRAX v Belgium State.*)

What about divorce or separation? In *Case 267/83 Diatta v Land Berlin* a German national and her spouse separated and they continued to live in the same member state. The ECJ held that spouse retained the right to stay. There was a continuing family link, which remained pending a divorce.

In *R v S.O.S. Home Office Ex p Sandhu (1982)*. Sandhu, an Indian national who married and then separated from a German national (who was residing in the UK but then returned to Germany) could not stay in the UK as the EU worker had left the UK and therefore Sandhu was no longer a qualifying spouse under EU law.

In *Case 431/99 R & Baumbast v Secretary of State for the Home Office*, the ECJ showed a more lenient approach to the right of third country nationals to remain after divorce. Changes contained in Directive 2004/38 reflect the ECJ's approach in *Baumbast*. Under Article 13 of the new Directive, the right to remain in the host State after divorce will be granted to the third country national if he was;

(a) Married or in a partnership to a Union citizen for at least three years, including one year in the host Member State; or

(b) The spouse or partner is granted custody of the Union citizens' children; or

(c) It is warranted by difficult circumstances such as having been a victim of domestic violence while the marriage or registered partnership was subsiding; or

(d) If the third country national has a right of access to a minor in the host Member State.

Again however, if the third country national is to receive a right of permanent residence under any one of these rules, they must also show that they have sufficient resources for themselves and their family so as not to become a burden on the social assistance system of the Member State.

7 RIGHTS OF A WORKER AND FAMILY ONCE INSTALLED IN ANOTHER MEMBER STATE

Once a worker and his/her family are installed in another Member State we need to consider what rights they can claim. It is important to note that generally migrants only have the right to equal treatment with nationals. They cannot expect certain minimum standards of education, health and so on. They must accept conditions in the member state where they are.

7.1 Non-discrimination on the basis of nationality

The general right of non-discrimination on the basis of his nationality is found in Article 12 EC. The key question is how wide the field of application of the EC Treaty is eg a French worker cannot vote in UK general elections (although he can in EU elections).

7.2 Discrimination

Articles 23 and 24 of Directive 2004/38 provide equality guarantees in the fields of employment, housing, trade union rights and tax/social rights for those Union citizens and family members who have a right of residence or permanent residence. The ECJ has outlawed both direct and indirect discrimination. Thus a rule that has more significant impact upon non-nationals can be said to be indirect discrimination and will be unlawful unless it can be objectively justified.

Direct discrimination – *Case 167/73 Commission v France* in which France operated a quota requiring a minimum percentage of French nationals to operate merchant vessels. Indirect discrimination – *Case 15/69 Württembergische Milchverwertung-Südmilch-AG v Salvatore Ugliola,* where an Italian (who had served in the Italian army) complained that his employer in Germany gave seniority to persons for having served in the German army. Ugliola argued that non-Germans were unlikely to serve in that army and that he was suffering indirect discrimination. The ECJ agreed and held there was no justification for the rule.

7.3 Non-discriminatory rules – the Bosman decision

Bosman was a Belgian footballer whose contract had expired with his Belgian club and he wished to transfer to a French club. His own club would not release him without payment of a transfer fee. This rule was standard throughout European football associations. The Belgian FA rules did not discriminate directly or indirectly against non-nationals. They were indistinctly applicable as between nationals and non-nationals. The rules also did not discriminate against players transferring internally or those going abroad. Both attracted a transfer fee.

It is important here to note the horizontal direct effect of Article 39 EC. It applies to private bodies – such as football associations – as much as government bodies.

The ECJ held that the transfer fee rules were a barrier to players leaving one country to work in another, because they were denied the opportunity to take up employment even though their contracts had expired. Their very access to the labour market was denied by such rules for which there were no adequate justifications. The *Bosman* decision led to a revision of the transfer rules, but not before players benefited from large wage increases due to a shift of power away from clubs.

7.4 Social and tax advantages

Article 7(2) of *Regulation 1612/68* provides that 'workers' are entitled to the same 'social and tax advantages'.

'**Social advantages**' have been taken to include:

(a) Fare reduction on railway fares – *Case 32/75 Fiorini v SNCF.*

(b) State childbirth loans – *Case 65/81 Reina v Landeskreditbank Baden-Württemberg.*

(c) The right to have a foreign partner install themselves in the member state where the national law allows such a right to its own nationals – *Case 59/85 Netherlands v Reed.*

(d) Funeral expenses benefits – *Case C-237/94 O'Flynn v Adjudication Officer.*

(e) Access to university courses – *Case 197/86 Brown v Secretary of State for Scotland.*

(f)   Access to maintenance grants whilst at university where these are provided for host-State nationals. In *Case 209/03 Bidar v London Borough of Ealing, Secretary of State for Learning and Skills,* a French national came to the UK to live with his grandmother. He started to read economics at University College London, but upon application for financial assistance to cover his maintenance costs, he was refused as he had not been resident in the UK for three years prior to applying for the loan. The ECJ held that the refusal to grant the maintenance loan was discriminatory and as a citizen lawfully resident in the UK, he was entitled to equal treatment under Article 12 EC in respect of social assistance benefits.

7.5   Education and training for workers and their families

Regulation 1612/68 confers rights to equal access to certain kinds of training in certain situations for workers, and rather broader access to education for their families. Under Article 7(3), workers have a right of equal access to training in vocational schools. Under Article 12, children of workers have rights of entitlement to general education, apprenticeship, and vocational training courses under the same conditions as nationals of that member state.

The scope of Article 7(3) is quite limited. Thus in *Case 197/86 Brown v Secretary of State for Scotland* the ECJ ruled that universities could not be considered 'vocational schools'. A worker must be given equal access to such schools, including the same level of fees and entry requirements.

Article 12 of the Regulation has by contrast been given a very wide interpretation by the ECJ, so that it covers 'any form of education, including university course in economics and advanced vocational training at a technical college' (*Cases 389 & 390/87 Echternach & Moritz v Minister of Education and Science*). Thus access to these educational establishments must be on equal terms for children of workers resident in another member state.

What about the award of grants, rather than simply equal access to the course? In *Case 9/74 Casagrande v Landeshauptstadt München* the ECJ ruled that, under Article 12, the child of a deceased worker was entitled to a grant to study which was paid to German nationals in similar circumstances. The more difficult area has been access to grants for study by workers under Article 7 of the Regulation. The ECJ imposed two limits upon the right of equal treatment in grants in these situations.

- Work which is obtained with a view to taking up later studies does not qualify a worker for a grant under Article 7(2) of the Regulation.

- A person who had worked previously and given up that job voluntarily must show some link between their former employment and studies in order to qualify for a grant

The second restriction would however not apply if the person became involuntarily unemployed and needed to re-train.

This is a confusing picture. The ECJ was trying to balance the concerns of Member States about grant-shopping against the need to encourage workers to migrate. This created a kind of 'quasi-worker' who has the right of residence but who may not have the full range of rights under Article 7(2).

Matters may however change again in the future because these cases were decided before the concept of EU citizenship had become part of the EC Treaty. Recent cases, concerning welfare benefits not education, have begun to hold that so long as an EU citizen is lawfully resident in another member state then they have the right to equal treatment under Article 12 EC in all fields covered by the Treaty (*Case C-85/96 Martinez Sala v Freistaat Bayern*).

The idea of rights for European citizens, rather than rights as 'member of a worker's family' was further demonstrated in *Case 431/99 R & Baumbast v Secretary of State for the Home Office*. Here *R*, a third country national, married a German national working in the UK. *R* had brought with her, a daughter from a previous marriage who was also not a national of an EU Member State. Upon divorce of *R* from the EU worker, he returned to Germany but *R* and her daughter from the previous marriage were able to stay on in the UK so the daughter could complete the studies she had begun here.

7.6 Rights of the spouse/children to equality in employment

Article 11 of *Regulation 1612/68* provides:

> *'where a national of a Member State is pursuing an activity as an employed or self-employed person in the territory of another Member State, his Spouse and those of the children who are under the age of 21 years or dependant on him shall have the rights to take up any activity as an employed person throughout the territory of that same state even if they are not nationals of any Member State'.*

Case 131/85 Gül v Regierungspräsident Düsseldorf concerned a Turkish-Cypriot who qualified as a doctor in Istanbul University, and married an English hairdresser who was working in Germany. He had worked in Germany on a temporary basis for five years. He applied for permanent authorisation to practice in Germany. He was refused on the basis of his nationality. The ECJ held that as long as he had qualifications and diplomas that were sufficient under German legislation and any specific professional rules, he was entitled under Article 11 of *Regulation 1612/68* to practice in Germany, even though he was not an EU National.

Thus Article 11 was interpreted as conferring a right of non-discrimination on the basis of nationality upon third-country nationals who are spouses/children of EU national workers.

Activity 2	(5 minutes)
What are the main rights of equal treatment for workers?	

8 GROUNDS FOR EXCLUSION OF WORKERS – ARTICLE 39(3) EC

Member States viewed exclusion of migrants on security or public policy grounds as an essential attribute of their sovereignty. The ECJ has, after a hesitant beginning, begun to read the derogations in a restrictive manner to ensure that they are used only where strictly necessary.

Article 39(3) EC lists the grounds under which derogations by Member States from the right of free movement can be invoked. These are public policy, public security and public health. Article 39(3) EC does not allow Member States to treat migrants differently as regards employment rights if they are admitted to the territory, they must either be excluded or given full equality. In addition, migrants cannot be restricted to residence in one part of the country (see *Case 36/75 Rutili v Minister for the Interior*).

The ECJ has also held that Article 39(3) EC does not allow Member States to require all migrants to demonstrate that they do not represent a threat to public policy as a pre-condition to their rights to entry eg no general border checks on all migrants to ensure that criminals are excluded.

Beyond these limits, Article 39(3) EC left a broad discretion to Member States without any procedural or substantive safeguards for migrants. The purpose of *Directive 64/221* is to correct this omission. It applies to workers, the self-employed and the recipients of services (this would include tourists – see *Case C-348/96 Donatella Calfa*).

8.1 The substantive limits on Member State discretion (Directive 2004/38)

The Directive limits the reasons that can be used by Member States to conclude that a person represents a threat to public security, policy or health when refusing to admit or wanting to deport a person claiming free movement rights.

Under Article 27 of the Directive, derogations are not allowed to serve economic purposes and therefore exclusion cannot be based upon a recession or others problems in the home economy. Under Article 27(2) any measures that are taken on the grounds of public policy or security shall comply with the principle of proportionality.

Certain diseases can justify exclusion under Article 29 of the Directive. The diseases justifying restriction on freedom are those with 'epidemic potential' as defined by the World Health Organisation, or other diseases subject to protection provision.

The key ground for exclusion is usually criminal conduct, or other conduct alleged to represent a threat to public policy or security.

Exclusion must be based exclusively upon conduct of the individual

Article 27(2) of the Directive states that exclusion must be based 'exclusively on the conduct of the individual'.

The ECJ has laid down a number of principles that derive from this limitation.

(a) The person must constitute a genuine and **sufficiently serious threat** to a fundamental interest.

(b) Member states must assess the likely **future conduct** of a person – not simply rely upon their past actions

(c)   Article 28(2) adds that EU citizens and their family members who have the right of *permanent residence* can only be expelled for 'serious grounds' of public policy or security. This appears to suggest an even higher standard of threat must be achieved over and above the seriousness of the threat that may be presented by an EU citizen and their family members who are merely lawfully resident.

    (d)   The ECJ in *Case 30/77 R v Bouchereau* by held that, not only must the person's presence represent such a threat, but that the threat must be to:

> '*one of the fundamental interests of society*'.

The following principles are further manifestations of the basic rules.

    (a)   **Deportation must not be arbitrary** – nationals must be treated alike. Although nationals cannot be deported, they must be subject to 'repressive measures or other genuine and effective measures to combat such conduct'.

    (b)   Deportation cannot be effected as an **example to others**.

    (c)   The question must be asked is whether there is a **future risk** of a breach of public policy/security which would affect the fundamental interests of society.

    (d)   Exclusion must be compatible with Human Rights and the principle of **proportionality**.

Criminal conviction not a ground for deportation in itself

Article 27(2) of Directive 2004/38 states that past convictions alone cannot in themselves justify deportation unless they showed a tendency to act in the same way again and that future conduct was in itself a threat to public policy/security (as confirmed in *Case 67/74 Bonsignore*). There may, however, be rare cases where a past crime is so serious that exclusion is justified solely upon that basis.

Certain outrageous crimes can in themselves be good grounds for deportation. In *Case 30/77 Bouchereau* a person convicted for commercial importation of cocaine on a large scale was deported. As an exceptional situation, a single conviction may be good ground for deportation, especially if it reveals that the person concerned may be a present danger to society.

Where there is evidence that a person has reformed, admission is to be allowed *Astrid Proll v Entry Clearance Officer Dusseldorf (1988) 2 CMLR 387*.

8.2   Procedural safeguards against exclusion

There are procedural safeguards which enable migrants to challenge decisions to exclude.

A party refused a permit must be given full notice of the grounds for that refusal.

Before making a decision to expel, the host State must consider elements such as the length of residence, the age, state of health and the family and economic situation, and the social links of the individual in its territory.

Articles 27 - 31 of Directive 2004/38 has introduced a number procedural safeguards combining the jurisprudence of the ECJ from several cases.

There is no right to a full appeal to a court of law on the merits against deportation or denial of entry under the Directive but it provides the following.

(a) **Refusal of entry or residence** – the worker should have the same right of challenge that a national has against administrative acts.

(b) **Refusal of residence** (but not entry) – if there is no means of appeal offered by national law (or if the appeal is non-suspensory or only by means of judicial review) then deportation can only occur after an opinion has been sought from another body (apart from the deporting one) where the individual can appear and present his case.

In the UK, in criminal cases the court recommends a person to be deported and the Home Secretary makes the final decision. Since a court makes the recommendation, the individual can present his case against deportation. It was held in *Case 131/79 R v Secretary of State for Home Affairs (ex p Santillo)* that the criminal court is considered to be an adequate reviewing body for the purposes of Article 9 of the Directive.

A person facing deportation or denial of residence must be able to utilise their remedies under Article 9 of the Directive prior to deportation, except in urgent cases, otherwise the safeguards would be illusory. However, the same does not apply to Article 8 of the Directive which allows execution of the deportation order prior to a final decision within legal proceedings. The migrant would then have to conduct the case from abroad (see *Case 98/79 Pescataing v Belgium*).

It is important to note that refusal of entry only attracts the limited Article 8 rights (not Article 9). In *Case C-65/95 R v Secretary of State for the Home Department ex parte Shingara* the ECJ ruled that this Article did not require migrants to be given the same remedies as nationals facing exclusion.

Activity 3 **(10 minutes)**
What are the key legal rules limiting member states' ability to deport workers?

---

9 PUBLIC EMPLOYEES

The EC Treaty provisions recognise that certain positions can reasonably be reserved to nationals. This is made express by Article 39(4) EC. Thus political posts and other sensitive public service posts can be retained for nationals. The ECJ has however been keen to restrict abuse of this exception by member states.

9.1 Definition of public service

In *Case 152/73 Sotgiu v Deutsche Bundespost* the ECJ ruled that the exception must have a Community meaning to ensure consistency between States. It also must be interpreted narrowly as it was an exception to a fundamental right.

The ECJ has held that public service involves work which is charged with the participation in the direct or indirect exercise of public law powers or duties designed to safeguard the general interests of the State or other public authorities. Hence, we can conclude that judges, heads of civil service, police and security forces would be covered but other tasks would be excluded from Article 39(4) EC eg nurses in public hospitals do not qualify under this test (*Case 307/84 Commission v France (The Nurses Case)*).

> **Activity 4** (5 minutes)
>
> Why does the EU allow 'public employment' to be restricted to nationals?

10 THE RIGHT OF ESTABLISHMENT – ARTICLE 43 EC

The basic right for a self-employed person is to move to another member state to establish themselves in business there - the right of establishment.

10.1 Definition of the right in Article 43 EC

Article 43 EC provides as follows.

> '*Within the framework of the provisions set out below, restrictions on the freedom of establishment of nationals of a Member State in the territory of another Member State shall be prohibited. Freedom of establishment shall include the right to take up and pursue activities as self employed persons ...under the conditions laid down for its own nationals by the law of the country where such establishment is effected...*'

The key decision is *Case 2/74 Reyners v Belgium* which declared the provision to be directly effective.

Directive 2004/38 applies to the right of entry, residence and the requirement of registration in the host State in exactly the same way as it applies to those rights discussed in the previous section on Article 39 EC. Directive 2004/38 also regulates the rights of family members accompanying individuals establishing themselves in a State other than their home State.

Be aware that in older case law reference will be made to Directives 64/221 and 73/148 on the rights of entry, residence and deportation. The provisions of these directives have now been incorporated into Directive 2004/38.

The case law in this area has been augmented by a number of different directives, both general and sector specific. The overall emphasis of both case law and secondary legislation is on 'mutual recognition' of training and practical experience. The system of numerous directives has now been combined into three chapters in Directive 2005/36 which we shall look at briefly below.

The original Directive 89/48 dealt with 'mutual recognition' of general higher education diplomas requiring training of three years or more. This was complemented by Directive 92/51 on recognition of lower-level training in industrial sectors. Certain sector specific directives encouraged mutual recognition in professional fields; for example in law, architecture and veterinary services. Directive 98/5 facilitates the practice of the profession of a lawyer in a Member State other than that in which the qualification was obtained. In *Case 340/89 Vlassopoulou* a Greek law graduate, who went on to obtain a doctorate in Germany, wanted to remain and work as a lawyer in Germany after finishing her studies there. It was held she was able to rely on Article 43EC, in the light of the (then new) Directive 98/5, and require the German authorities to consider her practical experience and knowledge of the German legal system obtained from her doctorial studies and paralegal work undertaken in that country when assessing her suitability to register as a solicitor in Germany.

The problem with these directives was that they only required a Member State to *consider* a non-national's qualification. It was not a requirement to *accept* qualifications obtained in other Member States. It was found that Member States could refuse access to a particular profession on the basis that after consideration, they deemed the qualification to be insufficient compared to their domestic equivalent. All directives in this field have now been consolidated in to one, rather large directive, Directive 2005/36.

Directive 2005/36 applies to those wishing to pursue a regulated profession in a Member State other than that in which they obtained their professional qualification. It provides clearer directions to regulatory authorities to accept equivalent qualifications received in other Member States and to consider an individual's practical experience if it is of two years duration or more. It also lists a number of sector specific qualifications that now have to be regarded as equal, no matter where they were obtained.

10.2 Discrimination on basis of nationality

Rules which amount to direct discrimination on the basis of nationality will infringe Article 43 EC. However indirect discrimination is also caught. *Case 3/88 Commission v Italy* concerned rules which stated that only companies which were mainly publicly owned could bid for data-processing contracts. The rule was neutral on the surface but in practice only Italian companies complied with it. It was indirectly discriminatory and unlawful because it could not be objectively justified.

10.3 Indistinctly applicable measures

Some national rules are not discriminatory at all but may discourage persons from moving between states. The ECJ ruled in *Case C-55/94 Gebhard v Consiglio dell'Ordine degli Avvocati e Procuratori di Milano* that national rules which were liable to hinder or make less attractive the exercise of fundamental freedoms guaranteed by the EC Treaty, including establishment, must satisfy the following tests.

- They must be **non-discriminatory** in application
- They must be justified by imperative requirements in the general interest
- They must be suitable for attainment of these objectives
- It must be necessary to attain them

Thus rules which might deter a person leaving their country to work elsewhere could be illegal under Article 43 EC (and Article 39) even though they do not discriminate against non-nationals.

10.4 Mutual recognition of professional qualifications

One of the key problems for professionals seeking to move between States is non-recognition of diplomas by other States. The ECJ used Article 43 EC to tackle this in *Case 71/76 Thieffry v Paris Bar Council* in which a Belgian had obtained law qualifications in Belgium which were recognised as adequate to practise in France by a French University, but which the Paris Bar continued to object to. The ECJ ruled this a breach of Article 43 EC as it was indirect discrimination without justification.

The case law on this has been augmented by *Directive 89/48*, as amended, which deals with the mutual recognition of professional qualification. It applies to most professional activities. It generally involves the recognition by each member state of certain qualifications achieved after at least three years' training. There are other Directives covering other types of education and professions. For example, lawyers' qualifications are regulated by *Directive 98/5*.

Activity 5	(5 minutes)
How is indirect discrimination caught?	

11 THE RIGHT OF RESIDENCE FOR THE RETIRED AND THE GENERAL RIGHT OF RESIDENCE

Prior to Directive 2004/38 there were two separate directives; one regarding the right for retired workers and the self-employed (together with their family members as defined therein) to remain in the host Member State (Directive 90/364) and another regarding the right of general residence for those not retired but not working (the so-called 'playboy directive', Directive 90/365.)

Article 5 of Directive 2004/38 is more inclusive in its approach. It does not differentiate between retired persons or persons simply wanting to move to live in a host Member State. Instead Article 5 grants a Union citizen and their family members a general right to enter a host State for a period of up to three months. Article 7 provides that if they intend to stay longer than three months without taking up employment, they may do so, if the Union citizen has;

(a)   Sufficient resources for themselves and their family so as not to become a burden on the social assistance system of the host Member State during their period of residence; and

(b)   Has comprehensive sickness insurance cover in the host Member State.

Then they may remain indefinitely.

It is not for the Member State to set a level of what is 'sufficient'. It will be a subjective amount, dependent upon the 'personal situation' of the individual. Under the new case law of the ECJ, incorporation of the European Convention on Human Rights has been invoked in cases of deportation. In the case of *R v Moustaquim* [1991] 13 EHRR 802 the European Court of Human Rights declared that before someone could be deported regard was to be had to their social, economic and familial ties with the host State. In this case a Moroccan boy had lived in Belgium since he was 1 year old. At the age of 21 as a result of frequent criminal activity, Belgium deported Mr Moustaquim. He claimed on the basis of Article 8 ECHR that his right to 'family life' had been deprived as all his family were in Belgium and he had no social links in his state of origin, Morocco, as a result of him having lived in Belgium most of his life. The ECHR held deportation was a breach of Mr Moustaquim's Article 8 right and ordered he be allowed back in to Belgium and a more proportionate action taken. This approach to deportation has been applied in a similar manner by the ECJ. Thus before a Member State can deport an individual, regard is to be had to his or her social, economic and familial connections in both the host State they are being deported from and in the State or country they are being deported to.

Chapter roundup

- The route to obtaining full rights under EU law is to be a 'worker'.

- However there is also a general right of entry and the right to remain for all Union citizens and their family members for a minimum of three months.

- Significant rights now accrue to Union citizens and their family members, even if they are not economically active. This incorporates the idea of a common European identity and a sense of (albeit incomplete) European solidarity.

- The EU prohibits discrimination on the basis of nationality.

- Non-national workers can, in limited circumstances, be excluded from other member states for security or public policy reasons.

- Public employment may also be restricted to nationals.

- Persons other than workers, such as the self-employed, are also entitled to certain rights.

Quick quiz

1 What is the key EU legislation supplementing Article 39 EC?

2 What is an 'economic activity'?

3 Who can a worker bring with him when working in another member state?

4 Where are the grounds for exclusion found and what are they?

5 What is the right of establishment?

Answers to quick quiz

1 *Directive 2004/38*, which covers entry and residence formalities such as visas and residence permits; *and* confers rights of equal treatment and residence for family members; *and* provides greater security against deportation for workers and families. (see para 1)

2 A person who claims to be a 'worker' must actually be performing an 'economic activity' (in the words of the *Lawrie Blum* test, 'providing services' of an economic value). (para 2.4).

3 Article 3 of Directive 2004/38 provides that a worker may bring his family with him, if he works in another member state.

4 Article 39(3) EC lists the grounds under which derogations by member states from the right of free movement can be invoked. These are public policy, public security and public health. (para 6).

5 It is the basic right for a self-employed person is to move to another member state to establish themselves in business there. (para 8).

BPP
LEARNING MEDIA

Answers to activities

1   The test of who is a worker must be set by the ECJ, not national authorities. The work must be effective and genuine, not marginal and ancillary. This test is met even if a person earns less than subsistence wages and relies on benefit. Finally a worker is simply someone who performs services for remuneration under the direction of another.

2   The key provisions are contained in *Regulation 1612/68* and Directive 2004/38 and give equal treatment in respect of housing, employment and tax and social advantages. This latter has a broad meaning.

3   The basic rules are contained in *Directive 2004/38*, which limits the power of States under Article 39(3) EC. The ECJ has built upon the Directive to further restrict the power to deport by requiring a State to show that the person is likely to act in such a way as to pose a genuine and serious threat to a fundamental interest of society.

4   Member states might be concerned about employing non-nationals in sensitive fields. There might be questions about security and loyalty to the State that could arise if foreigners were employed. The EC Treaty provisions recognise this and certain positions can reasonably be reserved to nationals and therefore discrimination against migrants practiced.

5   Indirect discrimination infringes Article 43 EC. See *Case 3/88 Commission v Italy*.

Chapter 18:

FREE MOVEMENT OF GOODS AND SERVICES

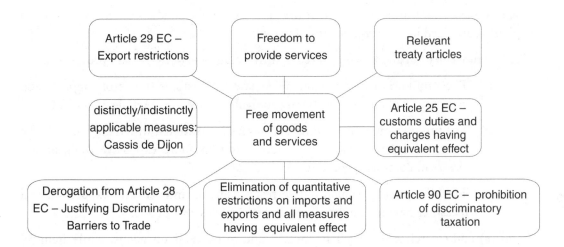

Introduction

The free movement of goods is one of the most important areas of the substantive law of the EU. It is viewed by the EU institutions as the cornerstone to securing integration of European markets.

For many years in the period up to 1987, however, it was difficult to secure the necessary agreement of member states to EU legislation that would make the single market in goods a reality.

After the Single European Act 1986, the EU began to act by qualified majority, not unanimity, to create the internal market, with the objective of removing all remaining barriers to trade by 1992. The internal market is defined in Article 14(2) EC as follows.

> 'The internal market shall comprise an area without internal frontiers in which the free movement of goods, persons, services and capital is ensured in accordance with the provisions of this Treaty.'

Since 1987, the EU has been passing laws harmonising the technical rules relating to the production of goods. These rules have built upon the case law of the ECJ.

Your objectives

In this chapter you will learn about the following.

(a) The concept of a financial barrier to trade and the case law defining this

(b) The difference between charges having equivalent effect and discriminatory taxes

(c)   The concept of non-financial barriers to trade using the case law

(d)   The difference between distinctly and indistinctly applicable measures

(e)   The ECJ's limitations on Article 28 EC through the case law on selling arrangements

(f)   The principles behind the freedom to provide services

1   RELEVANT TREATY ARTICLES

The **free movement of goods** is one of the 'four freedoms' (goods, workers, services and capital) guaranteed by the original EEC Treaty.

The free movement of goods was covered by three main sets of EC Treaty provisions.

(a)   The prohibition between member states of customs duties on imports and exports and of all charges having equivalent effect. See Article 23 – 25 EC.

(b)   The prohibition of discriminatory domestic taxation – which may impede the free movement of goods by making imports more expensive than similar classes of domestic goods. See Articles 90 – 93 EC.

(c)   The elimination of quantitative restrictions on imports and exports and all measures having equivalent effect. See Articles 28 – 31 EC.

Items (a) and (b) relate to illegal financial trade restrictions on goods, while item (c) relates to non-financial trade restrictions on goods.

2   ARTICLE 25 EC – CUSTOMS DUTIES AND CHARGES HAVING EQUIVALENT EFFECT

Article 25 provides as follows.

> '*Customs duties on imports and exports and charges having equivalent effect shall be prohibited between Member States. This prohibition shall also apply to customs duties of a fiscal nature.* '

2.1   Customs duties

In *Case 26/62 NV Algemene Transporten Expeditie Onderneming v Nederlandse Administratie der Belastingen (Van Gend en Loos)* the ECJ held that Article 25 EC would prohibit:

> '... *any charge however small imposed on goods solely for the reason that they crossed a frontier constitutes an obstacle to the free movement of goods*'.

What matters is not the purpose of the charge but its effect. If its effect is to create an illegal trade restriction, Article 25 EC will bite.

For example, in *Case 7/68 Commission v Italy (Italian Art)* Italian taxes on the export of artistic heritage aimed at the protection of national heritage from being sent abroad – and not seeking to raise revenue – were held to be illegal because they had the effect of imposing a duty upon the export of goods.

2.2 'Charge having equivalent effect' to a customs duty

Member states could try to dress up duties so as to conceal their true nature. The phrase 'charges having equivalent effect' is intended to prohibit attempts by member states to create financial barriers to trade which would not fall within the definition of a customs duty or charge, but which have the same effect.

Case 24/68 Commission v Italy (Statistical Data) concerned a levy imposed by Italy on goods exported to other member states, for the ostensible purpose of collecting statistical material for discerning trade patterns. The ECJ held that the levy breached Article 25 EC and that a charge having equivalent effect means:

> '... *any pecuniary charge, however small and whatever its destination and mode of application which is imposed unilaterally on domestic or foreign goods by reason of the fact that they cross a frontier and which is not a custom duty in the strict sense ... even if it is not imposed for the benefit of the State, is not discriminatory or protective in effect and if the product on which the charge is imposed is not in competition with any domestic product.* '

The charge need not be levied at the frontier, as long as it is levied by reason of importation.

The following types of charge have been held to be 'charges having equivalent effect':

(a) Charges for the collection of statistical information. *Case 24/68 Commission v Italy (Statistical Data)*.

(b) Charges for compulsory veterinary inspections for public health purposes on raw cow hide imports, which were not imposed as part of a general scheme on all producers in a like manner. *Case 87/75 Bresciani v Amministrazione Italiana delle Finanze*.

(c) Fees charged against traders by national authorities where Community legislation allows an inspection to be undertaken. *Case 314/82 Commission v Belgium*.

A fee/levy is not always an illegal charge having equivalent effect. There will be instances where fees/levies are not held to be charges of equivalent effect. The following are examples.

Fees charged for services rendered.

See *Case 132/82 Commission v Belgium* (1984) – The ECJ held that if the charge in question is:

(a) consideration for a service actually rendered; and
(b) of benefit to the importer; and
(c) an amount commensurate with that service given,

then it is not a 'charge having equivalent effect' to a customs duty.

Charges levied to cover the cost of a mandatory inspection required by Community Law.

See *Case 18/87 Commission v Germany* (1988), which concerned fees to cover the cost of certain compulsory animal inspections, required under a Directive. The ECJ held these would not be charges having equivalent effect if the following conditions were all satisfied.

(a) The fees do not exceed the actual cost of inspection.

(b) The inspections are obligatory – all member states required to carry them out.

(c) The inspections are required by Community law in the general interest of the EU.

(d) The inspections promote the free movement of goods. For example, the relevant EU law is intended to eliminate trade barriers and harmonise member state law.

The costs of the mandatory inspections/checks carried out as a result of rules imposed by international conventions.

See *Case 46/76 Bauhuis v Netherlands* (1977).

Charges on goods, which form part of a general system of internal taxation or charges which are systematically applied using the same criteria on domestic and imported products alike.

In *Case 29/87 Dansk Denkavit v Danish Ministry of Agriculture* the ECJ found that a charge levied to fund the cost of checking samples of feedstuffs for quality, which was imposed using the same criteria on domestic and imported goods, was not a 'charge having equivalent effect' but part of a general system of dues (Article 90 EC below).

2.3 Distinguishing between a charge and a tax

Genuine taxes fall within the ambit of Article 90 EC and are treated slightly more leniently than charges having equivalent effect (which are illegal subject to the limited exceptions set out above).

A genuine tax was defined in *Case 132/78 Denkavit v France* as one relating to:

> 'a general system of internal dues applied systematically to categories of products in accordance with objective criteria irrespective of the origin of the products. '

As such, even what may appear to be a genuine tax may be treated as a charge if it is earmarked to benefit only the domestic producers and not to achieve general public interest purposes.

Activity 1	(10 minutes)

What is the definition of a charge having equivalent effect to a customs duty?

3 ARTICLE 90 EC – PROHIBITION OF DISCRIMINATORY TAXATION

The purpose of Article 90 EC is to prevent the protection of domestic producers by making it illegal to impose taxes upon imported goods which are not imposed upon domestic goods.

Article 90 EC provides:

'(1) *No Member State shall impose, directly or indirectly, on the products of other Member States any internal taxation of any kind in excess of that imposed directly or indirectly on similar domestic products.*

(2) *Furthermore, no Member State shall impose on the products of other Member States any internal taxation of such a nature as to afford indirect protection to other products'.*

To fall within Article 90 EC at all, a genuine tax must be '*a measure relating to a system of internal dues ...*' *Case 90/79 Commission v France* . If the charge does not fall within this it will come under Articles 23 to 25 EC above.

3.1 'Similar products' – Article 90(1) EC

Direct discrimination

When a tax is imposed upon imported but not domestic goods this is obvious discrimination contrary to Article 90 EC and is illegal.

Indirect discrimination

When a tax is imposed, which appears to be non-discriminatory, but in fact affects imported goods more than domestic ones then this is indirect discrimination. It is also unlawful, unless it can be justified on objective grounds.

In *Case 112/84 Humblot v Directeur des Services Fiscaux* French laws relating to car tax were challenged by H who had paid a large tax on a 36CV car. The tax payable on purchase of a car was graded according to engine power up to 16CV. Above this there was a large flat fee. France produced no cars above 16CV all of which were imported. The court ruled the tax illegal. This meant that consumers would be influenced against such imported cars.

Objective justification for indirect discrimination

An indirectly discriminatory tax can be lawful if there is an objective justification for it and it does not have a protective effect for domestic producers.

In *Case 132/88 Commission v Greece* environmental concerns were sufficient to justify higher taxes on bigger cars even where all these were imported unlike in the *Commission v France* case. The distinction was that here the rules did not have protective effect because the tax was not set so high as to discourage consumers into buying domestic goods.

3.2 Non-similar products – Article 90(2) EC

In *Case 168/78 Commission v France (Spirits)* the ECJ ruled that Article 90 EC applies to goods which were not similar but which:

> *'are nevertheless in competition, even partial, indirect or potential, with certain products of the importing country.'*

National laws which imposed different levels of tax on drinks were subject to a number of challenges by the Commission which argued that the laws attempted to protect domestically produced drinks such as beer (UK) from imported drinks such as wine (from France).

Taxes imposed where no domestic producer exists

When a member state imposes a charge/tax on a product of which there is no domestic producer it might be thought that this would fall under Article 23-5 EC as a charge having equivalent effect because it is only imposed upon imports *de facto* (although not *de jure*).

However, the ECJ has held that such taxation may be imposed on imported products even where there is no domestic production of a similar or competing product, as long as it forms part of a general system of dues applying to the product as a class, irrespective of origin.

Activity 2   **(5 minutes)**

Why does Article 90 apply to non-similar products?

---

4 ELIMINATION OF QUANTITATIVE RESTRICTIONS ON IMPORTS AND EXPORTS AND ALL MEASURES HAVING EQUIVALENT EFFECT

Articles 28 – 31 EC are designed to eliminate non-financial trade barriers in contrast to the financial barriers that are covered by Articles 23 –25 EC and Article 90 EC.

(a) Article 28 EC prohibits quantitative restrictions, and all measures having equivalent effect on imports.

(b) Article 29 EC contains a similar prohibition regarding exports.

Suppose there is a UK national rule laying down a standard for the efficiency of car-brakes. If this standard is more stringent than that pertaining in France, a car sold in France may not be saleable in the UK without modification. The free movement of goods is reduced. This reflects national attitudes to cost, safety etc.

4.1 Who is bound by Article 28 to 30 EC?

Despite relating to 'measures' taken by member states, these articles also apply to the activities of any public body (legislative, executive or judicial) or semi-public body exercising powers derived from public law. For example, *Case 266, 267/87 R v Royal Pharmaceutical Society of GB* – an independent professional body responsible for the regulation of standards among UK pharmacists.

Note also that member states are required to take necessary and appropriate measures to ensure that goods are not impeded by members of the public seeking to block their movement. In *265/95 Commission v France* the court ruled that a breach of Article 28 EC had occurred where French police had consistently failed to prevent French farmers from blocking imports of agricultural products by public disorder.

4.2 Prohibition, as between member states, of quantitative restrictions on imports and of all measures having equivalent effect – Article 28 EC

Quantitative Restrictions

In *Case 2/73 Geddo v Ente Nazionale Risi* the ECJ held quantitative restrictions to be any

> '*measures which amount to a total or partial restraint, according to the circumstances of imports, exports or goods in transit'.*

Other examples include *Case 13/65 Salgoil SpA v Italian Minister of Finance*, concerning a quota system, and *Case 57-4/41 International Fruit Co NV* concerning a licensing system.

Measures having equivalent effect to quantitative restrictions (MEQRS)

Quotas are obvious barriers to trade but there are also disguised barriers caused by national rules that regulate the market so as to influence the free movement of goods. These have been given a wide interpretation by both the ECJ and the Commission.

Examples include:

- Regulatory measures designed to enforce minimum standards
- Tests/inspections
- Certification requirements
- Conditions on packaging, composition, identification, size and weight
- Minimum/maximum price fixing
- Payment conditions on products

The Commission's Definition of MEQR's

Commission Directive 70/50, although no longer in force, reinforced the standard categorisations of MEQR's. These are:

(a) **Distinctly applicable measures** – measures which do not apply equally to domestic or imported products, and therefore have some element of discrimination against imports.

(b) **Indistinctly applicable measures** – measures which are equally applicable to domestic imported and exported products. These measures are contrary to Article 28 EC where their restrictive effect on the free movement of goods are out of proportion to their purpose or where the same objective can be attained by other measures which constitute less of a hindrance to trade.

The ECJ's definition of MEQR's

In *Case 8/74 Procureur du Roi v Dassonville* the ECJ introduced its own definition of MEQRs. This definition is known as the '**Dassonville formula**':

> *'all trading rules enacted by member states which are capable of hindering, directly or indirectly, actually or potentially, intra-Community trade are to be considered as measures having an effect equivalent to quantitative restrictions'.*

It is not necessary to show an **actual** hindrance to trade between member states, only a potential to hinder member state trade. Further, there is no need to prove that there is discriminatory intent against imports on the part of the relevant member state. In fact, there is no need to show discrimination at all, as became clear in the later *Cassis de Dijon* decision (see below).

Discriminatory measures – Dassonville *applied*

There have been a large number of cases in which the court has ruled measures to be MEQRs where they discriminate against imports.

Conditions imposed on imports

Case 154/85 Commission v Italy in which the registration of imported cars required extra data beyond that for domestic cars.

Promotion of domestic goods

Case 249/81 Commission v Ireland ('Buy Irish') in which the Irish Goods Council campaign to promote Irish goods was held to be an MEQR because consumers and traders were likely to be affected by it.

Public procurement favouring domestic goods

Case 45/87 Commission v Ireland ('Dundalk water supply') in which the Dundalk council tendered for water supply contracts. The conditions of the contract specification included the use of a piping which conformed to an Irish standard. Only one company complied with the standard and this was Irish. The requirement favoured domestic companies and there was no need for it.

Measures which make imports more difficult or costly

Case 82/77 Openbaar Ministerie v Van Tiggele Dutch rules which set minimum selling prices for spirit drinks applied equally in law to home and imported goods but the court found that they discriminated in fact against importers because the latter had lower costs of production but would not be able exploit these by lowering their prices below the minimum. They would thus be unable to penetrate the Dutch market as easily.

Activity 3	(10 minutes)
Why does the EU prohibitive quantitative restrictions and MEQRs?	

5 DEROGATION FROM ARTICLE 28 EC – JUSTIFYING DISCRIMINATORY BARRIERS TO TRADE

Where a rule does constitute a quantitative restriction or MEQR under the Dassonville test then it is *prima facie* unlawful. However it may be justified under Article 30 EC, which provides member states with a range of justifications for derogation from Article 28-29 EC. The court has however interpreted these restrictively as they deviate from one of the fundamental rights under the Treaty.

Under Article 30 EC, therefore, prohibitions and restrictions on imports, exports or goods in transit can be justified on the grounds of:

- the protection of health and life of humans, animals and plants

- the protection of national treasures possessing artistic, historic or archeological value

- the protection of industrial or commercial property

It is important to remember that Article 30 EC must be interpreted strictly. Furthermore, the list of exceptions contained in Article 30 EC is exhaustive when considering discriminatory measures.

(a) **Public morality.** In *Case 121/85 Conegate v Customs & Excise Commissioners* customs officers seized inflatable sex dolls imported from Germany relying on Article 30 EC. The ECJ held that the UK government was free to determine public morality for the UK but could not **arbitrarily** discriminate against imports. The seizure was arbitrary because the UK had no domestic law against the sale of the items. By contrast in *Case 34/79 R v Henn and Darby* the seizure of imports of pornographic material was lawful because the UK did not have a legitimate trade in the items.

(b) **Public policy.** In *Case 231/83 Cullett v Centre Leclerc* the French government argued that minimum prices for petrol – which made it more difficult for importers to undercut French distributors – were necessary because otherwise French traders would cause disruption to prevent cheap imports. This was rejected because there was no evidence that the disturbances would not be controllable.

One case in which this justification was accepted is *Case 7/78 R v Thompson* where the ECJ recognised a member state's need to protect its right to mint and stop coinage from being destroyed as one of its fundamental interests. Thus a prohibition on import/export of coins was justified.

(c) **Public security.** Again this has a restrictive interpretation. In *Case 72/83 Campus Oil Ltd* the Irish government was allowed to require traders to buy a share of their oil from a state-run refinery because a national oil supply capacity had to be maintained for national economic reasons. However this seems to be a case peculiar to its own facts and has not subsequently been followed by the ECJ (see *Commission v Greece* Case C-367/89).

(d) **Protection of health, life of humans, animals and plants.** This heading has been employed by states on many occasions when faced with animal health crises. See *Case 190/87 Oberkreisdirektor v Moormann* in which a state could not rely on Article 30 to introduce its own checks because there was an EC measure setting out the rules on health inspections for poultry. Where there is no EU measure in place, member states have discretion under Article 30 EC. However, the court will scrutinise closely the evidence supporting a ban on these grounds. Thus in *Case 40/82 Commission v United Kingdom* the court ruled that a ban on imports of Christmas turkeys from France, apparently to prevent Newcastle disease spreading in the UK, was in fact aimed at protecting UK producers.

(e) **Protection of national treasures**. This heading is rarely invoked by member states.

(f) **Protection of industrial and commercial property**. This heading concerns intellectual property rights held by private companies, which can be used to prevent the sale of goods in member states where the company has registered such rights.

6 DISTINCTLY/INDISTINCTLY APPLICABLE MEASURES: *CASSIS DE DIJON*

Where a Member State enacts rules that are directly discriminatory against imports/exports, these rules can only be justified if they come within the derogations contained in **Article 30**. Article 30 has not changed in substance since the original Treaty of Rome signed in 1957. The ECJ has recognised that these derogations are no longer sufficient, especially with regard to indistinctly applicable measures. As a result there has been a series of cases that have operated to disapply Article 28 in certain situations. Member States do not have to rely on the derogations under Article 30, as they can claim that Article 28 does not actually apply. The Court did this by allowing that mandatory requirements were outside the scope of Article 28 (see below).

There are rules which are **indistinctly applicable** – they apply equally in fact and law to imports and domestic goods but they still inhibit the flow of goods. These are rules and policies on product standards, shop opening hours, advertising and so on. Even public spending plans, planning regulations, licensing laws for guns could be viewed as inhibiting the flow of goods from other member states if a broad view is taken.

The issue that came before the ECJ in *Case 120/78 Rewe-Zentral AG v Bundesmonopolverwaltung für Branntwein ('Cassis De Dijon')*. This concerned the legality under EC law of a German law, which specified a minimum alcohol level of 25% for certain spirits including cassis. German fruit liqueurs complied with this requirement, but French cassis did not. Although the law was indistinctly applicable, applying to both domestic and imported products, the effect of the measure was to prevent French cassis from being sold on the German market. The French importer challenged the rule, arguing that it was an MEQR under Article 28 EC.

6.1 The mandatory requirements

The court reiterated the Dassonville formula and noted that the national rules did, in fact, impede the movement of goods because they prevented the sale of French cassis in Germany. The court then stated that:

> *'obstacles to movement within the Community resulting from disparities between national laws relating to the marketing of the products in question must be accepted in so far as those provisions may be recognised as being **necessary** in order to satisfy **mandatory requirements** relating in particular to the effectiveness of fiscal supervision, the protection of public health, the fairness of commercial transactions and the defence of the consumer'.*

The court thus ruled that only national rules which were necessary to satisfy 'mandatory requirements' could be considered outside the scope of Article 28 EC. The rules must both pursue a legitimate aim and not go beyond that which is necessary to achieve that aim.

The court then went on to consider the German law which, it was argued, aimed to prevent alcoholism (!) and to protect consumers. The court decided that these aims were acceptable but that the means were excessive. They could be achieved by labelling rather than minimum alcohol rules. The court thus declared them to be illegal under Article 28 EC.

6.2 Rule of Reason

The Rule of Reason is a principle arising out of *Cassis de Dijon* whereby certain indistinctly applicable measures will not be prohibited by Article 28 EC if they are necessary to satisfy mandatory requirements (as above). Although the *Cassis de Dijon* judgment does not say so in so many words, later case law indicates that the **Rule of Reason applies only to indistinctly applicable measures**.

As such, the Rule of Reason provides member states with additional and wider grounds of justification, for indistinctly applicable measures than that provided under Article 30 EC. In addition, unlike Article 30 EC, the mandatory requirements permitted under *Cassis de Dijon* are non-exhaustive. The ECJ has expanded on the list set out in *Cassis de Dijon* itself.

6.3 Presumption of marketability

The ECJ established an additional principle in *Cassis de Dijon*, suggesting that there was no valid reason why '*provided that goods have been lawfully produced and marketed in one member state, that they should not be introduced into any other member state*'.

This principle gives rise to the presumption that goods which have been lawfully marketed in one member state will comply with the mandatory requirements of the importing State. This can be rebutted by evidence that further measures are necessary to protect the pertinent interest however, rebuttal will be difficult.

Cassis de Dijon has been used many times by the ECJ to strike down rules that impede the movement of goods without being necessary to satisfy a mandatory requirement. The case has therefore been a powerful tool in forcing EU integration. National laws that make it more difficult to sell goods in other member states by imposing **dual burdens** on importers who lawfully market products in their home market have been declared unlawful as in *Cassis de Dijon* itself.

6.4 Selling arrangements – Sunday Trading cases & *Keck*

In *Cases 267 & 268/91 Keck & Mithouard (Criminal Proceedings)* the ECJ effectively overruled its earlier decisions on Sunday trading and ruled that, subject to certain conditions, laws relating to selling arrangements (like Sunday trading) did not fall within Article 28 EC at all. **Such laws were in effect not MEQRs under the *Dassonville* test**. The decision in this case sought to counter the confusion that had arisen as a result of the Sunday Trading cases.

Keck concerned the prosecution of K and M in the French courts for selling goods at a price which was lower than their actual price (resale at a loss). This was contrary to French law. K and M claimed that the French Law was contrary to the free movement and competition principles of the EC Treaty.

The case was referred to the ECJ under Article 234 EC. The ECJ held:

(a) That it was necessary to re-examine the case law in this area, especially on rules which relate to selling arrangements for products, as opposed to those which relate to the goods themselves (composition, packaging and presentation), to combat the tendency of traders to invoke Article 28 EC to challenge trading rules which restrict their commercial freedom, even when those rules are not aimed at products from other member states.

(b) Article 28 EC does not apply to national legislation which prohibits resale at a loss (a form of selling arrangement) because the purpose of the legislation was not to regulate trade and its effect was not to prevent market access for traders from member states.

However, for this conclusion to be drawn the following conditions must apply.

(a) The legislation must apply to **all traders** operating in the member state; and

(b) The marketing of domestic products and those from other member states are **equally affected** by the relevant measure in the same manner, in law and fact by the legislation.

The *Keck* decision was followed by a number of cases where selling arrangements of various sorts were held to fall outside the rigours of Article 28 EC altogether and thus there was no need to seek to justify them as being necessary and proportionate.

6.5 Exceptions to Keck – the limits of selling arrangements

In *Case C-405/98 Konsumentombudsmannen v Gourmet International Products*, the ECJ looked at Swedish laws which prohibited advertising of alcoholic beverages in periodicals or other publications, unless the publication was distributed solely at the point of sale of the beverage. Gourmet published a magazine intended for subscribers with ads for alcoholic beverages, and the Swedish authorities sought an injunction against the publication.

The ECJ held that, unlike in *Keck*, this type of selling arrangement would fall within Article 28 EC as it impedes access by foreign producers to the alcoholic beverage market: consumers are instantly more familiar with domestic goods. As such, the Swedish law fell within Article 28 EC as constituting an obstacle to trade between member states, although it could be justified under Article 30 EC (protection of public health). The ECJ left that balancing act to the national court.

Activity 4	(5 minutes)

Why did the ECJ introduce the selling arrangements exception to Cassis?

7   ARTICLE 29 EC – EXPORT RESTRICTIONS

Subject to the exception that indistinctly applicable measures will not breach Article 29 EC, all other principles relating to imports under Article 28 EC will also apply to exports under Article 29 EC.

The *Dassonville* formula for imports does not apply to indistinctly applicable export measures, that is measures which apply in equal measure to the domestic and export trade of a member state. This is because there is no dual burden – the exporter and domestic trader both have one set of rules to comply with. There must be some form of overt discrimination against exports.

In order to breach Article 29 EC, such measures must have as their specific object or effect the restrictions of patterns of exports and thereby the establishment of differential treatment, between the domestic trade of a member state and its export trade, so as to afford a particular advantage for domestic production or for the domestic market of the State.

8   FREEDOM TO PROVIDE SERVICES

Article 49 EC provides:

> '*Within the framework of the provisions set out below, restrictions on freedom to provide services within the Community shall be prohibited in respect of nationals or Member States who are established in a State of the Community other than that of the person for who the services are intended*'.

As with the provisions on workers and establishment, the provisions on services only apply to situations involving persons/organisations/activities from more than one member state.

8.1   What is a 'service'?

Article 50 EC defines 'services' as being normally provided for remuneration, insofar as they are not already governed by EU provisions relating to the freedom of movement of goods, capital and persons. In addition, 'services' are in particular:

- Activities of an industrial character,
- Activities of a commercial character,
- Activities of craftsmen, and
- Activities of the professions.

Hence, not only must there be an interstate element but the service must have an economic element. The ECJ has ruled that recreational, sporting and similar services are 'services' covered by Articles 49 and 50 EC.

The distinction between the freedom to provide services and the freedom of establishment (dealt with in the last chapter) is that latter is concerned with actually setting-up business (with premises etc) in another member state whereas the need to visit the other member state (although some services may not even require physical travel by their provider).

8.2 The freedom to receive services

Article 49 EC expressly refers to the freedom to 'provide services' and Article 50 EC is concerned with the rights of providers. They do not cover those who may wish to receive the services concerned.

Directive 64/221 protects the position of those recipients of services who reside in or travel to another member state in order to receive the services concerned. *Directive 73/148 Article 1(b)* also prohibits restrictions on movement and residence by nationals:

> *'wishing to go to another Member State as recipients of services'.*

In *Cases 286/82 and 26/83 Luisi and Cabone v Ministero del Tesoro*, the ECJ held that the Treaties provided for the freedom for a recipient of services to go to another member state – without any restriction – in order to receive the said services. This was implied by – and reflected the – provider's freedom to provide the services to persons from outside his own member state.

8.3 Vocational courses

Directive 93/96 deals with students who move to another member state to undertake a vocational course. The student, his/her spouse and children all have the right to live in the other member state for the duration of the course. The ECJ has given a wide definition to 'vocational courses'.

8.4 Illegal or immoral services

There are, of course, some activities which are legal (or considered morally acceptable) in some member states but not in others. What happens if someone wishes to provide a 'service' which is entirely permissible in his own member state but not in the state in which he wishes to offer the service in question?

In *Case 15/78 Societe General Alsacienne de Banque SA v Koestler* the ECJ held that the German authorities were permitted to prevent a French bank providing financial services which, although entirely legal in France, were not permitted in Germany. The ECJ held that, provided German banks were also prevented from providing such services, there was no infringement of Article 49 EC.

In *Case C-159/90 SPUC v Grogan*, students distributed information in Ireland concerning abortion services available in the UK, such services not being available in Ireland and the distribution of such information being banned by the Irish authorities. The student activists received no payment for this activity – hence they could not rely on Article 49 to prevent the ban on the distribution of the literature. It was also argued, by SPUC, that the provision of abortion facilities could not amount to a 'service' under Article 49 EC as it was immoral. The ECJ ruled that it could not supplant the views of those member states where abortion was legal and permitted.

The current view of the ECJ on this area appears to be that, provided it is lawful in some member states, a service will be caught by Articles 49 and 50 EC. The individual member states will, however, be allowed to regulate any service provided their actions are proportionate (see General Principles in Chapter 16) and are not discriminatory between nationals and non-nationals.

8.5   Exceptions

The three grounds which permit member states to discriminate against the general freedom provided for under Article 49 EC are set out in Article 46 EC. These are:

- Public policy
- Security, and
- Health.

Article 55 EC states that these are to be applied to services. The ECJ has interpreted the scope of the public policy exception in narrow terms. In *Case 36/75 Rutili v Ministre de l'Interieur* the ECJ stated that any such restriction on public policy grounds was only acceptable when the individual's behaviour constituted a genuine and sufficiently serious threat.

See Chapter 17, Paragraph 6.1 on the operation of *Directive 64/221*.

8.6   Mutual recognition

None of the EC Treaty provisions require the member states to recognise the qualifications an individual may have acquired in another member state. Note, however, the provisions on mutual recognition referred to in Paragraph 8.4 of Chapter 17.

8.7   Professional qualifications and freedom of establishment

Two recent Directives are of significance. **Directive 2005/36** replaced earlier legislation dealing with the **recognition of professional qualifications**, with the aim of consolidating the law and creating a single legal system that liberalized the provision of services, increasing the automatic recognition of services and making it easier to amend the Directive in future.

Directive **2006/123** is a controversial directive that deals not just with services, but also with **freedom of establishment**. The preamble to the Directive notes that it is still difficult, particularly for small and medium sized enterprises (SMEs) to provide services beyond their own national borders. This is significant given that the growth of service industries throughout the EU means that these form at least 70% of the GDP of most Member States. The original proposal was that the country in which a service provider was established was to take responsibility for regulating that provider and its services, regardless of where those services were performed. This did not make it into the version finally adopted as there were many who feared that this would lead to a lowering of standards. Instead Member States have to ensure that service providers have free access to and exercise of a service provision within their own boundaries, regardless of where the provider is based.

NOTES

Chapter roundup

- The free movement of goods and services are two of the 'four freedoms' guaranteed by the EC Treaty.

- Article 25 EC prohibits customs duties and charges having an equivalent effect on goods.

- Article 90 EC prohibits discriminatory taxation of goods.

- Quantitative restrictions on imports and exports are also prohibited.

- Derogations are permitted on restricted grounds.

- The freedom to supply services is a freedom for suppliers and recipients of services.

Quick quiz

1   Name two types of charge that have been held to be 'charges having an equivalent effect'.

2   What is the distinction between a charge and a tax?

3   What non-similar products are covered by Article 90 EC?

4   Who is bound by Article 28 to 30 EC?

5   What are the exceptions under Article 46 EC?

Answers to quick quiz

1   Charges for the collection of statistical information. Case 24/68 *Commission v Italy (Statistical Data)*; Charges for compulsory veterinary inspections for public health purposes on raw cow hide imports, which were not imposed as part of a general scheme on all producers in a like manner. Case 87/75 *Bresciani v Amministrazione Italiana delle Finanze*; Fees charged against traders by national authorities where Community legislation allows an inspection to be undertaken. Case 314/82 *Commission v Belgium* (see para 2.2).

2   A genuine tax was defined in Case 132/78 *Denkavit v France* as one relating 'to a general system of internal dues applied systematically to categories of products in accordance with objective criteria irrespective of the origin of the products.' (para 2.3)

3   In Case 168/78 *Commission v France (Spirits)* the ECJ ruled that Article 90 EC applies to goods which were not similar but which: 'are nevertheless in competition, even partial, indirect or potential, with certain products of the importing country'. (para 3.2)

4   Any public body (legislative, executive or judicial) or semi-public body exercising powers derived from public law (para 4.1).

5   Public policy; security; and health (para 8.5).

Answers to activities

1   Case 24/68 *Commission v Italy (Statistical Data)* concerned a levy imposed by Italy on goods exported to other member states, for the ostensible purpose of collecting statistical material for discerning trade patterns. The ECJ held that the levy breached Article 25 EC and that a charge having equivalent effect means:

> *'... any pecuniary charge, however small and whatever its destination and mode of application which is imposed unilaterally on domestic or foreign goods by reason of the fact that they cross a frontier and which is not a custom duty in the strict sense ... even if it is not imposed for the benefit of the State, is not discriminatory or protective in effect and if the product on which the charge is imposed is not in competition with any domestic product. '*

2   To prevent the discrimination against products which may not be in direct competition with those of the member state's own nationals (ie like-for-like) but which nevertheless are directed towards the same market (ie food and drink).

3   Quotas are obvious barriers to trade but there are also disguised barriers caused by national rules that regulate the market so as to influence the free movement of goods. Hence not only quotas, which are clearly quantitative, but also MEQRs are prohibited as being contrary to the objective of the free movement of goods.

4   The ECJ was concerned that traders were invoking *Cassis* to challenge rules relating to the breadth of marketing opportunities. These applied equally to all traders (eg Sunday trading laws). Cassis had been aimed at product standard laws which prevented any marketing of an imported product. The Court therefore tried to exclude challenges to rules that merely limited options for marketing and did not relate to product standards.

GLOSSARY OF
BUSINESS LAW TERMS

Acceptance An unqualified agreement to the terms of the offer.

Anticipatory breach Renunciation by party to a contract of his contractual obligations before the date for performance.

Arbitration A means of settling a dispute outside the courts.

Bill of exchange A type of order to pay money.

Capacity The ability or power of a person to enter into legal relationships or carry out legal acts.

Claimant The person who complains or brings an action asking the court for relief (used to be called the plaintiff)

Code of practice A code which lays out a set of procedures and policies that a firm will follow.

Common law The body of legal rules developed by the common law courts and now embodied in legal decisions.

Condition Term which is vital to a contract. Breach of a condition destroys the basis of the contract which is itself then breached.

Consideration Consists either in some right, interest, profit or benefit accruing to one party contract, or some forbearance, detriment, loss or responsibility given, suffered or undertaken by the other.

Constructive dismissal Serious breach of contract by an employer which forces an employee to leave.

Consumer Any natural person who, in contracts covered by the regulations, is acting outside his trade, business as progression.

Contract An agreement which legally binds the parties.

Contract of employment A contract of employment is 'a contract of service or apprenticeship, whether express or implied, and (if it is express) whether it is oral or in writing.'

Control test Test used by the courts to determine whether a contract of employment exists, or whether a party is an independent contractor.

Damages The sum claimed or awarded in a civil action in compensation for the loss or injury suffered by the claimant.

Decision A source of European law, which may be addressed to a state, person or a company and is immediately binding, but only on the recipient.

Defendant The person against whom a civil action is brought or who is prosecuted for a criminal offence.

Delegated legislation Rules of law made by subordinate bodies to whom the power to do so has been given by statute.

Directive A term of European Community law, issued to the government of the EU states requiring them within a certain specified period (usually two years) to alter the national laws of the state so that they conform to the directive.

Dismissal Termination by an employer of a contract of employment.

Enforceable code of practice A code of practice that is enforceable by means of sanctions falling short of legal proceedings. It will set down codes of conduct that can be enforced against people engaged in a certain trade or business, even though they are not members of the relevant trade body.

Equity A source of English law consisting of those rules which emerged from the Court of Chancery.

Estoppel When a person, by his words or conduct, leads another to believe that a certain state of affairs exists. If the other person alters his or her position to his or her detriment in reliance on that belief, the first person is estopped (prevented) from claiming later that a different state of affairs existed.

Exclusion clause Contract clause purporting to exclude or restrict liability.

Executed consideration A performed, or executed, act in return for a promise.

Executory consideration A promise given for a promise, not a performed act.

Force majeure clauses Clauses inserted in contracts when the parties can foresee that difficulties are likely to arise but the parties cannot foresee their precise nature of extent.

Fundamental breach Doctrine developed by the courts as a protection against unreasonable exemption clauses in contracts.

Implied term Term deemed to form part of a contract even though not expressly mentioned by the parties.

In personam An action *in personam* is one seeking relief against a particular person.

In rem An action *in rem* is one brought in respect of property.

Independent contractor Self-employed person.

Indictable offences Are serious offences that can only be heard in a Crown court.

Injunction An equitable remedy in which the court orders the other party to a contract to observe negative restrictions.

Integration test Test used by the courts to determine whether a contract of employment exists.

Intention to create legal relations Element necessary for an agreement to become a legally binding contract.

Invitation to treat Indication that someone is prepared to receive offers with a view to forming a binding contract. It is not on offer in itself.

Lien A right to retain possession of property until a debt has been paid.

Minor A person under the age of eighteen.

Misrepresentation False statement made with the object of inducing the other party to enter into a contract.

Multiple test Used by the courts to determine whether a contract of employment exists.

Obiter dicta Statements made by a judge 'by the way'.

Offer A definite promise to be bound on specific terms.

Office of Fair Trading A government department staffed by over 300 people and financed by the Department of Trade and Industry. It is headed by the Director General of Fair Trading (DGFT), supported by a Deputy Director General. It does not usually deal with complaints received directly from members of the general public, but acts on information from the following sources:

(a)   Its own investigations
(b)   Information provided by local authority trading standards departments
(c)   The courts (who inform the DGFT of material convictions)
(d)   News media

Ombudsman Used to describe the provision of a final independent appeal that a dissatisfied customer may make against what he or she believes to be unfair or incompetent treatment. (The term is Swedish and does not have a satisfactory English translation.) Some Ombudsmen are provided with government support. In the private sector, banks, building societies and insurance companies may support Ombudsmen on a voluntary basis.

Past consideration Something already done at the time that a contractual promise is made.

Penalty clause In a contract providing for a specific sum to be payable in the event of a subsequent breach.

Per se By itself.

Persons at work Anyone who comes within the scope of the employer while undertaking their own work. This therefore would include employees, independent contractors, visitors who are visiting for business purposes (for example, suppliers or professional advisers).

Persons other than persons at work appears to mean any persons, extending to the general public.

Precedent A previous court decision.

Privity of contract The relation between two parties to a contract.

Quantum meruit As much as he has deserved.

Ratio decidendi The reason for the decision.

Re In the matter of. Seen in some case names.

Rectification An equitable remedy in which the court can order a document to be altered so that it reflects the parties true intentions.

Regulation A form of European Community law which became part of the law of each member nation as soon as they come into force without the need for each country to make its own legislation.

Remoteness of damage Relationship between a wrongful act and the resulting damage which determines whether or not compensation may be recovered. Different principles apply in contract and in tort.

Rescission An equitable remedy through which a contract is cancelled or rejected and the parties are restored to their pre-contracted position, as if it had never been entered into.

Royal Assent Final stage in the process by which a Bill becomes an Act.

Sale of goods A contract whereby the seller transfers or agrees to transfer the property in goods for a money consideration called the price.

Seller/supplier Any natural or legal person who, in contracts covered by the regulations, is acting for the purposes relating to his trade, business or profession, whether publicly owned or privately owned.

Specific performance An equitable remedy in which the court orders the defendant to perform his side of a contract.

Standard form contract A standard document prepared by many large organisations and setting out the terms on which they contract with their customers.

Standard of proof The extent to which the court must be satisfied by the evidence presented.

Statutory instrument Form of delegated legislation.

Summary offences Are minor crimes, only triable summarily in magistrates' courts.

Uberrimae fidei Of utmost good faith.

Ultra vires Beyond their powers. In company law this term is used in connection with transactions which are outside the scope of the objects clause and therefore, in principle at least, unenforceable. In an *ultra vires* contract the company would not have had the capacity to contract.

Unenforceable contract Is a valid contract and property transferred under it cannot be recovered even from the other party to the contract if either party refuses to perform the contract, the other party cannot compel him to do so

Void contract Not a contract at all. The parties are not bound by it and if they transfer property under it they can sometimes recover their goods from a third party.

Voidable contract A contract which one party may avoid, that is, terminate at his option. Property transferred before avoidance is usually irrecoverable from a third party.

Warranty Minor term in a contract. It does not go to the root of the contract, but is subsidiary to the main purpose of the contract. Breach of a warranty does not give rise to breach of the contract itself.

376

APPENDIX:
EDEXCEL GUIDELINES

This course book, and its companion volume Business Essentials Company and Commercial Law, between them cover the topics set out in the Edexcel guidelines for the HND/HNC Business qualification for:

- Unit 5, Common Law I
- Unit 25, English Legal System
- Unit 26, Business Law
- Unit 27, Common Law II
- Unit 28, European Law

The BPP Learning Media Business Essentials course books divide the material between them, one entitled Business Law and the other entitled Company and Commercial Law.

This book covers:

- Unit 5: Common Law I: all sections
- Unit 25: English legal system: Sections 1 to 3
- Unit 27: all sections
- Unit 28: all sections

EDEXCEL GUIDELINES FOR UNIT 5: COMMON LAW I

Description of unit

The aim of this unit is to provide an introduction to the law of contract, w ith a particular focus on the formation and operation of a business contract. Learners are encouraged to explore the contents of such an agreement and, in particular, to appreciate the practical application of standard-form business contracts. Additionally, the unit enables learners to understand how the Law of Tort differs from the law of contract and examines the Tort of Negligence and issues of liability pertinent to business.

Summary of learning outcomes

To achieve this unit a student must:

1   Understand the **essential elements of a valid** and legally binding **contract** and its role in a business context

2   Explore the significance of **specific terms in a business contract**

3   Examine the role of the **Law of Tort in business activities** assessing **particular forms of tortious liability**

4   Understand and apply the **elements of the Tort of Negligence**

Content	Chapter coverage
1 Essential elements of a valid contract	
Essential elements: types of contractual agreements and their application in business: the making of a valid offer and its unconditional acceptance; the essential existence of a clear and unambiguous intention supported by sufficient consideration; the parties to the agreement possessing the necessary capacity and being privy to the agreement.	4 – 6
2 Specific terms in a business contract	
Specific terms: contents of a valid agreement, and standard form business contracts; comparative analysis of express and implied terms; the effects of the breach of a condition, warranty or an innominate term; the legal effect on the agreement of the incorporation of an exemption clause.	7
3 The Law of Tort in business activities and particular forms of tortious liability	
The Law of Tort: fundamental aspects of tort; tortious liability and business operations; advantages of using tortious as opposed to contractual remedies	12
Types of tortious liability: the tortious liability of occupiers, employer's liability including vicarious liability for employees, health and safety issues, strict liability, difficulties of practical application	13, 14
4 Elements of the Tort of Negligence	
Negligence: the nature and scope of the duty of care and the standard of care; breach of duty, issues of causation and remoteness of damage	13, 14

Outcomes and assessment criteria

Outcomes	Assessment criteria for pass **To achieve each outcome a learner must demonstrate the ability to:**
1 Understand the **essential elements of a valid** and legally binding **contract** and its role in a business context	• Explain the different types of business agreement and the importance of the key elements required for the formation of a valid contract • Apply the rules of offer and acceptance in a given scenario, also considering any impact of new technology • Assess the importance of the rules of intention and consideration of the parties to the agreement • Explain the importance of the contracting parties having the appropriate legal capacity to enter into a binding agreement
2 Analyse the significance of **specific terms in a business contract**	• Analyse specific contract terms with reference to their importance and impact if these terms are broken • Apply and analyse the law on standard form contracts • Discuss the effect of exemption clauses in attempting to exclude contractual liability
3 Examine the role of the **Law of Tort in business activities** assessing **particular forms of tortious liability**	• Describe the nature of general tortious liability comparing and contrasting to contractual liability • Explain the liability applicable to an occupier of premises • Discuss the nature of employer's liability with reference to vicarious liability and health and safety implications • Distinguish strict liability from general tortious liability
4 Understand and apply **the elements of the Tort of Negligence**	• Explain and understand the application of the elements of the Tort of Negligence • Analyse the practical applications of particular elements of the tort of negligence

Delivery

This unit can be delivered in a variety of ways. Group work and other active methods of learning can be employed to enhance learners' experience and promote the required understanding. The use of case studies and specimen documentation is to be particularly encouraged, both as a means of assessment and as part of the normal learning process.

Assessment

Evidence of outcomes may be in the form of:

- Case studies to assess differing approaches to contractual liability

- Group work, presentations, and role plays used critically, to examine the essential elements of a valid contract

- Case studies to assess differing approaches to tortious liability

- Group work to examine critically particular elements of negligence

- Group role play to simulate situations where various forms of tortious liability apply

Links

This unit provides for the development of a solid understanding of the essential requirements of a valid business contract. This will be a foundation for *Unit 27: Common Law II* where the knowledge base and understanding gained will be further developed and enhanced. To a lesser extent there will be some common ground between the contents of this unit and *Unit 25: English Legal System* in relation to the forms of liability and the development of common law and equitable remedies.

This unit offers opportunities for developing common skills in managing tasks and solving problems, communicating, working with and relating to others.

Support materials

Textbooks

Sufficient library resources should be available to enable learners to achieve this unit. Particularly relevant texts are:

- Atiyah, P. S. *Introduction to the Law of Contract* (Clarendon Press, June 1995) ISBN 0198259530

- Beale, Bishop and Furmston, *Contract – Cases and Materials* (Butterworth, October 2001) ISBN 0406 92404X

- Cheshire, Fifoot and Furmston, *Law of Contract* (Butterworth, October 2001) ISBN 0406930589

- Cooke, J. *Law of Tort* (Prentice Hall, May 1997) ISBN 0273627104

- Elliott and Quinn, *Contract Law* (Longman, December 2002) ISBN 0582473306

- Elliott and Quinn, *Tort Law* (Longman, July 1997) ISBN 058243811X

- Harvey and Marston, *Cases and Commentary on TORT* (Prentice Hall, 2004) 5th edition ISBN 0406971382

- Hodgson, J. and Lewthwaite, J. *Law of Torts* (Blackstone, October 2001) ISBN 1841742759

- Jones, M. *Textbook on Torts* (Oxford University, August 2002) ISBN 0199255334

- Pannett, A. *Law of Torts* (Prentice Hall, March 1997) ISBN 0712110704

- Treitel, G. *Law of Contract* (Sweet & Maxwell, June 2003) ISBN 042178850X

- Young, M. *Cases and Commentary in Contract Law* (Prentice Hall, June 1997) ISBN 0273 625705

Journals

- *Law Society Gazette*
- *New Law Journal*

EDEXCEL GUIDELINES FOR SPECIALIST UNIT 25: ENGLISH LEGAL SYSTEM

Description of the Unit

This unit provides an introduction to the English legal system. It develops learners' knowledge of the court structure, court procedures, funding and legal personnel. Alternative methods of settling disputes are also covered, as are the sources of law, their development and interpretation. It also provides an introduction to the legal formalities required for the formation of the different business entities, their management and dissolution.

Outcomes and assessment criteria

Outcomes	Assessment criteria
	To achieve each outcome a student must demonstrate the ability to:
1 Investigate the **civil and criminal courts**, their structure, operation and **alternative methods of dispute resolution**	• understand the differences between criminal and civil law • identify the role of individual courts and assess their effectiveness within the court structure • apply knowledge of court roles to live case/case study material and present findings • explain the mean of ADR and assess its usefulness
2 Identify sources of **legal advice and funding**, including the roles of **different legal personnel**	• identify sources of legal advice • assess implications of changes in funding • understand and assess the role of solicitors, barristers and judges
3 Explore the relevant importance of the different **sources of law**, together with **rules of interpretation**	• understand the current day importance of the sources of law • apply knowledge of the sources of law to a case study and present findings • assess the effectiveness of the rules of interpretation
4 Investigate legal personality, particularly of **business entities**	• evaluate the legal principles which can influence choice of business entity • assess the difference with regard to management of partnerships and companies

Content	Covered in chapter(s)
1 Civil and criminal courts and alternative methods of dispute resolution	
Criminal courts: classification of crimes and methods of trial; magistrates' court – jurisdiction, personnel, procedure; Crown Court – juries, their role and structure, jurisdiction, procedure; grounds for appeal, Court of Appeal, House of Lords, European Court of Justice	1
Civil courts: Small Claims Court and jurisdiction; County Court and High Court, jurisdiction of both and allocation of cases to tracks; grounds for appeal; Court of Appeal, House of Lords, ECJ	1
Alternative dispute resolution: meaning – conciliation, mediation and arbitration; advantages and disadvantages; tribunals and enquiries	1
2 Legal advice, funding and legal personnel	
Legal advice and funding: sources of legal advice, duty solicitor scheme, funding, conditional fees	2
Legal personnel: solicitors and barristers, roles and training; overview of the judiciary	2
3 Sources of law and rules of interpretation	
Sources of law: judicial precedent, statute, delegated legislation – meaning, how they operate, advantages and disadvantages; rules of Statutory Interpretation; European law – types of law	3
Differences between common law and equity: role of equity today	3
4 Business entities	
Meaning and examples: sole traders, partnerships, companies	*Covered in Business Essentials Company and Commercial Law*
Advantages and disadvantages: of types of legal business entity	
Legal requirements: for the formation of sole traders, partnerships and companies	
Provisions: relating to the running/management of businesses, eg rights/duties of partners, directors and creditors; dissolution of business entities	

Delivery

Each section will require lecturers to provide an introductory factual framework. Learners should then take part in a variety of activities, eg visits, talks, research to access primary sources, case studies, group discussions and moots.

A good starting point for delivery is Outcome 1. Visits to a variety of courts generate discussion and enable learners to visualise the courts, their personnel and the procedures and types of cases dealt with. It may then be preferable to continue with Outcome 3, as some of the cases seen in the courts will generate discussion on the law involved and explanation of Statutes, Judicial Precedent and Delegated Legislation will follow naturally. It is important when looking at the rules of interpretation to use live case examples to explain the different results which can result from the application of different rules. Outcome 2 also follows on from the court visits and looks at where advice can be sought, how it can be funded and what responsibilities the different legal personnel have. Finally, Outcome 4 looks at the formation of businesses and the legal requirements involved. This Outcome is freestanding, but useful in cases where learners are not opting for further law units.

Assessment

The assessment(s) should aim in a structured way to test the different unit outcomes. They will develop and test a variety of skills and encourage use of primary and secondary legal materials. Examples of assessment could include:

- a record of a visit to a court/tribunal with an analysis of the role of that institution

- a case study including a number of incidents which require advice on the particular courts that would deal with the incidents, the availability of advice, funding and personnel

- a case study on a source of law

- a report on proposed or recent legislation

- an oral presentation on some aspect of the legal system

- a case study on a business, including choice of business entity, advantages/ disadvantages, management, dissolution.

Links

This unit forms the foundation for all the other specialist law units. It examines the structure of the legal system, the sources of law, funding and personnel. This is an essential introduction to the specialist law units covering contract, tort, European law and business law.

The formation, management and dissolution of business entities is a useful introduction to the company unit.

The sources of law section looks at types of European law and the court structure of the ECJ which is a useful introduction to *Unit 28: European Law*.

Resources

Learners should have access to a learning resource centre with a good range of legal text and case books. These should be supported by journals, statutes and law reports. Good newspapers are also necessary because of the topical nature of law.

Learners will also benefit from visits to courts and parliament. Crown Courts are usually excellent in arranging tours and talks by resident judges. Magistrates, solicitors and barristers are usually willing to talk collectively to groups of learners.

Suggested reading

Textbooks

- Elliot and Quinn. *English Legal System* (Longman, April 2002)

- Slapper and Kelly. *English Legal System* (Cavendish, August 2001)

- Ingman, T. *The English Legal Process* (Blackstone, August 2000)

- Stychin, C. *Legal Method: Text and Materials* (Sweet & Maxwell, April 1999)

- Darbyshire, P. *Nutshells English Legal System* (Sweet & Maxwell, March 2001)

- Smith and Keenan. *Advanced Business Law* (Prentice Hall, January 2000)

- Martin, J. *English Legal System* (Hodder & Stoughton Educational, June 2002)

Websites

World wide websites can be useful in providing information and case studies, for example:

- www.bized.co.uk — Provides case studies appropriate for educational purposes

- www.cps.gov.uk — The Crown Prosecution Service

- www.legalservices.gov.uk — Legal Services Commission

- www.dca.gov.uk — Department for Constitutional Affairs

- www.lawcom.gov.uk — The Law Commission

- www.criminal-justice-system.gov.uk — Criminal Justice System

- www.eurunion.org — European Union in the US

- www.courtservice.gov.uk — The Court Service

- www.bbc.co.uk/law — BBC

- www.cjsonline.org — Criminal Justice System

388

EDEXCEL GUIDELINES FOR SPECIALIST UNIT 27: COMMON LAW II

Description of the Unit

The aim of this unit is to build on the knowledge of contract and tort acquired in *Unit 5: Common Law I*, with a particular focus on business organisations. The learner is encouraged to investigate key concepts and principles in relation to specific forms of tortious liability. Additionally, the unit develops an awareness of possible defences against tortious action and the remedies available in relation to various form of loss. This unit also develops the learner's knowledge of contract by looking at factors which can initiate contracts, ways contracts can be discharged and remedies available.

Outcomes and assessment criteria

Outcomes	Assessment criteria
	To achieve each outcome a student must demonstrate the ability to:
1 Examine the **vitiating factors** that could impact on an otherwise legally binding business agreement	• explain the legal concepts of misrepresentation and mistake • discuss the legal concepts of duress (including economic duress) and undue influence
2 Explore the practical situations which could lead to the **discharge of a business contract** and evaluate the relative importance of the **remedies** available	• examine the legal consequences of discharge • examine the various remedies, evaluating their appropriateness in given situations
3 Analyse **specific torts** other than negligence which impact on business activities	• explain and apply nuisance, trespass, defamation and the specific business economic torts • evaluate the scope of these torts in terms of right to sue and who may be sued • apply the rule in Rylands v Fletcher • evaluate liability for fire

Outcomes	Assessment criteria
	To achieve each outcome a student must demonstrate the ability to:
4 Examine and evaluate **possible defences against actions in tort** and the **remedies** available	• distinguish and evaluate general defences from other defences relevant to specific torts • identify the particular types and classifications of remedies • understand the basis of the calculation of potential damages in particular situations • evaluate the effectiveness of particular remedies when applied to different forms of loss

Content

	Covered in chapter(s)

1 Vitiating factors

Identification of key vitiating factors: mistake, misrepresentation, duress, undue influence, restraint of trade, illegality — 8

2 Discharge of a business contract and remedies

Forms of discharge: agreement, frustration, performance, breach — 9

Remedies: damages (liquidated and unliquidated), specific performance, injunctions, restitution, rescission, remoteness, mitigation — 9

3 Specific torts which impact on business activities

The nature and scope of particular torts: trespass to persons, land and goods; nuisance, public and private; defamation – slander, libel; business and economic torts, right to sue and who may be sued; rule in Rylands v Fletcher; liability for fire — 12, 13

4 Defences against actions in tort and remedies

General defences: volenti non fit injuria, statutory authority, necessity, Act of God, special defences against specific torts, contributory negligence — 14

Remedies: compensatory and non-compensatory — 14

Damages: calculation of, and different forms of loss — 14

Delivery

This unit can be delivered in a variety of ways. Group work and other active methods of learning can be employed to enhance learners' experience and promote the required understanding. The use of case studies and specimen documentation is to be particularly encouraged, both as a means of assessment and as part of the normal learning process.

Assessment

Evidence of outcomes may be in the form of:

- case studies to assess differing approaches to tortuous liability

- group work to examine critically particular elements of negligence

- group role play to simulate situations where various forms of tortious liability apply

- time-constrained assessment analysing practical issues facing a client, including defences and remedies in tortious actions

Links

It is desirable to have completed *Unit 5: Common Law I* and *Unit 25: English Legal System* prior to commencing this unit, as they lay down the foundations for contract and tort and the English legal systems and procedures.

The unit provides for the development of a solid understanding of the law of tort and contract.

Resources

Learners need access to a library with the key texts and to case studies. The use of texts should be supported by reference to broadsheet newspapers, relevant journals and technology-based databases.

Suggested reading

Textbooks

Sufficient library resources should be available to enable learners to achieve this unit. Texts that are particularly relevant are:

- Elliot and Quinn. *Contract Law* (Longman, 2002)

- Young, M. *Cases and Commentary in Contract Law* (Prentice Hall, 1997)

- Atiyah, P. S. *Introduction to the law of Contract* (Clarendon Press, 1995)

- Beale, Bishop and Furmston. *Contract – Cases and Materials* (Butterworth, 2001)

- Cheshire, Fifoot and Furmston. *Law of Contract* (Butterworth, 2001)

- Treitel, G. *Law of Contract* (Sweet & Maxwell, 2003)

- Elliot and Quinn. *Tort Law* (Longman, 1997)

- Cooke, J. *Law of Tort* (Prentice Hall, 1997)

- Harvey and Marston. *Cases and Commentary on TORT* (Prentice Hall, 2000) (5th edition will be published in 2004)

- Jones, M. *Textbook on Torts* (Oxford University, 2002)

- Hodgson, J. and Lewthwaite, J. *Law of Torts* (Blackstone, 2001)

- Pannett, A. *Law of Torts* (Prentice Hall, March 1997)

Journals

- *New Law Journal*
- *Law Society Gazette*

EDEXCEL GUIDELINES FOR SPECIALIST UNIT 28: EUROPEAN LAW

Description of the Unit

This unit provides the learner with an introduction to the principles of European Law which relate to the integration of those legal rules within the domestic legal framework and the impact of European Union legal rules upon the individual and business organisations.

It will also provide an introduction to EU wide legal rules which impact upon persons seeking work in other member states and how business organisations are able to promote and set up branches of the business in other member states.

In addition the unit will allow the learner to identify anti-competitive practices and how these can impact upon business organisations and the individual.

Outcomes and assessment criteria

Outcomes	Assessment criteria
	To achieve each outcome a student must demonstrate the ability to:
1 Explore the **EU institutions**	• explain the constitution of the different EU institutions • distinguish the function of community institutions in relation to the formulation of legal rules • evaluate the roles of the different EU institutions
2 Investigate the **sources of EU law and issues of sovereignty**	• describe and evaluate the sources of European law • examine the principles of European Union law and analyse the solution to issues of sovereignty • apply and evaluate relevant principles relating to the implementation and integration of European law
3 Investigate the European legal principles concerned with the **free movement of workers**	• explain the concept of the 'worker' • analyse provisions relating to equal treatment for European nationals • apply and evaluate relevant worker rights • apply and evaluate derogations to workers' rights
4 Explore key European provisions relating to the **free movement of goods, services and establishment**	• distinguish goods and services • explain discriminatory practices which member states may use to curtail free movement of goods • evaluate the freedom to receive services • distinguish non-workers from workers and apply and evaluate the residence rights of non-workers

Content	Covered in chapter
1 **EU institutions**	15

Community institutions: Council, Commission, Parliament, European Court of Justice

Constitutional principles: European citizenship, federalism and subsidiarity

2 **The sources of EU law and issues of sovereignty**	16

Sources of European law: treaty provisions, regulations, directives, decisions

General principles of European law: direct and indirect effect of EU legal rules

Sovereignty issues: supremacy of EU law over domestic legislation

3 **Free movement of workers**	17

Sources: Relevant treaty articles, regulations and directives

Community citizenship: political and social rights

Defining workers: treaty articles, regulations and directives

Equal treatment of European nationals: right of entry, right of residence and right to remain

Derogations from free movement of workers: the grounds of public policy, public security, public health

4 **Free movement of goods, services and establishment**	18

Free movement of goods: cases, treaty articles, regulations and directives, discriminatory taxation and quantitative restrictions

Free movement of services: cases, treaty articles, regulations and directives

Free movement of establishment: recognition of qualifications, right to establish and residence rights of non-workers

Delivery

The unit may be delivered as a stand-alone unit, although there may be opportunities for mapping outcomes through the integration of assessed outcomes made up from other units which are being studied alongside *Unit 28: European Law,* for example, *Unit 25: English Legal System, Unit 26: Business Law, Unit 43: Employment Law* and other general business units as appropriate.

It is anticipated that much of the material in this unit can be delivered actively through the use of case studies and learner-centred learning both as small group and individual exercises. Wherever possible, a link should be made between the underpinning academic knowledge and its practical application through given cases and judgements.

Typical class sessions will begin with an explanation of the relevant legal rules from both statutory sources and leading cases appropriate to the outcome under study. This factual introduction may be followed by a learner-led discussion on how the relevant legal rules were applied within decided cases. In some instances the learner may be given a pre-prepared number of cases to read in advance of classes and then contribute during the session in a manner appropriate to set classroom tasks. The learner may also be given self-directed study handouts through which they present a seminar or lead a discussion on stated outcomes.

The use of case studies can be used as both a means of encouraging learning and also to provide a vehicle for assessment.

Small group, tutor-devised workshops can be used to direct learners and to develop the learners' understanding of individual outcomes. Their conclusions may be used to develop their knowledge base.

In addition learners should be encouraged to undertake self-directed study and present their findings during seminars and workshops which may be used as an assessment vehicle. This may be particularly effective due to the number of government Internet sites, both domestic and European, which provide free access to relevant information to broadening the learners' development and understanding of the unit in a broader context.

Alternative methods of delivery include online materials which may be centre devised using centre-specific resources such as hand-outs and assignments and the use of other non-centre devised electronic sources and materials.

Assessment

The assessment strategy should aim to encourage use of primary and secondary European legislation and relevant domestic provisions in addition to the application of relevant decided cases, again both European and domestic, to the outcomes.

The assessment of this unit can be through individual and group assignments. These may be in the form of submitted reports, written memoranda, business letters and presentations. The presentations may be formal and include electronic presentations using software such as Microsoft PowerPoint. Alternatively presentations may be in the form of a moot or discussion, or learner-led seminar on an outcome during which the learner, either individually or in a group, orally conveys assessment material to the group.

Evidence may be provided by the learner at outcome level only, although there exist opportunities for the design of assignments that cover different outcomes from, for example, *Unit 25: English Legal System, Unit 26: Business Law, Unit 43: Employment Law* and other general business units as appropriate. Class materials, eg handouts, may include case study material and which may be used in conjunction with assessments made under time-constrained conditions.

Alternative assessment methods may include peer assessment during presentations, seminars etc, multiple choice questions and in class open-book, timed assessments.

Outcomes may be combined to further the learners' understanding of European legal rules, again case studies may be used for assessment or self-directed study purposes.

The sections which look at sovereignty may be combined with free movement of goods and how domestic legislation was formulated.

Links

This unit has particular links to *Unit 5: Common Law I, Unit 26: Business Law, Unit 42: European Business, Unit 43: Employment Law* and to the units in the E-Business Strategies pathway.

Resources

Learners will require access to a library, which contains key texts and materials suitable to studying the law of the European Union.

Additional resources include Iolis, an interactive CD-Rom for law students available from the University of Warwick, and Seneca, a legal information service, also on CD. (See websites.)

Suggested reading

Textbooks

Sufficient library resources should be available to enable learners to achieve this unit. Texts that are particularly relevant are:

- Kent, P. *The Law of the European Union* (Longman, 2001)
- Owen, R. *Essential European Community Law* (Cavendish, 1994)
- Ewing and Bradley. *Constitutional and Administrative Law* (Longman, 2002)
- Tillotson, J. *European Community Law: Text, Cases and Materials* (Cavendish, 1996)
- Steiner, J. *Textbook on EC Law* 5th ed. (Blackstone, 1996)
- Foster, N. (Ed) *Blackstone's EC Legislation* (Oxford University, 2002)
- McLean, R. M. (Ed) *European Community Law Casebook* (HLT Publications, 1991)
- Cairns, W. *Introduction to European Union Law* (Cavendish, 1997)
- Kaczoroswka, A. *EU Law Today* (Old Bailey Press, 1998)
- Craig and de Busca, G. *EU Law* (Oxford University Press, 2002)

Journals

- *The Times*

Videos

- *An introduction to European Community Law*
- *Supremacy of EC Law*

Websites

- www.europa.eu.int   The Court of Justice of the European Communities
- www.curia.eu.int/en/index.htm   The European Union online
- www.jurist.law.cam.ac.uk   Legal information for educational purposes
- www.lawtel.co.uk   Legal information service

- www.lexis-nexis.com   Lexis-Nexis provides legal information
- www.timesonline.co.uk   website of *The Times* newspaper
- www.law.warwick.ac.uk/lcc/iolis   Iolis website
- www.senecaweb.co.uk   Seneca website

TABLE OF CASES

INDEX

BPP
LEARNING MEDIA

Review Form – Business Essentials Business Law (12/07)

BPP Learning Media always appreciates feedback from the students who use our books. We would be very grateful if you would take the time to complete this feedback form, and return it to the address below.

Name: _____   Address: _____

_____

_____

How have you used this Course Book?
(Tick one box only)

☐ Home study (book only)

☐ On a course: college _____

☐ Other _____

During the past six months do you recall seeing/receiving any of the following?
(Tick as many boxes as are relevant)

☐ Our advertisement

☐ Our brochure with a letter through the post

Why did you decide to purchase this Course book? *(Tick one box only)*

☐ Have used BPP Learning Media Texts in the past

☐ Recommendation by friend/colleague

☐ Recommendation by a lecturer at college

☐ Saw advertising

☐ Other _____

Your ratings, comments and suggestions would be appreciated on the following areas

	Very useful	Useful	Not useful
Introductory pages	☐	☐	☐
Topic coverage	☐	☐	☐
Summary diagrams	☐	☐	☐
Chapter roundups	☐	☐	☐
Quick quizzes	☐	☐	☐
Activities	☐	☐	☐
Discussion points	☐	☐	☐

	Excellent	Good	Adequate	Poor
Overall opinion of this Course book	☐	☐	☐	☐

Do you intend to continue using BPP Learning Media Business Essentials Course books?   ☐ Yes   ☐ No

Please note any further comments and suggestions/errors on the reverse of this page.

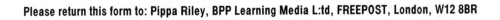

Please return this form to: Pippa Riley, BPP Learning Media L:td, FREEPOST, London, W12 8BR

Review Form (continued)

Please note any further comments and suggestions/errors below